WHY ARE WE ALWAYS INDOORS?

WHY ARE WE ALWAYS INDOORS?

(...unless we're off to Barnard Castle)

PAUL ARMSTRONG

First published by Pitch Publishing, 2020

Pitch Publishing
A2 Yeoman Gate
Yeoman Way
Worthing
Sussex
BN13 3QZ
www.pitchpublishing.co.uk
info@pitchpublishing.co.uk

A CIP catalogue record is available for this book from the British Library.

ISBN 978 1 78531 802 3

Typesetting and origination by Pitch Publishing

Printed and bound by TJ International, Padstow, UK

Contents

Week Ten

Week Eleven

Author's Note

I embarked on this book as a way of recording daily reflections on the most bizarre football close-season ever known, and to fill the long hours of lockdown. However, as events beyond our four walls grew darker, so the focus drifted from whimsical musings on football, TV and music to a growing unease with how a dreadful pandemic was being handled. Even then, it quite often drifted back again.

Unlike Dominic Cummings's blog about pandemics, this journal was written in real time, and sent to friends on a weekly basis. I've amended certain words and phrases where necessary in accordance with legal guidelines, but any misinterpretations or inaccurate forecasts have not been edited retrospectively to try to make me look clever. As a former TV programme editor with an academic background in politics and (some) economics, I tried to remain evidence-based and well-sourced, even when ranting.

I'd like to thank my weekly distribution list of friends and family for their encouragement and input. Especially Dick Clement, whose generosity and collaborative instincts from a lifetime of co-writing some of the greatest TV scripts of all time (*Porridge, The Likely Lads, Auf Wiedersehen, Pet*) were a godsend. All the attempts at silly or dark comedy herein are very much mine, though. And huge thanks to Jane Camillin from Pitch Publishing for her support. *Why Are We Always*

On Last? (2019), covering my time in charge of BBC's *Match of the Day*, was very much their patch; this isn't, but they've stuck with me, for which I'm very grateful.

Most of all, thanks and love to Amanda from Stockton for tolerating several months trapped with me in our small flat and still being prepared to improve my syntax, grammar and punctuation on a daily basis.

Foreword by Dick Clement

I haven't spent a lot of time in Paul's company. The most memorable occasion was a trip to Stockholm in 1998 with him and my son Andrew for the European Cup Winners' Cup Final between Chelsea and Stuttgart. Gianfranco Zola got the winning goal. Andrew and I got quite excited. I don't think Paul did as he supports Middlesbrough, as you will often be reminded in the pages that follow.

I feel I know Paul a great deal better now after reading his journal as it unfolded over the past weeks. When I read the opening segment, it hit me that a chronicle of living through this unprecedented crisis would be an invaluable document. I think I was the first person who compared him to Samuel Pepys and his *Diaries*, which chronicled the Great Plague.

Certain events feel like genuine watersheds. The attack on the Twin Towers was one. As I watched it on TV, I knew that the world would never be the same. We're living through another such event. This one is far more drawn out and unpredictable but in years to come writers will be asking themselves, 'Did this happen before or after COVID-19?' because it's hard to imagine that we will ever go back to the way we were. Already TV shows where people get together in groups for a party or a play or a sporting event seem as if they're from another era. I flinch when people stand too close or – God forbid – hug and kiss each other on the screen.

Back to Pepys, writing in 1664, 'On hearing ill rumour that Londoners may soon be urged from their lodgings by Her Majesty's men, I looked upon the street to see a gaggle of striplings making fair merry, and no doubt spreading the plague well about. Not a care had these rogues for the health of their elders!'

Full disclosure: I've never read Pepys but the quote is bogus. England didn't have a queen in 1664 and the plague only took hold the following year. Can't really blame the author. We all need to find something to do during lockdown.

There is nothing fake about Paul's sentiments. His fury with miscommunication, lack of leadership, bad decision-making and trepidation about the eventual outcome leap from the page. The fact that he was able to finish the document is its own spoiler alert. Let's just hope he never has to write a sequel.

Dick Clement, Los Angeles, June 2020.

WEEK ONE

Saturday, 14 March 2020

'Lord Olivier is indisposed and will be unable to take part in tonight's performance. The part of Macbeth will instead be played by Dave Lee Travis.'

That was the response of my Twitter account @armoaning to the news that tonight's cancelled *Match of the Day* (*MOTD*) will be replaced in the BBC One schedule by an episode of *Mrs Brown's Boys*.

For all my ambivalence about this country, I'm as British as it gets when it comes to expressing my feelings in public. I'm in London NW3, in the borough with the second-highest recorded infection rate in the whole of England to date, on the day official figures for coronavirus (or its latest incarnation, COVID-19, to be more specific) in the UK reached four figures and deaths almost doubled to 20. Italy, which seems to be about a fortnight ahead of us in the global science fiction movie currently playing out, is burying its dead (over 1,000 already), singing defiantly from balconies above the deserted streets and applauding its overwhelmed medical heroes. The best I can do, publicly at least, is to rubbish a hackneyed but harmless comedy show by reworking an old Paul Calf line my mate Rob Skilbeck has been using to express dissatisfaction for 20 years or more.

At least part of me is crapping myself, to be honest. I'm only ('only') 55, with a bit of a history of asthma, and Amanda is a little older with a strange auto-immune condition which can cause her to develop a cough even when nothing's ostensibly wrong. We're not in the highest 'at risk' group (though I suspect we're in the city which is going to get this worst, and first) but my parents absolutely are. Aged 80-ish with underlying health conditions, and living in Kent with my brother and his school age daughters, so potentially not able to isolate themselves properly.

As BBC Sport presenters, pundits and production teams would tell you, my tendency when I have no control over events is to absorb as much information as possible in the hope that whatever happens isn't going to catch me on the hop. That works fairly well when you're in charge of a live World Cup broadcast, and know what analysis and features you want, with a contingency plan if the star man doesn't start or the kick-off's delayed. It's an absolute nightmare in a situation like this. Even the scientists don't seem to agree, so how can I find anything to cling on to? Worryingly, the UK government in the form of Prime Minister Boris Johnson and his chief adviser Dominic Cummings appears to have taken its cavalier, maverick outlier approach to Brexit into the gravest health crisis this country, and indeed the world, has faced in a century.

The whole of Europe appears to be heading for a death toll far in excess of the Asian countries in which this virus first struck. Within Europe – and indeed the world, now that US President Donald Trump appears to have had his initial unhinged pronouncements overturned behind his back by the remaining adults in the room – Britain seems to have been ploughing a lone furrow. Maybe the 'herd immunity' described by Boris Johnson and his scientific advisers on Thursday could work in the long run. No one knows whether the populace can acquire immunity to this still-mutating virus in a way that they never did to smallpox, polio or AIDS.

In the meantime, I wasn't alone in feeling uneasy at the suggestion that 60 to 80 per cent of us need to contract this thing in order to test the theory. Call me Mr Picky, but when a man whose career has been littered with inconsistencies and controversies tells me that my elderly parents may have to be sacrificed, I'm not inclined to acquiesce. It's very difficult for broadcasters to question the government at a moment of unprecedented national crisis, though Sky and *C4 News,* as they have throughout what now seems like the comparatively trivial Brexit shambles, do so rather more often than the two traditional TV news outlets. At least they seem happy to ask ever so politely if the PM is absolutely sure that his new clothes aren't really his birthday suit. Unpatriotic treachery in the eyes of some, absolutely necessary journalistic scrutiny in desperate times as far as I'm concerned.

God, more than at any time in my life I hope I'm wrong, and I'm not going to foment further panic by speculating on social media, as so many are. Moreover, unlike Brexit, Trump's election and Jeremy Corbyn and Johnson being chosen as our respective main party leaders, no one's offering bets on how bad this will be. Even Paddy Power, with whom I closed an online account when they offered various jokey #bantz odds on the Oscar Pistorius trial, aren't sinking that low.

I won small fortunes on all the calamitous events above, by the way. I'll rephrase that: in retrospect, they were extremely unfortunate events, this is a calamity. Then again, I have a better nose for democratic madness than I have for medical and epidemiological science. Maybe, just maybe, someone qualified is steering the good ship Britannia through this unprecedented storm.

One small sign of sanity was the U-turn last night. Twenty-four hours after blithely telling the herd that mass gatherings were just the ticket to get the jolly old virus sweeping through us, Johnson backtracked. Or rather, he didn't do it personally – as is his wont, he's now completely disappeared again – but at least someone did. Stable doors and horses spring to mind since the sporting authorities belatedly and unilaterally shut themselves down. It's beyond scandalous that the Cheltenham Festival and Liverpool v Atlético Madrid both took place in front of huge crowds this week, and it shouldn't have been left to the Premier and Football Leagues to take the initiative and moral high ground after a Chelsea player and the Arsenal coach tested positive, thus presenting the government with a fait accompli, but at least it happened.

As a result, for the first time since I was six years old, I didn't spend an August to May Saturday watching football in person or on a screen, or at the very least, desperately trying to find out the scores. I was even born on a Saturday lunchtime, 3 October 1964. Appropriately, my team Middlesbrough made their longest possible domestic journey – to Plymouth Argyle – and lost 1-0. Even in summer, I've always spent as many Saturdays as possible watching cricket or other sports. Guy Mowbray, the *MOTD* commentator and club cricketer, wistfully asked his Twitter followers yesterday what on earth you can do on a Saturday that doesn't involve sport, and then pre-empted any possible answers by (rightly) opining that they were already boring him.

In retrospect, today may not have been the best day to try to find out. At the sacred hour of 3pm, we left our one-bedroom flat in Belsize Park for the first time today and headed out for a walk. At one point during the first half we were spooked at the top of Primrose Hill by an idiotic passer-by coughing without covering her mouth. By half-time, we were on the Finchley Road (like 'the coronavirus', using the 'the' in this context seems to suggest advancing years) buying some greetings cards and stamps. I tackled the still relatively civilised Waitrose shopping yesterday. I say 'civilised': in common with most of the country, there was no toilet paper or hand sanitiser whatsoever to be had, but I didn't see any actual fights break out.

In fact, I'm personally responsible for the most confrontational act I've ever seen in there. Amanda and I once saw the bejewelled, and very expensively dressed, 'outrage for hire' shock-jock Julia Hartley-Brewer in the underground car park. The best I could come out with was, 'Look, it's the Waitrose Katie Hopkins.' Just to reinforce that, a good friend passed on a tweet from JHB today in which she suggested that 'working from home' which, for many, is about to start in earnest, is a good chance for bosses to offload underperforming staff. Nice.

Then someone else I follow had retweeted Lady Karren Brady opining in *The Sun* (natch) that the Premier League should be declared null and void. Tough on champions-elect Liverpool, she admitted, but ah … oh, yes, now that you mention it, her club

West Ham wouldn't be relegated. Cor blimey, guv'nor, would you Adam and Eve it, eh?

Between that, and the incessant speculation about the virus from people who don't even have my clean sweep of science O levels, and the squabbling among those who know a lot more about it than I do, I've taken the drastic decision to delete Twitter from my devices. At the best of times, it's grim, albeit that's frequently countered by some very funny friends and acquaintances. Right now, it's potentially injurious to mental health, and no help whatsoever to our imperilled physical health, either. I've deleted Twitter before at the height of various political storms; it'll be interesting (to Amanda, anyway – she hates all forms of social media) to see whether that boycott or the peace and calm in Waitrose lasts longer this time. Amanda gives the Twitter shutdown a week at most. We'll see.

I'll stay on Facebook, though. For all the creepy amorality of its founder, Facebook allows me to keep in touch with most of my friends and family of a certain age. Especially since it doesn't look like I'll be seeing any of them face to face any time soon. I didn't grow up in an internet world, so it seems all the more bizarre that I (and governments and internet providers) can keep track of every movement and preference of anyone, anywhere, yet we're all seemingly completely at the mercy of a microscopic organism which mutated across the globe in three months from its starting point, an unknown animal in a wet market in Wuhan, China.

I'll keep checking into Facebook, but I really don't intend to post anything. For years I've irritated, entertained or possibly bored hundreds of Facebook friends with holiday snaps, intermittent bursts of dark humour or just straightforward rants about politics and the state of the world. The latter probably peaked in what seemed like the worst year imaginable back in 2016, but I've had my moments since. It all seems ever so slightly silly now.

In recent weeks, the magnitude of the coronavirus has become the nearest thing 95 per cent of us have ever known to September 1939. My dad was born that month, incidentally. On the fourth, the day after Britain declared war on Hitler. We lost 450,000 lives in World War Two (the Soviet Union lost 27 million people). If we have to wait for herd immunity to kick in, this virus could wipe out an even bigger slice of our population in a much shorter time frame. The evidence suggests that the oldest, weakest members of society will bear the brunt, whereas most fatalities in both world wars were young and male. And in 1939, the country had Churchill waiting in the wings, with Attlee ready in 1945 to preside over the peace and build the NHS and the 'cradle to grave' orthodoxy which I took for granted during my childhood.

At the risk of plunging myself into despair again, we currently have Boris Johnson and Jeremy Corbyn. Based on their pronouncements this week, I'd rather we had Jürgen Klopp and Nigel Pearson in charge. Pearson, managing Watford, a Premier League club which at the time had been told to play today despite having suspected coronavirus cases in their squad, wearily and adroitly dismantled Johnson's attempts at leadership. Klopp, whose Liverpool stood just six points away from a first league title in 30 years, sent a message to the fans which was chock full of common sense and fine human instincts. Sample line: 'If it's a choice between football and the good of wider society, it's no contest. It really isn't.' He also used a phrase I quoted throughout my time at *MOTD* and in my book: 'Football is the most important of all the unimportant things.' I'm not sure who originally came up with that, but I adopted it after working at the Hillsborough disaster, then watching the subsequent 30-year smear campaign and cover-up unravel. Klopp just got it instinctively, and brought his values and coaching genius with him from Dortmund to Liverpool.

I posted his whole letter, intending it to be my last Facebook contribution for some time, with a simple message of my own: 'In the weeks and months ahead, let's all try to be more like Jürgen Klopp.' I'm going to say whatever I like in this diary, but when communicating in public, I'll try to channel at least some of Klopp's decency and humanity for as long as this nightmare lasts.

Sunday, 15 March 2020

There's a long-standing tradition in our household, dating back to my days editing *MOTD*, that I have a lie-in on Sunday mornings, while Amanda watches the Sophy Ridge and Andrew Marr shows so I don't have to. A two-minute summary – 'May said Brexit means Brexit'; 'In the event of a nuclear missile being fired at us, Richard Burgon says he'll wait until he's consulted every local constituency Labour Party before responding'; a couple of expletives from me, and we can start thinking about lunch and what live football's on TV. People are amazed when they visit our tiny flat that we manage to co-exist peacefully in it. I would ascribe that partly to my night owl hours and Amanda's early-bird regime minimising bathroom and cupboard-sized kitchen interfaces. But it's mostly down to my wife's almost unbelievably tolerant and independent disposition, something she ascribes to going to boarding school aged ten while her parents worked abroad.

Anyway, this morning, her first words were, 'You don't want to know.' We'd read books from mid-evening, then I'd typed this diary later so we were about 12 hours – or 15, in my case – behind the news cycle. So, what had happened? Well, we're all still doomed, but rabbit in the aircraft landing lights Health Secretary Matt Hancock, had apparently been on both shows seemingly trying to claim that 'herd immunity' was all a misunderstanding and appealing for anyone who thinks they might be able to construct a respirator in their garage to get in touch. Hancock first came to my attention as Culture Secretary when he tried to get down wiv da kids by saying that Ed Sheeran's all-time low point, 'Galway Girl', was his record of the year. How we laughed. But as Bob Monkhouse once said about his own comedy career, 'They're not laughing now.'

Amanda also related South Korea's foreign minister's appearance on Marr, in which she calmly explained their strategy of using state-of-the-art technology to trace, test and treat those infected and, as importantly, being open and honest at all times with the general public and giving them as much information as is available. So, 20,000 people are being tested every day in South Korea; a mobile phone app locates the whereabouts of those with the virus; and life is carrying on, certainly to a far greater extent than in the similar sized European nations which are now in lockdown with no idea where those infected are. Just 75 people have died so far in South Korea, a figure we will pass in the next day or so, thanks to only testing people when they arrive in hospital, and not even then, if NHS friends are to be believed (see below). South Korea was the first country outside China to experience a COVID-19 outbreak, but they realised that tracing those affected was paramount, so launched testing in the street, at petrol stations, and in other public spaces.

I read yesterday that symptoms tend not to show within at least five days and that you're believed to be at your most infectious after three days. The UK is still advising people to self-isolate when they experience symptoms, that is, at least two days after you're at your most infectious. To paraphrase World War One *Blackadder*, 'There was just one problem with that plan. It was bollocks.'

In other news, we've retaliated pointlessly to Trump's belated decision to add the UK to his European flight ban, by telling Brits not to go there. Er, we already can't. Turns out that even though we're Anglo-Saxon and leaving the dirty Continentals behind so we can take back control, we're not 'doing very well' after all, eh, Donny? At least he's just acting as the front man with a squirty flower full of bile while (you hope) adults belatedly cobble together a strategy to minimise the carnage in the land of no public health provision whatsoever. Still, they've now said they'll try to test people, which is more than the UK is doing. Maybe now the herd immunity doctrine has gone away, officially at least, we could think about doing that? At the moment, the UK government is doing a passable impression of the guy in the control tower in *Airplane* who, when asked why the runway lights haven't been switched on, replies with a manic cackle, 'That's just what they'll be expecting us to do.'

Despite wanting to see how other people I respect reacted to the South Korean contribution in particular, I've managed to sustain my self-isolation from Twitter. As well as Facebook – where it seems most people are, like me, being publicly British about it all and avoiding expressing their inner fears – I'm in various WhatsApp and Messenger groups.

A bunch of guys I used to meet for a curry at the magnificent, but now sadly closed, Nepalese Gurkha in Wembley while Tottenham were playing there, is one. I'll come back to them sometime when I discuss the backlog of recommended TV series Amanda and I are planning to watch while in lockdown. Then there's a sub-group of four old friends from the Curry Club who all broadly agree politically – one works in finance, another has a tech business, another works with senior civil servants – in that we all thought, until the last week or so, that Brexit was the worst domestic development in this country in our lifetimes. It's called 'Special Measures for Eton' after I once suggested that any state school which produced Boris Johnson, David Cameron, Jacob Rees-Mogg and Cambridge Analytica's Alexander Nix in quick succession would be put in special measures. Our avatar is a picture of Johnson casting the shadow of a giant penis behind him, so although the chat is often of the gallows humour variety, it's a good way of letting off steam without inflicting too much of it on Amanda. As I said yesterday, she's far too sensible to touch social media with latex gloves while wearing a Hazchem suit.

The other much bigger and more fluid group is called 'Just for the Remainiacs' set up by Jake, an ex-colleague of Amanda's at the House of Commons – I'll return to that period another day – with assorted friends of friends from academia, nursing, campaign groups and so on. It's a bit gossipy – I've learnt things in the last couple of years about Dominic Cummings that I can't even tell this diary – frequently sweary and hilarious, but has also acted as a mental health support group as we've slowly watched our country descend into a dystopian nightmare. I went to it this morning instead of Twitter and the first post I saw was a link to an article by the 'Brexit Guru', ex-MEP and utter twat Daniel Hannan, on *The Telegraph*'s website. The headline, gobsmackingly removed from reality, even for the formerly respectable publication now remodelled as the Billionaire's Boris Beano, was, 'If coronavirus has a silver lining, it should be the return of the bow and the curtsy.'

I'm struggling to formulate a sentence to describe just how tone deaf that is right now. Derek and Clive's 'What a cunt, eh?' will have to do. Then a couple of health professionals un-hysterically described how consultants are being discouraged from testing elderly admissions and are simply categorising them as flu or pneumonia victims to keep the figures from being even more alarming. Oh boy.

While we wait for the full madness to play out in the coming weeks and months, Amanda and I decided earlier this week to fly in the face of government advice, so didn't go to the Cheltenham Festival to stand next to as many coughing hoorays in pink trousers, green jackets and silly hats as possible. As far as we can – and in London there are clearly limits – we're going to sit it out. Fortunately for us and unlike so many elsewhere, including my freelance friends in the TV sport industry – we are able to do it financially. Even so, yesterday was a troubling experience, and not just because there was no football.

We must have passed 500 people while walking to Primrose Hill then the Finchley Road. The government's Chief Medical Officer, Professor Chris Whitty, admitted the other day when there were 500 confirmed cases that there were probably another 10,000 out there developing herd immunity, sorry, regrettably untested. That will have doubled by now. London is the epicentre. Being cheek by jowl with 500 other people is a form of Russian roulette now, whatever the government advise, as is then visiting elderly relatives. I only noticed two people actually coughing yesterday, but it felt like the pre-titles sequence in a zombie apocalypse movie. We're going to have to work out a different walk and shopping routine, particularly at weekends. At least we have both local shops we should support in Belsize Village, and the more open Hampstead Heath ten minutes away.

If we are to be stuck here for months – and let's face it, unless we end up in a tent in the Royal Free Hospital car park, then one of the 24-hour cremation centres blithely being discussed, that's what's going to happen – we're pleased that our last taste of freedom, which ended a week ago today, was a visit to our native north-east. Despite its baffling decision to vote for Brexit self-harm and then Boris sodding Johnson (yes, I know Corbyn was dire) it was great to see the aforementioned Jake, some of his Messenger group and other friends for a birthday gathering in Newcastle and a sunny afternoon on the beach at Tynemouth. We then had a night in Bishop Auckland, dinner with aunties, uncles and cousins, and a very quick detour to Whitby before dropping the hire car off at York and coming back to that there London. We're so glad in retrospect that the timing meant we were able to do that. It will be some time before we can do it again.

The only sour note for me was spotting that one of the cafes on the gorgeous back streets of Whitby, one of our favourite towns, had reinvented itself as The Blitz Café, complete with a Mark Francois/Nigel Farage-style picture of a Spitfire in the window. Amanda's marvellous auntie, Irene, who hailed from Stockton and died a couple of years ago in her 90s, served in the WRENs in London during that war, lost loved ones, and absolutely hated the modern, misty-eyed faux nostalgia for a truly horrible era she actually lived through. And that's despite seeing Clark Gable taking a stroll in Ropner Park, Stockton while he was posted to nearby Middleton St George airbase. Auntie Irene cast a postal vote for Remain from her nursing home. We're going to find out now how the mindless 'two world wars and one World Cup' brigade cope with the first comparable period in British history since. It's not a good sign that the very same types are already hoarding all the toilet paper.

Monday, 16 March 2020

When we downsized from a two-bed flat in Bayswater to this one, it was a financial necessity. After a grim period of inner ear issues and operations, I'd been told by my ENT specialist that I couldn't work in TV any more, Amanda had left her PA job and we needed a financial cushion. That said, we were attracted to this place by a small but beautiful patio garden. Not much use for half the year, except for the bird life I've attracted with an array of feeders, but it comes into its own in spring and summer when we can finally throw the French windows open and emerge from the gloom. Today is that day: beautiful sunshine, the clocks go forward soon, and my favourite British garden birds – the almost tropically exotic goldfinches – have joined an array of tits and our resident robin hopping around the garden of flowering camellia and primroses. Goldfinches absolutely love nyjer seeds, if anyone's interested. Large bags are available from the RSPB website.

Such was the beauty of the scene, I took my guitar outside and played 'Blackbird'. We're not in Italy, so none of the neighbours joined in, but I hope the genius who recorded the track at Abbey Road a mile south of here, and after whom I'm named – my brother, born the year 'Blackbird' was released, is John – would have appreciated the spirit of the performance, and forgiven any bum notes. All in all, the sort of morning another genius who lived even closer in the other direction – John Keats – would have written an ode about, as 'light-winged dryads of the trees' flitted about. England at its absolute best and just three weeks until I can stride, Middlesex membership card in hand, just beyond the

McCartney back garden in Cavendish Avenue (then and now) for the start of a blissful summer at Lord's, the greatest sporting venue of them all. Oh shit, wait a minute.

'Back to life, back to reality', as Soul 2 Soul sang, though not in this context. Appropriately, given that we're being governed by Laurel and Hardy minus all the warmth and humour, the first catch-up conversation Amanda and I had this morning centred around Abbott and Costello. Diane Abbott and Professor Anthony Costello, that is. I'd foolishly looked at the newspaper front pages online before I went to bed: *The Guardian* has obtained a Health England memo suggesting that eight million British people could be hospitalised as this virus potentially lasts for a year. Well, I'm no health expert or mathematician, but I've read there are approximately 100,000 hospital beds and a paltry 4,000 intensive care beds (a fraction of most of our neighbours' ICU capability) across the UK. Eight million people in 100,000 beds in a year, even if it was evenly spread (which it clearly won't be) gives each admission four and a half days in hospital, if they were cleared of cancer patients and expectant mothers and no one has a heart attack. The average stay in hospital in Wuhan for COVID-19 sufferers was 11 days. And our NHS was collapsing in places this winter anyway, massively understaffed and just about kept going by the 40,000 mostly lowly paid (and therefore now defined as 'low skilled' by Priti Patel) EU workers who've stayed on despite the referendum result.

I know it's a trite observation, but do you remember the social media and newspaper column avalanche which descended on poor old Diane Abbott when she got into a muddle over police recruitment figures? Some of it wasn't even just because she's a prominent black woman – I wouldn't have her anywhere near the shadow cabinet, either, but not on those grounds – but I think we'd all agree that was a relatively trivial mistake compared to modelling which has eliminated testing (20,000 a day in South Korea, only 75 deaths), been laissez-faire on public gatherings and failed to change even when the better-equipped Italian health service, about a fortnight ahead of us, has collapsed under the strain, leaving doctors to play God and decide who lives and dies. That's presumably coming here, and soon. Again, Italy has 8,000 ventilator-equipped ICU beds, we have 4,000.

Twenty-six per cent of hospital admissions in Wuhan required ICU treatment for an average of eight days. Because the outbreak was largely shut down locally and back-up personnel and resources were flown in from across China, they got the treatment they needed. Twenty-six per cent of eight million is just over two million people who will theoretically need ICU beds in the UK in the next year. If that turns out to be accurate, they'll get, on average, 1.4 days each of ventilator treatment. Or if brutal triage decisions are made, roughly one in eight will get the 11 days they need, the others will get nothing. And that's assuming an even spread across the year and no one else at all being ill. And there will be regional variations – according to Jake's Messenger group which includes those on the front line, Sunderland's quarter of a million population currently has precisely two ICU units to go around. No wonder Matt Hancock looks utterly terrified and even Johnson, the last time he surfaced, reined in the buffoonery to a solitary 'squashed sombrero' reference, as he attempted to explain the graph curve they want to see.

I'm not sharing any of this with the wider world: a) because the figures are hypothetical and b) if remotely correct, they're utterly terrifying. A statistical footnote: 3,200 people have died in China to date, their huge population meaning that's approximately one in 437,500 people. By my (A grade at O level) maths, replicating that rate here would mean around 155 deaths. Even Diane Abbott can tell you that won't be the outcome.

So, what is happening? Sky News's online headline is currently 'UK to announce new measures today – Dominic Cummings'. As a former journalist of sorts, I've been shouting at my TV for a long time that they need to name him, so it's interesting that Sky finally have. Laura Kuenssberg and Robert Peston, the political correspondents at the two traditional TV news broadcasters, have spent recent times citing a 'Number 10 source' pretty much every time they appear on screen. Peter Geoghan has written in *The Guardian* that 'journalists should refuse to be played' and that 'many believe he (Cummings) has become the (very) thinly veiled source of a series of government announcements by anonymous briefing.'

One of the great tragedies of our times is that only maybe ten per cent of the UK population even know who Cummings is, and many of those only because Benedict Cumberbatch played a sanitised version of him in a Channel 4 drama about Brexit. Okay, he came across as weird, slightly unhinged and very Machiavellian, but I've been following his career closely for some time, and believe me, that was sanitised. Sometimes in life – when my musician friend David Eastwood handed me a brand-new copy of Radiohead's first album, or two weeks ago at the last football match I'll be attending for some time, when a teenager called Billy Gilmour ran the show as Chelsea put Liverpool out of the FA Cup – you can look back fondly and feel you were one of the first to know about something. I'm afraid that's not the case with Dominic Cummings – I knew about him before most people, but have watched on with horror as he's shaped our country, arguably more than any other 21st-century figure. I now get angrier about him than any other public figure, too, which is saying something in the era of Trump, Murdoch, Putin, Farage and Johnson.

I've no idea what will happen in the coming weeks to me or anyone else, and I don't know whether anyone will ever read this, but I'd like to have the following rant early in this diary. Scream Therapy was all the rage in the 1970s: I can't actually scream here in this confined space without scaring the neighbours, so I'll do it via the keyboard. And as I was typing that sentence, it occurred to me that Cummings bears something of a resemblance to the figure in Edvard Munch's famous painting 'The Scream', though to be honest that's the least of his – and our – problems.

The first time I really became aware of Dominic Cummings was when someone on Facebook posted footage of his appearance before the Treasury Select Committee as Vote Leave's director shortly before the referendum on EU membership in 2016. It's still on YouTube, and well worth a watch – the line I can remember without even having to look it up was 'accuracy is for snake oil pussies', sneered petulantly at the assembled MPs by an overgrown aggressive child with wild eyes, who seemed unable to sit still, then abruptly walked out saying he had to be somewhere else. This same man – whose contempt for accuracy ironically accurately reflected the fast and loose approach of the Leave campaign – is still in contempt of Parliament, having refused to attend later committee sittings intended to investigate Vote Leave's far from transparent funding.

I've been in some strange BBC meetings, but I had never seen a performance like his committee appearance, and already had a horrible feeling Leave was poised to win from my soundings in north-east England where everyone hated then-PM David Cameron and his Chancellor George Osborne, so planned to vote against anything those two supported, regardless of the economic consequences. Add in a proportion of decent people – some of whom we knew – who had misguided notions about regaining sovereignty with little else changing, and then the distinctly iffy claims of the two-headed Leave beast, and you had a potent mix which I backed heavily to win the day.

I wanted to lose that bet so badly, but there was the officially sanctioned People's Front of Leave, fronted by Johnson and Michael Gove and run by Cummings with their notorious '£350m a week for the NHS' bus and suggestion that millions might be on their way to the UK from Turkey, a country which has never been close to joining the EU. Add in unofficial Farage of the Leave People's Front, with his pint and jovial flag-waving and an infamous poster of Syrian refugees at an Eastern European border, and Leave seemed to be offering something for everyone, from the idealistic sovereignty seekers to the merely confused to the truly bigoted. That combination harvested 52% of the vote.

But before that, I asked around about this swivel-eyed committee loon Cummings, and discovered that a mild mannered but hugely intelligent friend had worked with Dom when Michael Gove brought him into the Department of Education. This chap moved to work in another government department as soon as he could because, and I quote, 'he was the most appalling man I've ever met'. I then read that David Cameron, hardly my favourite person, had described Cummings as 'a career psychopath'.

Even when Cummings disappeared back into the undergrowth after Brexit was secured – many credit/blame his ultimately meaningless, but appealing-sounding, slogan 'Take Back Control' for causing that outcome – I became mildly obsessed with the man and read some of the impenetrable, rambling blogs which he inflicted on the world in the name of 'The Odyssean Project'. From his overgrown Kevin the Teenager demeanour, random name dropping of academic theorists and dislike of 'drivel about "identity" and "diversity" from Oxbridge humanities graduates' (his words) of the liberal London metropolitan elite who he felt had a stranglehold on the law, civil service, BBC, you name it, I assumed Cummings was a self-taught and slightly bitter outsider. If you could penetrate his bizarre, rambling prose style, it seemed he raised some valid points about the often narrow and complacent upper echelons of our society.

Then I did a bit more digging. Like me, Cummings grew up mostly in the north-east, then went to Oxford University. Where he studied, hang on a minute, Ancient and Modern History? I could write a book about the shortcomings of the course I did – PPE (Philosophy, Politics and Economics, not the Personal Protective Equipment currently in worryingly short supply in the NHS) – and I'll probably reflect further on that on another lockdown day, but at least it taught me the rudiments of economics and quite a lot about present-day political systems. Ancient and Modern History is probably second only to Jacob

Rees-Mogg's Classics for creating those unworldly 'Oxbridge humanities graduates' Dom doesn't like.

But let's cut him some slack, it's an achievement for a northern state school type to get into Oxford. Ah, right – he went to Durham School, top of the private school tree in the region. But, like me, he married a sound north-east lass. Ah, okay. His wife is deputy editor of *The Spectator*, the publication responsible for a lorry-load of casual Boris Johnson stereotyping, and many other very posh right-wing libertarian outpourings. And her dad is called Sir Humphry and lives in Chillingham Castle in Northumberland. But Dom genuinely hates London and the metropolitan elite, surely? He keeps sneerily telling journalists to get out of the capital and 'talk to real people', doesn't he? Ah, okay, he lives in a townhouse in Islington, a couple of miles to the east of our flat. And he has a library and a tapestry room, just like any other north-east son of toil.

Does he actually just hate himself? His demeanour suggests as much. How has he got away with it? Well, we live in a world where his fellow Oxford humanities graduates Johnson and Rees-Mogg are apparently fighting for the people against the establishment. And they know their enemy all right, having shared a dorm with them at Eton. So, what else do I know about Dom? Straight after Oxford, he had three mystery years 'pursuing various projects in Russia' (his words, not mine), notably running an airline which never had a single passenger. That's becoming the norm in March 2020, but seems a strange way to have spent three years in the 1990s. Still, it's not like he was anywhere where anything odd, or in any way of concern to the security services, could have happened to him. He was just like any other young Englishman, spending the first portion of his graduate life in entirely-above-board 1990s Russia.

On coming home, he got involved in the successful campaign to get the north-east to reject a regional assembly. Decentralisation AND democracy? Bollocks to that. Then he disappeared for two and a half years. I'm going to quote from the Conservative Home website, in case you don't believe the next bit: 'He then proceeded to spend two and a half years in a bunker he and his father built for him on their farm in Durham, reading science and history and trying to understand the world.' To be fair, which of us can honestly say we haven't done that at one time or another?

So, what did he conclude? I'll quote from one of Dom's essays this time: 'We need leaders with an understanding of Thucydides and statistical modelling, who have read *The Brothers Karamazov* and *The Quark and the Jaguar*, who can feel Kipling's *Kim* and succeed in Tetlock's Good Judgements.' I'm clearly not cut out for leadership because that sounds like a pretentious, name-dropping, word salad to me. But somewhere along the line, he caught the eye of (cough) a true leader, Michael Gove, hence his Department of Education and Vote Leave stints. And when the largely octogenarian Tory membership chose our Prime Minister for us last year, the notoriously lazy Alexander De Pfeffel Boris Johnson knew just the man to do most of the work, concoct some cunning plans and deal with dissenters ... sorry, assist him. Better call Dom.

Again, one of Cummings's appealing, but ultimately over-simplistic slogans – 'Get Brexit Done' – did almost as much as Jeremy Corbyn and our wildly-biased newspapers to secure a Tory majority. OK, so Boris and Dom shut down Parliament, unlawfully as it turned out, expelled the remaining 20 Tory MPs with a backbone and a conscience, watched on as decent people seeking a compromise or a non-lemming Brexit were branded traitors and faced death threats, and sent the Leader of the House of Commons to Scotland to smooth-talk the monarch. Then again, you don't make an omelette without breaking a few eggs. And, potentially, the rule of law and centuries-old doctrine of Sovereignty of Parliament. Johnson's connections with the billionaire tax-exile media barons, who already loved him for preventing their subjection to proposed greater scrutiny of their financial affairs by the EU, did the rest.

I'll discuss what I know about Johnson (I was vaguely in his presence in the mid-1980s, when even the poshos at Oxford saw him as a joke) another time, but suffice to say, if you'd told me a year ago that Johnson, as frontman for Cummings, would be steering this country through an unprecedented and truly alarming pandemic, I think I would have been physically sick, but we are where we are. There would have been no pleasure in watching Brexit go horribly awry in 2021, and it would be positively psychotic not to pray for those at the helm right now to make the right decisions. Firstly, I hope they are listening to the right advice and that we won't rue an apparent schism with the thinking in the rest of the world and the World Health Organisation (WHO). Secondly, I wouldn't be in charge of this for anything. There are going to be some truly horrible, virtually impossible decisions to be made in the coming months, unprecedented in peacetime.

It may have been my state school background, but I never felt remotely entitled to run anything, let alone the country, just because of a middling degree from Oxford. Boris Johnson has seen it as his birthright from the age of five when, according to his sister, he proclaimed himself 'World King', and has never been disabused of the notion by those around him. This may turn out to be the greatest example of 'be careful what you wish for' in history. Neither he nor Cummings presided over austerity, to be fair – last week's budget was the first departure from a dry-as-dust approach to public finances in a decade. Chancellor Rishi Sunak is even proposing to ask Google, Facebook and co. to stump up a minuscule slice of actual tax. Given that interest rates have been at a historical low for that entire time, and because I broadly subscribe to the Keynesianism which got the world out of the Great Depression in the 1930s, I would argue that the UK's coronavirus death rate is going to be much higher than in many other countries, as much because of Cameron and Osborne (also substantially to blame for Brexit) as the chaotic strategy pursued since the virus first appeared in Wuhan.

So, what do I think Johnson and Cummings have got wrong? I really don't know about the science. My brother to whom I spoke earlier about the plan for my parents (I'll come back to that another day) brought up the South Korean foreign minister and the strategy which has kept the death rate so low there. The counter-argument seems to be that there'll be a second spike in Asia, but the mass testing and tracking there, in Singapore and elsewhere, must have been the right approach, surely? A government's first duty is to try to keep its citizens – or subjects in our case – safe. Too late for that now, but the WHO's obvious concern about the UK's maverick approach, and the recent letter of alarm from 200 of our own scientists, still worry me silly. I think I do know a reasonable amount about politics and media communication, though, and it seems to me that the Vote Leave campaign which now runs Downing Street tried to adapt the approach which won them the referendum to a radically different context. It's proved counter-productive to say the least.

Much as I dislike almost everything about Dominic Cummings, and rue the damage he's caused to Britain, there's no doubt he pulled a strategic rabbit out of the hat with the Leave victory. Leaving the question of funding aside (both in terms of volume and origin) and the 'accuracy is for snake oil pussies' level of truth-telling, the messaging around both Leave and the 2019 General Election was undoubtedly effective. His three-word slogans (the second of which, 'Get Brexit Done', was every bit as superficially appealing and vacuous as the first) triumphed over a mishmash of complex arguments once again, and left the country bitterly divided.

This time, though, there's a common enemy and a craving for national unity. Plenty of ordinary people – Welsh miners, veterans of Gallipoli, and many in his own party – didn't like Johnson's hero Churchill when he got the gig in 1940. Winston's record as Chancellor in the 1920s was almost as widely lambasted as Johnson's more recent tenure at the Foreign Office. But cometh the hour, his sense of calm and oratorical prowess was exactly what was needed. By contrast, even though he was on his best behaviour last Thursday, even Johnson's fans – the ones we saw saying 'he's one of the lads' and 'I'd love to have a drink with him' in those incessant vox pops which were broadcast during the 2019 election campaign – know he's basically a chancer. I don't particularly want to knock around with people like that, though some people, usually men, clearly do, but that raffish persona is diametrically at odds with what any sentient being needs at the helm right now. Being flanked by two scientists calms that down a little, until one of them produces a graph projection of the herd immunity theory. We'll only know the truth if someone in the inner circle is keeping a diary, but my bet is that Cummings's curiosity about science and behavioural theory was stimulated and he encouraged Sir Patrick Vallance, the government's chief scientist, to whip it out at the press conference (so to speak) forgetting that the demise of people's actual parents and grandparents was thereby being bandied about in the name of abstract theorising.

Unless you're a member of the Westminster lobby, it's difficult to assess whether, as Peter Geoghan has suggested, Cummings' obsessive level of control means he's always the 'Number 10 source' of all briefings. Within media and political circles, though, the approach adopted by the current regime is identified at least as much with him as it is with the actual Prime Minister. Unless we include the fictional Malcolm Tucker of *The Thick of It*, only Alastair Campbell has ever acquired such prominence as an unelected component of government. Campbell's take on Cummings appeared in *The Sunday Times* recently; former BBC managers and New Labour figures may have quietly chuckled to themselves as Alastair extolled the virtues of 'good manners and a desire for harmony'. Even so, Campbell worked alongside Tony Blair for nine years, so when he condemns the reported Cummings line to a team of special advisers – 'I'll see half of you next week' – and speaks of a 'culture of fear' and 'contempt for all but a chosen few', it all begins to sound potentially problematic, to say the least.

The fact that I'd already read about herd immunity the previous day illustrates another problem. ITV's Robert Peston, as he has regularly throughout Johnson's prime ministership, ran an exclusive story, this time explaining the principles behind it. As ever, a 'Number 10 source' was quoted. Now, as I mentioned earlier, there's nothing new about this. You can question journalists becoming conduits for 'sources', though it's happened since time immemorial even in the sports world I inhabited. Both during the Brexit campaign and the torrid parliamentary period after Johnson's accession, Number 10 frequently nudged ideas into the public domain through selected journalists. Sometimes they were genuinely testing the water; by contrast, other scoops were seemingly intended as a 'look over there' distraction, the so-called 'dead cat' theory. At a time of chaos and misinformation, that scattergun approach proved successful for Cummings and Johnson.

In this context, though, it's proved a PR and communications disaster. A simple slogan up front, backed up with a volley of mixed messages and throwing things against the wall, hoping something sticks, might get you to the 52 per cent you need to win a referendum or 40 per cent for a general election, but it's not what's needed now. There's no 'suck it up, losers' when we're all on the same (losing) side, and antagonising some media outlets by favouring others, and slipping them little 'exclusives', has to stop. The announcement of a daily press conference is a small step in the right direction, though Amanda watched today's (again, so I didn't have to) and is none the wiser afterwards.

Yet again, individuals and organisations are taking matters into their own hands, and imposing restrictions upon themselves. If you're not being governed properly, that's what you have to do. Though quite how much we can do as individuals in the absence of mass testing and with some people still going to the theatres, bars and restaurants that even US cities are shutting, is another question. I feel desperately sorry for those industries, and in happier times I regularly use their services, but Jürgen Klopp's words about football apply to all leisure pursuits right now. One advantage we have over the World War Two generation is that there's an awful lot more available for us to do virtually at home now, and in any case, boredom is infinitely preferable to infecting, and potentially killing, your loved ones.

That rant about Cummings – or Kuntings as one of my WhatsApp groups calls him – meant today's entry is longer than I intended it to be. At least I won't have to repeat all that again, especially since an over-long typing session has left me with tight upper body muscles. In these febrile times, I briefly wondered if I was developing ominous tight chest symptoms, but Amanda reminded me the same thing happened when I was hunched up at the computer writing *Why Are We Always On Last?* In those days, you could pop into the nearest spa every now and then for a back massage. It's extraordinary how the most straightforward everyday activity now has risks attached, and probably won't be happening at all for much longer.

I'll quickly summarise the rest of the day, then carry on with the novel I'm reading. Last week, I bought a few of those modern classics I should have read but haven't, once a London lockdown started looking inevitable to pretty much everyone except the government. The first is *My Brilliant Friend* by Elena Ferrante. We're also ploughing through piles of TV series, so I'll try to write about them on one of the many quiet days ahead.

Having not gone anywhere yesterday, we decided to drive to the municipal dump in Kentish Town to get rid of some masonry which fell on to our patio during the winter – God knows when the missing chunk of the soffit above our flat will be repaired now – and then park up and walk on Hampstead Heath. We ended up parking at the western limit of our Belsize Park permit, in South End Green just across from the former bookshop, now a Pain Quotidien, where John Wyndham once worked. He used the back alley to the side as the setting for Bill Masen's escape from the grocery store attack in *The Day of the Triffids*. Then we walked past the now-abandoned Magdala Tavern, outside which Ruth Ellis, the last woman to be hanged in Britain, killed her lover in 1955. Just up the street we passed a blue plaque to George Orwell and we went on to the Heath by the little passageway where an iconic photo was taken of Nick Drake during the recording of his final album, *Pink Moon*. We might have much the highest incidence in the country of this horrible virus here in London, but pretty much every neighbourhood has a lively back story.

We were surprised to find the Heath as busy as we'd ever seen it on a weekday. Thinking about it, many people will probably have started to work from home, and on such a beautiful day, a large open space is a safer place for a break than most. As I keep saying, people are making up their own rules at the moment, but it seemed like they were trying to employ social distancing.

We kept hearing snatches of passing conversation, almost all of it about the virus, with the exception of a woman talking to her young son about how well Kieran Trippier is doing at Atlético Madrid. It must be really difficult trying to strike a balance with youngsters right now. They are almost certainly not in danger themselves, but they may have to live with the lifelong guilt of inadvertently killing an older relative.

We saw a couple of school groups out there – again, there's probably less risk of passing on the virus than in a confined classroom, but are we right to still be sending them to school when pretty much everywhere else in the western world is now keeping them at home? Once again, let's hope to God we're getting this call right. Either way, it slightly marred our walk, as we entered the narrow section of pavement behind the pond at the Vale of Health, to encounter a gigantic crocodile of primary school kids coming the other way. Usually, it's a heart-warming sight to see a multicultural gaggle of young Londoners holding hands in twos and getting some fresh air. Right now, as with so much else, you don't know what to think.

Right, back to Elena Ferrante's lockdown-free, but still dicey, 1950s Naples. No statistics or social media before bedtime tonight.

Tuesday, 17 March 2020

Despite having gone to bed with nothing more disturbing to fire my thoughts than Signorina Ferrante's insight into the mind of an adolescent Neapolitan girl 60 years ago, I was wide awake at 5am, as was Amanda. Having not stockpiled, and naively assumed that everyone else would be sensible, we were starting to run low on most day-to-day basics, other than hand sanitiser which we've made ourselves to an online recipe (two parts rubbing alcohol, one part aloe vera gel – if that's useless, it'll be too late to let us know by the time a wider audience reads this) so we decided to investigate an online shop. The first available slot is three weeks away, and on reflection, the elderly and infirm need to be first in line, anyway.

I glanced wistfully at my online calendar. There was an Italian theme to my long-since abandoned plans for today. I'd deleted Juventus v Lyon and the early BA flight to Turin this morning when they bit the dust, but for some reason the words 'Hotel Residence Star' are in faded type with a line through them. I suspect if it's open at all, that establishment will be an emergency overspill hospital by now. If they, and we, emerge out of the other side of this, I'll be taking a trip there.

I phoned Expedia when the flight was cancelled by BA a couple of weeks ago when Italy's pandemic was about where we are now. The helpful young man on the line asked me to hold and phoned the hotel, and even though I'd booked a non-refundable room rate, the money was back in my account a couple of days later. Above and beyond all round.

Juventus, by contrast, the one Italian club I would have thought won't be in too much financial peril just yet, aren't refunding a penny of the rather pricey match ticket. That's allowed under Italian law, apparently, though pretty much every other club has done the right thing and Atalanta of horribly affected Bergamo have even given their advance ticket sales to the local medical fund at the behest of their fans. If and when I do get to Turin, I might try to sit in the away end for Juve v Atalanta. Bonkers one-season Boro misfit Marten De Roon is on the books of the Nerazzurri. In the meantime, have a jar of designer hair gel on me, CR7.

Since I left BBC Sport, and once I got through a year of dizziness, nausea, anxiety and inner ear operations, I've tried to have an annual outing to an iconic Champions League venue: Dortmund, for example, or last season Roma v Real Madrid on a Tuesday and Napoli v Red Star the next day when the fixtures fell kindly. Amanda came for the long weekend in Rome then bailed out, just in case you think I'm an even worse husband than I probably am.

So, no Champions League trip this year, though I was at the first leg of Spurs v Leipzig what seems like a lifetime ago, in the still-unfinished round of 16, when Timo Werner and co. somehow only won by a goal, despite having fashioned three glorious chances in the first 90 seconds alone. The Spurs Curry Club were not happy. They like Jose Mourinho about as much as I like Dominic Cummings. Not that they're simply bad losers – one of my fondest football memories is Spurs 2 Barcelona 4 at Wembley in 2018. I'd landed a ticket late in the day and was sitting separately from my friends as Lionel Messi ran the show in a fashion rarely witnessed before or since. Big bruising Norf London types around me were virtually making sex noises as Leo beat men at will, played angled passes which sold the crowd a dummy and caressed in a couple of goals for good measure. I'm a Boro fan, and merely a member at Spurs and Arsenal because of where I live, so I was essentially a neutral who felt blessed to be in the presence of football's Mozart or Vermeer. Even so, I could happily join in the post-match curry knees-up after the 3-1 mauling of Real Madrid or the day Harry Kane v Dejan Lovren and a 4-1 mauling left Jürgen Klopp simply writing 'Virgil van Dijk. ANY price' on his notepad.

That Barça evening I approached the Nepalese Gurkha expecting my pals to be feeling slightly beaten up. Instead, I was greeted by a passable impression of six kids at Christmas, beaming from ear to ear. They knew there was no disgrace in being beaten by a genius, and that it was a privilege to have been there, and I loved them for it. I remember Boro fans giving Thierry Henry a standing ovation when he was subbed, with that glorious turn of the century Arsenal team 6-1 up at the Riverside. I edited a live FA Cup tie at Fratton Park when the Portsmouth fans did likewise, and just last week the Curry Club was discussing the night Ronaldinho was given a standing ovation at the Bernabéu during El Clásico. It doesn't happen often – and nor should it; we're all partisan and don't want our teams to be beaten – but those moments separate true fans of football from the tribal herd.

Oh God, the herd. 'Back to life, back to reality' again. I decided since I was awake and I would have been on my way to Gatwick if I'd been implementing 2020's Plan A, I'd head off to the Finchley Road Sainsbury's for its 6am opening instead. I told you I wasn't an entirely bad husband. What a strange experience it was. For a start, it was as busy as you'd expect it to be at peak time. An old couple I talked to in the (very long) till queue – we kept the two metres distance I think the government advised at one point this last week – told me they'd given up yesterday and that the shelves were generally well-stocked at this hour, which indeed they were. And to be fair, if I hadn't spent a long time looking for the last item on Amanda's list, I wouldn't have found myself at the very back of the early birds' queue. By the way, Amanda – polenta? How NW3 is that? Perhaps polenta will see the metropolitan elite through anything, even the zombie apocalypse.

The only items clearly not on the shelves were paracetamol – apparently, the French medics have discovered that ibrupofen and coronavirus are a bad mix – and hand sanitiser. Luckily, I'd brought my own. It is an absolute minefield, though. Best intentions were almost immediately scuppered when I realised I didn't have a pound coin for the trolley. In normal times, trading two 50p is the simplest thing in the world, and a smiling lady was happy to do so, but then you try to remember for both of our sakes how long the virus can survive on a metal surface. And then you touch the trolley and the goods on the shelf and the PIN code buttons when you pay and the parking ticket machine and the car door handle and the handles of the bags you brought and the steering wheel and the front door at home. I tried to remember to spray my hands and pretty much anything I touched, but in a city where this virus is clearly spiralling out of control and there are a hundred people in the vicinity even at 6am, is any of this really going to work? There are a growing number of people in face masks and the employees were all wearing gloves which presumably they wash, then re-use.

I've only previously seen face masks worn by the public in the Far East where it signifies that you're being socially conscious by trying not to pass on a lurgy, and I'm told the non-fitted variety are not all that effective, but I think we'll be seeing more and more of them in the coming weeks. We might have to wheel out the latex gloves we keep under the sink for when the oven needs cleaning. To be honest, what I mean is, when Amanda cleans the oven. At the risk of sounding like that excruciating *This Morning* interview with Theresa May and her husband Arthur Askey, we do have some boy and girl jobs: I'm currently the supermarket hunter-gatherer, lightbulb changer, sous chef, washer-up, cleaner of the bathroom, bird feeder and designated driver.

We walked up to Primrose Hill again at lunchtime and touched absolutely nothing en route; this time there were very few people about. If we've caught this thing already, it wasn't on that outing. Not that it would matter, since we're not in South Korea. No testing or tracking, please – we're British. I've read yesterday's diatribe back, and although I'm leaving it there for posterity because I'm trying to convey the honest emotions of this weirdness, I may have gone a bit too far.

I always said to young producers, reporters or commentators when inevitable mistakes happened, that I wasn't going to emulate the legendary Fergie hairdryer-style 'bollockings' of the previous BBC Sport era. Even if I'd let out an exasperated yelp at the time, all I needed to know once the dust had settled is that they understood what had gone wrong, cared about it and would try to learn from the experience. Again, we won't – and probably shouldn't – know until an insider's diary appears, but I suspect something similar has happened in Whitehall. There appears to be a division in the scientific world as to whether 'herd immunity' was always a bad idea, or whether the data emerging from the rest of Europe was such that this shift towards a 'suppression' phase is a case of adapting when the facts change. It's immaterial until the inevitable massive scale post-mortem is held – there can be no cover-ups this time – the important thing is that there has been a decisive shift away from a course of action entirely out of kilter with the rest of the world.

I still don't understand the abandonment of testing and why we seem to have far fewer restrictions being formally placed on us than many other countries, but at least this week has finally seen much of the population largely shutting itself away, and saving lives put ahead of economics and speculative theories. Johnson and Cummings are, in their distinctive ways, an absolute pair of arses, but neither of them entered public life expecting this to land on their plate. Anyone would struggle in these circumstances.

After the awful mess of mixed messages and a 'source said', there are to be regular daily briefings: Rishi Sunak will be conducting today's, and I suspect will try to mothball the entire economy as far as possible with a view to adding the coming months of economic inactivity to the national debt. Or at least, I hope so. For all his unfortunate Winchester Head Boy manner (no surprise really since he was) and Brexitiness, he seems like the brightest of the young Tories to me. Admittedly, the plant pot I can see through the window would be ahead of Andrea Jenkyns, Daniel Kaswczynski and Dehenna Davison, the new MP for my family's home town of Bishop Auckland, and it's still beyond belief that the other two top cabinet jobs are in the hands of Messrs Raab and Patel, but Sunak seems to be a good operator.

There are going to be some staggering problems to solve as whole sectors shut down, not least given the extent of the gig economy of zero hours contracts and freelancers and the shambles that is Universal Credit, but his Budget suggested he may at least try. He'll certainly try more than George Osborne, who seemed to positively glory in shafting the undeserving poor. Quite how Osborne dares raise the issue of London's chronic hospital bed, staff and equipment shortages in the *Evening Standard* he now edits, is a question only he could answer. If he deigned to do so, which he won't.

It's also right that they're now starting to publish the data fuelling their modelling. The figures which seem to have brought about the recent change of direction came from a specialist Imperial College team of scientists, not the top of Cummings's chrome dome, which is something of a relief – the potential ICU shortfall they've cited of one bed to eight desperately ill patients is horrendous, but it saves amateurs like me from wasting time doing their own sums like I did yesterday. And therein lies the problem – there have been almost no actual edicts and where the football authorities led, so too, spasmodically, are other places of entertainment and hospitality. There are massive insurance implications until the government officially closes bars or restaurants, for example, but the numbers coming through those establishments' doors are rightly in freefall as people act ahead of the curve.

Despite the 'herd immunity' theory seemingly being sent to its bedroom to think about what it's done, I still worry that there's too much behavioural psychology input going on behind the scenes – the Sergeant Wilson-style 'would you mind awfully not going to the cinema?' approach is of course more stereotypically

British than imposing curfews, but I'm really not convinced we're getting this right. Boris Johnson is both politically and personally the epitome of laissez-faire, libertarian licentiousness, so trying to stop people from doing things is not in his DNA. In normal times, I'd see his permissiveness as a small redeeming feature, but he's going to have to change the habits of a lifetime now. He's also clearly finding not cracking bad jokes all the time about as difficult as I would, but he really has to keep that under control, too.

I've been communicating with my online groups and have talked at length on the phone to both my 80-year-old dad and my best mate at the BBC, their lead football director in precedented times, Andrew Clement, in the last 24 hours. It's safe to say we'd all rather have the South Korean foreign minister in charge here, and moreover, that none of us have liked the direction in which the UK has travelled this last decade. Austerity reducing public services and living standards for the most vulnerable in society and then cutting ourselves off from our neighbours, all cheered on and funded by shady billionaire tax exiles, isn't really our thing. We all feel this virus disaster has to lead to a 1945-style recalibration of our nation's values – my dad actually lived through the first one. That's the only way anything good can come out of what's about to happen.

There are, however, two snags: 1) Control of the means of communication; the billionaire tax exiles still control the media that older people consume, so they won't be told about South Korea's comparative figures. Meanwhile, the young are bombarded with unchecked disinformation on the morally neutral platforms they use. 'No one knows anything' as the screenwriter William Goldman once wrote, although it's more a case of 'no one wants you to know anything' now. 2) Timing: a general election was overdue by 1945. The nation saying 'thanks for your service Winston, old boy, but we want homes and a health service' therefore happened shortly after the end of World War Two. This time we're stuck with Churchill the insurance dog

– 'Oh, yes' – and his collapsible car cabinet of deeply unfunny horror clowns until 2024.

And unlike in 2017 and 2019, it seems the Labour Party may have a potentially electable Prime Minister and deputy leading it from next month. That is, not Rebecca Long-Bailey or Richard Burgon. As is my wont, I've put decent-sized bets at very favourable odds on those two winning on the grounds that either would represent yet more hopeless Continuity Corbynism, so I might as well cushion the blow should the worst happen. But that was back in the heady days of January when we still had an economy in which money had a tangible value. I could be wrong, but I don't think Betfair will be prepared to send me a barrowload of turnips as the barter equivalent of my winnings, but we'll see.

Evening footnote – I can't bear to watch any press conference involving Boris Johnson, but Sunak has indeed announced a range of measures – mortgage holidays and loans at 'attractive' rates to businesses affected by COVID-19 – which represent unprecedented state bail-outs from a Tory Chancellor. Even so, I'm not sure how many firms and jobs it will save. Many friends and family are extremely worried, and the government need to remember most of us don't have a tapestry room in which to self-isolate, and lots of people pay rent, too. I'd hope that will be reflected in further announcements, but while 'don't worry about your mortgage or company' is welcome news for property and business owners, everyone else should not be made to feel like an afterthought.

And, sadly, I spoke too soon about Johnson reining in the buffoonery – in a conference call with leading CEOs, designed to rustle up some extra ventilators to supplement the lowest capacity of any Western nation, he couldn't stop himself from dubbing it 'Operation Last Gasp'. The sort of thing you might think to yourself, or whisper after lights out in the dorm, but pitiful from a Prime Minister in this grave a situation. I hope with every fibre of my being that his government succeeds in minimising the death toll ahead, and I suspect that would have to mean that he isn't making a single decision about our futures himself.

Wednesday, 18 March 2020

Belsize Park was just that, a park adjoining Belsize House, until the mid-19th century. Hampstead, up the hill to the north in the highest part of London – Whitestone Pond is 135 metres above the London basin – was an upmarket village famed for its fresh air, an important consideration given the London environment of those days. Consumption, not coronavirus, was the terror of its day – even moving to Hampstead in 1817 at the age of just 22 failed to save the already sickly John Keats from his untimely demise in Rome four years later. He knew the end was nigh, but still conjured up some of the greatest poetry ever written – the odes *To a Nightingale*, *On Melancholy* and *To Autumn* all came to him in the one single Hampstead spring of 1819.

Fellow Hampsteadian John Constable painted numerous views looking down across the Heath to a far-distant City of London skyline with miles of greenery in between. Then someone bought the Belsize estate and built a planned district of white stucco-fronted houses to accommodate the burgeoning Victorian middle classes, and Hampstead was a separate entity no more. Hampstead has looked down on Belsize Park, literally and metaphorically, ever since, but on the plus side, that lesser cachet meant we were (just about) able to buy something here, equidistant from the Heath and the more earthy Finchley Road.

My indissoluble north-east ties mean I'm well aware of how London is viewed by some of the rest of the country. Until recently, Dominic Cummings over there in Islington talked of little else. I was going to add as he sipped sherry with visitors to his tapestry room, but I suspect he didn't have many visitors even in happier times. That said, not all of the resentment is misplaced: the City got completely out of control in the 'Greed is Good' 1980s, there's been a frightening surge in knife crime (often cited by tweeters in, er, the gun-crazed USA), property prices have historically been ridiculous to the point where none of Home Secretary Priti Patel's 'less-skilled or unskilled' workers – the nurses, cleaners and other NHS staff who are about to put their lives on the line for us all, for example – can do anything other than rent a flat towards the end of the Tube lines and commute every day.

There is a certain brand of irritating Shoreditch hipster who'll only drink artisan coffee from one farm in the Costa Rican rainforest, and even then, only if it's served with organic armadillo milk. And, if you're not a fan of diversity, having a Muslim mayor or eating Ghanaian, Turkish or Jamaican food at midnight outside Spurs' new space-age stadium when a game's gone to penalties (been there, done that), it's definitely not the place for you. I love the north-east, but I left it when I was 14, and I had a great time living in Oxford and later on, outside Manchester, but London's home. The Queen Mother was advised that she and the king should withdraw to Windsor or Sandringham during the Blitz, but famously stayed put because 'we could never look the East End in the eye again'. And, though it has no symbolic importance except to the two of us, and won't save the monarchy like that decision arguably did, Amanda and I feel a bit like that now.

The atmosphere is increasingly odd around here, though. Perhaps early September 1939 felt a bit like this, I don't know. But whereas that generation brilliantly lampooned Hitler by cutting newsreel footage of Nazi rallies and goose-stepping to the 'Lambeth Walk', it's not easy to satirise a microorganism, so around here people seem to have adopted the 'Belsize Shuffle'. Few people are on the streets, other than small numbers going in and out of our local late-night convenience store and the Belsize Village pharmacy. Those who are, seem to be doing what Amanda and I have begun to do, that is, gently straying towards the opposite pavement if someone's coming towards you. That works most of the way to Hampstead Heath, where we took a walk today, but then it gets worryingly random.

Despite, or perhaps because of Piffle-Paffle Wiff-Waff Johnson's suggestion that we avoid congregating if we 'er, um, er, wouldn't mind awfully', the cafes around the Heath are still all open, and plenty of people are in them. It could well be that, as small businesses know they're about to have no customers for an undefined amount of time, they're waiting to be ordered to close, so they're then covered by their insurance policies. The time lag while De Pfeffel and gang work that one out and actually just shut the bloody places makes us distinctly uneasy. I remembered the Jam song '"A" Bomb in Wardour Street'. That was about the thuggishly anarchic fringes of the punk movement, but it seems apt: 'If this is freedom, I don't want to know, because it seems like madness to me.'

I was just the right age to absolutely love The Jam, play their stuff on my first guitar, then find out more about their 1960s influences, but in retrospect, the young Paul Weller was actually a chord-thrashing prophet and virtuoso poet of Keatsian proportions. The whole of the lyrics to 'Eton Rifles' and 'Going Underground' could have been written yesterday. Weller wrote both when he was 21, Keats wrote those Hampstead odes aged 23. I might just cut and paste a selection from both here instead of diary entries as I become increasingly lost for words.

The Heath worried me as much as the cafes had: some walkers were being cautious, some weren't. A family of four strode at us, taking up the entire width of the path, the mother coughing fairly violently when she wasn't talking extremely loudly in a New York accent. Amanda was less freaked than I was as we jumped aside – that boarding school upbringing again, maybe – and I think I may have spoilt the rest of our outing with my constant slightly neurotic chuntering of 'being American doesn't mean you won't catch it, you silly cow', 'oh Christ, let's avoid sneeze features over there' and 'they won't die, but their grandad might' at one of a number of groups of teenagers I would never normally have noticed. I know the messaging's been muddled, and apparently Macron lost his rag when he saw similar gatherings in Paris at the weekend, but four people who don't live together, mucking around with each other like nothing has happened, is bordering on criminal negligence. You might be feeling fine now, and yes, they're your mates, but if you're in that first five-day plus symptom-free incubation period, you've just given the virus to three other people, and you and they will have, at the very least, a houseful of it. How fucking difficult is it to grasp?

Sadly, I think this tells you all you need to know about where society is now. Some people are on top of things, or ahead of the official guidance, others live on a planet comprised of inane reality TV, *FIFA 20* and social media influencers. I'm not singling out teenagers, there were also some really old people out there, who may, for all I know, have been burying themselves in the *Emmerdale* omnibus and Glenn Miller CDs and missed the whole of the last month's news coverage. In a way their recklessness is even less explicable than that of the younger lot, they're playing dare with their own lives. Not only that, but they're likely to clog up the NHS in the process, thereby causing other people to die. Maybe every TV ad break right now needs to feature footage from the front line in northern Italian hospitals to bring home the reality of the World War One-style carnage to the hard of thinking. Nice multicultural, well-educated, politically savvy middle-class Belsize Park largely seems to have grasped what's happening, but that's all going to count for nothing if a certain percentage of the wider public aren't following developments, or worse still, have decided it's for other people to worry about. Especially here in London where I fear the statistics in a fortnight's time are going to look very grim indeed.

The Twitter ban is still in force, so I'm getting my news in dribs and drabs online, on other social media and from the selected TV news I can bear watching. A decade's worth of events are happening every day, ranging from the trivially imbecilic –

Dominic Raab, our actual Foreign Secretary, thinks Lima is the capital of the Philippines, while Stanley Johnson, the human apple tree closely aligned with at least one of his fallen fruits, airily announced he was off to the pub last night – to the predictably horrific, i.e. all the stats, which still show us inexorably following where Italy was roughly 13 or so days ago in pretty much every respect. Johnson has a degree in classics, but Cummings studied history, so should be aware of the phrase, 'Those who fail to learn from history are doomed to repeat it.' It may only be 13-day-old history, Oxford historians tending to regard even the events of 13 centuries ago as a bit vulgar and modern, but the graphs are not difficult to interpret.

The one comfort is that Imperial College's input appears to have brought about a swift U-turn from the 'herd immunity' with 250,000 projected deaths insanity. How and why that was ever mooted – or even whether, as has been suggested, reporters all too readily accepted the government line that the science had changed and that the previously unheard-of 'suppression phrase' was the next stage of the plan all along – is something to be saved for the eventual official inquiry once this is all over. As long as it's not another Hutton Inquiry or the police's initial Hillsborough 'investigation'. I've had great respect for Imperial College ever since our college team was soundly thrashed by them at football on the first plastic pitch I'd ever played on, just along from The Oval in the mid-1980s. And, rather more importantly, they produce some world-class scientists. If we can't get the South Korean foreign minister in before the transfer deadline, we will have to put our full faith in the lads and lasses from Imperial.

Elsewhere, it transpires that an NHS dummy run for a flu epidemic in 2016 concluded that we would be woefully short of all manner of equipment if the real thing ever transpired. And to quote Derek and Clive again, 'Who listened? Fucking nobody, that's who.' Another topic for the Nuremberg trials, sorry, inquiry which has to follow all of this. And staggeringly, *The Telegraph*, of all publications, has conducted a survey which has discovered that two-thirds of Brits now think health and care workers should be exempt from Priti Patel's 'if you don't earn a wad, you ain't gettin' a job' immigration rules. Most of the other third will work it out in the coming weeks, and, as with the Polish chef who took on the (British-born) London Bridge terrorist armed with only a narwhal tusk, we're going to discover that, guess what, people from the EU contribute enormously to our country. Some 40,000 or so of them will be on the NHS front line and I'd wager there'll be a few 'forrins' in that Imperial brains trust, too. Putting aside their settled status applications, obscure English history tests and casual racism in the streets, to give every fibre of their being to a populace which (marginally) chose to tell them they're not welcome here. Coming over here, saving thousands and thousands of people's lives. Scrounging bastards, the lot of them.

Johnson – Kuntis Kuntson – as he is sometimes called on one of our WhatsApp groups when we descend to mindless vulgarity ('k' instead of 'c' makes it okay, apparently) is still sticking to the 'No Deal if necessary' exit on 31 December line, even in the face of desperate pleas in the Commons today, from the DUP of all people. Everyone in business or government on both sides of the Channel has infinitely more pressing fish/blue whales to fry right now, and in these circumstances, surely only a maniac could contemplate food and medicine supply chains being blocked at Calais or Dover, and the economy being even further destroyed? Even Nigel Farage or the *Daily Express* would surely accept a year's delay now on the grounds of the biggest sodding set of unforeseen circumstances ever known. If Johnson continues to plough on regardless for much longer, it will be an act of reckless self-destructive insanity to rival the Charge of the Light Brigade or Tony Blair's illegal (according to the UN) Iraq War in the history of British infamy. The kind of madness Oxford historians may well be studying in the 34th century AD.

After I wrote that last little lot, three things have happened: the schools are finally shutting on Friday, Professor Neil Ferguson, the man in charge of that Imperial data modelling has come down with COVID-19 symptoms and I had a somewhat fraught conversation with my dad, then my brother. All family situations are complex in their own way, but this one is very tricky now. My brother John and his two daughters are currently living with my elderly parents in Sevenoaks: Dad is mobile but with respiratory problems; Mum, not very mobile at all having had a couple of strokes, is visited morning and evening by an excellent local carer. The girls attend a primary school in Tunbridge Wells, where they formerly lived with my brother and their mother, a nurse and his then partner. Sadly, that relationship broke up acrimoniously and my brother and his kids were thrown out of their home by his partner. Court proceedings are ongoing, as and when family courts reconvene – the issue of the flat (my brother pays the mortgage) is not yet resolved but it was decided that the girls would live with John while having a certain amount of access to their mother. Not at all ideal, but between John and my dad, the girls have been driven to and from school for a while now, and it's generally been a manageable operation. Uncle Paul went down and did the school run a couple of weeks ago then took them to play football for the school, and actually thoroughly enjoyed himself.

The big snag is that John co-manages his own small law firm in London, specialising mostly in criminal cases. So, my parents, who really cannot afford to get this virus, face two dangers – the girls could bring it home from school or after visiting their mum who's a nurse, and John certainly could bring it back from London. His business, like so many others, may well go under if the work dries up, say, if the police start only dealing with the most serious of crimes, so he's continuing to commute for the time being. Both he and I think they need to divide the house and get my parents to self-isolate as far as possible – luckily, there are two bathrooms – with some kind of rota for the kitchen and maybe a sofa area each in the living room. It's still a minefield virus-wise, but my nieces are 11 and 9 now, very bright and caring and they're apparently being given hygiene lessons by Mum's lovely visiting carer, Tracey.

John and I don't see each other all that much these days except when I visit my parents, and he was already having a rather rough time one way and another, but I have to say I've never felt closer to him than I did tonight. He's trying to find a route out of coming to London as soon as he can, even if he loses his business in the process – he's going to explore using video conferencing from Sevenoaks – and other than the worry of accidental cross-infection, I'm glad he's going to be on hand. I've told him – and told him to tell my nieces in particular – that however this pans out no one is to blame for anything that happens. I've heard horrendous stories of kids starting to have nightmares about accidentally killing Grandad. No one should have that on their conscience for the rest of the lives, and as long as they have tried their best, no one is going to try to trace the microbiology back. If the government isn't tracking anything, we're certainly not going to do so.

Talking to John and my dad in particular made me realise how immersed I am in the news compared to most people. They're both highly intelligent – Dad has an extraordinary mind in many ways, as both the first grammar school boy and then university graduate in the family, but I think he thought I was exaggerating when I said with some conviction that we're seemingly on an unstoppable path to be roughly where Italy is now – 450 deaths in the last 24 hours – in around 13 days' time. They passed 100 deaths in total 13 days ago, we passed it today – the 13-day gap has been an eerie constant since I started to follow it last week when a clearly agitated US contributor to *Channel 4 News* flagged it up, and pleaded with the UK to abandon all notions of 'herd immunity'. I can't get my head around it, either, and I've been thinking about little else, so two men with little spare time on their hands to crunch the numbers can be forgiven for being sketchier than I am on the details. After all, the Prime Minister is sketchier still and he's allegedly running the show. I've left Dad thinking about it all, and I hope they'll come up with a concrete plan and crack on with it very soon.

In the meantime, Amanda and I are planning to lie even lower than we have been, until the government actually does something. My hunch is that London is the petri dish which will suffer horribly for the aborted herd immunity gamble in the next couple of weeks, while the rest of the country will see smaller localised outbreaks for now, many of which could well have spread from Cheltenham Races. That said, we don't have South Korea's technology, so we'll probably never know.

We ended a very, very strange and somewhat overwrought day wonderfully. Amanda made a superb chicken curry, we opened a beer and watched the latest episode of two comedies we always record on series link. Despite, or perhaps because of my background in live TV sport, I have absolutely no idea of the slot or channel for anything but we series link quite a lot, and made a timely, but totally coincidental investment in Netflix a few weeks ago. It might have been the stark contrast with what's going on in the world outside, but Larry David's pedantry and misanthropy in *Curb Your Enthusiasm* and Steve Coogan and Rob Brydon riffing on their Mick Jagger impressions on the stunning-looking island of Hydra in the *Trip to Greece* was the TV equivalent of a warm bath, and neither has ever seemed funnier.

Then my mate Ron Chakraborty, knowing I occasionally mess around on the ukulele, sent me a clip of a ludicrously talented exponent playing the whole of 'Bohemian Rhapsody' live. I occasionally try to copy bits and piece from musical performances, but I wouldn't even have a go at any given bar of this one. Jake Shimabukuro is his name – if people ever start travelling again, I'll look out for him on tour. Of my eternal triumvirate of the 'most important of the unimportant things in life', we've lost sport for the time being, but at least comedy and music are still at our disposal. For that, I'm genuinely thankful. I have a guitar, uke and a rarely used (rather antisocial) harmonica here but no piano. I only ever play that at my parents' house (my dad played church organ, and would be at the more accomplished end of the spectrum if he played his American songbook repertoire in a cocktail lounge) but I've just remembered there's an electric keyboard under the bed. As long as the headphones still work, that's coming out of mothballs very soon.

Thursday, 19 March 2020

It's 4am, the alarm's set for two hours from now, and for the first time in a long time I've been awake all night. The Friday in a Manchester hotel before we did a somewhat fluid two-hour build-up to the England v Greece qualifier (Beckham free kick, 90+3) may well have been the last time. Making late-night live TV most of my life after three years as a student means I've never really got out of the 'late to bed, late to rise' cycle. The only time that ever goes awry is when I'm ill or when I know I need to be up early. The latter applied tonight, but the fact that we've now moved somewhere beyond unprecedented times didn't help either.

The behavioural science experts have clearly told the government that it's best to moot something by planting a rumour about two days before they do it. I sort of get that in principle – getting people used to a notion before it happens may well breed acceptance – but since we're a fortnight behind the curve, and that's being generous, for the first time in my life I want martial law or something equally draconian to have happened yesterday, or maybe last week when '13 days behind Italy' seemed to become a fact of life and indeed death. So, when the media whispers that London may go into lockdown tomorrow, you assume it's going to happen. And this time the government might actually enforce, rather than just recommend, it.

Quite what a lockdown amounts to in a British context – Dixon of Dock Green asking those kids on Hampstead Heath to cover their mouths when they cough, probably – we don't yet know. It wouldn't entirely surprise me if our government asked for air raid warden volunteers to ensure we all have blackout curtains so the enemy can't see us. The patrons of the Blitz Café, Whitby, would expect no less.

In any case, I knew what was coming in advance of the media briefing, because Lee from the Spurs Curry Club WhatsApp group told us yesterday lunchtime that the schools were finally closing and London was going into some kind of lockdown. Quite how a project manager in the building industry finds that out before anyone else is one of life's great mysteries. He, Tall Paul and Mark all seem to know Spurs insiders who once in a blue moon tip them off about something that then actually happens, but you knew shit had got real when the Curry Club conversation moved beyond football, favourite *Inside No 9* episodes and music trivia quizzes. Actually, it's not even the Spurs Curry Club any more, Lee changed the name to Poncey Horse Club to register his contempt when three of us blagged some Royal Ascot tickets last summer. We won't be going there again this summer: the fact that it will almost certainly be cancelled is a secondary consideration, we wouldn't have upset Lee's sensibilities by attending a sporting event in suits, then posting him selfies. Not twice, anyway.

Amanda got up when the alarm went off at 6am, and we embarked on the frankly weird plan we'd hatched last night. Everyone knows London is supposedly going into lockdown tomorrow – no one knows exactly what that means, but the supermarkets were going to be bedlam squared, and judging by the very shaky statistics for the untested capital herd, becoming more and more likely to contain unwitting spreaders. Plus, Sainsbury's had rightly put aside the first hour of shopping today for the elderly and vulnerable – good for them, by the way – so by the time that was over, things would be even worse than usual. We had a look at a league table that Sky have been publishing of confirmed cases per 100,000: London is snowballing, whereas Reading to the west has only five confirmed cases – clearly, with no testing, it'll be a lot higher than that but it was still much better than anywhere in London, plus with no lockdown talk there, we shouldn't see the same sense of panic.

So, at 7.30am after a very easy drive we were at Waitrose in Reading: no loo paper, sanitiser, flour (extra home time is seemingly being used for a household bake-off) and no eggs or tinned vegetables, either. People are clearly bunkering down for the long haul, and to be honest they're right to do so. We didn't take too much of anything but now have enough dry goods, tinned soup, porridge oats, etc. to see us through for a while as well as some fresh stuff so we can front-load with vitamins, before we develop scurvy at a later date. There was nothing like the sense of urgency we're seeing everywhere in London, there was only a vague attempt at social distancing, but everyone was polite to the point where the till lady wanted a good natter while I mentally calculated how far away she was. We actually used the latex gloves for the first time; we only have a couple of flimsy and therefore presumably suspect masks, but I think that may be the order of the day from now on in London.

The weird part is that self-isolation didn't seem that big a deal when you thought life would go on normally again afterwards as long as you'd remained symptom-free. Footballers, musicians and others have been cheering people up with home-based clips. Pretty much anyone can deal with a week at home. I had three months more or less housebound when my ear problems were at their worst in 2015. I could just about walk 400 yards to Hyde Park for half an hour's fresh air if it was dry, and I can step out on to our patio now. Even so, if we spend seven straight days at home, which we're lucky enough to be able to contemplate doing, at best all we'll know at the end of that is whether we've had the virus yet. Even if the answer is no, one excursion to the nearest chemist or food store, and you'd have to do another week's self-isolation to make sure you hadn't contracted it on that latest trip.

I guess I underestimated the importance the behavioural psychologists were placing on the boredom factor. Even so, if I lived in China, I'd rather have gone stir crazy for the last three months in Wuhan or experienced various restrictions elsewhere, if it meant achieving the zero new infections they've announced today. Their 3,000-plus death toll, while still tragic, is clearly going to be dwarfed by the eventual figures here, in the US and in Italy. There'll doubtless be new outbreaks in Asia as people start to work and move around again, but at least their relative success so far means they can ease restrictions, and be ready to swoop with tests and localised restrictions as required. When this all settles down, if it ever does, you suspect that the axis of global power will have finally and firmly moved east. Not only are the Asian nations living up to the stereotype of efficiency, technological wizardry and ability to persuade (or force, in China's case) the public to comply, they're frankly trouncing the US and most of Europe in the most basic area of all: keeping their people safe, and indeed alive.

I really don't want to harp on about the inadequacy of the preparations and response here in the UK, but Liz, a consultant at a London hospital, has texted us today saying, 'Chaos. Scary stuff. Staff very much at risk.' And she's the most capable, dedicated person I know, so that's an ominous assessment, given that the process has barely even started yet. It seems to me that there's more than a whiff of World War One in the air – understaffed, under-equipped, undervalued, under-supported lions being led (if that's the word) by government donkeys. I'm not party political and have mostly voted for neither major party in the past, but the Tories have sold the necessary 40 per cent or so of the electorate the pipe dream of low taxation and top-class public services for the last four decades. Just string these thoughts together: 'There is no such thing as society' (Margaret Thatcher); Jacob Rees-Mogg's notion that environmental and safety regulations could be rolled back 'a very long way' post-Brexit to a 'good enough for India' level; and finally, a line from a book, 'Churchill ... put his shirt on a horse called anti-Nazism ... and his bet came off in spectacular fashion'.

That last one from Boris Johnson, in his biography of the wartime leader he claims is his hero, is in many ways the most disturbing of all. The one war every other British person I've ever met thinks was necessary and morally justified was no such thing, it seems. It was simply a cynical gamble with no moral dimension. Red or black on the roulette table. Could just as easily have gone the other way, rather like the pro- and anti-Brexit articles Johnson wrote for *The Telegraph* in 2016. He ultimately sent the Leave version for publication, but David Cameron has subsequently told ITV News that he believes that Johnson wanted to be the 'romantic, patriotic' hero, thinking that the Leave campaign would be 'crushed like a toad under the harrow'. The implication being that Johnson's enhanced standing with the Eurosceptic Tory membership would ensure him the leadership when Cameron eventually left office. The shell-shocked expression Johnson wore when giving his 'victory' speech the morning after the referendum did rather suggest that his NHS and Turkey claims had exceeded their objective. Meanwhile, Sarah Vine had joked to her husband Michael Gove, 'You were only supposed to blow the bloody doors off.'

Boris Johnson epitomises a certain right-wing type. Life's a gamble, you wheel and deal, bluff, bend or break the rules if you have to, then winner takes all. It's a lot easier when you start at the top, like he did, but you see it in a certain type of businessman, too. JD Wetherspoon boss Tim Martin, the only prominent businessman to back Brexit other than James Dyson (and Dyson promptly moved his HQ to Singapore) is currently warning the government not to shut all 800 or so of his pubs in an attempt to halt the spread of the virus. And the problem is that Johnson and his ilk see Martin, or the Cheltenham bookmakers and probably the insurance brokers who have to pay up if businesses are forced to close, as the voice of the risk-taker, to be accorded enormous weight even in a conversation about tens of thousands of people dying.

There's a story in the *Daily Mirror* today about two young hospitality workers who were told to carry on working at the

Cheltenham Festival by the Jockey Club, despite developing a fever and dry cough. 'It's only a cold,' they were told, so they worked for all four days, infecting God knows how many people who've probably since infected lots more. Having read that, I'm genuinely never attending a horse racing meeting again, and the Jockey Club and the Cheltenham organisers may need to be answerable to a bit more than a stewards' enquiry in due course.

While I was typing that, Radio 4's *World at One* has just announced that London isn't in fact going into lockdown, so I'm off to Tim Martin's nearest establishment for a pint and a game of darts. Like hell I am – provided Amanda and I show no symptoms, we've decided not to go out of the front door for seven days, then review our options. We could drive out of London at that point knowing we weren't infectious, if we had anywhere obvious to go. I had calmed down a little from the other day, and I don't want to keep radiating terror and pessimism, but if we're not even aping the Milan epicentre lockdown, we're going to narrow the 13-day gap with Italy, then presumably overtake them, all in the name of no strategy whatsoever.

Are we back to herd immunity or are the government so incompetent – and presumably divided – that 'indecision rules', as Alan Hansen used to say? That was just a back four getting in a tangle, not an actual government of my country adopting a laissez-faire 'put all your chips on number 32' approach to the greatest health threat for a century. I hope to God I'm proved wrong, and if I am, will admit as much with absolute delight, but it's little wonder that the only message most people have picked up from our non-leader during this infinitely more serious continuation of the Brexit insanity, is 'Wash Your Hands'. Yes, Boris – we can see you doing it, and we're all absolutely shitting ourselves out here.

I took a siesta after that, and came back into the living room as the daily press conference was in full flow. I haven't watched him unedited in a very long time, but my God, Boris Johnson was awful. Not a single meaningful sentence came out of his mouth, other than we'll 'turn the tide in 12 weeks'. Okay, so we'll be through the worst by June? Well no, it wouldn't …wiffle-waffle, piffle-paffle … necessarily be on the way down as such by then. He started to study the carpet, as if that would provide inspiration, but to no avail. The scientists didn't really know what he was talking about, either – they're both better, steadier orators than Johnson, but so then was Marcel Marceau – and I'm afraid their skill sets, whatever they are, are being dragged into the vacuum of his leadership. Nothing new was on offer at all, no need for all that lockdown bally-hoo: Tim Martin continues to gurn and pull his pints, there's not remotely enough equipment to go round and, as for the WHO recommendations on testing … ha, ha, you're joking, aren't you?

They all seem to have given up, especially our PM who is pretty much all out of a vocabulary, let alone ideas – in summary, minus the ums and ers, sideways glances and weird hand movements: 'We don't do draconian, we've known for years that the NHS's resources are third-rate while its remaining staff are first-rate (yes, yes, all right – even the unskilled forrins) the virus will do whatever it will do, the public can react as it sees fit, the roulette ball will land where it lands. Life's one big gamble. Best of British luck to you all, and let's see what the body count is in 12 weeks' time. Oh God, you're going to hold me to that "turn the tide" thing, aren't you? Why are you media johnnies suddenly expecting me to mean anything I say? Don't you know anything about me?' As Gareth Southgate said after an uninspiring half-time World Cup team talk from Sven-Göran Eriksson, 'We needed Winston Churchill, but instead we got Iain Duncan Smith.' That was a football match, this is a global pandemic.

British exceptionalism is an insidious thing: we don't salute the flag in our schools (yet) and only a minority of us feel a tumescence in our underwear when human nicotine stain Nigel Farage and his frog face make an appearance on *Question Time*, or when fat, tattooed men sing 'Ten German Bombers' as they throw plastic chairs around a mediaeval Continental town square of a summer's evening. I'm not sure what it's like now, but my schooling was based on the unstated truth that this is the best country on the planet, doling out lashings of civilisation and invention to a grateful planet. It was only when I reached my late teens, and was left reeling by the 'Kill an Argie, and win a Metro' jingoism of the Falklands War, and Margaret Thatcher's 'rejoice, rejoice' reaction to the sinking of a vessel full of conscripts, which swung the opinion polls decisively back in her favour in a recession-ravaged nation as a result, that I began to suspect that we might have a slightly deluded self-image.

I got the principle – there had been an invasion, by a dismal and desperate military junta, of a disputed territory whose inhabitants saw it as British, so technically it was no crime to evict the invaders. And yes, our professional – and much larger then than now – military efficiently and bravely did its job. But it was a diplomatic failure, decades in the making, as the patrician Lord Carrington recognised when he resigned as Foreign Secretary on the basis that it had happened on his watch. Just compare that reaction with the 'cockroach in a nuclear holocaust' survival skills of Priti Patel, Chris Grayling and Boris Johnson himself, despite calamity after calamity. Just Google Nazanin Zaghari-Ratcliffe if you haven't followed the latter's career too closely. His political career should have been over when her sentence in an Iranian jail was increased after he misspoke as Foreign Secretary, but then so should Donald Trump's when he launched into an impersonation of a disabled journalist which you'd hope would lead to the expulsion of a seven-year-old from infant school. These are not normal times. They weren't even before the coronavirus.

I saw a cartoon a while back – from a European newspaper, I think – of a man in a bowler hat jumping out of a plane holding a Union Jack. A concerned steward was saying, 'Shouldn't you take a parachute, sir?' and the reply was simply, 'No, thank you – the flag will do.' Well, it seems we're taking that same Brexit 'Britannia waives the rules' approach even to our greatest crisis for 80 years. We were all alone for a while in World War Two, and I have nothing but admiration for the generation which stood firm in the face of terrible danger. But we didn't win that war on our own – those 27 million dead Soviets are part of the reason the Russians admire Putin, the US's entry was key, so too were the Polish airmen in the Battle of Britain, and thousands of Canadian and other then-Empire servicemen and women, as well as the resistance movements in every occupied country.

I sincerely hope there is more co-operation going on behind the scenes than it appears – international science must be seeking answers and antidotes in a co-ordinated fashion, but the news that Matt Hancock doesn't join the pan-European Health Ministers' daily phone conference, and that we've turned down an offer to be involved in a joint EU trawl for more ventilators and protective equipment makes me want to cry, to be honest. I don't care if you're a Remainer or a Leaver, this is way, way beyond that; I was very much the former but would have taken a sensible softish Brexit as being regrettable, but as close to the democratic verdict as we're ever going to get. I will never understand as long as I live why Mark Francois MP feels it necessary to tear up a document from a German business leader on national TV, or why Nigel Farage and his gang feel the need to be so swaggeringly rude and cheaply xenophobic on every jolly to Brussels. I want England to win at football or cricket, am generally pleased by any British Olympic gold medal, and love the fact that I come from the home of the Beatles, Shakespeare and the NHS, but that doesn't make me intrinsically better than anyone from any other country. I'm just not. It's infantile to think otherwise.

Frankie Boyle talks ruefully of people who complain of visitors or immigrants that 'they don't speak English', then go to Spain every summer and point at a picture of egg and chips when they're hungry. The distinction some Brexity Brits abroad made between themselves – ex-pats – and people from elsewhere living in Britain – immigrants – sums it up, too. You'd like to think that a tiny upside of the impending nightmare would be a gradual realisation that we're no longer a significant nation globally and that we need to take part in as much international co-operation as possible. Even if the EU does eventually fall apart, our departure will have helped the process of everyone looking after themselves, and I can't see that as anything to celebrate.

We were in Arctic Norway on 31 January when Britain technically left the EU; we were deliberately avoiding the spectacle of Farage lighting his own farts in Parliament Square. I presume that's what he did. We were also out of the country as the previous two deadlines came and went, and were hoping to be away on 31 December this year when No Deal was poised to cause unimaginable chaos. It's all too imaginable now, but still best avoided in my humble, and doubtless irrelevant, opinion. Incidentally, if you think trying to be abroad to avoid those landmarks is a bit extreme, I'd like to quote Woody Allen on the subject of death: 'It's not that I'm afraid of it. I just don't want to be there when it happens.'

One footnote to another strange day: I put one of my random playlists on in the car to and from Reading. Being the age that I am, it's skewed towards my era, but it's nothing if not eclectic. What struck both of us, though, was how many songs had suddenly acquired a new poignancy: the beautiful 'Only Living Boy in New York', despite actually being about Art Garfunkel leaving Paul Simon behind when he went away to appear in the movie *Catch-22,* suddenly had lockdown connotations. Then there was an Abba masterpiece – in a very cliquey era, my teenage music collaborator David Eastwood and I always maintained that it was all music, so you could like the Jam and Rush and Bob Dylan and Stevie Wonder and the Specials and Abba … and we were right. In 'The Day Before You Came', Agnetha relates, almost as an actor as well as a singer, an ordinary day of commuting and work. This is intended to show how grey life was before a certain someone entered her life, now it actually felt like something to aspire towards: normality. Sam Cooke's stupendous 'Bring It On Home', as well as providing me with the chance to attempt to sing Lou Rawls' counter-harmony – even in the car, I'm not going to try to be Sam – gave Amanda an idea for an advert for home food delivery. Neat any time, but it could almost be a public safety message right now.

Then, as we approached home, one of my favourite tracks of all time – the utterly sublime 'Ain't That Enough' by Teenage Fanclub – guided us down our street. There's a Byrds-style harmony on that one; and for some reason, since my ear problems, that's where I'm naturally drawn. I wish I'd worked out 40 years ago that I was a natural backing, not lead, vocalist. I digress. What a song: and if there's a better springtime, lockdown, 'taking pleasure in small things' message in music than 'Here is a sunrise, ain't that enough. True as a clear sky, ain't that enough', I'm not aware of it. I have a week alone now with a beautiful woman who mostly (not Dylan) shares my taste in music, and we have a patio garden and enough food and a roof over our heads. Who knows where we'll be by then, but for now, yes, that is enough.

Friday, 20 March 2020

'I'm torn between the desire to be well-informed and the desire to remain sane' was the caption to a cartoon I remember posting on social media towards the end of 2016. Brexit and Trump made me a lot of money from the bookies, but I'd much rather have lost the whole stake. I'm not a sociopath.

And there was a serious point to posting that line – in 2015 when my world closed in and I was stricken with the inner ear condition which cost me my job and wrecked my balance for a while, I developed anxiety. I've been known to get a bit down in the dumps at various moments in my life, and stress was an intrinsic part of my job, but I'd never had anxiety before. It got so bad I was actually writhing around on the bed at times, and coupled with the dizziness, it was a pretty grim time, not least for Amanda.

I was very lucky that our then GP in Bayswater had trained with the Royal Free psychiatric team; he prescribed medication which together with some ENT operations and a programme of vestibular exercises – basically walking backwards and forwards and building up ever quicker and more vigorous head movements – meant that I largely got through it. My ears are far from perfect and I'm stuck with tinnitus, but compared to that part of 2015, I was in better shape to cope with the rotten following year for the planet, both politically and in terms of the deaths of a seemingly never-ending stream of fantastic people including – off the top of my head – David Bowie, Garry Shandling, Prince, Jo Cox MP, George Michael and Muhammad Ali. That's some dinner party and late-night jamming session, right there.

'The pleasure of small things' was the philosophy of Marcel Proust, whose works I read extensively while laid up in 2015. He could spend several pages describing the pleasure of dipping a madeleine into a cup of tea, or dissecting the way one of his characters talked or thought. It was about as racy a read as I could cope with at that time, and a course of mindfulness at the local Buddhist centre (yes, really) turned out to be a modern twist on the same philosophy. And working on reducing anxiety triggers, I had a few psychotherapy sessions which helped me understand and address some long-standing family-related issues more directly, and I realised that consuming news 24 hours a day via a plethora of outlets had to stop. I cut out anything featuring people like Trump, Farage, Johnson or the rash of new professional libtard-baiters like Katie Hopkins and Tommy Robinson. I have a less violent reaction to reading a print précis of what an awful person has said or done than I have after watching their press conferences or YouTube posts. In that, I differ completely from Amanda who wants to observe everything in full. But then she's an English graduate who reads everything several times and spots subtleties I've missed in films and plays. While we're getting on amazingly well in confinement, we often separate between bedroom and living room TVs. In normal times, that would be me watching a football match too many; right now she wants to watch the daily press conferences, and it's best if I read a summary.

I'm afraid I came as near as I have in over four years to an anxiety relapse overnight. I imagine mental health is an even bigger issue than usual everywhere at the moment, but the combination of the best and worst of people got to me. Watching a man who's always wanted to be Prime Minister but is currently absolutely, gob-smackingly awful at it, then reading that Cummings thought London was shutting down but Johnson decided against it, then reading a truly harrowing e-mail from Liz the doctor on the front line and seeing images of feral fights in supermarkets and stories of people ripping hand sanitiser off the wall of cancer wards, proved too much.

I read an open letter from a publican pleading for his establishment to be closed: he feels he's endangering the public but can't do so, unless the government orders it, without going bankrupt. Then I think about Tim Martin. As a revered 'risk-taking' (we might need to re-evaluate that term once our 1945 arrives) capitalist, he has influence and media outlets galore (R4's *Today* this morning, just before the health secretary, according to Amanda) in this mad world. Liz the doctor and the scarcely believable footage *Channel 4 News* shot in a Bergamo hospital yesterday, much less so. Is Johnson listening to anyone other than his inner libertarian telling him on no account ever to be the Nanny State? How can London pubs still be open? Every unwitting carrier infects God knows how many others, making Dr Liz even more likely to have to choose who lives or dies, and taking us ever closer to the Hieronymous Bosch vision of hell that we're now seeing in Italy.

A comparable death toll here seems simply inevitable now – there's surely zero chance of averting it. The government seems to live in some long-lost world where the herd: a) all follow the TV news every evening; b) can make any sense of whatever message the bumbling idiot of a PM is trying to convey. I fail the second of those tests miserably, too. It's an absolutely hopeless situation

– it was never going to be pretty, but they're currently completely failing on every level. I'm not going near Twitter, but beyond the usual WhatsApp groups, two university friends I rarely hear from contacted me last night, completely spooked by Johnson's impossibly inept and incoherent display.

You almost begin to wonder if he's actually as bad as the Mango Mussolini across the Atlantic – Trump's a truly moronic figurehead with a tiny vocabulary researchers say equates to that of an eight-year-old, and with which he chose to malign the Chinese for no discernible reason today, but at least he doesn't seem to be running their whole show. I've come to the terrifying conclusion that Johnson actually is in charge here, which seems to mean no one is in charge. Hence the square root of fuck all happening as my city and the NHS are poised on the brink of collapse.

Then you see the best of humanity: a beautiful letter a Teesside headteacher, and wife of Boro's former head of PR, wrote to her pupils; the wonderful NZ PM Jacinda Arden holding a kids' press conference to address their fears; the spontaneous help groups supporting the elderly and vulnerable, outlets giving out free food and football clubs handing their hotels over to the NHS staff, our front line troops in what is effectively World War Three. One thing that simply has to emerge from this – NHS staff are, at the very least, on a par with our armed forces: genuinely brave heroes who will do everything to save the lives this miserable virus and miserable country have imperilled.

I hope never again to see some smiling young American woman representing the 'Institute of Economic Affairs' or other Tufton Street-based, shadily funded pressure group, on the BBC, telling us in honeyed tones that the socialist NHS should be broken up and sold to whoever's behind the whole sinister shit show we've somehow been in thrall to for the last decade. Tragically, we're stuck with Johnson, Mogg, Patel, Raab, the European Research Group (ERG) and all the rest of this shower until 2024, but public pressure has to be such that they can no longer contemplate the sort of heinous dismantling and profiteering they were expecting to engineer with their majority of 80. Thanks, Jezza. Speaking of Corbyn, there are moves afoot to suspend the Labour leadership election, thus letting him continue to fail to oppose this horrible government. No, just no. You're in London and over 70, Magic Grandpa, get yourself into isolation now. Or preferably get in a Tardis and do it in 2015.

I've always been wary of extremes. I've never voted Tory, although I guess I might have done so in the 1970s when there wasn't much to choose between them and Labour – 'cradle to grave' was a given – except that Heath and company had booted Enoch Powell out, were pro-Europe and not in hoc to the Len McCluskeys of the age. I've not voted Labour very often either – I saw Lewis Mooney, then Labour's Culture and Media spokesman, praise Rupert Murdoch to the hilt a week into the Dirty Digger's Damascene conversion to the Blair cause just before the 1997 election (Rupe knew what the result was going to be, and he only backs winners) so I can proudly say I never voted for the man. Despite some fine domestic achievements, merited interventions in Kosovo and Sierra Leone, and his later sound common sense on Brexit, Iraq and the never-ending repercussions are the things for which I – and history – will most remember Blair. And to a BBC veteran who has seen the corporation put on the back foot ever since, Alistair Campbell's part in spinning the specious case for the illegal Iraq War, then David Kelly's death and the subsequent preposterous Hutton Report, paved the way for Dominic Cummings, imho.

At least Blair, other than over Iraq, was a pragmatic man. That's a bit like *This Country*'s Martin Mucklowe describing Fred West thus: 'I know he done some iffy things but as a builder he was top notch.' But dogma is the real killer. Literally at the moment. In the Johnson world, 'risk-taking' is always a good thing – he once cited the mayor who keeps the beach open in *Jaws* as a political inspiration – and the Nanny State is always bad. Corbyn is the other way around; they're both utterly unshakeable in those views and therefore seemingly incapable of changing tack in changing circumstances.

Maybe it's the job I did – if I'd said, 'Look, I drew up this running order on Wednesday, so Spurs 0 Liverpool 0 is leading the show and Portsmouth 7 Reading 4 is staying in last place,' I'd rightly have been fired. And that's just football (that 7-4 'last to first' scenario actually happened on a *MOTD* I edited, by the way) so it's just plain nuts to view pub closures as unthinkable right now. We'll all be in one (as long as it's not a Wetherspoons) having a VE Day-style celebration as soon as this is all over, but even *The Sun* and *Daily Mail* are splashing on the utter irresponsibility of what's happening now. They're blaming the punters rather than Johnson and Tim Martin, so they're only halfway there, but it's a start.

Tory backbenchers demanding the Chancellor goes much further than mere loans for business and gives the public a basic state income and/or Universal Credit funds in these wartime circumstances is also something I never thought I'd see, but like the DUP pleading for a Brexit delay, they're showing some much-needed if belated pragmatism and above all they're right. Johnson, so far, appears to be immovable on all of this, though I think Sunak is likely to go further in financial terms. But, with a majority of 80, Johnson's not obliged to listen to the howl of dissent, even in his own party and among traditionally supportive newspapers. And he doesn't have to be irritated by the independently minded coterie of Tory MPs – the Ken Clarkes, Dominic Grieves and Anna Soubrys – who would be asking some really probing questions right now. They were expelled last year: first from the party and then by the electorate.

Private Eye's front cover the other week portrayed the new cabinet in a series of photos of poodles. Again, how we laughed, but Amanda and I were discussing earlier who in the current cabinet might be intelligent and well-established enough to raise some urgent objections. The only name we could come up with was Michael Gove. Yes, I know, but these are desperate times.

The problem there is that Gove's back-stabbing reputation goes before him, and even at this alarming moment, any attempt by him to rustle up support for some belated stable-door shutting is going to look like a self-serving plot.

My only distant hope is that Johnson does what Kevin Keegan did as England manager in 2000 and says, 'You know what? I always wanted this job, but I'm just not suited to it. I'll step aside and let someone else have a go.' Keegan got a lot of flak, but I thought it was a very decent and honest thing to do. The trouble is it required some self-awareness and presumably a frank discussion with those around him. Johnson appears to have been encouraged for much of his life to believe that he's the greatest, sexiest, funniest and most brilliant man who's ever lived. Amongst those who've seemed unwilling to suggest otherwise are his father, parts of the media, the changing cast of male and female courtiers who've surrounded him, and now Carrie, whose two most noteworthy contributions to 2020 have been to dress their dog in a Union Jack waistcoat for Brexit Day, then allow Bozza to bring yet another human life into the world.

I'll reflect on Johnson at Oxford at some point, but to be honest, this diary was meant to provide therapeutic diversion. I really did hope I'd simply chronicle life in lockdown, and though I'd make a few wry observations, we could safely assume that whatever happened out there, and even to us and our families, everyone across the board would be giving it their best shot. Tragically, it's not panning out like that. As I'm typing, *The World At One* is leading on the SAGE (Scientific Advisory Group for Emergencies) finding that our current massively restricted life will most likely carry on for the next year. That's no huge surprise to me, but it's clearly a hastily released response to Johnson inventing a 12-week tide-turning schedule yesterday as if he was riffing to his usual crowd of pissed City traders at their annual dinner. '£25k for talking absolute shit off the top of the old tousled bonce to the red braces brigade? Don't mind if I do. What-ho and pip-pip.'

Sorry, mate, this is a frightened nation you're addressing now and mixing up 12 weeks and 12 months really won't do at this juncture. Apart from anything else, you've embarrassed the *Daily Mail* and *Express* who chose to regurgitate it on their front pages today, and may have to backtrack quietly. Again, we'll have to wait for the inquiry and the publication of diaries, but the silence of the two science sidekicks who flanked Bojo at his briefing seemed to speak volumes. They sensed there'd be yelps of anguish from the guys at Imperial and the wider scientific community, and bingo, the government have had to issue a clarification (ie contradiction) with undue haste. Good luck to Dom if he's going to try to brief reporters that 'the science has changed' in the last 18 hours. Unlike the 'herd immunity' shambles, this one's squarely on the PM. As is the public confusion – occasionally in the word soup he emits, he says something which is absolutely vital, like 'wash your hands' and 'employ social distancing'. The problem is, because it's Boris 'letterbox women', 'grinning picaninnies with watermelon smiles', 'tank-topped bum boy', 'one of the lads' Johnson relaying crucial messages amidst a sea of waffle and bluster, many of us are struggling to understand, let alone abide by, his guidelines.

Speaking of which, I'm sending what I've written to a few chosen friends. Firstly, I'm vain enough to share the fruits of my labour with the odd person (some of them are very odd indeed) beyond Amanda. And secondly, whether posterity tells me my observations were right or wrong, or more likely, somewhere in that grey area Johnson and Corbyn have never discovered, I won't be rewriting this after the event and I'd like that fact to be verified independently. I reserve the right to get Amanda or someone else to tidy up the grammar and punctuation, though.

And with that, I'm knocking this on the head for the day and will just play the guitar, read my book or do some Sudokus. We're even having steak and chips later. We're up to date with our various comedies, and *University Challenge* and *Only Connect*, and though it's a lavish, beautifully acted production, we're losing it a bit with *The Crown* on our newly acquired Netflix. I have a problem with British dramas which seem to be aimed at reassuring American audiences that we're merely a collection of royals, aristocrats, posh bumblers and serfs. I gave *Downton Abbey* one series – basically, until the pouting dreamboat Lady Sybil was unforgivably killed off – and got increasingly sick of Richard Curtis's ever lazier Hugh Grant vehicles. Curtis co-wrote *Blackadder*, for God's sake, and we saw in *Paddington 2*, and when he played Jeremy Thorpe, that Grant is capable of far more than just ruffling his hair while saying, 'Um, er, um, er, would you mind awfully?'

Hang on … Johnson saw how those movies went down and stole the whole persona, didn't he? Johnny Public doesn't like the sound of the Bullingdon Club with its frock coats and braying, and upper-class hooliganism. Charm them, Bozza – that way they'll think the non-PC air of entitlement is all a bit of a joke, and that you must be really clever deep down. I'm sorry, but Curtis and Grant will also be summoned to the eventual Nuremberg trials for seemingly planting an idea in that calculatingly ambitious brain. *Blackadder*, Hugh's role in the Hacked Off campaign, and the fact that they didn't mean to do it, may mitigate the sentence handed down.

Back to *The Crown*: the, at best, speculative account of intimate scenes featuring living people, and depressing evocation of the 1950s, that dismal-looking decade of Nigel Farage's dreams – like World War Two, he can say that because he wasn't there – seems like something we may not stick with. We gave up on two all-time classic series after one episode of each not so long ago. The first was *The Sopranos*: I don't care how good it is, I've had it with mafia dramas after we sat through the interminable, self-indulgent *The Irishman* at the cinema (remember those?) and all I could think about was where, as an editor or studio head, I'd make the necessary two hours of cuts.

'Marty, I know you made *The Last Waltz, Raging Bull* and *The King of Comedy*, but since then it's been non-stop fantasising about gangsters. Oh yes, you're right. Your Dylan documentary was excellent, and yes, granted, nobody was shot in the back of the head, called a "fucking fuck", or both, in that. Even so, have you ever wondered if it's time you retired?' The last hour of *The Irishman* should have been five minutes, max – De Niro's character is a horrible, banal and unrepentant thug, so don't give us this 'ah, bless, he talks to the priest in his retirement home' crap.

Where was I? Oh yes, abandoning box sets one episode in. Our other biggie was *The Wire*: again obviously superbly made, but Christ, life's short enough and possibly getting shorter by the day. Seeing how apocalyptic Baltimore seems to be in normal circumstances won't provide escapism from London right now, either. Not that we can't finish a box set: Tina Fey is a goddess and her *30 Rock* is just magnificent – US comedy on a par with *The Larry Sanders Show* or *Cheers/Frasier* or *Curb Your Enthusiasm*. Hey, I never really watched *Seinfeld*, but I think it's all available on All 4 (*makes note, possible plan for lockdown weeks 30–40*) And I can sometimes stick a drama series out, too. In the same way that I think Tarantino is simultaneously both a genius and a menace to civilisation, I watched the whole of *Breaking Bad* during the time I was working for BBC Sport at Media City in Salford. My more morally consistent better half abandoned it after the first sordid drug deal or vicious murder of a Mexican (I forget which) but she was still working a couple of days a week in London at that point, so it helped me to cope in her absence, and to compensate for the inferior quality of my dinner on those evenings.

Well, that's been a stream of consciousness of almost *Finnegan's Wake* proportions. Joyce had no excuse – he could go outside without a mask and latex gloves on. Maybe I should write a few shorter entries as we enter the second week. If I can dodge the bug, there could be 51 more to go. Sorry, I'll wash my mouth out with home-made sanitiser, there are 11 weeks to go. The Churchill of his generation said so. 'Ohhh yursssss' or possibly 'ohhh noooo'. As they say in *Breaking Bad*, 'Hasta mañana, diario.'

WEEK TWO

Saturday, 21 March 2020

Saturday, 3pm. The title of an excellent set of short essays on the '50 Eternal Delights of Modern Football' by my fellow Boro fan, Daniel Gray. Like me, Dan has been a regular contributor to the superb (irrespective of our input) Boro fanzine *Fly Me to the Moon*, itself possibly the 51st eternal delight of football. It's currently resting, along with its editor Rob Nichols, for the first time in over 30 years. In happier, almost carefree times, Dan and I shared a stage at the 2019 Edinburgh Book Festival where we read extracts from our books, followed by a Q&A and exotic beer-tasting with a fabulous, mostly Scottish, audience. The question I remember most clearly came from a middle-aged guy, and was along the lines of, 'Since I was a lad, I've dreamt of scoring the winning goal in a World Cup final. Against England. With my hand. Why are they introducing a VAR system which will take my dream away from me?' I've just taken Dan's book down from the shelf and reminded myself of such evocative chapter headings as 'Seeing a ground from a train', 'Catering vans' and 'Jeering passes which go out of play'. Just like last Saturday and many more to come, there'll be none of that today, I'm afraid. We're not even risking going out for a walk this Saturday.

And I am afraid, it may sound weak, but I simply can't watch or read any more of the news reports from Italy. They're a 21st-century TV reportage reprise of Wilfred Owen's World War One poem *Dulce et Decorum Est.* Owen's unflinching portrait of death in the trenches was written while he rested with shell-shock in 1917, and was published posthumously after he was killed in action just a week before the armistice. It's right that those reports are broadcast, though, and I wish being frank about the harsh reality wasn't largely limited to Sky and *C4 News*, the broadsheet newspapers and the parts of social media mostly inhabited by those who've already changed their lifestyles. I understand it's difficult to reach other parts of the population who don't know or don't want to know, but we've reached the point where every ad break during a soap or reality show, and the short bumper when you first click on YouTube, needs to be replaced with the most harrowing of the images. It's still too late, but it might just help to slow down the inevitable, at least partial, collapse of the NHS.

It's a bit flip to say it in the circumstances, but you know you're in trouble when Ireland closes its pubs a week before you do. And I'm saying that out of love, since three of my great-grandparents were Irish. None of them had their children in Ireland, sadly, otherwise I'd have retained an EU passport. Johnson finally overruled the proprietor of Wetherspoons yesterday teatime, but still allowed one final chance for another multiplication of cross-infection before he did so. And on a Friday night, too.

It doesn't matter that 90 per cent of the nation will have been shouting furiously at their TV screens – we were, anyway – as the news outlets showed the most witless ten per cent laughing and drinking in our faces. That number included a couple of prominent former UKIP MEPs who finally pushed their usually loyal social media following too far and were roundly and rightly savaged, apparently, as too was 'Father Jack' Martin. The juxtaposition of the pictures of what appeared to be a normal Friday night to some – hugs galore, drunken revelry and zilch social distancing – and the delayed results of the doubtless more civilised gatherings in northern Italy's restaurants and bars which were finally halted, 13 days ago (yet again) is unbearable, frankly. All the more so if you work for the NHS and happened to pass a pub at the end of a harrowing 20-hour shift last night. Isn't there a line from Einstein about the definition of insanity being doing the same thing over and over again while expecting different results?

This could be the first time I've ever praised either publication in print, but it may just be that *The Sun* and *Daily Mail* alerting their largely Tory-supporting readership to the madness unfolding in the bars and clubs forced the World King (of Laissez-Faire) to knock it on the head. Who knows – their intervention could mean we only continue to copy Italy's statistics, rather than surpass them. A total of 627 deaths in one day there yesterday is the equivalent of 16 Heysel Stadium disasters. I watched some footage yesterday of an exasperated Chinese expert who's been flown into Milan, raging at the Italian failure to do what the Chinese did in Wuhan, and properly shut the place down. Italy closed all the roads and trains in and out of the Milan area, but in a UK government-level display of incompetence, flagged the move up 24 hours early, so some of those who were carrying the virus but didn't yet know it fled and dispersed it all over Italy.

Despite London bearing the brunt of our spread, we already have regional clusters everywhere, whereas I believe Italy's outbreak was almost all in the north at this point. That could explain why London hasn't been sealed off yet, or at least I hope it's that and not another 'Oh cripes, the five-year-old Bozza didn't envisage this in the old King of the World scenario. Can I have a think about it for a week or so?' Again, I wouldn't be making these decisions for anything, but as an eloquent WHO spokesman said the other day, in the absence of perfect solutions, try anything and everything you can and do it decisively. The same WHO have guidelines about front line staff being issued with PPE (Personal Protective Equipment) and we're routinely breaking them already, as Doctor Liz's message earlier in the week flagged up.

There was also an unforgivable time lag between the reduction in Tube services and the announcement of bars, restaurants and non-essential shops closing. There were stories and photos galore of a reduced number of passengers taking a similarly reduced number of trains. Net result: the usual crowding at busy times, exacerbated by stations which were neither near a hospital nor at an intersection having closed. That may improve now people don't have to travel to businesses which should have shut at least a week ago, but forcing low-paid Londoners, including NHS staff, into an environment where they can't employ social distancing carries echoes of Grenfell in this city, I'm afraid. And seeing the horrendous queues still forming outside supermarkets all over the country doesn't inspire any confidence that social distancing will, or indeed can, be observed there, either.

Amanda and I have realised for a while that at some point, possibly very soon, we may have to settle for subsistence and volume, rather than epicurean or even nutritional value, of whatever food's available. That's assuming the supply chains don't collapse, which is by no means guaranteed, though I can see why the government is saying it's all in hand. Like many urban dwellers, and by contrast with most of our non-London friends and family, we only have a small fridge and tiny freezer compartment, so can only store extra dry goods, tins and jars. We haven't even panic-bought a huge stash of those, but unlike many Londoners we do have a car, a 12-year-old Clio which I almost sold for scrap when it failed its MOT in November. It got a last-minute reprieve, so all being well it will take us somewhere when we next need to shop.

We really have reached the latex gloves and mask stage outside the home, though. There's no chance of acquiring anything now beyond the flimsy semi-protective gear we have in the flat, but at least we're not health professionals woefully underequipped for the front line. At worst, we'll spend half an hour in whichever supermarket or convenience store we opt for next. And we'll check if the neighbours need anything before we go. Believe you me, we're wrestling with our consciences on all fronts here, and in a perfect world I'd rather be a very, very long way from London right now, but we can't think of a way to make that work that wouldn't further endanger us or others.

In other news, I think my Twitter absence has left me behind the curve, but I see Farage has started to parrot Trump's dog-whistling term, 'the Chinese Virus' and that Brendan O'Neill of *Spiked* has railed against the 'North Korean-style' closing of the pubs. O'Neill has a large social media audience – I'm unable to check how many of his Twitter followers are also devotees of Trump, Farage and Katie Hopkins, but I bet there are some significant Venn diagram intersections. Suffice it to say, I see him review the papers sometimes on Sky News, and never read his tweets or blogs, but he has an almost comical ability to take a contrarian stance in every possible circumstance, and defend the seemingly indefensible: Meghan Markle leaving the country and Dom giving a eugenicist a job in Downing Street are two recent examples of seemingly unfortunate developments he was happy to endorse. Normally his followers lap this stuff up, but apparently, on this occasion, most acolytes weren't having this 'don't close our pubs' stuff at all. That development does provide one tiny glimmer of hope for the future: even some of the alt-right Twitter brigade think for themselves, and don't always hold a blanket set of views.

It's trumpet fanfare time. I'm about to give a Conservative politician some credit. Rishi Sunak was excellent in the daily press conference yesterday, calmly and cogently introducing the most radical single set of economic reforms in modern British history. Hugh Dalton and Sir Stafford Cripps oversaw many huge changes as they rolled out the welfare state and NHS between 1945 and 1950, but that wasn't set in motion with this alacrity. And they were Labour chancellors, so a spot of socialism was to be expected. With the exception of the freelance world which will need some reassurances in the coming days, Sunak assuaged most people's worst economic fears, effectively nationalising the economy for the time being, with employees continuing to get 80 per cent of their usual salaries.

Sky went over to the Shadow Chancellor, and frankly, his response was pathetic and depressing. John McDonnell sneered that Sunak hadn't gone 'far enough'. What would you have done, Johnny boy? Increased tractor production to supply the collective farms out on the Steppes? It was a tone-deaf, clapped-out default reaction worthy of Farage at the other extreme. Just go into self-isolation somewhere with no modern methods of communication, and take Corbyn, McCluskey and the whole Momentum gang with you, would you, pal?

With Sunak shining alongside him, Johnson's prepared bit on shutting gathering places wasn't bad, for once. He only went off-piste once, in the Q&A section when he said he hoped to see his mother on Mother's Day which it turns out is tomorrow. Is it? Oh shit … no, I did remember. It was possibly the best performance I've ever seen from him – not stunning in any way, but more Gordon Brown than Mrs Brown, for once. It must have been okay, because I stuck it out. Now he's finally closed everything, there's not a lot more he can tell us day by day, other than if he wants to get more draconian or needs to bring in the army. We can see the rising death toll on every news outlet, and the comparative trajectories of other countries online at worldometers.info.

Even Classic Dom had played to his strength. In fact, he'd surpassed himself by providing three-word slogans for all three Kraftwerk gig-style podiums in the press conference. For 'Take Back Control' and 'Get Brexit Done', read the genuinely helpful 'Stay At Home' and 'Protect the NHS'. He let himself down slightly with the third: a mere 'Save Lives' when he could have gone with 'Save Some Lives', but it's still probably the most constructive day he's spent since he rearranged the furniture in his tapestry room in 2015.

For the first time since the Spanish flu pandemic of 1918–19, a huge casualty toll will mount up rapidly in the immediate vicinity of much of the population of this country. The fallen will be not be killed by a human enemy in some faraway corner of a foreign field. Fifty-three more people have died from the virus in the last 24 hours here in the UK, taking the total death toll to 233. Some 793 people died in Italy alone today, the highest number so far. That's the equivalent of a reasonable-sized village expiring in one day; 793 individual stories of a human being dying a slow, grim death away from their loved ones, with wildly overstretched health professionals offering what comfort they could.

And yet, here in the UK, people still went to the pub last night and had one – or six – for the road. I genuinely hope it's a case of 'they know not what they do' and not utter indifference to the fatal ripple effect. The figures are now inexorable and on an irreversible trajectory. All we can do is to hope that as few people as possible die because of a shortage of staff or equipment. We'll probably never be able to calculate that either.

In among the overwhelmingly grim news, there are small sparkles of hope and human decency. Almost every e-mail we've received from a company with which we deal has focused on making life more bearable for all of us, rather than their own fears for the future. From the arts world streaming all the archive material at their disposal, to the typically superb message to all registered England fans from Gareth Southgate, to our local physio practice setting up virtual exercise sessions via Skype, it really does feel as if profits and the rat race have been stood down at least for a while.

And the environment is presumably getting a little respite, too. Satellite pictures reveal the relative absence of air pollution in conurbations and companies will start to re-evaluate the need for people to turn up at a desk every day or to fly all over the world for meetings which can just as easily be conducted through a teleconferencing app. The wider BBC beyond national news has absolutely come into its own at a critical moment, too. As we heard in February when visiting flood-ridden Shropshire, BBC local radio is a lifeline and provides a unique area-wide network of information and support to a beleaguered population. Never more so than now. Dom may have to shelve his plans to either close it altogether, or make Rebekah Brooks director-general and retain just a few subscription services, as 'a Number 10 source' floated the other week. It's just a hunch, but I suspect Radio Cumbria has more reporters on the ground keeping people up to date with the spread of the pandemic across that region than Netflix and Amazon could ever rustle up.

Most importantly of all, as I've said before, almost everyone now knows that the NHS is our country's single most important institution – even Farage and his main backer, the insurance industry's own Arron Banks, may be less openly keen to see it sold off than once was the case. Wembley Stadium is sporting a huge illuminated 'Thank you, NHS' sign, there is a universal will to see the staff fed and protected properly and a nationwide minute's applause is being mooted for this week. And rightly so. A deal has been struck to use the private hospitals' facilities and 4,500 doctors and nurses who've left the NHS have agreed to return temporarily. Quite how there were 100,000 unfilled NHS vacancies before this is yet another question for another day.

I hope to God the story on Sky News earlier is true and that British engineering capability is poised to help ease the ventilator crisis. One firm – vacuum cleaner manufacturer G-Tech – thinks it can start to deliver up to 1,000 a day within a week, to try to help reach the government's target of 30,000 new machines. Off the top of my head I think that would belatedly put us on a par with Germany where the case to deaths ratio is currently extraordinarily low, albeit in these very early stages. This manufacturing effort may be just too late to avert mayhem this week in London, and begs the blindingly obvious question of why the cry for help only went out last Sunday, when we rank amateurs have known for a while that the system couldn't cope, but it sounds like some effort by the companies involved.

Andrew Clement phoned earlier from Manchester; he was one of the friends to whom I'd sent the first week of this diary. He'd forwarded it to his dad, who lives in Los Angeles, read it in one go and e-mailed both of us straight back. This isn't just anyone's dad, by the way – it's Stanley Johnson. Not really. Dick is one half of Clement and La Frenais: *Porridge, The Likely Lads, Auf Wiedersehen, Pet* and *The Commitments* feature among their many, many credits. He also produced Peter Cook and Dudley Moore in *Not Only, But Als*o. I've met Dick a few times down the years and grilled him on comedy long into a beery night in Stockholm after BBC Sport had covered Chelsea's European Cup Winners' Cup win in 1998. The two Clements are Chelsea through and through, Andrew being as obsessed a supporter of any team as I've ever known. To answer the old terrace charge, he actually was there when they were shit, so I had to forgive him his excitement when they started winning things. We shared a small sub-office at that time: the endless trip-planning calls from his own Curry Club led me to post a notice reading 'Thank You for Not Discussing the Champions League'. That was before I became equally boring, and well-travelled football-wise, during Boro's two UEFA Cup runs.

I'm slightly taken aback by how enthusiastic Dick is about my fear-fuelled ramblings and rantings, to the point where he thinks they deserve a wider audience. He even mentioned Pepys, whose famous diary featured being trapped in London during the Great Plague of 1665. I've replied that I'll take that: the boy Samuel eventually emerged to tell the tale, so he'd be my precedent of choice. I'd take 0.001 per cent of his accumulated readership numbers, too. In normal circumstances, I'd be floating on air to be encouraged by one of the great TV writers. I'm still very flattered, but everything is utterly surreal at the moment, with added flashes of absolute terror, so I'm not sure how to feel. It's certainly given me a push to keep ploughing on, although I need to start to rein it a bit, and I think I will to an extent as the numbers phase gains a momentum which is going to leave even the great writers struggling to find the right words.

Speaking of great writers, Marina Hyde is still somehow managing to pull it off. If I can come up with a phrase a week that would earn its place in any given paragraph of hers, I'll be happy. My proudest hour on Twitter was when I earned a retweet and a 'hahahaha' from Marina. In a sincere post, she congratulated *The Telegraph* for an enlightened new policy of giving fathers who work there six months' paternity leave. I replied asking whether it could be applied retrospectively to (their former Brussels correspondent) Boris Johnson. Here's just one of many great barbs in her latest column: 'Cummings is interested in behavioural science in the way I'm interested in Olympic figure skating. Which is to say, I like it, but I'm unbelievably, lethally shit at it.' Chapeau, as they say.

And on top of all that, Kenny Rogers died today. Still, he picked a fine time to leave us.

Sunday, 22 March 2020

A beautiful sunny day, and before I've even started a first coffee of the day, another mind-boggling juxtaposition: my old Stockton-on-Tees schoolmate, Susan, in one of social media's happier outcomes, has turned out be an absolute kindred spirit even though she lives in rural Scotland and I haven't seen her in 40 years. Her latest Facebook post is a sober, informed account from the immunologists at Johns Hopkins University of how the coronavirus originated in that unknown animal in a Wuhan wet market, mutated within a fortnight to allow human-to-human transfer, spread as it has because humans have no immunity, and has now mutated into two known forms and will carry on doing so unless checked. I broke my silence to re-post it in the hope that others will do the same. Then I saw a report from Skegness: decent weather has created volumes of day trippers akin to those on Bank Holidays, and they're wandering around gormlessly with their families, partying like it's 1999, or 2019, or 1959. And Snowdonia and the Scottish Highlands are awash with urban visitors, too.

I have to say, despite my often cynical take on human nature, I did not see this one coming. Whatever the government projection was – 20,000 deaths were quietly posited as a reasonable outcome last week – this weekend may have blown it out of the water. If a Tory chancellor can unveil the most socialist policies ever seen in the UK, then I think I can reverse my usual aversion to overbearing authoritarianism. Get the army on the case right now. Not when the daily figures in a fortnight's time reflect this weekend's madness. Right now.

I stand by my criticism of our government's handling of this crisis, but at some point the population has to shoulder some responsibility. In this particular situation, assuming we're all agreed now that there is, after all, such a thing as society, we're only as strong as the weakest-minded. You can add 'absolute fucking morons' to that sentence, if you want. Whether they think it's just a 'that there London' thing, or a touch of flu, or something only the old can catch, I genuinely don't know, but we need to copy Australia pronto. Idiocy one day, Bondi Beach closed the next – an action as totemic as Ireland closing the pubs or France shutting the Eiffel Tower, but they all did it. Then there was another level of stupid being shown on Sky News – thousands of Beavis and Buttheads queueing up on their spring break in Florida to share drinks, snogs and fried chicken of dubious provenance (does chlorine kill COVID-19? I doubt it) with any passing camera crew. 'If I get it, I get it, dude. Yeee-haaa' was the median vox pop in evidence.

Now, obviously, these aren't the only countries where people have failed to get it (as opposed to get 'it') but what do the UK, US and Australia have in common? Yes, they all speak English; yes, they're generally a bit more right of centre politically than most democracies; and yes, they all patronise a smaller neighbour whose population quietly thanks the Lord they live in a kinder, less self-congratulatory country: that is, Ireland, Canada and New Zealand. I'm going to posit a different, somewhat simplistic yet, I believe, valid answer. Rupert Murdoch has had a stranglehold on the means of communication in each of those countries for many decades. He's chosen to use that power to pump well-reported and produced sport (so far, so harmless) and craven nationalistic xenophobic bilge (not so good) into people's letter boxes and living rooms, and he's exercised an outrageous degree of political influence. He's on record as saying he dislikes the EU because 'they take no notice of me', whereas at Downing Street 'they do what I say'.

His UK tabloid *The Sun* has not supported a losing party in a General Election since 1970, and was predictably, rabidly pro-Leave before the 2016 referendum. *Sun* editor-in-chief Rebekah Brooks, emphatically not connected in any way to the phone-hacking scandal because a court found her not guilty so there, was even obliged to knife fellow Chipping Norton 'kitchen supper' stalwart David Cameron for his insolent defiance of Rupe in backing Remain, and for the added crime of allowing the Leveson Report to investigate press standards. Theresa May and Boris Johnson have since quite independently (ahem) decided to let that wither on the vine, hacking the phones of dead schoolgirls and actors whose partners are terminally ill being just one of those things. I know less about Australian politics, though Rupe's outlets gave an especially big thumbs-up to the clearly appalling wolf in Speedos Tony Abbott and the, at best, below average current incumbent Scott Morrison. There can be no doubt, however, that without Fox News there would be no President Trump, no debasing of all previous norms of behaviour and truth-telling, and no initial dismissal of COVID-19 as a 'Democrat hoax'.

The fact that so few people believe anything they read or hear, and so many simply think only about celebrity gossip, their football team and themselves, to the point that they're swaggering around Skegness, Miami and, until yesterday, Bondi despite clearly contributing to many thousands of imminent deaths is the logical, if extreme, consequence of Murdoch and his fellow travellers mushing the pack (let's not use 'herd' again) into unknown territory, then feigning surprise when the blizzard clears and we find we're in mid-air freefall down a cliff face.

As ever on a Sunday, Amanda watched the politics shows, and I didn't. Sophy Ridge is one of many good journalists working for the former Murdoch asset, Sky News. Unlike the newspaper industry, TV news is subject to strict neutrality guidelines, so Sky News has always appeared to be balanced, even under News International's auspices. BBC News – in my humble opinion –

has in recent years turned that into an increasingly meaningless game, to whit, 'Climate: here's 30 seconds from a panel of climate scientists, countered and thereby balanced by 30 seconds of Darren and his mates in a Wetherspoons in (insert name of town which voted 70 per cent Leave)'. Nobody thanks them for it, anyway – the Corbynites squarely blame their demise on the Corporation, Classic Dom is one of many on the right who still see it as a hotbed of pinko treachery – so why not start asking some searching bloody questions?

Sky and *C4 News* are seemingly less worried about ruffling feathers, so naturally the day I quit Twitter, the outstanding Sky reporter Beth Rigby was the number-one trend for an hour or two. She'd dared suggest to Johnson during the Q&A which followed that disastrous 'herd immunity' press conference ten days ago, that advising old people not to embark on cruises and school groups not to venture abroad may not suffice. Naturally, every crimson-faced man (and it did seem to be entirely men) with a Union Jack as their profile picture, and a variation on @truepatriotnigeforpm as their handle, raged and railed long into the night about that traitorous, libtard, remoaning (insert an abusive epithet for a woman) and what cruel and unusual punishment they'd like to inflict on her. They're probably still doing it from the depths of an amusement arcade in Skegness as I type. Or West Wittering, another hotbed of cretinous coastal congregation yesterday – let's not be northernist about this.

According to Amanda, who tends not to provide me with fake news, the most striking moment on TV this morning was Andrew Marr speaking to two hospital consultants – one in Birmingham, one in London – who both emphasised the terrible risks their staff are taking because of inadequate protective equipment that does not meet WHO regulations.

This country is built on an adversorial system – my brother is all too aware of the Punch and Judy show in the courts, based on prosecution vs defence rather than a dispassionate dissection of the evidence, and Parliament has been like that since Gladstone and Disraeli's time and beyond. Margaret Thatcher got lucky with her adversaries; Michael Foot dwarfed Corbyn intellectually but like Jezza, seemed to the public to be behind the times, too far to the left and moreover, not prime ministerial material. General Galtieri invaded the Falklands to distract his people from domestic woes and gave her the perfect opportunity to do likewise. 'Wallop' and 'Gotcha' (the second in particular, as hundreds of young conscripts perished outside our exclusion zone on the *Belgrano*, was a particular favourite of the then middle-aged *Sun* proprietor) and the SDP-Liberal Alliance, who had been leading in the opinion polls, and for whom I cast my first vote, were swept aside along with Labour at the 1983 General Election.

Then there was Arthur Scargill. As someone who had moved after the Thatcher victory in 1979 from Stockton-on-Tees, where a sign on the town hall kept tally of the skyrocketing local unemployment figures, to Sevenoaks, one of the richest towns in the country, I had my own take on how the north-south, left-right divide of the time played out. When I moved to Kent, my Teesside accent (I still say 'bath' not 'barth') earned me the nickname 'Jock' for a while. My grammar school sixth form politics group, led between 1981 and 1983 by two great young teachers, Mr Ford and Mr Moth, whom I'd love to be able to thank one day, contained two SDPish types (me and my friend then and now, Jon Rycroft, whose family hailed from Carlisle) and one socialist (Richard Dewdney, later at Balliol with Boris Johnson – wish I hadn't lost touch with him), while the rest of the class were default, no-holds-barred Tories.

This was a useful lesson for me: every single teenage classmate in Stockton pitied me for moving to a south-east England they'd only seen on TV and pictured as a prissy, snobbish bastion of *Terry and June*/*The Good Life*-style suburbia, with a *The Sweeney* underbelly in the rough bits; that is to say, those not populated by the smart-arse families Robert 'Pray tell all, Mr Smithers' Robertson indulged every week on *Ask the Family*. Ian Ramsey was a good comprehensive which has given me lifelong friends all over the world and in all manner of professions (all Remainers, I think) and a rump who were clearly never going to leave Stockton (anecdotally, mostly Leavers). Although there were social subdivisions developing within our adolescent year group, I think we'd all have been united by the degree of antipathy, and possibly violence, which would have greeted those *Ask the Family* youngsters should any have ever turned up in our school.

Conversely, the perception my A level politics set had acquired from their Kentish parents was that the north was lazy, scruffy and in hoc to the unions, so therefore needed a good Thatcherite kick up the arse. So too, all but the same three of us slavered excitedly, did the Argies. The miners' strike cemented those divisions. Again, Margaret Thatcher had the perfect enemy: NUM leader Arthur Scargill, a hardline Soviet-leaning militant of a type which disappeared under Neil Kinnock before resurfacing in Momentum more recently, was the donkey in charge of those particular lions. He refused to call a ballot, so as with Galtieri's invasion of the Falklands, the subsequent bloodshed and mayhem could be pinned on an illegitimate action. There's little doubt the miners would have voted to strike, and that the government was indeed planning to shut down their industry, but Scargill was essentially not a democrat so took his troops into a battle they were only ever going to lose.

As with her cry of 'Rejoice' when the *Belgrano* was sunk, Mrs Thatcher was all too enthusiastic a warrior and effectively employed various police forces as a private army. One particularly brutal deployment, the so-called Battle of Orgreave, and subsequent whitewash of police brutality by both government and national and local newspapers, is seen by some as contributing to the air of invincibility and negligence the same South Yorkshire Constabulary displayed at Hillsborough five years later. The hotline to Kelvin Mackenzie at *The Sun* to instigate the smear and cover-up campaign was re-activated almost instantly in 1989.

I had no intention of going there or of typing as much as this today, but there you go. The point I wanted to make was that the UK all too often becomes a divided society in which one side comes out on top for a while, and is bitterly resented by the other. The southern part of the UK broadly backed Margaret Thatcher; the rest of it broadly hated her. Now the young, urban and Scottish mostly hate Brexit and its figurehead Boris Johnson, the old and those in left-behind towns put their faith in both, or possibly decided they had nothing left to lose. I've been on the losing side of both of those major schisms – though I'd argue only a handful of disaster capitalists and tax exiles were ever really likely to benefit from Brexit – but having lived in different parts of the country and mixed with all sorts of people both here and around the world at one time or another, I know that most people are not motivated by malign intentions. More often than not, they're products of their upbringing and environment and tend to become more open-minded the more they travel and the more people they meet. Just look at the range of food Britain now eats, or how homophobia has gone from a default setting to minority position in the West even in my lifetime.

Returning to the miners' strike for a moment, I remember one very surreal visit to Plough Lane in the 1984/85 season, a year when my own horizons were being expanded as I went to university and gradually discovered that state school didn't always equal good and private didn't mean bad, and that most stereotypes are lazy twaddle borne of ignorance, even when employed by me. A struggling pre-bankruptcy Boro were visiting Wimbledon, a former non-league club travelling in the opposite direction. The knot of Boro fans in the segregated away end, with their Durham/Yorkshire roots, started to sing 'there's only one Arthur Scargill'. For the reasons I outlined above there was no way I was joining in, but neither could I identify with the police reaction which, while it didn't descend to Orgreave-style baton charges at a very low-key, poorly attended fixture, created a hostility which was tangible for the rest of the game, and throughout the tightly marshalled march back to Wimbledon station. As it usually did back then, that enforced crocodile probably also swept up the away fans who'd actually driven there and then had to turn around and go back to find their cars. A divided society and tribalism at its pettiest, and as so often in my life, I didn't really agree with anyone.

In 2020, however, having successfully divided society and got 40 per cent of it to back them at elections, or 52 per cent at the referendum, the right will not be able to turn a government vs doctors battle into Thatcher vs the miners. We've heard of at least three London doctors who are now in intensive care with the virus, many of their Italian counterparts having already died in Lombardy. In the absence of testing and tracking – that ship has sailed now – we don't know for certain that they've caught it in hospital, but the cries of anguish about the lack of protective equipment are not going to be assuaged by government denials.

Even the tabloids aren't going to shy away from highlighting it, I suspect – their reporters are mostly intelligent people who toe a line because they're paid to do so, but unlike the miners' strike era, they and their families could be in the firing line now, so it's self-interest as well as in the general interest to start holding power to account. Proper treatment for NHS staff will, I suspect, be our generation's unstoppable 'Homes for Heroes' demand once this is all over, the dead have been counted and the walking wounded have limped home. And if we never again hear Nigel Farage describe the WHO as a 'club for clever people who want to bully us' or Michael Gove say 'we've all had enough of experts', then a scintilla of good will have come out of it all. Gove, an intelligent man if nothing else, did at least eventually say that he regretted that remark. I bet he really, really regrets it now.

So, what else is going on? Our last fresh meat supply is in the oven for a late Sunday lunch, I've talked to my dad – he loved the latest Marina Hyde article, and put my mum on so I could wish her a happy Mother's Day, but not before he pointed out that the list of 'key workers' now allowed to leave their children at the skeletal school service mostly comprised groups recently dismissed as 'low-skilled' by our Home Secretary. As it stands, unless they're already here, they would not be allowed into Britain in Priti Patel's grisly vision of the brave new world of immigration, one which would have precluded her own parents from fleeing Idi Amin. It's just possible that she may quietly have to reassess that once this is all over and the public has fully understood that nurses, cleaners and care workers are every bit as important – whisper it quietly, perhaps even more important – to our society than advertising executives and merchant bankers.

I'm knocking this on the head for the day, having just logged on to the internet for the first time since this morning, to the alarming breakdown of confirmed cases figures, especially for the London boroughs, some of which have more than 100 tested cases, a figure which will in reality be in the thousands by now, and therefore pretty much unstoppable. London appears poised for an unintended de facto test of 'herd immunity' theory. It also could be goodbye universal health care in the capital at some point soon, and in a fair world, the 20- and 30-somethings who were in the pubs on Friday and who are seemingly crowding Richmond Park today wouldn't be at the front of the queue when ICU rationing starts in earnest. Sadly, unlike most daredevils in history, they're not likely to pay the ultimate price themselves. The old person they stood next to later in the supermarket will pay it instead, and nobody will ever be the wiser.

If I think about all this for much longer, I may break down, which will be no use to anyone. My thinking about it cannot cancel out the actions of anyone who's clearly not thinking about it, so I'm going to spend this evening playing the keyboard which now stands next to the bedroom window (headphones placed prominently but silently by Amanda, as if to say 'bloody use them, Vangelis') read the novel I haven't touched for three days and try to find something utterly silly to watch, like a *Family Guy*, or one of those great music documentaries on BBC Four.

Monday, 23 March 2020

Amanda was up before me again, and left me the following hand-over note:

News item on R4's Today *which (again) beggars belief: supermarket shoppers (don't know where from) blatantly disregarding the hour set aside for NHS workers and barging past staff who were powerless to stop them.*

Inexplicably, at a time of national crisis, Johnson appears largely driven by a desire to be loved: patting us on the head for following his advice and threatening the naughty step when we don't. Afraid to do anything that will make him unpopular, even though resisting or even delaying draconian measures – like locking down London – will directly result in additional loss of life.

According to an article in Liberation, *France and Continental Europe in general have been so alarmed by Johnson's paralysis that last week Macron threatened to ban all movement between France and the UK, effectively cutting the UK off as a 'pays tiers' (third country). On Friday Johnson responded gingerly by giving restaurants, bars, pubs, gyms and leisure centres only hours to close their doors while politely asking the public not to take advantage of the limited remaining hours – which many promptly did. The trend continued over the weekend with crowds gathering in markets, parks and beaches, while an exodus of Londoners travelled to second homes in rural areas, to the understandable anger of locals whose services will soon be overwhelmed.*

There are now reports of cabinet mutiny, amid the growing clamour of NHS frontline staff, some of whom are already struggling to cope with the daily influx of infected patients, to enforce social distancing and self-isolation where appropriate. The entreaties from, among others, the Mayor of Bergamo, Italy's worst affected city, to lock down as the only hope of stemming the tide, should give Johnson nowhere to go but temporarily remove our freedoms and make us stay at home. We will find out soon if he's listening.

Further proof if it was needed that Amanda is the brains behind this operation. I sent her the *Liberation* article last night having understood the terrifying gist of the headline. Since she lived in France both as a child and after university, she's filled in the gaps. Macron was absolutely right to threaten Johnson and the French government branding the UK's approach as 'benign neglect' is, I'm afraid, spot on. Amanda was less accurate, however, when she gave my Twitter boycott a week. It actually lasted eight days – I reinstalled it last night, then deleted it an hour later. As more than one busted wrongdoer has claimed, 'I was only doing some research, m'lud.'

Before the BBC Sport hours made it impossible for me, I briefly played Sunday morning football at Wormwood Scrubs for a team called Lokomotiv Knightsbridge (the other option considered was Red Star Belgravia) with a bright, finance- and statistics-minded Arsenal fan called Pete. I haven't seen him for some time, but he married a Kentish woman I knew, and I befriended him on Facebook. He's often raised the alarm about the economics of Brexit, but of late, he's posted every day on the statistical trends of the coronavirus. Like me, and my university friend and frequent text-exchanger Justin, whose speciality is global finance, he's all over the ominous correlation of our figures and those of Italy, roughly two weeks apart. Last night he mentioned Tim Shipman's report in the *Sunday Times* (Emma Tucker, who was a PPE contemporary of mine, and whom I saw at a University College reunion in the autumn, has just taken over as Shipman's editor) but since it was behind a paywall, I logged on to Twitter to see what the article had contained.

Going back on there after eight days' absence was like opening an overfilled cupboard. On to my head tumbled 'Stanley Johnson applies for French passport', 'Cabinet to mutiny unless PM clamps down', and that *Liberation* article. All of those stories would have fuelled a month's worth of outrage and vicious spats at any other point in Twitter's history, but not today. I eventually found the kernel of the Shipman article: 'At a private engagement at the end of February, Cummings outlined the government's strategy. Those present say it was "herd immunity, protect the economy, and if that means some pensioners die, too bad".'

Chilling, and yet all too believable for those of us who've followed the progress of the 'career psychopath' (copyright: D. Cameron). Jake's online group has been using the term 'Domocracy' since Parliament was prorogued months ago. Tim Shipman proved the quality of his sources in his remarkable, definitive Brexit chronicle *All Out War,* so although 'a Downing Street source' denied his latest account yesterday, I wouldn't hold your breath for the heavyweight libel case of Dominic 'The Source' Cummings vs the *Sunday Times*. One per cent of me was glad I sent the first week of the diary out so that my current readership knows I wasn't wise after the event; 99 per cent of me just wanted to scream. How in God's name did this unelected weirdo end up seemingly in sole charge of the most important strategy in our country's post-war history?

We know why: Johnson is shallow and irredeemably lazy, the cabinet has had almost all experience and competence Dom'ed out of it, and the government scientists appear not to have spoken up until 'herd immunity' terrified both the British and international scientific community. Only then did a Domascene conversion take place. Or, if you were certain journalists, 'the science changed'. The government's Chief Scientific Officer, Sir Patrick Vallance, in particular, will one day have to explain why he seemed to present herd immunity as government policy (with an accompanying slideshow) to the media the week before last. Stats Pete, not unreasonably, thinks that Sir Patrick has to go right now as he was either unforgivably weak, complicit or both, but what signal would that send out? In any case, Downing Street had already given Robert Peston that exclusive. By a terrible irony, Peston's partner, Charlotte Edwardes, has now developed symptoms and has posted a poignant blog about spending Mother's Day in isolation in the family attic.

Being able to delegate to the right people can be a strength in a manager, but even as Mayor of London, Johnson surrounded himself with the 'I've got this, boss' brigade, and a BBC documentary about a year in the life of the Foreign Office showed he got away with that hands-off approach less well in his next job. His civil servants were seen on camera begging him not to quote the imperialist Kipling in a Myanmar temple and wincing as he mangled the most basic of briefings on a Eurostar ride to Paris. Some half-arsed Franglais and 'they love it when I speak French' was the best he had to offer, as the highly intelligent diplomat beside him cringed up her kidneys.

My brief Twitter return also coincided with the excellent Faisal Islam – the first journalist to flag up that Cameron and Osborne had no plan whatsoever in place after Leave won a binary referendum – reporting that Dom's behavioural scientists are under fire in Whitehall for trusting the Bozza gentle touch to persuade the public not to flock to the beaches and parks at the weekend. Yet again, 'we've got this, chaps' has blown up in their faces and set in motion a frantic scramble for Plan B. I didn't think the public would behave quite this appallingly, either, but I'd still have gone with the total lockdown that medics, and even benevolent figures abroad, have been demanding.

The Mayor of Bergamo, Italy's epicentre, has taken his children away from college in England because he thinks the lockdown at home is safer for them than the extraordinary footage of loucheness he's seeing from England. I don't blame him, to be honest. A Czech friend of a friend on Facebook reports total calm, compulsory masks and no stockpiling in Prague. Amanda spent time there in the 1970s during her parents' Foreign Office posting, and suggests that nation's experiences under the Nazi and Soviet occupation may be a rather better preparation for current circumstances than Mark Francois installing a giant picture of a Spitfire on the wall of his parliamentary office. Which he has, of course.

One wartime precedent we maybe should follow is to establish a national government, as suggested by the impressive Labour leadership candidate Lisa Nandy. So far, Dom and Bozza have kept things rigidly partisan, to the point where the Labour Mayor of London was only finally permitted to attend COBRA (Cabinet Office Briefing Room) briefing meetings this week. Amanda, meanwhile, has suggested that COBRA be renamed VIPER – Vacuous, Inept, Procrastinating, Egotist's Room – in honour of its tousled chair. Faisal Islam also reports that the EU Health Ministers' daily teleconference has been flagging up the deteriorating situation in Italy for weeks, so we may have learnt something useful if only Downing Street hadn't decided we would opt out of that bureaucratic nonsense. 'Co-operation' is two letters away from 'co-operative', and that's leftie talk.

As for Nandy's point, almost equally tragically – and I don't use that word lightly – Corbyn's replacement as Labour leader will not be announced until 4 April, so the opposition figures who might contribute some flexible, fresh, non-partisan thinking in the spirit of Sunak's economic measures – Nandy herself and Keir Starmer, for example, emphatically not Corbyn or McDonnell – are not currently in place. And I'm told many Momentum Moonies are still calling for that election to be suspended, so that the Dear Leader can stink the place out for a while longer. Donald Trump will doubtless be poised to do the same with this autumn's scheduled presidential election in due course. Oh boy, are we all in a mess. Bigly.

Amanda mentioned earlier the justifiable fury felt by residents of North Wales, the Highlands and Southwold in Suffolk, to name but three, as relatively unaffected areas are descended upon by the 21st-century equivalent of wartime evacuees. The difference is that the powdered egg incarnation was sensible, this artisan bakery version is nuts. A huge sign has gone up in North

Wales saying 'Go home, idiots' and while in normal times that would seem akin to *The League of Gentlemen* and 'local shops for local people', these are not normal times. I hope this isn't a permanent state of affairs, but neither 'travel broadens the mind', nor the difference I outlined yesterday between outward-and inward-facing Teessiders, applies right now.

In the absence of testing, all current figures are only a guess, but Middlesbrough is currently joint-bottom of the virus league table among all the English boroughs with just one confirmed case, by contrast to the 100-plus already in most inner London boroughs. The others in the bottom five are Stoke-on-Trent, Hull, Blackburn and Gateshead; unlike many Londoners I've been to all of those places, bar Gateshead, to watch Boro play. And we drove through Gateshead just over a fortnight ago on our way to visit Jake in Newcastle. All five places have plenty in common: they're emphatically not like Royston Vasey, the village in which *The League of Gentlemen* was set – they're too big and diverse for starters – but they are all classic examples of the so-called 'left-behind' towns and cities which voted overwhelmingly for Brexit. And in the cases of Stoke, Blackburn and the southern half of Middlesbrough, they then voted for Boris Johnson last December for good measure.

I'm no sociologist, but I'd guess a significant common factor is that a lack of money among the citizenry, and few major visitor attractions for outsiders, means there is not the same movement of people in and out of those towns as would be the case in some similar-sized places nearby, say York or Chester. Once, or if, this is all over, and if those 'left-behind' places and rural outposts have also been left behind by the virus to whatever extent, academics will need to study how that new 'them and us' divide plays out within the pre-existing societal schisms. Of course, if Johnson continues to stare at the boiling pot, and merely asks it to 'simmer down, old boy, if you wouldn't mind, what-what' while holding the lid aloft, those particular divisions will be close to non-existent before long.

The afternoon was spent outdoors, flexing – and possibly pulling – a few muscles. In a cross between one of those corporate team-building exercises and the classic two-reeler *Towed in a Hole* in which Laurel and Hardy fail catastrophically to renovate a fishing boat, Amanda and I have been out on the patio assembling a kit of parts garden bench which arrived a few days ago. Our grunting and muffled swearing at an incomprehensible diagram drove away all the birdlife. All, that is, except for our resident robin which true to form – it doesn't even observe social distancing when I'm filling up the birdbath – hung around glaring at us contemptuously. Robins are the cats of the bird world: bold, utterly selfish, viciously cruel to smaller beasts, and yet somehow loved by most of us. If the bench stays up, it will be a proud practical achievement to rival the IKEA chest of drawers I once finished assembling at 5am, or the driver's side rear tyre I once changed on the hard shoulder of the M25 after a blowout. It remains to be seen whether it ends up falling apart and flattening our car when we try to use it as L&H's boat did, but we managed to avoid any slapstick fights, which is some achievement after a fortnight spent entirely in each other's company.

Tuesday, 24 March 2020

To quote one of Mr McCartney's soppier lyrics, on an early single released under the guise of Wings ('the band the Beatles could have been' – Alan Partridge): 'Only my love holds the other key to me.' She also set the password for this laptop, and got up early as usual so, once again, here's Amanda's handover note:

The announcement that there would be a televised statement by the Prime Minister at 8.30pm suggested we were in for something far more serious than the daily 5pm Q&A format. Was he really going to take that extra step and lock us down? At 8.30pm a different Boris Johnson appeared on our screens. No hair ruffling or fist pumping.

He looked straight into the camera and told us what to do. Beth Rigby's take on it (and I'm sure this is a widely shared view) is that he really didn't want to do it (as he admitted during his address, no Prime Minister would) but there was simply nowhere left to go. The science hasn't changed, the number of infections is rising inexorably and European levels of catastrophe await us down the road. He got there in the end but it's been a frustrating fortnight for those of us who've voluntarily gone into self-isolation, waiting for official government policy to catch up.

As far back as 5 March, during a hearing of the Health and Social Care Select Committee, the government's Chief Medical Officer Professor Chris Whitty spoke about moving beyond the containment phase towards the delay phase. Nothing happened. We were only exhorted to keep washing our hands frequently, singing 'God Save the Queen'. It's taken a full 18 days for the PM to do the right thing. How many infections and deaths might have been prevented in the meantime?

This morning, there is confusion about what the new measures actually mean. Commuters are reporting packed tubes and trains. Some businesses appear to be looking for wriggle room, though Mike Ashley's attempt to keep his shops open because they supply 'essential' exercise equipment has been kicked into touch by the government and all Sports Direct stores will now close. There is conflicting advice for the construction industry – something that needs immediate clarification. Just when we thought Johnson's hand was firmly on the tiller and set on the right course, it appears he hasn't even locked down the lockdown.

Or you can opt for the following verdict: among the hundreds of comments under Mark Bright's entirely straightforward Facebook reiteration of the new measures, was one from a Julia B: 'Boris is the new Churchill.' Let's give Julia the benefit of the doubt, she may not be following events as closely as Amanda is, and may also have missed yesterday's *Times* editorial which likened her man instead to Neville Chamberlain. Who knows, that rebuke from the august 'The Thunderer' (a nickname for *The Times*) – a publication which, even under Rupert Murdoch's ownership, sacked a young reporter called (checks notes) Boris Johnson in the late 1980s for fabricating quotes – may have shamed him into belatedly taking action, as the right-wing tabloids seem to have done when he shut the pubs on Friday.

Politicians, vain creatures that they usually are, often have one eye on their 'legacy'. No Prime Minister wants one catastrophic debacle to provide most of the content in their paragraph in the history books: from Lord 'He lost the American colonies' North to Anthony 'Suez Crisis' Eden to Tony 'Iraq' Blair, that can all too easily happen. Johnson knew on the morning of his downcast 'victory speech' after the 2016 referendum that he might be heading there, even before he'd landed the top job. Indeed, on that day after the night before, he and Michael Gove did a passable impression of Dustin Hoffman and Katherine Ross in that magical last scene of *The Graduate* where the adrenaline rush of their daring escape ebbs away and a wordless 'what the hell have we done?' look spreads across their faces Johnson and Gove had got off their bus rather than leapt on to one, but I think the parallel stands up. A clever friend of mine mocked that image up – Gove in a wedding dress, and all – after I suggested the comparison on Facebook, if anyone ever wants to be both amused and traumatised at the same time.

Bozza's at-times scarcely believable handling of the Brexit situation as PM hasn't done much to prevent future historians from referring to him as Boris 'Brexit Debacle' Johnson, but at least he'd be fighting his two predecessors Cameron and May for the podium positions in that unwanted legacy contest. It is, though, his genuine misfortune to have a nightmare to dwarf even Brexit appear in his in-tray in his first year in office. At least last night he looked like he'd grasped the enormity of what was unfolding, and at the age of 55, he may just finally have become an adult.

By contrast, a bored and fidgety Donald Trump tweeted that he's set to lift the US's haphazard economic shutdown minutes after a rogue host on his favourite channel Fox News (Steve Hilton, once David Cameron's right-hand man) said he should. Hilton even dared to cite his former boss's UK austerity measures as a precedent of stifling an economy too much, begging the question of how he, Hilton, failed to raise his concerns at the time with anyone influential. Far be it from me to intrude, but perhaps he could have contacted Steve Hilton, chief adviser to David Cameron? At least we know, if we ever doubted it, that Johnson isn't the worst, least stable leader in the western world right now. A *Private Eye*-style apology is due if I've ever suggested as much.

Another football Facebook friend of mine, Dean Gordon, formerly of Boro, is now running a football school in Sunderland, and like Brighty, magnanimously lets all comers befriend him on Facebook. I keep my friends list to people I know, or at a pinch are friends of friends, so although my feed is by no means an echo chamber, it rarely takes me into the farthest reaches of societal thinking. Except, that is, when a friend decides to rant about the latest inflammatory 'look at me, look at me' thing some cuntraversialist (misprint) has said.

Rather than take a dip in the Twitter sewer or look at the unhinged comments on online news platforms, I find the replies to the two footballers' posts often cast some light on the wider public response. For example, Dean, as a black ex-footballer and moreover a thoughtful, civilised bloke, occasionally raises an eyebrow at the utterances of Donald Trump. A good 20 per cent of his (mostly north-eastern, sadly) respondents aren't having any of it, and say they would like Trump to run the world or at least their corner of it. Likewise, the responses to Brighty's post last night contained a few positive takes on our PM, a few more who think like us that this had to happen but is happening too late, and a lot who are understandably very confused about what they are, and aren't, now allowed to do. A salutary reminder that my online echo chamber, in openly discussing a new 1945 as if everyone would sign up, may be in for a nasty surprise once this is all over.

That really is all best left to another day and a national post-mortem, on public forums at least. The vital thing now is that the world pulls together to see if something approaching normality will ever actually be possible again. Suspicion of outsiders, both within and between countries will be matched by a huge curtailment of travel I suspect. The only now-shelved travel plans we had this year were to Dublin and Baku, then the Caucuses, in the summer based around Euro 2020 tickets I'd landed in UEFA's ballot. That, with a following wind and a vaccine, could conceivably be parked for another year as the tournament itself has been. Likewise, the Tokyo Olympics has also just been moved to 2021 in arguably the least surprising announcement since Philip Schofield told his daytime audience that he's gay.

Sitting on our new bench this sunny morning, we chatted from a distance to our lovely neighbour Elaine, with whom we share a side gate to the block. Her partner Ian, who has been ill most of the winter with various bronchial complaints but is now on the mend, is holed up in his house in rural France. Her nonagenarian parents are staying indoors at the family home in Nottingham where Elaine's sister still lives and keeps an eye on them, but also works in the intensive care department of a local hospital. My brother's ex-partner, who still has access to their daughters twice a week, is a nurse, too, so we understand all too well how complex the cross-infection lottery now is for previously functioning family set-ups.

Elaine said she is going out for a walk every day and has been using the Belsize Village shops 200 yards away – the convenience store, greengrocer and chemist all still remain open and 'one in, one out' is being observed, as is the Belsize Shuffle on the pavements. The whole small square, where the cafes would have moved outdoors in earnest this week and schoolchildren would be laughing and making a mess with their sweets and ice creams by now, featured in a much-broadcast Direct Line insurance advert, presumably because it looks like the quintessential London neighbourhood. Harvey Keitel played his usual menacing gangster type sitting in the passenger seat of a parked car who gives an ordinary Joe driver a lecture about unlimited cover. The Hollywood actor left a signed note for the wall of the greengrocers' where he wandered off looking for a healthy snack between takes. We've also seen Dame Joan Bakewell in there – now that would have been a meeting of minds.

Johnson's address last night specifically told us that we're allowed out for shopping for essentials, and can take exercise once a day alone, or in pairs with someone from the same household. Elaine rightly pointed out that Italy has now forbidden exercise outdoors, a measure which will probably head our way in the usual fortnight's time. So, feeling a little stir crazy, we opted to drive to Hampstead Heath to try taking a walk. The gloves were on, the masks – which I increasingly suspect are pretty useless in this context – strapped on to our chins to be raised if anyone got too close.

The volume of people was noticeably lower than usual, until we reached the fence which surrounds Kenwood House and its grounds, which constitute maybe a quarter of the Heath. We knew the house would be shut, but the grounds in front contain wide spaces where they stage huge open-air concerts in a normal summer. With it being dry underfoot now, it would be a perfect place for social distancing, but shut it is. I guess some of this will be ironed out in the coming days (coming hours or minutes would be a lot better) but quite how a huge open patch of green in London is shut while NHS workers, construction workers and God knows who else are squeezing themselves into a skeletal Tube service in the same city, is yet another contradictory and potentially catastrophic conundrum.

Kenwood House, with its Robert Adam library, and free entrance for all enshrined in perpetuity in the Guinness family's bequest to the nation, contains an extraordinary collection of Constables, Gainsboroughs, one of the world's 34 confirmed Vermeers – *The Guitar Player*, by common consent not his best work – and a truly incredible 'warts and all' Rembrandt self-portrait. The boy Van Rijn actually painted that when he was an old man and seemingly looked like Leo McKern's weathered, but defiant, grandad. He added a perfect circle freehand in the background, simply to show off, apparently. The overall message of 'This is me, now, as I am. I'm the sum of my experiences – take it or leave it' has the same effect on me as that unforgettable promotional film for a cover version of the Nine Inch Nails' 'Hurt', featuring the elderly, and equally brutally honest, Johnny Cash.

Amanda volunteers at a National Trust property (like her unpaid stints with the Witness Service at Highbury Magistrates' Court, all in mothballs right now) so we like to talk to the people on duty in the rooms. An old chap somewhere in the vicinity apparently goes to drink in Rembrandt's masterpiece as he takes his morning walk every day, all year round. We thought of the poor fellow unable to do so now, before quickly being distracted by a violent sneeze from a bench in the distance. Back to reality – among the muddled advice we've read was a warning that the coronavirus particles can hang around in the air. We couldn't remember how long or how far that applied but took another route back to the car, nevertheless. It could be research into incidents like that which has led Italy to ban all outdoor exercise.

We took a drive through Hampstead and down to the Finchley Road to get home. All looked orderly and fairly quiet, and the only functioning businesses appeared to be the essential ones (so not Sport Direct, Ashley) which are supposed to stay open – garages, food shops, chemists – and they didn't appear to be mobbed. We've pretty much run out of milk, so in a moment of foolhardiness decided to swing by our nearest convenience store; Amanda in gloves, mask and contactless card would jump in and out again. Bad timing – it was lunchtime and The Late, Late Shop was almost bustling, presumably with those working from home. Then we remembered a seemingly empty Tesco Extra we'd passed on the corner of Finchley Road and Fitzjohn's

Avenue. I dropped Amanda at the door, but to avoid the bus lane, parked up just around the corner.

By the time I got inside the shop, she was in a state of agitation, for the first time in this entire ordeal. As she'd waited in one of the aisles, a man wearing no protective gear had been opening the egg boxes and deliberately handling the individual eggs. Amanda asked him what he thought he was doing, was told to 'fuck off', and by the time I arrived and instinctively wanted to chase after him, he'd disappeared. The lone young woman manning the checkout looked bemused and was clearly unable to leave her post, so maybe nothing happened – I hope they either thoroughly washed or threw out all the eggs – but we took our milk and some yoghurt and went straight home where we washed everything: gloves, masks, car keys, milk and yoghurt containers, even our carrier bag, in soapy water. On reflection, we suspect the chap may have had mental health problems: let's hope those are the only health problems he currently has.

Unless we've been unlucky during that outing, it's one to put down to experience, but it really did make us think about the supermarket workers, front line health staff and everyone who has to take the Tube right now. We had a glass of wine and an unchilled Kronenburg respectively with our lunch, and Amanda's okay now, but it's the first time she's been really unnerved since we locked down.

I got emotional for the first time since this started earlier, too. As so often it was music, and the simple act of people coming together through it, which set me off. Lynne, from Jake's messenger group posted a video which starts with people greeting each other from their living rooms, then gradually reveals they each have a musical instrument with them. A lone double bass picks out a tune, three violas join in after a few bars, and so on, until eventually the entire Rotterdam Philharmonic Orchestra is giving Beethoven's 'Ode to Joy' full welly.

The poignancy of their performance brought back memories of a moment I related in *Why Are We Always On Last?* I devoted a chapter of that book to my experiences as a young producer who turned up to supervise the slow-motion replays at an FA Cup semi-final in Sheffield in 1989, on a sunny spring day much like this one. That became the Hillsborough disaster, and was reflected 30 years later in the chapter I separated from the rest and agonised over for far longer than any of the others. I was never in danger, so went through nothing compared to those who were, and their friends and families, but I saw things which I can never expel from my mind. That day changed the 24-year-old me for good. Among other lessons I learnt: sport is only a pastime, parts of the media can be utterly disgusting and to be wary of what authority figures tell you, especially when something's gone horribly wrong.

I was in a bit of a daze for the next few days, but kept working as planned on the World Snooker at the Crucible in Sheffield. Then came the moment I fell apart – *Sportsnight* the following Wednesday featured highlights of a European Cup semi-final between AC Milan and Real Madrid. Naturally, a minute's silence was to be observed. Somehow, the Milanese crowd – from the city which is so stricken right now – took it upon themselves to fill the silence with a spontaneous rendition of 'You'll Never Walk Alone', and I was a helpless puddle on the floor. I'm tearing up again now just remembering it. In the midst of this mess when we're all separated from each other, it's vital to remember that a group of human beings can sometimes come together to provide something absolutely beautiful, as they offer what comfort they can to those who are suffering. Forza Milan and Dank U Vel to the Rotterdam Philarmonic.

There are some other wonderful things going on amidst the darkness: I was particularly moved to read the story of a 72-year-old Italian priest – Father Giuseppe Berardelli – who died after giving up his ventilator to a younger stranger. I'm not a religious person – though as with politics, I'm suspicious of extremes, including aggressive atheism – but if that's not the ultimate expression of what the message is supposed to be, I really don't know what is. I'm also impressed by the community efforts and attempts to help the vulnerable which are springing up all over the country. I took out a year's subscription to *The Big Issue* today – I usually buy one from the lady who sells them outside Finchley Road tube when I remember, and I have been known to stuff a few notes into the nearby Shelter store's collection box when a cold snap pricks our consciences. But right now, we can't do that, and being homeless amidst this unfolding horror must be even more harrowing than usual, so £130 up front for what is often excellent content is not much of an ask, especially when we're all spending so little elsewhere.

I can't claim I thought of the idea, though: my half an hour back on Twitter saw it suggested by Armando Iannucci, who memorably contributed an especially sweary interview with his creation Malcolm Tucker of *The Thick of It* to the magazine a while back. Armando was already at University College when I arrived, performing revues and toying with the English language just as he subsequently did for *The Day Today, Alan Partridge, The Death of Stalin*, the excellent recent *David Copperfield* movie adaptation and much more. He was quite a serious and moral guy outside of his comedy writing, working hard enough to get a first in English and become a post-grad. Along with ITN, then the BBC's, own Nick Robinson, who I thought would become a Tory 'wet' MP, Armando was the one person we foresaw would become well known once we left.

And finally, on the Twitter front, there's Peter Reid, a great bloke with whom I notably spent a wonderful fortnight in Japan at the 2002 World Cup. When he and Ian Wright appeared together for the first time, I gave Gary Lineker this slightly cheap shot as we scripted together: 'Alongside Alan Hansen, something most footballers can't do, Reid and Wright.' That may or not have been #classicbantz, but it was entirely untrue of all four of them and most of the other ex-footballers I worked with. Wrighty was the guest for as reflective and astute an episode of *Desert Island Discs* as I've ever heard, the other week – his tribute to Mr Pigden, the teacher who showed faith in him when he was a troubled kid, left both presenter Lauren Laverne and this audience choked up – and Reidy was trending on Sunday for performing a public service in conducting his Mother's Day visit through the window of her outhouse. He live-streamed the whole thing, and it was trending during my brief return to Twitter. That in itself may have helped counteract Boris Johnson's blunder on Friday when he said, contradicting official advice, that he would be seeing his elderly mother on the day. He meant he'd see her via Skype, a 'spokesman' assured everyone belatedly.

Reidy and Bojo go back a long way – a typically slapdash and offensive article in *The Spectator,* then edited by Johnson, chose the aftermath of the murder of a Liverpudlian civilian Ken Bigley in Iraq to bemoan the alleged wallowing in 'a victim status' of the entire city of Liverpool, and repeated the long-since disproven lie that drunken fans had contributed to the '50-odd' deaths at Hillsborough. There isn't a football fan in the country who doesn't know there were 96 deaths, but no one at Spectator Towers could be bothered to check a reference to plebeian soccer. Then fate threw the pair together when an 'England Legends' football team managed by Reidy for a charity match somehow included Johnson. 'A fat lying disgrace' was a phrase which featured in the earthy Scouse tirade which was hurled at the cowering future PM. Bojo still came off the bench and rugby-tackled a bewildered opponent, but the point had been made. That mid-'80s Everton side contained at least three original thinkers: Neville Southall's Twitter timeline being as likely to have something trenchant to say about our society as those of Messrs Reid and Lineker. I'm still staying off there for now, though.

Very sombre early evening news – the daily death toll in the UK is 87, taking us close to Hillsborough territory. Twenty-one in one west London health authority suggests this city is indeed going to be our Lombardy. We're now 15 days behind Italy on the graph, but I suspect the wanton irresponsibility of many at the weekend, and that slow response from government means we're truly out of the holding pattern and plunging towards the ground. The collective tension is now palpable.

I still feel that putting the most harrowing pictures from Italy into every single ad break and online bumper would ram home the peril we're in. The government, which not so long ago blew £100m on asinine Brexit ads, has failed to run anything at all so far during this mounting crisis, and hasn't even taken advantage of an offer to run whatever content they want for free on Facebook and other platforms. Twenty-seven million watching Bojo's address on TV may be 'England go to penalties in a tournament' territory, but it still means 41 million of us didn't see it. I suspect the Tesco egg man, unless he's dangerously psychotic, may have been one of them.

Wednesday, 25 March 2020

I was wide awake at 4.30am, so ahead of today's diary entry, I drew up the kind of key-word plan I used in exams before I ploughed into an essay. Returning to the keyboard at 10am, I found Amanda had left me the following:

Every morning there's a segment on the Today *programme which features a musician or actor giving an extract from their cancelled performance. This morning the two actors from Hampstead Theatre's production of Pinter's* The Dumb Waiter *performed a short scene from the play. Two hitmen are sitting in a lonely basement waiting for their target. As actor Harry Lloyd ruefully remarked, 'A good example of self-isolation.'*

Harry told Mishal Hussein that the play's January 1960 premiere took place in a village hall which housed the then Hampstead Theatre Club – a far cry from its new home, a plush, purpose-built theatre in Swiss Cottage. Back in the village hall in 1960, the set was dismantled every evening and carried across the road until it was time to put it up again for the next performance.

We are lucky to have Hampstead Theatre on our doorstep and we're enthusiastic patrons and supporters. We were really looking forward to its revival of The Dumb Waiter *and had booked tickets for Saturday, 11 April. For now, while the theatre is dark and the building is locked, the set is staying put until the cast and audience can return.*

An excellent anecdote there from Amanda, albeit one which rivals her sending me out for polenta last week for making us sound like a pair of NW3 'it's grim up north London' fops. Just as well no one knows I also scraped the last of our past-its-sell-by-date pot of guacamole on to my toast this morning. Yes, we are both from Stockton-on-Tees and no, we don't have a tapestry room. Pinter's long-time lover, Joan 'thinking man's crumpet' Bakewell does use both the local greengrocer's I mentioned and the longstanding old-school Greek restaurant three doors down, though.

Since this isn't supposed to be the complete history of this virus, here's a quick summary of some of the worrying developments which had us both staring at the ceiling in the middle of the night. The Tube, that obvious Achilles heel in the great social distancing plan, has become the subject of a hugely depressing battle between local and central government: the Health Secretary says Transport for London must run more trains; our mayor says an alarming 30 per cent of drivers are off work so it can't be done. The main problem seems to be construction workers: some contractors in the building industry are insisting their workforce comes in every day, seemingly so they're not sued for abandoning projects. Unless they're building hospitals, that's insane. If this is found to have anything to do with the building industry's Tim Martin-like Tory/Brexit credentials, it'll be another item for the Nuremburg charge sheet.

Meanwhile, Michael Gove, who despite his gigantic character flaws usually seems like one of our more competent ministers, had to make two appearances on ITV's *This Morning*, that 'oh no, not the comfy chair' TV interview outlet for all ministers (including the Prime one) who can't face a real inquisition with Andrew Neil. His first attempt to explain the new restrictions so confused viewers that he was obliged to have another go. Pete on Facebook has found some figures suggesting that 6,000 people were tested in the UK yesterday; at that rate, it would take 30 years to test us all. Jake's group disagrees with my suggestion of a national government, not unreasonably suggesting that it would be a trap designed to tarnish the other parties with the consequences of the Tory party's inadequate preparations; bin Corbyn, then join COBRA, is their view.

Worst of all, Spain, which employed similar measures to ours about a week earlier, but while at a similar point on the graph, has now overtaken China's death toll with figures that unlike Italy's are still rising exponentially. The USA will almost certainly overtake all of them in due course, a price their deranged commander-in-chief appears willing to pay. State and city governments in New York and California in particular are poised to defy any Trump attempt to loosen restrictions. The President seems to be advocating a blindfolded leap into 'herd immunity' territory, and you can only imagine the divisions and panic behind the scenes in Washington. Whitehall, where all hell has clearly been breaking loose, too, probably sounds like a Quaker library by comparison.

We've been watching bits of Sky News, most of *C4 News* and very little BBC TV news, but last night we gave the corporation's main *News at Ten* a whirl. A decision seems to have been made, with or without menacing input from the 'Number 10 source' who so loathes the place, not to show anything unpleasant either from here, Italy or elsewhere, or to question anything the government has done or is still doing. I presume they've never retracted that 'the science has changed' regurgitated line, either. Last night's running order was mostly sensible public service advice, usually expressed as 'the government says' with a reassuring Auntie overtone of, 'it's all going to be all right'. Maybe that is the way it should be right now, as it was during World War Two, but it's certainly not the full Reithian 'Inform, Educate and Entertain' mission statement of the training courses I once attended.

Even so, whenever this is all over, the BBC ought to feel a little of the same protection from the vultures and Tufton Street think-tank maniacs as the NHS undoubtedly will. Local TV and radio, the now mercifully John Humphrys-free Radio 4 and the BBC website are informing the populace quite brilliantly and, the infliction of extra repeats of *Mrs Brown's Boys* notwithstanding, the entertainment quotient of BBCs Two and Four in particular are proving more than enough to sustain us, without yet dipping into any box sets.

We Sky+ *Only Connect* and *University Challenge* and watched the latest instalments of both yesterday – it's good to stretch the brain, just a shame both current series are nearly over – and savoured the last-ever episode of the wry fly-on-the-wall spoof Cotswold comedy *This Country*. As usual, it was well into its second series before someone – Jan from the Curry Club this time – urged us to watch it. Thanks, Jan – it just got better and better, and managed over three series to make these viewers really care about two seemingly hopeless cousins from broken families, living in a sleepy rural backwater.

Like the now internationally acclaimed *Fleabag, This Country* was a fantastic piece of commissioning from the scaled-back BBC Three. As David Attenborough once did with *Monty Python*, someone at Radio 4 did with the then unknown Armando Iannucci, Chris Morris, Steve Coogan, Rebecca Front and friends and the ground-breaking *On the Hour*, or Jane Root did this century with *The Office*, the BBC can still experiment and innovate. Because its funding model isn't built around advertising, poor initial viewing or listening figures aren't the end of the world – hardly anyone watched the first series of *Only Fools and Horses*, for example – and you can take a punt on something you believe in. Netflix and Amazon Prime, while employing admirable production values, mostly opt for big name actors and writers who have already proven their box office credentials. A further example is the eclectic, often new, music I'm listening to right now on BBC Radio 6. Good luck to most of these bands if they want airplay on Heart FM or even daytime Radio 2.

Dick Clement mentioning Samuel Pepys in his e-mail made me think I should check the old boy out for the first time since we skimmed through his diary in history lessons when I was about 12 or 13. There's a quote doing the rounds now about youths still roistering in the street outside as the plague begins to spread, but sadly it comes from a reworking by a modern author. I bet there are loads of parallels with 2020's London in the original Pepys's diary, though. Marina Hyde, and the occasional stunning one-liner from the ever sharper and less gratuitously nasty Frankie Boyle, are the nearest thing Twitter offers to Pepys as chroniclers of our era. Fortunately, the prolific output of the former, at least, is also regularly available at Guardian Online.

Marina is on imperious form today: a serious and fair preamble where she rightly says of Boris Johnson, 'Thank heavens he finally did it,' is followed by a stupendous dissection of preceding events. His 'we shall fight on the beaches' moment was indeed preceded by days of 'I want people to be able to visit our great beaches! I want to keep our great beaches open! I have to tell you that, should my beach waffle prove demonstrably unclear to millions, then I may be forced to bring forward measures to lay the ground for some kind of beach-fight.' As good a summary of the far from Churchillian Great British lost weekend just gone as you're likely to read. And I saw a line of Churchill's today which, though it was aimed at the American administrations of his day, seems to apply equally well to our current UK government: 'They will always do the right thing … after they've exhausted all other possibilities.'

It's probably as well for national morale that only we politics wonks followed the tortured, excruciating build-up to that half-decent, pre-recorded address seen by 27 million viewers. In that spirit, I've just deleted a long account I'd written of the Boris Johnson I didn't know but whose membership of the once respectable, but by the mid-'80s, notorious 'smash up a restaurant, make the staff cry, pater'll write a cheque' Bullingdon Club, and whose desperate need to fulfil what he saw as his birthright by becoming President of the Union en route to World King, were part of the backdrop to my time at Oxford. I went on at length about the bizarre spectacle the Bullingdon Club (including Bozza) once made of themselves in their frock coats at largely state-school Univ, when invited by our resident Buller and only (I think) Old Etonian, one Toby Edmond Luard Morton Mansell-Pleydell. That's one bloke, not the whole club, by the way. Crazy name, crazy guy – or at least I assume he was. I never exchanged one word with him in the two years we overlapped in our cosily intimate college.

In the end, though, what's the point? I've actually met one or two extremely pleasant and well-mannered Etonians since then, but Alexander Boris De Pfeffel Johnson and his ilk are what they are. This country has always deferred to them and largely continues to do so. We simply have no option but to put whatever faith we can muster in the man who would be Winston – the fact that he thinks so highly of someone who was a mere Harrovian is, I guess, a relative sign of broadmindedness – and we'll just have to batten down the hatches as best we can, hope someone does something very quickly about the Tube, and wait as the numbers continue silently to swell.

Thursday, 26 March 2020

A truly gorgeous spring morning, nothing on *Today* or Sky News had agitated Amanda enough to leave a handover note, so I headed outside where she was already sitting in the sunshine reading the last instalment of Hilary Mantel's Wolf Hall trilogy, *The Mirror and the Light*. I'll be reading that too at some point, having loved the last two books and the adaptations we saw both on stage and TV. The former featured Ben Miles as Dom

Cummings's Tudor predecessor Thomas Cromwell, the latter Mark Rylance. She says it's superbly written but all a bit too unsettling for current times with beheadings always looming and (spoiler alert) Cromwell destined to meet the same fate.

I took a coffee and the guitar out there and gave Amanda and our robin my finest rendition of 'Here Comes the Sun'. Not very imaginative, I know, but George Harrison wrote it 51 years ago in an English garden in springtime, and I can actually play and sing it reasonably accurately. The garden in question was Eric Clapton's so may have been more than a patio. George borrowed an acoustic guitar from Eric, just as Eric later borrowed George's wife and eventually married her. That's just how it was in the 1960s. Eric wrote 'Layla' about Pattie Boyd while their relationship was still clandestine and 'Wonderful Tonight' once it was official, George having previously written the sublime 'Something' for her. If you're going to be cast as a muse by unreliable artistic types, you may as well entice some masterpieces out of them, and Pattie certainly did.

We've attended a number of Hyde Park concerts over the years – Simon and Garfunkel's second and last ever gig in London with support from their heroes The Everly Brothers was one; the great Tom Petty a couple of months before his untimely death, was another. When Clapton and Santana headlined two years ago, the young Spanish man next to me waited to act out the 'You've got me on my knees' line in 'Layla' and promptly proposed to his girlfriend. She accepted, to much delight in our section. A lovely moment.

By the way, just in case you get the impression that we're completely stuck in an old fart's musical rut, I should point out that the last gig we were due to go to was the magnificent Brittany Howard, formerly of Alabama Shakes, and a latter-day Mavis Staples, at the Forum in Camden. That was a couple of weeks ago, immediately before the pubs and venues were belatedly shut – I believe it took place, but having seen Teenage Fanclub there last year, I know it's a sweaty, cramped standing venue of the old-school variety, so we reluctantly swerved it. I hope the audience are all okay now and that Brittany and her band got home safely to the States. Next time, eh?

Speaking of music, among the many regular e-mails I receive is one from an app called Bandsintown which syncs up with your music apps and tells you if anyone you listen to is touring. It's often a useful service and is probably how I found out Brittany was coming to town. Nevertheless, I was surprised to be greeted today by the following e-mail header, 'Hi Paul, You got (sic) a new message from Jimi Hendrix'. Christ, the virus really is mutating, I thought. Disappointingly, they were just commemorating the 50th anniversary of the release of *Band of Gypsies*, so, much as I'd love to have seen my fellow left-handed (all comparisons end there) guitarist live, it's not to be. I've been to the flat he lived in, though – remarkably it's at the same 25 Brook Street, Mayfair address where Handel lived two centuries earlier, and the two men now share a museum. Quite right, too – it's all music, as my late friend David Eastwood used to say.

Back to our current bizarre times. The UK's daily death figures actually went down a bit yesterday, due to the announcement being made at 9am instead of late afternoon, but there's no doubt it just means the maelstrom has been pushed back slightly. It makes you wonder what a complete lockdown a fortnight ago might have achieved, but it wasn't to be and a week more of open pubs, then that lost weekend of unforeseen public stupidity, won't show in the statistics for another couple of weeks. I switched on Sky briefly: there's now a dispiriting squabble and disconnect between politicians, notably the Health Secretary, and manufacturers and those on the NHS front line over the blithe assurances given yesterday of the imminent arrival of protective equipment, testing gear and ventilators. Various vital components seemingly can't be sourced because, guess what, other countries snapped them up first.

It could well turn out that our non-participation in the EU's collective scheme to buy equipment has cost us, either because of their far greater collective purchasing power or because we were slow off the mark, or possibly both. A 'government spokesman' has claimed today that a 'communications error' rather than a doctrinaire take on Brexit stopped us from participating. I'm tempted to suggest that the 'communications error' may simply be a euphemism for Classic Dom Cummings having told the Europeans to 'fuck off', but who knows? I really don't want to think about how idiotic any version of our going it alone is right now, or indeed to think too often about how the 'herd immunity' wrong turning may have impacted on that situation, but I can't help but be reminded of an infinitely more trivial episode from my BBC Sport career.

The Atlanta Olympics of 1996 was a nadir for the British team (I will never, ever call them Team GB, so up yours, branding gurus) with only the rowers Steve Redgrave and Matthew Pinsent winning gold. The undoubted star of the games was the American athlete Michael Johnson, later to become one of the greatest of all sporting pundits with the BBC. The day after he'd smashed the 200m world record – I'd rushed to the stadium after my shift with my mate Carl Hicks and I'll never forget watching both him and the clock simultaneously as he won by about 20 lengths. His time of 19.32 took 0.34 of a second off the figure Johnson had set at the US trials, which in itself had shaved six hundredths of a second off Pietro Mennea's 27-year-old mark. That 19.32 was seen as our generation's Bob Beamon moment until a Jamaican nine-year-old called Bolt grew up and ran even faster.

So, next day, the whole world naturally wanted to talk to Johnson – Brian Barwick, later head of BBC then ITV Sport, and then the FA, was editing the peak UK time show presented by Des Lynam, so told Carl in his role of chief news gatherer to drop everything else and get Johnson. The impeccably well-connected Brendan Foster knew Michael from the athletics circuit and tracked him down as he was doing the rounds of his sponsors. Brendan fixed a time and phoned Carl who dashed off with a crew to produce this major scoop. Michael was where they were told he would be and would indeed be delighted to talk to Brendan and the BBC.

Just as they were about to set up their camera, Carl took a call on his brick-sized mobile phone. It was Brian – he'd spoken to an agent and Johnson would come into the studio to talk to Des pre-recorded for the main evening show, so Carl could stand his interview down. 'Hadn't we better get something in the can, just in case?' asked Carl. 'No, stand Brendan down and get back here,' was the answer. When later that day MJ came into the International Broadcast Centre and started to do the rounds, he got behind schedule to the point where his agent, spooked by the endless faffing about with studio lights and cameras in the BBC studio, pulled him out 30 seconds after he'd sat down with Des – who unlike Brendan, he didn't know from Adam – to rush him off to NBC or wherever he was supposed to be half an hour ago. No usable BBC interview at all was the outcome.

All hell broke loose. I was in the room when Carl – who, although he went on to be the editor of *Grandstand* was very much the junior figure at this point – threw a pen at Brian and launched a volley of epithets closely resembling that Peter Reid verbal assault on Boris Johnson. It seemed quite an important dropping of the ball at the time, but it was only TV Sport and 'no one died' was, as ever, everyone's attitude once the dust had settled. Carl still remembers it, though, and so do I.

Again, although Tim Shipman felt confident enough of his sources to write that *Sunday Times* article on the herd immunity U-turn, I'd never speculate about this in public right now, it would only frighten and enrage people who have enough to contend with at the moment. Only the eventual national post-mortem – assuming it's truthful – will tell us exactly what happened in Whitehall, and whether Cummings was the Barwick figure, and the NHS and scientists effectively Carl, over the last couple of months.

On a lighter note, both Amanda and I are probably having more conversations and interactions with our friends than we ever did when we were free to physically get together. Two of the girls, women now of course, with whom Amanda was at her Darlington boarding school, set up a conference call with her. They're all predictably coping with this as well as Amanda is. Tall Paul from the Curry Club invited me to join an app called Houseparty – a sort of FaceTime via which 30 people can interact at any one time. That sounds a bit like bedlam, but we managed a good chat with just me and Amanda here and Paul, his wife Joyce and daughter Charlotte in south-west London as they took their permitted daily walk in an open space. It turns out I'm late to this trend, too; dozens of friends are already on there, including Lucy, our lovely ex-neighbour from Bayswater who'd tried to speak to us earlier and left me a wave instead. We were supposed to be staying with Tom and Lucy down on the Berkshire-Hampshire border last weekend, and watching their eldest son – Amanda's godson – play school rugby, but that all bit the dust, so a virtual chat would be the next best thing.

Speaking of friendly neighbours, we had a hand-written note pushed through our letterbox yesterday. Aline from Flat 6, whom we've never met properly, wanted to check that everyone was okay and to know whether anyone needed any shopping or other errands doing. I called her to tell her what a lovely gesture that was and had a spirited 20 minutes or so conversation in which I discovered she was Brazilian, a former Unilever employee turned sustainability and environmental consultant, had been in London for more than a decade and had moved a while back to share a flat with Alex. Although we and Elaine in the adjacent ground floor flat have a completely separate entrance from the rest of the building, we're in touch with Alex, largely because everyone's electricity meters are in our hall cupboard, and we take their readings for them. This is presumably a remnant of this once being the sort of family house Charles Pooter of *The Diary of a Nobody* might have lived in when the street was first built.

It turns out Aline has been here nearly a year, so I felt slightly ashamed and stereotypically 'that there London' that we hadn't spoken before, especially when she turned out to have an extremely interesting take on the pandemic and life in general. As concern about the environment has reached the alarm bell stage in recent years, those in charge of countries and industries and their associated lobbyists have often countered it: firstly, in some cases, by abusing the remarkable teenager Greta Thunberg on social media, and secondly by saying it's unthinkable that we'd stop chopping down forests, wiping out thousands of animal species a year, belching factory fumes into the air and racing around the planet in cars and aeroplanes. 'It's the economy, stupid,' as George Bush senior once said, and that's been almost everyone's orthodoxy ever since. Amanda and I calculate a carbon-offsetting donation every time we fly and almost always use public transport to get around, but to be honest, we've flown away on cheap flights for long weekends or football matches as much as anyone, and I've been fixated on GDP figures with the best of them, especially with regard to the likely effects of Brexit. The economy not growing, and therefore not using up more resources, has previously been unthinkable, too.

Aline thinks there'll be some negative impacts in that suspicion of the 'other' will only increase around the globe and that companies will initially just want to get up and running again, meaning that sustainability may slip down the corporate agenda for a while. But, as Amanda and I have been discussing, everyone will now be aware of the needless journeys they regularly insist on taking and may increasingly look to return to locally sourced food, rather than prissily demanding that a punnet of strawberries be flown in from Kenya in December. The next generation, including my nieces and their primary school, are already way ahead of their leaders on that front – old and narrow-minded voters largely installed Trump and Brazil's own fascistic, Amazon-destroying, demagogic monster Jair Bolsonaro. The young are being handed the ultimate in hospital passes from what I've just heard 70-something Max Hastings describe on Radio 4 as the 'most selfish and privileged generation in history'. This episode, calamitous though it is, may precipitate some necessary changes rather more quickly than anyone envisaged.

So too could the extraordinary economic transformation, epitomised by Rishi Sunak's latest pronouncement of help for the self-employed. We're moving back towards the 'safety net for all' society I felt I'd grown up in, and at least some of it is going to have to stick. The 1970s in the UK were crap in many ways, but no one dreamt back then that the UK would have more food banks than branches of WH Smith by 2020, or so many homeless people, or schools and teachers holding whip-rounds to buy basic equipment and counter widespread vitamin deficiencies among their pupils. All of that is a disgrace in one of the richest countries in the world, and needs to be re-examined.

If that means that Mike Ashley or Tim Martin have to hand over some of their personal fortunes – approximately £2bn and £500m respectively – then bring it on. After his reckless plea to keep his pubs open was eventually ignored, Martin has since had to U-turn on a threat not to pay his employees for a month, and Ashley is rightly being lambasted, both for trying to say that Sports Direct is an essential service, and for taking next season's money in advance out of the accounts of Newcastle United season ticket holders before anyone even knows what next season might be. I'm not sure what planet those two inhabit, but I think they may find that some of their regular customers won't be returning to avail themselves of their services when they're allowed to reopen.

Along with huge corporations like Amazon and Starbucks who pay no tax in the UK despite their dominance of their respective markets, Ashley and Martin have long since had this reassessment coming to them. Even though we're stuck with a Tory government which would instinctively be intensely relaxed about such matters, and a press which traditionally protects its own tax-avoiding proprietors, they may all find that public opinion has shifted and that they're forced to play their part in the emergency resuscitation our economy is going to need. I sincerely hope so, anyway.

The news cycle has gone eerily quiet today, a bit like the lull where the tide goes out before a tsunami. Although we've heard no more from Doctor Liz on the front line, there are mutterings elsewhere among my groups that her fears about the failure to protect her staff are proving to be well founded. I can't find this anywhere official yet but a worrying proportion of the staff at some hospitals are said to be ill or self-isolating, a call has gone out for volunteers to assist the NHS and though a remarkable half a million people have signed up, it's all beginning to sound a bit ominous. Oh, and Russian warships have apparently been hanging around the Channel and North Sea. Like their official COVID-19 death toll – three to date – it's all a bit suspicious.

One sad item of news unrelated to the virus – as his family were at pains to point out – was the passing at the age of 92 of the co-creator and illustrator of the *Asterix the Gaul* series, Albert Uderzo. Along with Charles M. Schulz, the man behind *Peanuts*, Uderzo drew a gently humorous but essential decent world in which this Teesside youngster immersed himself.

Back here in 2020, the British love of gallows humour means the jokes and wry lines are already flying around. 'We'll be home for Christmas' was the notoriously over-optimistic claim as World War One broke out in 1914. My mate Philip has adapted that to, 'We'll still be home for Christmas.' And someone was very quick off the mark when the news broke that the Prince of Wales has tested positive for the virus. Within the hour, I was sent the following: 'Prince Charles is isolating in Scotland with COVID-19. Prince Andrew is isolating at Windsor with Jennifer-14.'

Friday, 27 March 2020

Something genuinely remarkable and moving happened last night. Inspired by similar events in Italy and Spain, there was online chatter about everyone applauding our NHS workers at

8pm. A great idea, clearly, but one which I suspected would be a damp squib here in cynical, disorganised old Britain. Not a bit of it – there was football crowd-level noise all around here; clapping, cheering, the banging of saucepans, and I hope the heroic workforce around the corner at the Royal Free Hospital felt the love.

I suspect they'd rather have enough protective equipment, ventilators and the chance to be tested, even so. The BBC's coverage from around the country segued into *Question Time*, which I promptly switched off. I've been boycotting that independently produced show since seven-time parliamentary election loser Nigel Farage was about midway to his 32 appearances tally, and when it began to emerge that some of the more outspoken questions from the selected audience were from far-right activists. In at least one case in Scotland, the same angry little man asked questions on three separate programmes in different towns within about a year. The Special Measures WhatsApp group told me afterwards that I'd missed something very different: no audience and the editor of *The Lancet* tearing the government a new one over its ill-preparedness and for 'wasting the whole of February'.

A glance at the newspaper headlines Google offered me this morning, and even the normally rabidly loyal *Daily Express*, has reported the chief scientific adviser to the Italian government's interview yesterday in which he expressed incredulity that having seen disaster mounting there, we didn't go into lockdown ten days earlier. A key moment in the spread there appears to have been what's now being dubbed Game Zero: the Champions League tie between Atalanta of Bergamo and Valencia on 19 February. The game, like all their other European matches so far, had been switched from Atalanta's tiny stadium to the San Siro in Milan, so a third of Bergamo's population travelled by car, train and bus, and thousands more gathered in bars and homes to watch what had been billed as the club's biggest-ever fixture. In retrospect, an almost perfect breeding ground for the incipient virus to spread.

At that point only three coronavirus cases had been recorded in Italy, none in Bergamo or Milan, so there seemed to be nothing foolhardy about the game going ahead or 2,500 away fans having travelled over from Spain.

By contrast, on 12 March, when a crowd of around 60,000 attended the third day of the Cheltenham Festival, and Boris Johnson's contribution to the 'herd immunity' press conference was to say mass gatherings were still fine, there were 590 confirmed cases in the UK, with a death toll already in double figures. Furthermore, pubs still had what turned out to be another nine evenings' grace. By then, Italy had more than 15,000 confirmed cases and 1,800 deaths. I'm not being wise after the event, and nor is the editor of *The Lancet*. I'd capitalise the whole of this next bit if Donald Trump hadn't ruined that technique for ever, but – What The Fuck Were We Thinking???

Sorry, researching and writing that last paragraph has tipped the 'desire to be well-informed' gauge close to the 'endangering sanity' reading. Some extraordinary – albeit temporary – moves are afoot in British politics, even beyond the fiscal Sunak Socialism: councils have been ordered to house all homeless people by the weekend, and the red-faced potato lookalike and hitherto very, very right wing Edward Leigh MP is now advocating a basic minimum wage for all. Finland, the happiest country on the planet three years running according to surveys, has that in place permanently, but the fact that it's being discussed even within a Tory party stripped of all its moderates, is absolutely amazing.

Oh, and like the 'Number 10 spokesman' claiming yesterday that the cat ate the e-mail from the EU about procuring ventilators and protective equipment, Mike Ashley is 'deeply apologetic' for his various 'communication errors' of recent days. I think 'rumbled' was the word you were looking for, Mike. Having been knocked back by the government when he proclaimed Sports Direct 'an essential service', he closed his stores but, according to newspaper reports, kept his warehouses open and added a 50 per cent mark-up on exercise equipment for delivery. Supervisors in his Derbyshire warehouse failed to implement social distancing and staff were having to turn to social media to say they weren't being allowed time off even if they were developing symptoms. The sort of 'Victorian workhouse' conditions a parliamentary committee chastised Ashley for overseeing a few years ago or, if you're Jacob Rees-Mogg, a shining example of the 'Indian-style' health and safety regime Brexit could free us up to implement. Jacob, like Priti Patel, has wisely been kept out of the limelight for the last couple of weeks – it's probably not the moment for another quip along the lines of his zinger, 'I find food banks rather uplifting.'

Oh, my God. I had various more trivial matters to record, but Amanda has just passed me her iPad. Boris Johnson has tested positive for coronavirus. Her first, and correct, thought was that he has a pregnant girlfriend; mine was that whatever you think of him he is a known figurehead who probably has provided an illusion of stability for much of a frightened country thus far. Then you think of the people he's been around, not least the chief scientific and medical advisers who regularly flank him at his press conferences. Finally, you remember that Dominic Raab – the man who thinks Lima is in the Philippines and discovered that the Dover to Calais route was significant only after he'd lobbied for a No Deal Brexit – is now in charge. Assuming he hasn't caught it, of course.

I'd better stop there. I'm tempted to go back and moderate some of my criticism of Johnson, but that would be inauthentic, so I won't. It's also not the time to pass on what I know about Dominic Raab's temperament, from those who knew him when he was a lawyer at Linklaters. Suffice to say, it all suddenly feels deeply unstable. This diary's at the fortnight mark now, so I'll wrap it here for the day and send it to my distribution list.

WEEK THREE

Saturday, 28 March 2020

'The first thing Boris said to me was, "We need more ventilators."' – Donald Trump in his latest press conference, as shown to me on her iPad by Amanda when I emerged this morning.

With the obvious caveat that Trump isn't the most reliable of sources, this is not what I wanted to hear, especially having developed a sore throat overnight. All week we've been hearing on various TV and radio shows about British ventilator manufacturers who responded to Matt Hancock's desperate-sounding appeal two weeks ago, but have since been turned down or ignored by our government, who in turn also turned down/lost the e-mail from that EU initiative to acquire them from around the world. I believe we've now handed a contract to Dyson, who've never, ever manufactured a single ventilator before, and need to clinically test the one they've just designed in a week. Still, on the bright side, Sir James Dyson is a long-standing Conservative Party member and backed Brexit, before shifting his HQ to Singapore after Leave won. Entirely coincidental, I'm sure, that the move gave Dyson access to Singapore's trade deal with the EU.

To be honest, the whole story is so frightening and depressing – I outlined the sums relating to the shortfall on here days ago – that I can't face researching it any further. If the whole ventilator/protective equipment/testing saga turns out after the event not to be one of our greatest-ever national scandals, and doesn't cost thousands of lives, I will be both surprised and delighted, assuming I'm still around. Let's just leave it there.

Despite the iffy throat, it turns out my temperature's normal, but a dodgy throat frequently leads to ear infections and, with T-tubes inserted into each eardrum, I've had a few blockages cleared in the last four or five years, the latest about a month ago. My perennial ENT issues are emphatically not going to be London's health priority any time soon, so I just hope it clears. In other personal health news, I've lost 6lb in weight in about three weeks – I suspect mostly from having no access to sugary non-essentials – and have been riding the exercise bike Amanda bought on the internet last week, and not from Mike Ashley's Sports Direct, either. Being Chinese-made, it was also remarkably easy to assemble, so it's out on the patio and already getting plenty of use.

Pete on Facebook, the stats man who's called most of this correctly so far, has posited a new world order which he thinks may emerge out of this crisis. The developing world, especially most of Africa, lies outside of this assessment for the time being, having far fewer cases to date, and more worryingly, generally less-developed medical provision, and some very densely populated cities. Amanda lived in Nigeria for a while when her parents worked there and I covered the World Cup in South Africa and made a filming trip for Sport Relief to the shanty towns of Kampala in Uganda. We're both picturing the places we visited and wonderful people we met, and hoping to God this thing doesn't sweep through them in due course.

The top tier of Pete's new hierarchy of nations would be China and the more high-tech of its Asian neighbours – although they can't eradicate this thing altogether without a vaccine. Two of the first three affected countries, China and South Korea, recorded three and five deaths respectively yesterday; the third country, Singapore, has only recorded two coronavirus deaths throughout this crisis. South Korea has had 144 deaths in total so far and, officially at least, China has never had as many deaths in one day as the 181 the UK registered yesterday. Germany, with less than half the UK's death total so far and four times the number of people tested, is the only major European country who might stake a claim to be included in the top tier. I hate just spouting numbers like this, by the way – each individual component of these numbers is a human being, a loved one mourned by friends and families. It's just that mounting numbers equate to mounting grief and lives lost before their time, so the cold statistics are our only way of trying to understand the macro, rather than tragic micro, picture.

The second tier is most of the rest of Europe, who despite some national variations have ended up on the same page, putting their economies second in a (belated, in some cases) quest to save as many people as possible. Sweden is an interesting, and puzzling to me, outlier – while they're not citing 'herd immunity' theory, they've toned down rather than curtailed day-to-day life it seems, other than banning crowds of more than 500 people (I can hear Alan Shearer telling me 'Well, Boro would be all right, then'). This Swedish policy stands in direct contrast to their neighbours Denmark and Norway who are broadly in step with the rest of Europe. I travelled across Sweden in 2013 for the Women's Euros and outside of three reasonably large cities a long way apart from each other, population density is thin, and although we didn't test them, I would imagine the medical facilities and provision level would be on a par with those in Germany. While they're clearly trying to strike a balance between limiting the spread of the virus and shutting down economic activity, only time – and a sober comparison of the eventual statistics with the countries around them – will tell if it was a good judgement call. Sweden has currently recorded 105 coronavirus deaths. Across the Baltic, Poland which has four times Sweden's population, has only recorded 16 deaths to date, but these are early days.

I've been dredging my mind for the moral philosophy tenets I once studied: Kant's categorical imperative would, I think, always put preventing deaths first but the Utilitarian calculus of the 'greatest happiness for the greatest number' is more difficult to measure against a situation like this. For a start, you'd somehow have to factor in the worrying number of domestic abuse victims now stuck indoors with their assailant, or neglected kids living in poverty who may only get a square meal when they go to school. Then there are the incalculable effects of shutting down much of the economy. John Rawls's hugely influential *A Theory of Justice* posited the 'invisible veil'. Hypothetically, if we took away everyone's current health, wealth and status and said, 'How would you like a future society to look?' he suggested that we'd all want to shore up the less fortunate, given that any of us could now be one of them. You could argue that most of Europe has, albeit temporarily, chosen a Rawlsian path.

Or you can go down the lines of Pete's third category, the countries governed by maverick populists who seemingly don't obey any established norms. Our quarantined PM has a touch of that about him, but in the end, he hasn't gone the whole hog like Trump, or Bolsonaro in Brazil. It's no coincidence that the latter and his entourage visited Trump's Mar a Lago three weekends ago as this crisis began to escalate. Neither believes in climate change: Trump quietly sneaked through 'the most radical dismantling of environmental regulations in 50 years' (CNN) yesterday; the rainforest is the first casualty of Bolsanaro's hostility to science, 'The Amazon is Now Completely Lawless' (*NY Times* headline).

Trump has not a clue about science: the photo op to commemorate the economic aid package he signed today showed his whole team huddled around him as if the concept of social distancing hasn't reached any of them, and he told the governor of New York only yesterday that he had 'a feeling' that the figures were wrong and that the Big Apple wouldn't need the ventilators the projections were demanding. Governor Cuomo responded despairingly that he'd rather deal in facts and science.

That 21st-century existential 'emotion versus fact' battle again: as Arron Banks boasted, the former certainly won the day back in 2016 when we'd 'all had enough of experts' (M. Gove) but I strongly suspect it's not going to defeat this virus. Back when reported US cases were still in double figures, Trump wanted to leave a returning cruise ship stranded off California, because, 'I like the figures the way they are.' Perhaps he thinks those passengers – despite being tested and quarantined as they came ashore – are directly responsible for the USA now moving ahead of China and Italy into the top spot in the reported cases league table. Then again, one of his election slogans was 'America First'. Or maybe it's still a 'Democrat plot' or man-made in China, or something to do with Mexican 'rapists and drug dealers' – who knows? Clearly not the 49 per cent of Americans who are currently giving Pee 45 his highest approval ratings since just after his inauguration. Ninety per cent of Republicans say they trust his handling of this crisis, in which case I have a bridge straight from the heart of London I'd like to sell to them.

Both presidents are also currently at odds with their state governors: 36 out of 37 in Brazil are imposing their own restrictions, despite Bolsonaro telling them not to do so, while Rio's Favela gangs have imposed their own lockdowns. Many of the most populous US states – New York, California and Illinois – are doing likewise. I honestly think Trump is cynical enough not to worry too much about those three states: they were never going to vote for him in the autumn anyway, and with the electoral college system it doesn't matter by what margin they oppose him. He didn't win a plurality of the popular vote in 2016, Hillary Clinton receiving 2.8 million more votes than he did, and he won't need to do so this time. He'll only start to panic if and when he thinks the swing states – Ohio, Michigan and co. – are turning on him.

Oh, and the other thing Bolsonaro and Trump have in common is that they were mentored, and encouraged to stir up mayhem, by one Steve Bannon, former chief aide to Donald Trump. Here are a few sample Bannon quotes: 'Fear is a good thing'; 'Lenin wanted to destroy the state and that's my goal too'; 'I want to bring everything crashing down, and destroy all of today's establishment'. Lovely, sane sentiments, I'm sure we can all agree.

On our own referendum night in 2016, another close associate of Bannon's, the human nicotine stain that is Nigel Farage, falsely conceded victory when the polls closed, entirely coincidentally allowing a handful of people to cash in on the currency markets when the pound leapt in value for an hour or two. It then crashed a little later when Cuddly Nige finally put down his cigarette and pint, admitted he'd won after all and what's more 'without a shot being fired' (er, what about the late Jo Cox MP?) then directly thanked Bannon (and the closely associated, now-disbanded Cambridge Analytica) for making it all possible.

I suppose we in the UK should be grateful Bannon never got Farage into Parliament, or into a powerful executive role like another of his protégés, the sinister and openly racist Matteo Salvini, formerly deputy prime minister of Italy. Bannon is a big fan of Boris Johnson's, though: an interview he gave last year revealed that the two men regularly went 'went back and forth' around the time of Johnson's resignation from the May government and Steve could hardly contain his glee when Bozza took a leaf straight out of the Bannon-Trump playbook and likened some Muslim women to 'letterboxes'.

But what of our own Poundshop Bannon, Dominic Cummings? Well, a widely shared clip showed him hurriedly leaving Downing Street yesterday shortly after his nominal boss, the PM, tested positive, but before the Health Secretary (confirmed) chief Brexit negotiator (suspected) and Chief Medical Officer (suspected) were revealed to have gone into self-isolation too. Dom being Dom, though, he couldn't help but provide the unfortunate ten per cent of us who know who he is with the darkest of laughs. Jake posted the footage of him trying to sprint towards the back gate of Downing Street, dressed like a tramp as usual and showing the sort of sporting prowess which would definitely have seen him picked last in games – so often the core problem with his type.

I responded by describing the spectacle as Pythonesque: the Ministry of Silly Walks meets Neil Innes's marvellous *Holy Grail* ditty, 'Brave Sir Robin bravely ran away.' And Britain being Britain, within an hour someone had soundtracked his stick-insect sprint with 'Brave Sir Robin', someone else had sped it up to the Benny Hill 'Yakety Sax' theme, and the Scottish comedian Janey Godley had dubbed on one of her inimitable commentaries, 'Plenty o' fluids, Boris, d'ya ken? See you on the WhatsApp group and tha'. Byeee.' There'll be plenty more where those came from on Twitter, I suspect. On a serious note, Sam Coates of Sky reports that Dom went back to Downing Street later in the day – is self-isolation when you've been around those with symptoms just for the herd?

Before the core of our government began dropping like flies, I'd decided that in the interests of balance (I'm not exactly adhering to BBC editorial guidelines in only doing this after 40,000 words which have not been particularly supportive of those in charge) I thought it was time to see what the formerly sane voice of the right, *The Telegraph*, has been saying.

My dad is one of the few people I know who still reads print editions of the papers; for years he bought *The Times, Guardian/Observer* and *Telegraph* and devoured them all. *The Telegraph* had a particularly good sports section and some reasoned Tory-leaning opinion pieces, but it all began to fall apart when good journalists like Henry Winter and my college friend Christina Lamb left for Times Newspapers and the whole thing has degenerated into a far-right morass.

The excellent *Telegraph* Brussels correspondent Peter Foster, who we saw share a stage with Sky's Adam Boulton and another ex-Univ friend, Professor Anand Menon, (someone else I miss on Twitter) last year, has gone to the *Financial Times*, and even TV's Graham Norton packed in the agony aunt column he'd been writing when he woke up to the toxicity of the surrounding content. My dad scaled back to just *The Times* and *Guardian/Observer* a while back and because I have an illogical (given that I pay fortunes to Sky Sports) aversion to newspaper paywalls, I've only seen recent *Telegraph* headlines second-hand, and to my great shame I only read the now-*Sunday Times* chief foreign correspondent Christina's superb stuff when I'm down at my parents on a Sunday, or when she publishes a book.

My interest in *The Telegraph*'s current stance was piqued this week when the Remoaners WhatsApp group said that that paper had turned on Boris Johnson. Given that they've slavishly supported their ex-'Bendy Bananas' 1990s Brussels correspondent through thick and thin, this came as a surprise. Perhaps, like the hitherto equally loyal *Daily Express*, they were fretting at the tardiness of the imposition of measures which would potentially save lives? Or perhaps they too, had spotted the considerable Venn diagram intersection between the most at-risk categories and those who still buy newspapers?

Not a bit of it: they were furious with the PM for the polar opposite reason, namely that he'd gone much too far for them. They'd prominently placed an article hailing Sweden's approach and assistant comment editor Sherelle Jacobs had written an opinion piece slamming Johnson for capitulating to the liberals when he should have emulated Donald Trump in prioritising the economy. 'Herd immunity,' Jacobs insisted, was controversial but 'correct'. It would be interesting to know whether their remaining, mostly elderly, readership agrees. I was going to ask the same question about the *Telegraph* proprietors, the 85-year-old twin brothers Sir David and Sir Frederick Barclay, but they live in glorious tax exile on the tiny island of Brecqhou, off Sark in the Channel Islands, so have probably reassured Sherelle that they think they'll be okay, and to say whatever she likes.

In other happier news, it appears that mass testing of front-line NHS workers is at last going to start happening this weekend, and despite the high-profile exceptions, it's clear that more organisations than otherwise are behaving well. Middlesex Cricket Club sent an absolutely lovely note to their membership: club chairman and former player Mike Selvey made no reference at all to what must be the desperately worrying financial impact of most, if not all, of the 2020 season being in jeopardy. Instead, he talked about teamwork and community, and implored any member who needed help or just wanted a chat to call the usual office number, now redirected to the staff working at home. Norwich City – always one of the great community-based football clubs – have enlisted their playing and coaching staff to call all 6,000 of their season ticket holders aged over 60 to check they're okay. And the Great British bleak humour is still to the fore: my Boro mate Andy posted the following on Facebook today: 'I've been having a chat with Kev the Cushion and Artie the Ironing Board this morning about which one of us is going to crack up first.'

Then there's Marina Hyde. Her latest column is so good, I'm tempted just to reproduce the whole thing here, but instead, here's her take on Prince Charles testing positive: 'The royal toothpaste will still be squeezed on to the royal toothbrush by a key-worker servant; only they'll do it in one of the rubber-gloved laboratory boxes they use to handle Prince Andrew's bedsheets.' I can't just leave it there, here's a couple more: 'The WHO recommends the sort of full-body armour you'd want to attend dinner at Michael Gove's, though current government largesse only allows for a Kiss the Cook apron and a cardboard Simon Cowell mask;' 'Every night is Halloween at Wetherspoons, and Tim Martin always wears the same costume: coarse fisherman whose wife is missing after 30 years of coercive control. Neighbours say she planned to leave him.'

I stumble around all week trying to channel my anger and disbelief at these people into furious, protracted bouts at the keyboard, then Marina dissects each of them in a handful of seemingly effortless sentences. I'm getting my coat – I might need it on the exercise bike, the weather's turned – for the rest of the day, at the very least.

Sunday, 29 March 2020

The clocks went forward overnight. I normally love that annual harbinger of spring, but this time I'd prefer them to have gone forward several months, or maybe back to the halcyon days of London 2012, and that glorious Olympic opening ceremony. Then culture secretary, and permanent startled meerkat lookalike Jeremy Hunt, wanted the section celebrating the NHS to be removed (too political, he thought) but when creative director

Danny Boyle threatened to walk out, PM David Cameron in one of his better moments went with Boyle. The net result was that joyous evening – Bond meets the Queen and all – where the world just may have thought we were a sophisticated, funny, inclusive nation. Jonathan Coe's superb novel *Middle England* starts on that high and gradually takes his characters down the slippery slope to the rancour and stupidity of 2016.

Mind you, I'd turn the clocks back even to that miserable year in a heartbeat just now. The UK has now had more than 1,000 deaths, 260 alone in one day yesterday. The graphs still show us on a trajectory 15 days behind Italy and just eight days behind Spain. Both countries registered close to 1,000 deaths yesterday alone. In the grisly contest no one in their right mind would want to win, the USA is inevitably going to emerge as the developed world's clear leader before long – New York on its own has similar numbers to the UK now – with the large European nations, bar Germany, vying for the most morbid of podium finishes behind them. Germany seemingly has such an excess of facilities and a quasi-Asian testing regime, that it's been able to airlift some Italian patients to be treated in German hospitals.

Meanwhile, poor, wonderful Italy is in a terrible place. The south in particular, where cash in hand is often the norm, is now seeing genuine deprivation and hunger among those who are off the grid to such an extent that raids on supermarkets are openly being planned on internet forums. Bannon and Farage's mate Salvini has decided that this is the right moment to revive his demand that Italy leaves the EU. All EU countries, having watched the Brexit car crash unfold, have been polling strongly to remain in the organisation. An emboldened Nigel Farage strode into Ireland a while back extolling the benefits of an 'Irexit' to solve the border issue. Instead he was amazed to trigger a new high of 93 per cent Remainers. It's almost as if Irish people weren't persuaded by a posh, arrogant English fox-hunting fan trying to tell them what was good for them. Who knew, eh?

Italy, by contrast, has for some time been second only to the UK in its ambivalence towards the EU: something like a third say they would vote to leave – a slightly smaller fraction than Salvini's Liga Nord polled at their last general election. There's no doubt that Europe has retreated into 'nation state' mode during this crisis, borders shutting and each country ramping up and timing its reactive measures differently. While this proves once and for all that 'taking back control' from the Brussels bureaucrats didn't have to mean actually leaving the EU – the UK has always remained outside the Schengen zone and the Euro, for a start – you can understand why the people of Italy might be wondering why it's had more help from China and Russia than from its EU partners to date.

China presumably feels a degree of responsibility for having been the source of the virus and now has empirically based expertise to share. Russia, I suspect, is just playing cynical power games as usual. Trump, as anyone who is prepared to do so can see, is in hock to Putin for whatever reason. Bannon, Farage, Salvini and all who sail on the bad ship Cambridge Analytica/WikiLeaks have been doing Russia's dirty work, either inadvertently or deliberately, for some time now. WikiLeaks releasing Hillary Clinton's largely innocuous e-mails allowed Trump to whip up the 'lock her up' chants and employ the 'dead cat' strategy to get his followers to ignore the graveyard's worth of skeletons in his own closet. And Putin wanted Brexit and the potential break-up of the EU as much as, if not more than, Farage and Arron Banks did. That'll be Arron Banks with the Russian wife with a colourful background, the XM15 5PY personalised number plate and the confused accounts of his trips to his wife's motherland, as reported by the *Sunday Times*. And why exactly did Farage go straight from meeting Trump and Bannon in Washington to a clandestine rendezvous at the Ecuadorian embassy in London with Julian Assange of WikiLeaks?

If you want to attempt to join a few more dots, I'd highly recommend Carole Cadwalladr's award-winning and extremely brave pursuit of the truth for *The Guardian*. Unless, that is, you're the sort of person who thinks those two rather brutish-looking Russians accused of poisoning Sergei and Yulia Skripal actually did make a mid-winter trip to Salisbury simply to gaze adoringly at the cathedral spire. In which case, nothing to see here.

I listened to Radio 4's excellent *From Our Own Correspondent* yesterday. Their woman in Singapore related the story of a friend who answered the phone one evening in late January. 'Were you in a taxi going from x to y at 18.47 on Wednesday?' she was asked. It turns out she was; the taxi driver had tested positive for COVID-19, so a team in hazmat gear arrived at her doorstep, tested her, and took her into a magnificently appointed hospital. A couple of weeks later she was back at home, fully recovered, a fact made available to her employers, passers-by and anyone else via a phone app. Now, you may argue that you don't want the government to know where you are at 18.47 on any given Wednesday, and in normal circumstances I'd agree, but if your social contract with your government allows them to solve a problem that quickly and efficiently, and keep the national total death toll to three (according to today's figures), I think most of us would sign up for that kind of nanny state.

So, where was Britain in late January? Well, *The Lancet*, written for – and by – doctors, flagged up the impending global pandemic on 21 January. Unfortunately, the British government and newspapers were otherwise occupied, with a big clock. 'Bung a Bob for Boris's Brexit Big Ben Bongs' screamed the headlines as 31 January – Farage's Independence Day – loomed, with our totemic symbol of God knows what any more undergoing repairs and therefore out of action. 'Bung a bob' was Johnson's own phrase, by the way – they were actually trying to crowdfund this idiocy. Never mind that the 'bob' or shilling was replaced by the 5p in 1971, it was alliterative and Bojo loves that. Boris buses, Boris bridges, Bung a bob for Big Ben bongs – he never got over that nursery school thrill of hearing the first letter of his own name.

In that very same 1971, I remember being delighted that a Partick Thistle team including Alan's older brother, John Hansen, shocked mighty Celtic 4-1 in the Scottish League Cup Final. I had no connection to Scottish football so I decided I'd keep on an eye on a team which, like my name, began with a P. I was six years old.

My unscientific survey of other people's Facebook posts and the replies suggests that our infant World King still attracts and repels exactly the same people in exactly the same proportions as before this crisis. I know I'm one of a small minority who risk their sanity in an attempt to stay well-informed, but even my level-headed wife said she was 'speechless' when a friend told us that #clapforboris was trending on Twitter. My immediate reaction was that while I don't like the man, I wouldn't wish gonorrhoea on him as well as the coronavirus, but it turned that wasn't the clap in question. There were actual people living in my actual country who thought that if NHS staff deserved a national round of applause on Thursday evening for putting themselves in harm's way for all of us, then so did De Pfeffel for, er, boasting of shaking hands with COVID-19 patients, procrastinating like Corporal Jones playing Hamlet, failing to observe social distancing in Downing Street and all the rest of it. I'm pleased to report there was a deathly silence in this neighbourhood as 8pm came and went. I can't vouch for the new 'he's one of the lads' Tory strongholds of Blackburn, Stoke and Blyth.

I'm not spending the majority of my time consumed with rage though, not least because I need to stay mentally strong. I've almost finished *My Brilliant Friend*, which despite some Scorsese-lite mafia intrusions, has become quite gripping; we finished the latest very silly, but equally funny, series of *Curb Your Enthusiasm* and have taken to watching *Vic and Bob's Big Night Out* via the iPlayer in bed last thing at night. Our bedtimes are finally reasonably synchronised after all these years, but I'm still generously giving Amanda a head start in the kitchen and bathroom of a morning. We've always loved the surrealism of Vic and Bob, and their gruffer characters are the most Teesside thing you'll ever see, even if Vic actually comes from Darlington a few miles west.

Bob Mortimer has been a totally approachable, if shy, fixture at Boro games home and away for years, in later years with one or both of his sons. I may be biased, but of all the famous fans a club could have, he's the one I'd choose. Especially if you heard his simply lovely *Desert Island Discs* appearance, or have watched that beautifully gentle and reflective fishing programme he made with Paul Whitehouse. We were supposed to be seeing Bob, along with Sunderland's own Andy Dawson, at the Leicester Square Theatre last week, as they brought their joyous *Athletico Mince* podcast to the stage. That's another thing to look forward to being rescheduled if and when we can go outdoors – or, in this case, indoors into a venue – again.

Relaxation of the restrictions is now being pushed back from April to June, it seems, and the current ones may well become even tighter soon. I watched Sky's newspaper review last night, somewhat against my better judgement. I increasingly feel that giving over half an hour of airtime – or big chunks of R4's *Today* – to a regurgitation of what is mostly a load of tripe dictated by billionaire tax exiles for a dwindling elderly readership, has maybe had its day. It seems to have come as a shock to most of the Sunday papers that the government is saying that 'this is going to get worse before it gets better'. Rearrange the following words: 'Sherlock', 'Shit' and 'No'.

Then there's the *Mail on Sunday* claiming that 'Number 10 plans a day of reckoning with Beijing' over the pandemic. 'Ooh, you're hard,' as David Brent once said. Not only is this straying dangerously into Trumpian 'Chinese Virus' territory, but what exactly does Dom – sorry, 'Number 10' – have in mind? Shall we send our one remaining gunboat to the South China Sea? And on an inside page the *Mail* also asks 'Did Barnier infect Boris?' There you go – whatever happens, it'll all have been down to the dastardly yellow peril and of course Bonkers Brussels, for good measure. Simple solutions for simple people.

Back to more agreeable distractions. We had a parakeet on the feeder earlier – only the second I've ever seen in our garden, although they're widespread in other parts of London, sometimes to the detriment of other species. A single bright-green visitor is quite welcome at the moment, though. I've heard two apocryphal stories about how a tropical bird came to flourish here at 52 degrees north: one says there was an escape from Shepperton Studios while Humphrey Bogart and Katherine Hepburn were shooting *African Queen* in the 1950s; the other claims that Jimi Hendrix released a pair a decade or so later. It seems both stories are 'fake news', sadly. Speaking of Jimi, inspired by the great man sending me that message via Bandsintown, I've watched a YouTube tutorial and have now worked out the intro to 'Hey Joe' pretty much perfectly, if I say so myself. It's taken quite a few attempts, dozens, maybe hundreds to be honest, so I've tried to keep it away from Amanda.

I've also connected Spotify to the TV to give us a musical backdrop to crossword or Sudoku sessions, or to the stretches I do before getting on the bike outside. They have a great feature where you select a band and they give you a long playlist which is a few songs of the band in question and lots more from artistes of a broadly similar ilk. I opted for Big Star radio yesterday – Teenage Fanclub cite Big Star as a huge influence on them and you can see why. If either of those bands had given themselves a better name or had a Brian Epstein or Peter Grant managing them, they would both have been as huge as they deserved to be.

The playlist shuffled agreeably to 'Mrs Robinson' by The Lemondrops. I've always loved the original, especially the stunning acoustic guitar part from Paul Simon, but also thought it worked as a rocking, slightly grungy '90s cover. A good song should work whether the tempo shifts, and whether orchestrated or stripped back. If it doesn't, my entire repertoire is absolutely screwed. The Spotify notes which accompanied Evan Dando's reworking on the TV screen were like a soap opera, though. Evan and company, it seems, recorded that version of 'Mrs Robinson' to be used on a trailer for the 25th anniversary re-release of *The Graduate*, a movie he (rightly) loved. When it became a hit single, Lemonheads fans rebelled, claiming they'd sold out by recording an old fart pop song. Evan then publicly dissed Paul Simon and said he 'hated' the song, Simon responded by being equally rude about the new version, Art Garfunkel mischievously said he loved it, presumably to wind Paul up, and so on. Sadly, the track ended before what I assume was the tale of a full-on tortured artiste punch-up, live on pay-per-view from Madison Square Garden, but even so, you learn something new every day. Especially when you're stuck indoors every day.

Despite having the keyboard now available to me, I'm sticking to playing the guitar at the moment. I may as well delay ringing the changes for a month or two – I'm not going anywhere, unless it's to hospital. Another ex-Univ friend has been inspiring me, guitar-wise. Stewart Wood was in my younger brother's year at our Kentish grammar school. Because I took a gap year and worked in an office with ten women and just one other bloke (a valuable insight into feminine wiles and an almost blokeish coarse outlook on life), Stewart, their star pupil, applied to university when I was already in my second year doing PPE. He came to visit for a day, liked the look of our down-to-earth college and ended up two years below me, in the same college and studying the same subject. He completely surpassed me on several fronts: he was elected president of Univ's Junior Common Room two years after Anand Menon had held the post, got a first in his finals, became a university lecturer and ended up as Gordon Brown's right-hand man through the 2008 financial crisis and beyond. He is now Baron Wood of Anfield; he's a massive Liverpool FC fan, for reasons which have never been satisfactorily explained to me.

He's remained a refreshingly normal bloke – one particularly fond memory I have is of attending a reception for Sport Relief at

11 Downing Street where Stewart made a beeline for me with the newly appointed PM for a chat about *MOTD* and Raith Rovers, Brown's boyhood team. The especially satisfactory part of this was that our then BBC director-general, Mark Thompson – Greg Dyke's less popular successor, who unlike Greg, hadn't given anyone in Sport the time of day – was forced to hang around like a spare part at the fringes of our conversation. He had no idea what to say, who I was, or why the PM and his adviser were talking to me instead of to a very important person like him, but it was hilarious to watch him hopping about in irritation when he'd expected to be doing some political schmoozing.

Stewart is an extremely good musician, too – I remember once getting him to explain the tuning of his balalaika to me (not a euphemism) – and a lover of all forms of the terpsichorean muse, to quote the Python cheese shop sketch. He, his son, Amanda and I went to see Graham Gouldman's touring incarnation of 10cc at Stevenage a while back. Stewart's Twitter account – another one I miss – features a photo of the original four-piece 10cc at about the time they recorded their great second album, *Sheet Music*. He also shares our love for Steely Dan, and mine for Bob Dylan, but his favourite band of all time is Jethro Tull. He still complains whenever I see him that John, my brother, once borrowed their LP *Minstrel in the Gallery*, only to leave it on a train. Stewart has now taken to posting his rendition of a Tull song from his home on the opposite side of the Heath every day throughout this lockdown, and the quality is remarkably good. I knew he was a good guitarist, but was previously unaware of his uncanny ability to channel Ian Anderson's singing voice.

I'm not sure I'm going to be brave enough to do likewise. I got carried away during England's run to the 2018 World Cup semi-final and posted my spirited attempt at 'Three Lions' on Facebook, but that was about it. The two songs I'm working on assiduously at the moment are 'Near Wild Heaven' by REM, effectively two rather lovely three-chord sequences, but significantly with a repeated background chant of the phrase 'living inside'. My biggest accomplishment of recent days, though, is pretty much nailing ELO's 'Telephone Line'. This was inspired by my exchanges of e-mails with Dick Clement, one of whose exile friends in LA is the great Jeff Lynne. I've never been too sure about the DJ/presenter Chris Evans, but I'll forgive him most things for persuading Jeff that there was an appetite for him to return to the stage back in 2014.

Amanda and I were there when he made a low-key entrance after Blondie's set in Hyde Park and, accompanied by his long-time keyboards man Richard Tandy and the BBC Concert Orchestra, blew the place away. The voice, guitar and songs were as good as ever. Despite having been praised to the hilt by John Lennon in the 70s, chosen by the three remaining Beatles to oversee the production of their *Anthology* project, reviving Roy Orbison's career and being Tom Petty's collaborator both in Petty's own solo career's *Full Moon Fever* era peak and then as two-fifths of the Travelling Wilburys, Jeff looked and sounded genuinely amazed that anyone still wanted to hear his songs.

Of course they bloody did. ELO were yet another of those bands that David Eastwood and I loved, despite the perms and beards making them look out of step when punk and new wave arrived. They were just great songs, brilliantly produced by Jeff himself, and it was your loss if you were too cool for school and preferred some band who thrashed three chords badly or played the synthesiser with one finger. For my money – and George Harrison's too, as I discovered in Martin Scorsese's superb documentary *Living in the Material World* – 'Telephone Line' is one of the greatest songs of all time. There are three parts to it: the intro and instrumental break in the middle are a bit like a subdued variation on the keyboard part in Del Shannon's 'Runaway', the verse is the most glorious honeyed progression of diminished and major 7th chords, and the chorus is an A, F# minor, D, E progression of many a wistful 50s doo-wop record. Put all that together and with perfect harmonies from the second verse onwards (that first multilayered 'I just can't believe' gets me every time) and drums and orchestra, it's a 'Be My Baby' or 'Waterloo Sunset' of pop perfection. Give it another listen, and tell me it isn't. Even the lyrics seem to have taken on new meaning in these days of uncertainty and separation when we are picking up our telephones more than some of us have done in decades.

That 'pleasure of small things' again. I've always loved that song, but now I have the chance to dissect it and learn how to play it to the best of my ability, I've finally given it the hours it deserves. If you're still with me at this point, Dick, please tell Jeff how good he is because for all the world, he behaves like he doesn't realise. Maybe the fact that his football team Birmingham City run out to 'Mr Blue Sky', one of a number of blue references – and none to claret, as far as I know – in ELO's output, has given him the accolade he most prizes.

Monday, 30 March 2020

It's not Monday by all that much, but for the second night running, I've woken up with a start from an anxiety dream. Last night, Amanda was awake at the same time and we were able to compare notes. Sigmund Freud wasn't needed, we had both pretty clearly been riffing on a social distancing mishap – mine involved greeting Peter Reid with a hug at some kind of reception, bizarrely enough.

I haven't seen him since our mutual friend Chris Lewis's 70th birthday bash a couple of years ago, but we follow each other on Twitter and tend to agree in our interpretation of current affairs, so I guess there was some logic to me greeting him warmly before my blood ran cold. There was a particularly strange episode in our Twitter kinship, which Gary Lineker also chipped into a while back, after their 1986 World Cup team-mate Peter Shilton had expressed his huge admiration for Jacob Rees-Mogg. Reidy, neither a Tory nor a Brexiteer, succinctly replied, 'Bad call, keeper,' and I piled in with something – probably a Cuthbert Cringeworthy reference – which was intended as a joke, but clearly went down badly at Shilton Manor. My next tweet read, 'I've just achieved something neither Maradona nor any German penalty taker ever managed. Blocked by Shilton.' Reidy replied with, 'You cad, sir,' and Gary made a punning glove joke which now escapes me. Ah, those innocent times.

Tonight's anxiety dream was worse than last night's and was triggered by the fact that I know I have to go to Waitrose tomorrow. If you think that sounds prissy now, it would have been unimaginably ridiculous a month ago. We're completely out of fresh food, supermarkets are suggesting people go in one at a time and are rightly devoting their first hour to the elderly and vulnerable, so I plan to be there just before 9am when they let the rest of us in. There is now a set maximum number of customers allowed in at any one time and socially distanced queues form outside. I'm just going to the Finchley Road this time, non-essential travel outside your immediate area having rightly bitten the dust. 'Having studied the stats, officer, I feel I'll be safer shopping in Reading' might have been acceptable ten days ago, but not now.

So why has going to the supermarket at all become so worrying? Well, we had a chat via Zoom with three other couples who are friends of ours, all based in west and south-west London. An extraordinary number of people they know well, and some of whom we've met, have gone down with the virus. An elderly friend of one of the couples has died, the best man at their wedding has it, as do the couple who run the travel agency through whom we'd booked our planned Euro 2020 travel, and so on.

Later in the evening, I found out that my BBC friend Isobel, thankfully now on the mend, has had a relatively mild bout but still can't taste or smell, then an old friend of Amanda's told her that her son has (almost certainly) had it. All of those cases are here in London. We've clearly been in our own bubble as this has mushroomed and even more clearly the virus is now properly rife here in the capital. Even the official figures show that 19 of the top 20 English boroughs for confirmed cases to population are in the London area, and only the one fatality from that anecdotal list above would have been picked up by those official figures.

Just to add to my sleep problems, the Sky paper review I really should stop watching included coverage of a leaked memo from Kings College London's Hospital Trust querying why their official death toll was only one third as high as they knew it to be. *The Telegraph* is reporting that a consultant in London has said that they're already picking and choosing who gets a ventilator. Doctor Liz has understandably gone completely quiet, although we spotted with alarm that one of the two NHS consultants who, tragically, have died today was based at her hospital. The great Dyson contract is still 'a couple of weeks' from producing anything, meanwhile there's yet another mad 'no, thanks' tale. This time it features a company who'd got hold of 5,000 ventilators after the Matt Hancock appeal, but having not heard back from our government despite increasingly urgent repeat queries, have now sold them elsewhere. We have 8,000 ventilators in total now in the UK, apparently. New York State, with a mere third of the UK's population, has asked Trump for 30,000 of them. I'm sorry to keep repeating myself but this makes me genuinely fearful of exposing myself or Amanda to potential harm.

There's also a (genuine, sadly) Twitter exchange doing the rounds featuring Andrew Sabisky, the young man appointed to a Downing Street role earlier this year after Dominic Cummings had advertised for 'freaks and weirdos' to come and help him. He subsequently resigned after it turned out he'd previously made a whole host of pro-eugenics remarks on social media (Dom didn't sack him, tellingly). Sabisky could well be out of the loop now that 'herd immunity' is no longer the weirdo and freak policy of choice, but he casually tweeted that the cut-off at which there would be automatic palliation, i.e. preparation for death rather than treatment, would be 'literally everyone over 60'. He breezily added 'dunno if it's been reported' in a conspiratorial insider fashion and added a friendly exclamation mark at the end. I bet he thought about adding 'lol'. This just confirmed my opinion that the man is an absolute danger who shouldn't have been allowed anywhere near any government, with the possible exception of Pol Pot's. Amanda is 60 in July, by the way, so I'm wrapping her in cotton wool for as long as it takes.

Most people knew even before ventilator and protective equipment statistics became of such vital importance that the NHS has been creaking for some time. Even then, there was usually a division between life-threatening and merely chronic conditions: my mum received truly amazing treatment when she had her strokes, much less so when she was through the worst and booked in for follow-up tests. I spent most of a day in January with her in an outpatient ward, waiting in conditions which reminded me of the last time I took a train in India, only without the majestic spectacle beyond the window. I had a series of high PSA readings last year and was told there was a 20 per cent chance I had prostate cancer. Compared to how I feel right now typing this at 3.17am, I was reasonably calm as I undertook tests and waited for the (thankfully negative) results. I felt, whatever happened, that the system would do its best for me, just as it had my mum with a stroke. It was a reassuring thought at an uncertain moment. Right now, while I know the NHS personnel plus wonderful volunteers will keep as many people alive as they possibly can, I can't say I feel that the powers that be have done anywhere near their best for any of us as we face our biggest modern-day health crisis.

Some mildly encouraging things are happening, though – Michael Gove managed to keep a straight face yesterday when he told people to listen to the same 'experts' we'd 'all had enough of' four years ago, and Boris Johnson said something truly remarkable from his quarantine room: 'There is such a thing as society,' after all. I know David Cameron fleetingly toyed with a 'Big Society' project, but credit where it's due, this is the first time any Tory leader has directly rebuked that infamous Thatcher mantra. Even now, some in his party will take umbrage, but they needed that wake-up call from one of their own, albeit a somewhat tardy 33 years on from that grim *Women's Own* interview. Of course, this welcome new line would sit far more comfortably if the man who said it hadn't appointed the man who then appointed Andrew Sabisky. Moreover, the spectre of the recently much-shared 2017 clip of Tory MPs cheering, waving order papers and banging the benches in ecstasy as a motion to freeze the pay of NHS workers was passed, still hangs over all of them. Even so, I'm glad he said it.

And, as if proof were needed that we don't have the worst leader in the western world, a superb Joe Biden campaign ad has simply documented the unhinged sequence of Trump quotes of denial and aggression towards journalists this year as the tally of US coronavirus cases mounts in a corner of the screen. The fact that he dismantled the White House pandemic unit in 2018, seemingly simply because Obama had set it up, is perhaps the most damning indictment of all. New York in particular is clearly heading for utter disaster, but then as I said yesterday, it always votes Democrat. It's also instructive to see what counts as an 'essential' activity over there: gun shops are open, of course – to be fair, the Armageddon-fearing people Louis Theroux has featured, who hole themselves up with tinned food and a year's supply of ammo, look somewhat less bonkers now than they used to – but I'd have to question the governor of Arizona's inclusion of golf courses in his list of protected all-American essential locations. That said, the president of Belarus was out playing competitive ice hockey yesterday which may have put ideas in the Trump head, but only if Fox News showed the footage.

Back up in the daylight, and two welcome interfaces with the outside world. Jake FaceTimed us, and was his usual well-informed, darkly witty self. He immediately, and logically, trashed the 'stay local' mantra. The whole issue is population density, he says, so providing you've been isolating for a week or more, you're better off driving to Reading to an out-of-town supermarket and then taking a walk in the middle of nowhere than hoping to dodge the Belsize Shuffle/London supermarket Russian roulette bullet. I think I've argued both for and against that in the last ten days. He's right, but not if lots of people, especially those who haven't been self-isolating, try it. And furthermore, there are now police checkpoints on the motorways to stop you. Again, while I have been clamouring for tighter restrictions to be imposed, especially over the bonus Bank Holiday weekend, I can see how a Home Secretary – especially the current one – might be tempted to exercise that degree of control even when it's no longer necessary.

Even now, Jake tells me, a mutual civil service legal friend of ours is drafting huge wads of emergency legislation in the morning and watching it assume the full force of the law by evening. With Parliament now in recess, we're effectively living in an authoritarian dictatorship. As Jake said, 'They nationalised the railways the other day, and no one even noticed.' I think Sunak has done about as well as a new Chancellor could have done in these circumstances, but there's no doubt some very radical moves are having to be waved through without the slightest scrutiny. Only a small percentage of the public, plus the majority of the NHS, will be aware of the ventilator and PPE procurement debacle, hence the 'government's doing well' line being trotted out by wishful thinkers on Facebook.

At least Corbyn will have been replaced by a statesman-like lawyer in Keir Starmer (please, God) by the time Parliament returns. Jezza's valedictory interview sees him claim that the current measures show that he 'won the argument'. No, you didn't, you silly narcissistic old sod – you oversaw Labour's worst result in 85 years, then the world turned on its head and the party that beat you displayed the pragmatism of which you've proved yourself entirely incapable all your working life.

Then I had my latest e-mail from Dick Clement in LA. He's written a lovely article for *The Telegraph* about what he and Ian La Frenais are doing at the moment. Writing remotely, albeit via FaceTime, for the first time in 55 years is the answer. He's also listening to lots of music of the Count Basie era and catching up on TV comedy. He rightly recommends *Parks and Recreation*, Amy Poehler's creation and one which gives her friend and sometime partner Tina Fey's *30 Rock* a run for its money. He's also enjoying the YouTube output of one Randy Rainbow. I'd seen Randy's brilliant reworking of Gilbert and Sullivan for the Trump era – 'I am the very model of a very stable genius' – but there is seemingly lots more where that came from. Best of all, though, is a guided mediation session set to peaceful images and soothing music, but overseen by J.B. Smoove, co-star of *Curb Your Enthusiasm*. Amanda and I dissolved with laughter watching it and I suspect 'breathe in yo' mouth, exhale through yo' ass'; 'a couch – now fold yo' body in half and lay the fuck down on that bitch'; and 'A stream flows by. Damn, streams are sexy' will join our repertoire of in-house catchphrases.

Oh, blimey. Dominic Cummings, last seen running in and out of Downing Street like he was in a Brian Rix farce, has come down with COVID-19 symptoms. I guess herd immunity will be tested after all; it seems as if most of us in London will get it now. At least, despite appearances, Dom is only 48, so he should be in luck if he needs a ventilator.

Tuesday, 31 March 2020

I was frequently told by people who worked in other walks of life how fantastically lucky I was to be in charge of programmes at major sporting events. Nobody ever wanted to hear the reality of stupidly long days and stupid amounts of pressure – the editor's role being one I always saw as that of worrier-in-chief, and even more so when 20 million or more might be watching. I guess

I have had a glimpse of some amazing places, at least once the rest days came around three weeks into a World Cup, worked and had the occasional meal with some great ex-footballers, and could get to the odd game we weren't covering live. That said, the only time I ever felt I could really enjoy it was when it was all over, and it seemed to have gone okay. I feel a bit like that now, only without any sense that it's all over.

Yes, I'm back from Waitrose and am typing this while drinking the first sugary drink I've had in weeks: a large bottle of raspberry-flavoured – and disturbingly crimson – Lucozade Sport. I did my best to avoid catching this bloody virus, donning my rubbish mask and latex gloves, and to be fair, Waitrose are doing their best, too. They've drafted in a lot of the workforce from their currently mothballed partner, John Lewis, and about 90 per cent of Amanda's shopping list was in stock. No Gaviscon – I had a horrible attack of heartburn yesterday – and no paracetamol, so if my current slightly worrying gunky ear turns as painful as it can do, I'll have to choose between the allegedly COVID-19-enabling Nurofen or some of Amanda's remaining Malbec. The queue outside is marked for social distancing, the numbers inside were sensible, maybe half were wearing masks and a trolley variation on the Belsize Shuffle took place with lots of 'sorry' and 'after you' comments. Although the stats for London would suggest that some of the dozens of people I saw will have this virus already (maybe I'm one of them and don't know it yet) I felt everything humanly possible was being done to minimise the odds of catching it on their premises.

If only the UK government were as competent as Waitrose. I should preface this by saying that an opinion poll claims that 74 per cent of Britain thinks that 'the government is doing a good job', and that if there was a general election, a whopping 54 per cent would vote for yet another five years of the people who've criminally neglected the NHS for the last decade and have failed utterly to prepare for this. Applaud the key workers AND

#clapforBoris says Joe Public. I mistyped that as Joe Pubic and maybe shouldn't have altered it.

I'm tempted to quote a line from Sid Vicious which I occasionally cited in the office when a particularly ridiculous *MOTD* viewer complaint had to be answered respectfully, 'I've met the man in the street, and he's a cunt.' I'm told by my ex-colleague Chris Lewis that Garth Crooks once laughed at that line all the way from Manchester Airport to Anfield. To be honest, though, if people have turned into Young Mr Grace from *Are You Being Served* and think 'it's all going terribly well' and, as long as they are doing what the medics are advising, then I guess the Utilitarian 'greatest happiness of the greatest number' criterion is being met.

For that reason, I'm not posting on Facebook. Why depress people? I have intervened on the feeds of friends a couple of times though: one chap unknown to me slated a friend who actually works for the NHS, for being a gloom merchant. Those in charge are, apparently, 'our brightest and best' and any criticism is both treacherous and seemingly fuelled by envy among lesser types who aren't in among 'the movers and shakers'. Yes, he really did use both of those (horribly misplaced) clichés. I used a variant on a previous line and told him that if he really believed that, perhaps he'd like to buy the Transporter Bridge from me. He won't have watched *Auf Wiedersehen, Pet*: he'll be a *Mrs Brown's Boys* or Michael McIntyre viewer if ever I encountered one.

A group of us also found ourselves embedded in a squabble with a friend's cousin Sue from Cornwall who simply wasn't having it that Richard Branson had a nerve asking for a government bail-out, even though: a) one per cent of his personal wealth would pay his staff for months b) he sued the NHS for millions from Necker Island not so long ago. Sue had read Branson's autobiography which portrayed him as a national hero and inspiration to all risk-takers (*Mein Kampf* did something similar, Sue) and took some shifting from that position. An old tabloid article in which racing driver Jenson Button claimed that

Branson had groped his wife finally did the trick. If there's one thing middle England likes more than a 'self-made' man, it's Formula One.

Maybe I shouldn't be so sneery. If you don't have friends and relatives on the front line – in a dreadful irony, Doctor Liz's elderly mum now has the virus – or don't read the science or high-end articles, or watch C4 or Sky News, and weren't cynical about this government in the first place (perhaps because you lead an incredibly busy life) you probably will think it's all going terribly well. We're watching very little of it, but from the bits we see BBC News is mostly toeing the 'don't frighten the horses' line. The three minutes I saw of the *News at Ten* last night before I gave up was effectively a giant PR exercise for the new 'Nightingale Hospital', which the army has constructed at the Excel Centre in Docklands.

I saw how the British Army saved the 2012 Olympics when they stepped in during the rehearsal week to take over the security operation from a clearly failing G4S team, who'd been contracted by then Home Secretary Theresa May. The public sector baling out ideologically driven private sector ineptitude, eh? Hmm. The day before the Army stepped in, it took two hours for hundreds of media people to get on site. By the Saturday when all the events started, the soldiers were cheerfully and efficiently processing tens of thousands of spectators in minutes. So, I know the Army will have done brilliantly to knock up a facility containing 4,000 beds in three weeks. But what happens then?

Yesterday's figures tell us there are currently 9,000 people in hospital nationally with the coronavirus and we're nowhere near the peak yet. Thanks to years of neglect and the acquisition fiasco, we currently have 8,000 ventilators available, so there's already a shortfall if you were hoping to give everyone the best chance of survival. Furthermore, despite the optimism expressed at the weekend (I now feel like a fool for believing it) we tested a princely 7,000 people in the UK yesterday. Germany, by comparison, tested 70,000. It's estimated that between a quarter and a third of NHS staff are currently off work. Some are ill, many feel fine but, because they can't be tested, they have to stay in self-isolation if they've been around someone else with symptoms. I have a horrible feeling this Nightingale Hospital is effectively going to become Death's waiting room: no ventilators, nowhere enough trained staff and the volunteers all holding people's hands (metaphorically, it would be far too dangerous to do it literally) as their lungs finally give in.

I'd heard a couple of stories of 5,000 ventilators being offered, but I'm not across everything, so it took my dad to point me towards the tale of a Cheshire company called Direct Access which responded to Matt Hancock's desperately belated appeal – 'herd immunity' having ruled the roost until well into March, remember – and said it could access 25,000 ventilators and 50 million coronavirus testing kits. With the glaring exception of protective equipment, this might have been all the NHS shortfall problems solved in one transaction. For whatever reason – loyalty to Dyson, the Singapore-based Brexit vacuum-cleaner man, or just breathtaking (literally) incompetence – Direct Access got no response, and the whole job lot was bought up by other countries, including the US, which had woken up even later than we had but then emptied the market.

My dad had seen Michael Gove, thrust into the press conference on Sunday because most other alternatives were by now out of action, say he was 'very sorry' to hear this and 'would investigate'. I don't think the results of that 'investigation' will be released until what may have to become criminal hearings. As an 80-year-old man with bronchial issues, my dad is naturally all over this story. I'd like to challenge any of the 74 per cent who pronounce themselves 'satisfied' with the government's handling to read the last two paragraphs and put themselves in his position.

The one exception to the BBC's largely compliant coverage appears to be Radio 4's *Today* programme, which since the insufferable John Humphrys retired to write the *Daily Mail* column which should have been his full-time occupation all along, has become listenable again. They had Amanda's ex-WHO director friend Professor Anthony Costello on this morning – I heard it, too, because I was awake early, psyching myself up for Waitrose – and he was excellent again. Calmly, reasonably skewering the government for all of the above but in such a rational, gentle fashion that it was only afterwards that you were fully aware of how damning he'd been.

According to *The Independent*, front-line doctors have been threatened with losing their jobs if they speak publicly about the shortages. Well, that'll help – we can add sacked, insubordinate doctors to those who are currently unavailable due to a lack of tests, or because they're ill or dead. We desperately need Keir Starmer (I'm assuming he's going to be the new Labour leader) to step up to the plate from next week, but even then, the 74 per cent will just think he's being unpatriotic. Just like that Corbyn, who wouldn't sing the national anthem.

It seems that the USA now has the right person for that opposition role: governor Andrew Cuomo of New York is conducting a news conference every day which currently has America spellbound. He's everything Trump isn't – a Democrat, yes, but also smart, with diagrams and statistics at the ready, a bit folksy (he's missing Mama's meatballs) and crucially not an absolute narcissist who will make each and every item on any agenda all about himself. Even Fox News are showing Cuomo live every day, and in a nation which is even more divided and partisan than we've become, he's getting a remarkable 70 per cent approval rating from Republicans. He'd clearly stroll the presidential election, assuming Trump doesn't try to cancel it, but he isn't running (this time) so the rest of the world is going to have to pray that dopey old Joe Biden can secure an electoral college majority as well as the popular vote.

It has been revealed today that Trump has said the Republicans would never win again without the blatant voter suppression which has increasingly taken place in recent years. That may be the most truthful thing he's ever said. The (single figures) cases of voter fraud here in the UK in December have led some on the extreme right to demand similar electoral engineering here. Which reminds me, I didn't see the bejewelled Julia Hartley-Brewer sweeping through Waitrose earlier. Maybe she sent her key worker personal food-taster instead.

There isn't much other news, but for once we went with the actual TV schedules for an hour last night. Monday evening has traditionally seen us watch the second half of Sky's live Premier League game (actually, that bit's usually only me while Amanda has a bath) preceded by a BBC2 double bill. Victoria Coren-Mitchell's fiendish *Only Connect* quiz is followed immediately by *University Challenge* on which Jeremy Paxman, in his dotage, appears to have reined in the fury and incredulity he used to express at certain wrong answers: 'Tennyson? Tennyson? It's Wordsworth, of course. My cat knows that.' He never did that with wrong science answers, we noticed – like us, it looks like he might as well make a cup of tea during those rounds. *Only Connect* had its Grand Final last night, *University Challenge* has just reached the semi-final stage, so the full quiz hour will be no more until studio recordings are possible again.

One of *Only Connect*'s sequence rounds last night contained clues which led to the following sequence: Gloria Steinem's *My Life on the Road*, David Brent's *Life on the Road*, Kerouac's *On the Road*, followed by a question mark. The answer was Cormac McCarthy's *The Road* which reminded me it's in my pile of 'novels I ought to have read' which I'm currently tackling to fill some of the long hours. Having finished *My Brilliant Friend,* and while I'm waiting for Amanda to plough through all 800 pages of Hilary Mantel's tome, a journey through 'a burned-out America' might be just the ticket. That's just reminded me of yet another cartoon I posted on Facebook in 2016, once I'd ranted myself dry of original observations. A sign in a bookshop reads, 'Our "Dystopian Fiction" section is now housed under "Current Affairs".'

After a couple of days where the coronavirus death rate for the UK stayed at around the 200 mark, it shot up to just under 400 today. That's effectively four Hillsboroughs in one day. Unlike Hillsborough, not all of those deaths will have been unavoidable in as much as the hospital system hasn't yet completely collapsed anywhere as far as we know. How many fatalities can be traced back to the Cheltenham Festival three weeks ago, where someone may have caught it there and died, or brought it back to their home town and passed it on unwittingly to someone more vulnerable, we'll never know. Nor will we ever know statistically exactly how big a part inadequate protection equipment is playing in the daily figures we're seeing, or likewise, the imminent impact of the huge shortage in ventilators. Michael Gove announced at today's press conference that the first newly produced one will appear this weekend and reach the NHS by next week. Quite apart from the tens of thousands the government appealed for, then somehow let go, around a fortnight ago – a grisly version of *Bullseye*'s 'just look what you could have won' – we've heard 'this weekend' bandied about with regard to testing and PPE too many times before, and it simply didn't happen.

I'm turning into one of those people I've always been wary of, who stops believing anything they're told. It's estimated that the actual death toll is at least 25 per cent higher than the one we're being given, because deaths outside hospitals, at home or in care homes aren't included. If coronavirus is mentioned on the death certificate, a different tally will take that into account at a later date, though without testing equipment that has to be a guess at best. Our confirmed cases tally is meaningless in one sense since we're only testing at hospitals, but ominous in another sense in that the 3,000 cases confirmed today – which you have to assume is mostly the seriously ill – is the highest so far, and that probably means our death rate will still be climbing in ten days or so.

It's all exceedingly bleak, and looking at the Italian and Spanish precedents which our graph still most closely resembles, we'll be collectively mourning 800 or 900 people a day by then. The Italian figures – still roughly 15 days in advance of ours – have flattened out at that level; Spain, which registered almost exactly today's UK death toll nine days ago, had its highest daily figure so far yesterday with 849 deaths, but the rate of increase has slowed considerably. We're going to end up at around the same point in the next week to fortnight, you'd think, and let's hope to God (I'm citing him a lot, despite being an agnostic) none of us becomes the first country to see 1,000 deaths in a day. The USA is probably on course to get there first, sadly.

Still, Priti Patel, mercifully not asked so far to front the daily conference and answer any questions (the country's terrified enough already, thanks), has generously extended the visas of all overseas NHS workers for a year. It must be a real fillip to hear that you won't be deported (yet) and will continue to be allowed to be paid a pittance for putting your life on the line every day in a job which has probably seen you routinely abused by the general public, many of whom you know don't want your 'low-skilled' foreign type to be here in the first place. Including Home Secretary Priti Patel until yesterday afternoon, when she also muttered something about revisiting the 'piss off, not paid enough' post-Brexit immigration categories she drew up just over a month ago.

Foolishly, I put the BBC's *News at Six* bulletin on tonight expecting a sober summary of the horrendous, part act of God/part self-inflicted, nightmare ahead. They gave the latest toll, told us that there would be a story later about a presenter who has the virus (fair enough, I suppose), and a piece about when football might be back (even I don't really care about that right now) and then went straight into a lead item about the car park at Chessington Zoo having been turned into a testing site for NHS workers. Maybe they went on to explain that this is just a trial and is as yet making no real inroads into our monumental, and increasingly critical, backlog, but it had the same effect on me as the triumphant report the previous day from the Nightingale project at the Excel Centre. 'It's just another puff piece for the government to keep the 74 per cent placated,' I said, although possibly more swearily.

Unlike Amanda, who generally keeps her cool, I have been known to explode at times when watching TV news – but normally, one of us can go for a walk or we can go together to one of our nearby cinemas or restaurants and forget about it. Right now, for the first time since we've been stuck indoors, I knew I'd overstepped the mark, especially in such a confined environment, so I left Amanda to a pre-arranged Zoom session with some old school friends and went into the bedroom. For the first time in the four years since I was able to control my ear-fuelled anxiety, I lay on the floor and did a guided mindfulness meditation. And not the J.B. Smoove one. A full half-hour with Jon Kabat Zinn's soothing hippy tones and whale-noise music in the background was the order of the day. And it worked, at least until the next time I watch an analysis-free news bulletin.

I was in a much better place after that, as I believe they say in mindfulness circles. They also say that 'if you're breathing, there's more right than wrong with you', which makes some sort of sense, I guess, and in that spirit – and with Amanda still rabbiting away to her friends – I had my first session of this whole lockdown on the keyboard in the bedroom. The various settings are staggeringly good these days, so my okay-ish take on 'A Whiter Shade of Pale' sounds cathedral-like on one of the organ settings, appropriately enough, since Bach wrote the sequence Procol Harum borrowed on a church organ in Leipzig. Most of the time, though, I just keep it on the grand piano setting.

I grew up listening to the piano being played in our house by my dad, especially on a Sunday morning. In the unlikely event that I'm ever invited on to *Desert Island Discs*, I'll definitely take one of the Fats Waller songs he used to play with gusto to the probable annoyance of our neighbours in Grosvenor Road, Stockton-on-Tees. I played the three I can give a go – 'My Very Good Friend the Milkman', 'Two Sleepy People' and 'Ain't Misbehaving' – and though my stride left hand in particular isn't as good as either Fats's or my old man's, I thoroughly enjoyed myself. I said in my book that, especially at World Cup time, I genuinely feel sorry for people who don't like sport, and that applies equally to music. I just wished I'd stuck at the piano lessons my dad sent me to back then – knowing guitar chords and improvising bass piano parts accordingly is no real substitute for being able to read music.

Back down to earth with a bump. Someone in one of my groups posted a harrowing story from the *Hackney Gazette*: 'Devoted father-of-seven NHS worker died alone of coronavirus after treating infection.' An awful, awful story but the quote from one of his colleagues should – but won't – lead every news bulletin and front page: 'They asked us to fight a war but they have not provided us with anything to fight this war.' That's why I'm angry with anodyne, unchallenging BBC One main news bulletins. The public has dragged an unwilling government into most of the measures so far, outrage needs to get them to nationalise the clothing industry or whatever it takes to make some bloody protective equipment, and then address the testing shambles. As it is, 74 per cent clearly have no idea what's going on behind the platitudes. Even Trump has apparently abandoned restarting the economy for Easter because opinion polls suggested that would, rightly, be deeply unpopular. Governor Cuomo alone is providing a more widely seen critique of government policy than anything we've seen here.

I have a nagging suspicion that how this crisis may pan out is going to mirror the same cities v the rest division we've seen in recent elections and in Brexit. Someone who should know better, and who lives in a town where the threat of the virus seems less immediate, said to Amanda of London the other day, 'Well, that's what you get for living in the cesspit of England.' He would claim that it was a joke, but we distinctly got the impression that some people we knew from the north-east and elsewhere were not as bothered about the Grenfell Tower disaster as they might have been. They certainly won't be as fearful of civil unrest as we are when we look ahead to the summer. Conversely, many

Londoners know much too little about the rest of the country, and the capital has dominated central government and economic thinking for far too long. Even our Skype conversations at the moment vary according to whether we're talking to Londoners (who know NHS workers and others caught up in this) and some (often lovely) people from more rural parts who don't entirely seem to get what's happening. Many small London boroughs have 400 or more confirmed cases now; the city of Hull, with a population of 284,000, has just 11 cases. It's perfectly reasonable to feel altogether less edgy about the situation if you live there at the moment, and it must seem an even more distant issue if you're living in a small town or village. I hope this doesn't become yet another British 'them' and 'us' – this country has had more than enough of that already.

Finally this evening, we spoke via Skype to Doctor Liz. Her mum's seemingly pulling through, thank goodness, and she gave us her take on life on the front line and the differing reactions of colleagues under duress. There are three broad categories, she says – the 'roll up your sleeves' brigade, those who fall apart (not always the ones you'd expect) and a group who do the bare minimum, and often even then with reluctance – not dissimilar to the accounts you read of how soldiers coped in the trenches, for example.

She's not optimistic that we'll see a 1945-style reboot after this: 'People want an amazing service but won't vote for tax rises' is the upshot. Then she tells us that five boxes of surgical masks have been stolen from her hospital trust by a member of the public, and you can understand her limited faith in human nature. She also says the guidelines they're given have completely departed from those laid down by the WHO, and moreover, change by the hour – 'Everyone must wear a mask.' 'We don't have enough masks.' 'Okay, then not everyone does need to wear a mask,' – and it sounds like some unacceptable risks are still being taken. All we can tell her is that we're thinking of her constantly and that we see her and her colleagues as genuine heroes.

Wednesday, 1 April 2020

Someone posted this morning's *Daily Mail* headline on Facebook. I looked at it, looked at the date and wondered, but it's true; they've absolutely hammered the government. 'Fix Testing Fiasco Now' they demand, quite rightly, with an adjoining editorial containing word like 'shambles' and 'catastrophe' in close proximity to the words, 'government' and 'Mr Johnson'. He's not even 'Boris' any more. I think it's the first time since they named Stephen Lawrence's killers that I've truly admired a *Daily Mail* front page. That courageous and justified stance was at least partly prompted by then editor Paul Dacre knowing Stephen's father, Neville, who had helped install a bathroom at Dacre's house. I think there may be a personal angle to this morning's remarkable broadside, too: the *Mail*'s associate editor, Andrew Pierce, is currently recovering from a bout of coronavirus and I suspect he and his anxious colleagues have now had enough of the government's ever more pathetic excuses.

I missed most of this by not being on Twitter, but apparently Gove's latest 'the dog ate my homework' excuse at yesterday's press conference was to claim that there's a global shortage of a vital chemical component used in the manufacturing of testing equipment. Having clocked that Germany for one doesn't seem to be experiencing the same problem, Robert Peston spoke to his contacts in the UK's chemical industry and was told that there's no shortage as far as they're concerned. They're just waiting, as exasperated as the rest of us, to be told what the government wants.

Fair play to Peston – his partner has been ill with the virus, and he's probably smarting over having been dragged into the 'herd immunity' water-testing. With *The Telegraph* also turning on the government (albeit for not being libertarian enough) and *The Times*'s front page today bringing up both testing and the staggering extent to which the UK underestimated the pandemic, only *The Sun* and the main BBC TV bulletins seem to remain firm as the purveyors of unquestioning deference to our rulers. *The Sun*'s 'War We Can Win' front page today has taken exactly the same line as that *BBC News at Six* lead item. 'Our boys have built a field hospital, who cares if there's no equipment or staff? Gawd bless us, one and all' is pretty much the gist.

I love the BBC – we watched a stunning BBC4 Howard Goodall documentary about the making of *Sgt Pepper* only last night – and would defend the wider organisation to the hilt, but the main TV news bulletins have been pretty poor for a while. The parroting of 'sources', utter failure to analyse, fear of upsetting power rather than holding it to account, and never-ending brainless vox pops were a dereliction of duty before and after Brexit, but are plain inexcusable right now.

This is not World War Two: asking questions which might save thousands of lives is not a treasonable offence. Unlike the Nazis, this virus is not going to get a morale boost from the national broadcaster at least hinting that this is rapidly turning into the most appalling and deadly display of inept leadership in our country's modern history. Dr Jenny Harries, deputising for the stricken Professor Whitty as the face of science at the same press conference at which Gove spoke about chemicals, had to apologise for assuring everyone ten days ago that the protective equipment debacle had been addressed, when we now know that it hadn't. Either that volte-face, fact-checking Gove's chemicals line, or a combination of both should have been the headline story on the *News at Six* last night, not, 'Isn't it marvellous? A couple of test tubes and some swabs have finally been delivered to the car park at Chessington.'

This whole thing has just taken a new and unexpected nose-dive. We're now being rubbished by the president of the United States, and worse still, the chief scientist in charge of their coronavirus response. Dr Deborah Birx must have briefed

Trump before they took to the stage because his takedown of the Johnson government was pretty much spot on: the initial response had been 'catastrophic', and while he wouldn't refer to 'herd immunity' by name, he said, 'I guess it's a concept. If you don't mind a lot of death.' Can you imagine having a recent official policy so unhinged and distasteful that Donald Trump doesn't even want to name it? It then got worse: Dr Birx focused on the UK's 8,000 ventilators figure and revealed that the US has 200,000, a figure which presumably includes thousands of those the UK government passed on because we'd rather wait for their mate James 'Singapore' Dyson to adapt and trial a vacuum cleaner. It turns out that the US, with its universally derided approach to healthcare, has five times the UK's number of ventilators relative to population.

Irrespective of the tosh Trump initially came out with about the virus, the adults in their room seem to have finally succeeded in turning the tables on us. For four years, troubled Brits have consoled themselves with, 'At least we don't have Trump/we're not America.' The UK is now the yardstick by which the States can show they're not so bad after all. This press conference happened in the middle of the night UK time so, fools that we are, we thought we'd listen to Radio 4's 9am news summary to see how this monumental breach of the fabled 'special relationship', and savage indictment of our government, was being covered.

We really should know better by now: the main headline was struggling small businesses, then a minister called Robert Jenrick (his name and tone suggestive of a Dickensian play on words: Jenrick = generic Tory flannel) dismissed suggestions that there wasn't a shortage of chemicals to make the testing equipment.

No right of reply was granted to chemical industry figures or the German government who might have contradicted Mr Generic. Then there was the dreadful story of the death of a 13-year-old boy in south London from the virus. Then, finally, the story we were all waiting for: yes, Derek Jarman's garden on the Kent coast has been saved for the nation. No disrespect to the innovative late film director but, really? Not a mention of that historically unprecedented trashing of 'Britannia waives the rules' from across the Atlantic.

I think I might have to take a break from this temporarily, or at least post a good deal less. My throat and ear are both now sore, which I hope is an ENT issue, not a sign of anything else. I'm also now struggling to find light and shade in the wider situation – it's becoming difficult to write anything light which doesn't seem clodhopping and trite.

And I'm becoming bogged down in far more research than I ever intended to do. I just wish certain leading journalists with a public platform would do some of it instead. I'm cursed with a mind which demands answers every time something doesn't seem to make sense, and that's happening every time I log on, or switch on the TV or radio. I can achieve absolutely nothing by screaming 'Fire!' into the void on a daily basis. The best I can do right now for Amanda, myself and those who know us, is to try to stay sane and healthy and add my weight to those calling for a proper inquest and harsh lessons to be learnt when the time is right.

Thursday, 2 April 2020

As usual, I didn't watch yesterday's government press conference. Amanda angrily summarised it as 'pointless' and 'evasive' in the face of some challenging questions, but I did watch the BBC's *News at Six* and, credit where it's due, they are finally asking the right questions about testing and protective equipment in particular. The ventilator shortage hasn't yet come into sharp focus, but that must be imminent, and was mentioned in passing. Maybe a different editor was on duty, or maybe they'd spotted that, other than *The Sun*, pretty much every other news outlet has stopped worrying about keeping in with the PM and Dom, especially since they're both still self-isolating.

The UK has recorded its highest tally of 563 deaths in 24 hours – and that's just those who've died in hospitals. There were also more than 4,000 new confirmed cases in a day, truly alarming considering that probably means they're almost all now in hospital and that the figure only passed 3,000 yesterday. Seven thousand more patients in 48 hours, and growing, to further overburden the NHS. That extra ten days or more of work, school, pub and restaurant normality when the Italian distress signals were there for all to see, plus that weekend of Bank Holiday-style madness, is starting to filter through in a truly grotesque fashion, especially here in London. The confirmed cases in this borough alone went up by 26 yesterday, to 210. If we don't overtake Italy and Spain's figures in the coming weeks it will be a miracle.

But now that it's being covered properly by almost all of the media, I probably don't need to scream in terror on here at length every day. Not that it was doing any good anyway. My throat and ear have been quite sore, but my temperature is normal, so I just hope neither of us has to test the NHS any time soon. So, for today, I'm going to do what I intended to do from the off with this diary, and leave what I can't change alone, and instead concentrate on the 'pleasure of small things'.

Marcel Proust – that proto-mindfulness exponent – and I have a few things in common. We both have/had slight hypochondriac tendencies, tend/tended to have a few opinions and not to rise early for breakfast, struggle(d) to self-edit when the words come tumbling out and, for three weeks in my case and his last three years in his, never go out anywhere. I can't write eight pages on dipping a madeleine into a cup of tea, much as I'd like to try, but I can – and just did – spend a day doing nothing very much, without beating myself up about it.

There have been no madeleines to savour around here, but the pleasure of fresh food is certainly one I'll take less for granted in future. My 'Raid on Entebbe' mission on Tuesday has granted me one whole banana a day for the week to accompany my breakfast, and Amanda rustled up a fabulous chicken in tomato and pepper sauce with rice and vegetables for our main meal yesterday. The birds on the patio have also had a gastronomic treat – my last remaining pack of suet and sunflower seed cake has gone into its holder to join the nyjer seeds and squirrel-proof feeder of a seed and nut mix. The latter is an ingenious device which closes if too much weight is brought to bear on it – that also frustrates the pigeons, but they're cunning (and unhygienic) enough to forage on the ground. And crap every now and then on Amanda's new bench.

I've liked birds ever since I found out about the nesting tawny and little owls in Kensington Gardens, back when I had my ear problems and the royal park was at the end of our road in Bayswater. That was at about the same time that I was reading Proust, come to think of it, as well as ploughing through the entirety of every series of *30 Rock*. I'd break off for a while each evening to read Ralph Hancock's labour of love, his daily *Birds of Hyde Park and Kensington Gardens* blog. Ralph uses his retirement to walk right round both adjoining parks at least once a day and photograph and chronicle every avian development. He even drew maps so that others could find the owls' nests.

Prior to falling ill, I'd probably have sniggered at this in much the same way as we used to laugh on our way to a match at the gaggle of men cataloguing train numbers when we passed through Crewe or Doncaster, but seeing owls perching in the daylight at the end of our street was remarkably therapeutic. Amanda and I absolutely love to travel – having no interest in expensive cars, gadgets or clothes, it's been our major self-indulgence for most of our time together – but as Proust said, 'The real voyage of discovery consists not in seeking new lands but seeing with new eyes.' I really do hope to be able to travel more widely again in due course, but being obliged to watch one small contained landscape change slowly and subtly through an English spring is indeed like 'seeing with new eyes'.

I'm cycling 10km every day on the exercise bike, and I'm starting to inject some uphill stretches into it. I might do more as the weather improves, but right now it gives me long enough to savour the now fully bloomed tulips and pink Japanese magnolia which forms the backdrop to the bird feeders. Bird activity slows down when an adult human is puffing away on a barely socially distant machine. A blackbird will use the birdbath; presumably because of their relative sizes, the resident robin lets that go. A great tit moving in on the suet cake is an entirely different matter, though – it was dive-bombed then chased out of the garden by a little angry blur of red and brown. Unlike the tits and the greater spotted woodpecker I've only seen once, the robin seems unable to land on the mesh which surrounds the suet. Instead, it does a passable, if less delicate, impression of a hummingbird by beating its wings frantically, allowing it to stay in one place in the air long enough for a good peck. When I finished on the bike yesterday and came indoors, two absolutely beautiful pink-tinged long-tailed tits descended on the main feeder, and three goldfinches arrived for their nyjer fix. It might not get you out of your seat like football or cricket, but it'll do for now.

Twenty minutes on a bike has also become a musical challenge. Like most people, I deploy playlists and random shuffle, especially in the car, and now rarely listen to the format I grew up with: whole albums from start to finish. So once a day, I'm trying to think of approximately a side of an old LP or another sequence of consecutive songs where I won't be tempted to press 'skip'. No compilations – that's cheating. The second side of *Abbey Road* was an obvious starting point, Stevie Wonder's *Songs in the Key of Life,* centring on 'I Wish' and 'Sir Duke' was next, and any stretch of *The Stone Roses* or Green Day's *American Idiot* works for me. Then I came to the contentious subject of prog rock. Being the age that I am, the album rock of the early to mid-'70s initially passed me by. Then late in the decade, Genesis released 'Follow You, Follow Me', Yes had a hit with 'Wondrous Stories' and Pink Floyd had the last number one of the decade with 'Another Brick in the Wall'. I loved all three of those, and a lot of punk and new wave, and from there started exploring Paul Weller's 1960s recommendations like the Kinks and the Small Faces. The only pop albums my dad had among his jazz and classical collection were Beatles and Simon and Garfunkel compilations, so I already knew about them.

I wasn't old enough to realise that you weren't supposed to like Pink Floyd if you also liked The Clash, so I bought or recorded whatever appealed to me. The three singles above, in retrospect, were pretty much the first thing any of those bands had recorded all decade which could be released as a single, and prefaced a downhill slide for each of them into the commercially successful, but musically less interesting, output they all released in the post-punk era. But having explored all their back catalogues and eliminated some horrible excesses, I still to this day appreciate few albums more than *Dark Side of the Moon* and *Selling England by the Pound*. I was fascinated to read recently that Peter Gabriel once heard John Lennon on the radio in New York extolling the virtues of that latter album, and almost wept with joy. 'Lennon loved early Genesis' would confuse a lot of people, Liam Gallagher for one, but he was right, imho.

I'm fortunate that I've always had friends who don't care what's hot and what's not. Amanda is completely, unshakeably, that way, Ron Chakraborty and Graham Wellham (an excessive love of *The Lamb Lies Down On Broadway* notwithstanding) were two more at BBC Sport. Ron places Yes, especially, on a pedestal (some of their stuff, anyway – even he recognises that *Tales from Topographic Oceans* was four sides of self-indulgent twaddle) and when bassist Chris Squire died not so long ago, Ron posted the song 'Parallels' as an example of his brilliance. I like a good bass part – just have a listen on YouTube to the isolated McCartney bass on 'I Want You, She's So Heavy' or indeed pretty much the whole of *Abbey Road* and marvel. Especially if you think he's just a twee, thumbs-aloft pretty boy like at least one of my regular readers. Anyway, I've now discovered that playing Yes's *Going for the One* album, from the title track onwards and including the aforementioned bass-fest 'Parallels', sees my exercise bike session end during the still lovely 'Wondrous Stories' but before the frankly boring and overlong 'Awaken'. The pleasure of small things, eh? The way it's going, I'll be on to Black Lace albums before this lockdown is over.

Again, just like me, Marcel Proust was a big fan of sleep, 'Dream all the time' was one of his mottos – it's no 'Take Back Control' or 'Get Brexit Done', admittedly, but it fits with the rest of his philosophy. I'm not sure he'd want some of the dreams I've been having lately, though.

With no alarm clock ringing or strict deadlines to meet you can doze off again, but I'm waking up with a start most nights at 4am or 5am. This morning featured a particular bizarre slumber interrupter – it centred on my mum's mum, Alice Allen, despite her having died over 20 years ago. I'd gone to visit her, but found her engrossed in making a handmade card for Boris Johnson, to my intense annoyance. To put this in context, in the mid-1920s, at 12 years old, my gran won a County Durham grammar school scholarship, but her family situation was such that she had turn it down to go into service in the south of England, to a home of Downton Abbey proportions. This shaped her firmly held view in later life that deference and starchy convention were nonsense; she couldn't see why people had to bow and curtsey to royalty, or why Elton John coming out (to the disdain of the tabloids) was anyone's concern but his, and even as an old lady, she could do a fantastic impression of Margaret Thatcher's scuttling walk with her handbag over her arm and all.

So, she absolutely wouldn't ever have been found making a card for Boris Johnson. He's exactly the sort of entitled twerp to whom she had to dole out turtle soup and venison back when she was in service. So sorry for even dreaming that about you, Gran. I can only blame unprecedented times. That said, you lived through two world wars, so there's no excuse.

Friday, 3 April 2020

I really did just type Thursday until I glanced at my phone. 'He doesn't know what day it is' is no longer simply a figure of speech. The way to remember it's Friday from now on is to think of it as the morning after we applauded the NHS. That gesture has rightly been extended to all key workers and was riotously observed in these parts, a whole orchestra section of banging saucepans adding a tuneless edge to proceedings. I think the tone may gradually shift from upbeat to sombre as the weeks go by, but it's an unequivocally good national development. What they're all going through at the moment makes them the front line soldiers of this bizarre war, and needs to be commemorated permanently with, say, an annual NHS Day. And it wouldn't hurt if 40 per cent or so of those out there clapping didn't vote Conservative next time, but let's not expect too much.

On the subject of key workers, I saw a line the other day from an exasperated but nameless online attendee at the regular virtual gathering of Premier League chairmen: 'Most of them are struggling to comprehend that they're now less important than a Tesco's delivery driver.' The Curry Club isn't overenamoured with their chairman at the best of times. Daniel Levy is seen as a zealous guarder of the purse strings to rival Philip Hammond, but his decision to ask the government to pay his non-playing staff's wage bill has made my friends cringe, and the wider country angry. I imagine the debt on that new stadium must be astronomical and can only be serviced by 20-plus massive paydays known as matches a year, but even so.

What does seem slightly unfair is that the heat is now being applied to Premier League footballers by some in the media, and as a 'dead cat' strategy in the case of the now fit-for-selection Health Secretary. Of course, they're paid stupid amounts of money, and Aston Villa's Jack Grealish was unimaginably cretinous to crash his car after a clandestine party this week, but they're young men, often poorly advised by greedy agents and their almost equally rich union boss, Gordon Taylor. Many of them do all manner of unseen good deeds through their club's community schemes, or off their own bat. The real villains of the piece are the Ashleys, Martins, Murdochs and Bransons who emerged in a 'greed is good' era, squirrel away their billions, and seem to struggle to take corporate responsibility, even in a global crisis. West Brewery from Scotland have just announced that they'd 'rather sweep the streets' than supply any more beer to Wetherspoons, so let's hope we've reached a tipping point. Sadly, in the looming recession, people with time on their hands but little money to spend will probably still shelter in Father Jack's establishments.

After the 8pm applause last night, Amanda and I sat down to watch the film *The Two Popes* on Netflix. This was a dramatisation of the abdication of the German Pope Benedict XVI, played by Anthony Hopkins, and his replacement by the Argentinian Pope Francis, played by Jonathan Pryce. The acting and writing – albeit in *The Crown*'s territory of invented conversations between living people – were worthy of their Oscar nominations and we were transported out of our time and place for two hours.

Until this happened: the young Argentinian, not yet a priest, is seen in a flashback working in a laboratory. His boss Esther tells him, 'Test, test, test. We live and die by facts.' That's almost word for word the WHO's appeal to the UK government. Is there no escape?

I still enjoyed the rest of the film, not least when a friend unexpectedly popped up to provide the soundtrack to the closing sequence. Guy Mowbray's BBC commentary on the 2014 World Cup Final, in which the two Popes' home countries met, was used as they sat watching the match on a sofa together. I'm guessing this never actually happened, and I certainly don't think Guy's words, excellent though they were, would have been available on Italian TV. Even so, it was a neat device from director Fernando

Meirelles. He also made *City of God*, by the way. Now that is a film.

I'm having a TV and radio news blackout for a day or two, though I will stay aware of the numbers. The statistics are too grim for words, and not just the COVID-19 death toll, which will today see the UK total figure exceed that for all the lives lost on 9/11. And just think how that changed the world: travel and other security procedures ramped up for ever; the spurious deposing of Saddam Hussein resulted in regional instability, a refugee crisis, and a worldwide clamour for isolationism and nationalist strongmen.

Even the EU's member states seem largely to be looking after themselves at the moment, while the story of a Chinese plane full of medical aid bound for France being flagged down on the runway by American government representatives offering three or four times the money is genuinely chilling. So too are the awful pictures from India of migrant workers scrambling to get on buses or even walking hundreds of miles to isolate at home as decreed by Prime Minister Modi. Far too reminiscent of the horrors of Partition for comfort. Then there are the refugee camps now being left to fend for themselves and horribly susceptible to a pandemic – the Syrians on the Greek island of Lesbos, and the estimated million Rohingyas who've fled across the border from Myanmar to Bangladesh. There's a stark contrast between the current anarchic mess and the 2008 banking crisis when Gordon Brown, Barack Obama and many others worked together across national divides to save the global economy. Right now, what we're seeing is more like an international version of William Golding's *Lord of the Flies*, and unless co-operation between countries kicks in pronto, there will be no lasting solution.

Domestically, there's an extraordinary clip of BBC News anchor Jane Hill reading some copy about a Cabinet Office statement that 30 new ventilators will be delivered to the NHS this weekend. It's not unlike one of those *Grandstand* teleprinter moments where Manchester City 10 (ten) Huddersfield 1 had to be reiterated because it was so unlikely. But 30 (three-zero) it was, and Jane tried to remain professional as a voice in her ear told her that, no, there were no noughts missing. That's your lot for now, good luck in that Nightingale field hospital everyone. At least someone named that appropriately, since the conditions may be similar in due course to those Florence encountered during the Crimean War.

Much of the press, glancing at the headlines, appears to have been placated by Matt Hancock's wildly improbable claim that 100,000 tests a day would be carried out by the end of this month. Why we're supposed to believe this after our now-indisposed PM said there'd be 250,000 a day within weeks, weeks ago, is anyone's guess. No country in the world has a definite exit strategy and evidence is mounting that China is being economical with the truth to put it mildly, but South Korea and Germany have half a chance of keeping further outbreaks under control until a vaccine is developed precisely because of their levels of testing.

I continued my press conference boycott yesterday, so didn't watch Hancock's half-hour, but apparently the largely inoffensive Matt H (he didn't even vote for Brexit) at least fielded supplementary questions and admitted that current testing levels weren't good enough. But then he seems to have floated the idea of an 'immunity passport' as a possible way out of lockdown. Again, that's made headlines because people are understandably desperate to find a possible chink of light, but even as a layman, I can see immediately that there are two gigantic problems there. Firstly, you'd have to test huge numbers of people for that to work and, secondly, as with immunity of the herd variety, the virus can potentially mutate and render your previously acquired antibodies potentially irrelevant.

One other observation about the press conferences: I only look at the cast list and a summary of what's been said, but they keep dragging out different scientists every day. The Chief Medical Officer is self-isolating, but the Chief Scientific Officer who isn't, as far as I know, hasn't appeared in some days. It may be coincidence that he was the chap wheeled out to give credence to the 'herd immunity' leak to Robert Peston. It's difficult to imagine how heated the blame game will now have become behind the scenes, and you can see people already manoeuvring ahead of the eventual inquiry.

For example, Jeremy Hunt in his role as the chairman of the Parliamentary Health Select Committee has, not unreasonably, been demanding that the government and NHS ramp up testing, protective equipment provision and ventilator acquisition. In 2016 as the actual Minister of Health, however, he had the actual findings of that NHS pandemic dry run, Exercise Cygnus, delivered to him. As we now know, that report, despite highlighting all our current issues, led to no action whatsoever. Like that other more recent government report, into Russian interference in the workings of British democracy, the details of Exercise Cygnus have never been released into the public domain, but let's guess what we'll discover when it's all too late. Jeremy Hunt will probably say he wanted to up our preparations but will blame Theresa May and Philip Hammond for refusing to release the necessary funds. May and Hammond will say they were far too busy cleaning up the Brexit mess Cameron and Osborne left them to read it, if indeed they were ever sent a copy, and so on, until it's eventually Harold Wilson's fault.

It probably is true, given the pre-occupation with Brexit, that everything else including pandemic preparedness, has been sacrificed these last four years. The absolute priority given to 'taking back control' has led to most senior civil servants, and the attention of the government, being almost entirely devoted to 'Get(ting) Brexit Done'. I have no words for Mark Francois and the ERG who are still insisting we decline the chance to park the whole thing beyond 31 December even now that both the UK and EU chief negotiators are stricken with this virus. Our limited resources, at least for the time being, would so obviously be infinitely better employed elsewhere, and we simply cannot countenance our food or medicine supplies being stuck at Calais in January. But then the ERG modus operandi (Jacob Rees-Mogg would like those two words, at least) has always been based on *Blackadder*'s World War One General Melchett: 'If nothing else works, a total pig-headed unwillingness to look facts in the face will see us through.'

I can't remember whether I've used this analogy before in this diary, but I definitely have on Facebook. If the government, or more specifically Johnson, is Melchett, then Dominic Cummings is very much Melchett's sidekick Captain Darling. A weaselly, vindictive little sneak who you only have any time for in the last episode, where they're about to go over the top and he confesses that he's scared, and only ever wanted to go back home to 'marry Doris and keep wicket for the Croydon second XI'. The big difference is that Cummings wasn't actually enlisted, his iconoclastic, ego-fuelled, intellectually arrogant mania being such that he enlisted himself as the only possible man for the job. Up to the point where he literally ran away from Number 10 last Friday, he seemed to be lapping up the power and notoriety. I hope he has sufficient self-awareness to know, as the German Pope did in that film, that he's not what's needed right now and therefore steps back from the fray.

I thought of Classic Dom when I saw a photo from the press conference and realised that another of his three-word slogans has bitten the dust. 'Stay at home' on the podiums is now 'stay home'. Possibly for the first time ever, Amanda and I are on Dom's side: removing the preposition turns that English sentence into an American one. What's next? 'Don't be a dummy', 'I'll be with you momentarily' or even 'You're the man – missing you already, Dom'?

WEEK FOUR

Saturday, 4 April 2020

For nearly three decades of my life, a sunny Saturday in April would have meant working on sport. Before and after my career, I'd still have been watching piles of it, in person, live on TV, or both. When I first joined BBC Sport in the pre-Sky late 1980s it had pretty much all the live sport the country and indeed world had to offer. I've written at length in *Why Are We Always On Last?* about those days, before there were red button and online options, when the *Grandstand* editor was effectively the person with the remote control flicking around the sporting world. April meant, among other events, golf's Masters, the London Marathon, the first cricket scoreboards of the year, the FA Cup semi-finals, and of course, the Grand National.

Horse racing has severely blotted its copybook by staging Cheltenham last month – yesterday's *Times* pointed to considerable anecdotal evidence suggesting that 250,000 people attending over four days helped spread the virus all over the country. I've since learnt that while I was shouting into the ether about the insanity of staging the Festival given what we already knew, Piers Morgan was apparently doing likewise on ITV's *Good Morning Britain.* I'm afraid he's another of those people who I'm physically unable to watch, or even read too much about on Twitter, but he has been right (i.e., agreed with me) at least three times in his long career: firstly, with his anti-Iraq War stance as editor of the *Daily Mirror* (sadly curtailed by printing what turned out to be fake atrocity photos); secondly, his hostility towards the gun lobby when he hosted a CNN show in the States (unfortunately, it didn't go down well, especially from a Brit), and now. I've seen quite a few 'I can't stand him, but …' posts from Facebook friends in recent days praising his fierce questioning of the government position, and (sadly) contrasting it to the rather anodyne offering that is *BBC Breakfast.*

We will be watching ITV this afternoon, though. Someone in the ITV Sport team headed by my old BBC friends and colleagues Niall Sloane, Mark Demuth and Paul McNamara has come up with the brainwave of turning what would have been Grand National day into a virtual race to be shown live in the National's slot. A group of my old Kent school friends and partners have pitched into a sweepstake and will be Skyping or Zooming or Housepartying or something to have a virtual get-together.

Sport's governing bodies and individual organisations on the whole have behaved with some decorum through this. Wimbledon has joined Euro 2020 and the Olympics in being cancelled already this summer, but chatting to Andrew Clement, I discovered that all of them have waived their usual tight archive restrictions – as have the Premier League – so that the BBC can run the best of the historical material in some of the vacated slots. Andrew is co-ordinating the European Championship archive pull-togethers, and we spent a happy half-hour on the phone swapping notes and remembering the Platini-, Van Basten-, Shearer- and Zidane-tinted memories of our youth and early middle age. With the technology now available in the home, Gary Lineker or whoever can record some links, and producers and videotape editors can access the archive on their laptops to put together perfectly transmittable packages. *Have I Got News For You?* returned last night and actually worked reasonably well with Merton, Hislop and guests contributing from home, and the Boro's own Steph McGovern (we exiles always find each other, so we sometimes had a Riverside-themed chat when we were both working in Salford) hosting from her home.

Speaking of Boro, I belatedly discovered that the club are running classic matches (yes, we have had some) in full on YouTube to keep the fans occupied. At 7.45pm precisely on Thursday, it was exactly 14 years to the minute since the greatest game I've ever attended, and probably ever will, kicked off. So, at that exact time, Boro's 2006 UEFA Cup semi-final second leg v Steaua Bucharest got under way once more for a watching audience of over 10,000. The club even provided its usual regular updates on Twitter. On the actual night, I was one of capacity crowd of 34,000 (see – it can happen, Shearer) at the Riverside, so have never heard what has become an iconic commentary in full. Alistair Brownlee, a delightful gentle Teessider with a lovely broadcast voice, worked wherever the local commentary rights went for over three decades. He died in 2016, but will always be thought of as 'the voice of the Boro' – his extraordinary words from that Steaua night are immortalised in big letters on the side of the bridge as you arrive at the ground. Steve Gibson hasn't got everything right in recent years – as an ex-Labour councillor, he shocked many of us by endorsing a controversial local Tory candidate in 2017 – but his club is rooted in the community, and chose to commemorate a much-loved local commentator within the stadium precincts, just as it has its greatest players – the superb statues of Wilf Mannion and George Hardwick in action – and its roots, with the original Ayresome Park gates also on prominent display.

I watched the whole game again, and after half an hour, I still couldn't see how the men in red with a white hoop (the only kit we should ever play in, in my opinion) were going to score the four goals they needed in an hour against accomplished, technically gifted Continental opponents. But then they'd done precisely that against Basel in the quarter-final a mere three weeks earlier. In that round I went to the wrong leg – Amanda and I were in Switzerland for a 2-0 defeat, then watched TV with incredulity as Boro went one down at home, pulled one back before half-time, then scored the last of the three more needed in the 90th minute, through the previously underachieving club record signing Massimo Maccarone. An unbelievable turnaround, and the commentary at 2-0 (3-0 on aggregate) against Steaua was, like it had been around me in the stadium, very much along the lines of 'lightning never strikes twice'. Ali's co-commentator, Bernie Slaven, had just questioned the decision to start with Maccarone when he made it 2-1 on the night, late in the first half.

The weirdest thing then happened: all the talk on the concourse at half-time turned into 'we've done this before' and Steaua, who'd looked imperious for a leg and a half started to look as if they knew it, too, and retreated deeper and deeper. It was amazing to see what then unfolded without the stomach-knotting tension and adrenaline of being there. Boro brought on Yakubu (oh, for an option like him on the bench these days) to replace our left-back and we switched to 4-2-4 bordering on 2-2-6. Stewart Downing on the left (why did Boro fans never appreciate him more?) became the default outlet ball and he slung cross after cross in the direction of Mark Viduka (on his day, as gifted a centre-forward as we've ever had) who held it up, flicked it on, or went for goal as the occasion required. A 2-1 deficit became 2-2 as Viduka headed home Downing's umpteenth precision ball from deep, then 3-2 as Chris Riggott, nominally a centre-half, scrambled home after a Downing cross-shot.

Steaua were still going through on away goals but by the 89th minute, they were so deep that wing-back Downing was permanently stationed on the corner of their box. He duly won the ball back from a visibly wilting Romanian, beat another man on his outside, slung in the best cross of his life and a bald head beat the remaining eight defenders to the ball. I have a collection of photographs from different angles of that moment when Massimo flew through the air. I'd always thought until then that the phrase 'the world stood still' was just sports journalism purple prose.

I was side-on to the action, not far from the camera gantry, so I could see that Maccarone had got to the cross first, but would only know if the header was on target if and when the net bulged. I can't imagine what it would have been like to have been in line with the header – actually, I can, I was right behind Keith Houchen's similar moment for Coventry in the 1987 FA Cup Final – but this was my team, on the threshold of the only

European final it could ever possibly reach. An audible intake of breath could be heard all around.

Then ball hit net; lightning had indeed struck twice and even the pensioners around me in the genteel West Stand pogoed in the arms of the person next to them. I looked around the ground, all the aisles had disappeared into a sea of utter bedlam. Boro being Boro, injury time was chaos, Steaua remembered they were allowed to play in the other half and the late, great Ugo Ehiogu did exactly what he'd done in injury time at Cardiff when we won our only ever trophy two years earlier, and leapt heroically to block a goalbound shot with his body.

The full-time whistle went, more utter bedlam ensued, as did the almost Shakespearean monologue from Ali which is now emblazoned on that bridge. 'We go back to 1876, the Infant Hercules, fathomed out of the foundries of Teesside, mined out of the Eston Hills,' he intoned, eventually ending with the slightly more prosaic, but still marvellous, 'Everybody round my house for a parmo.' I hadn't really been missing football until I watched all that back, then spent another self-indulgent half an hour just now trying – and probably failing – to capture the majesty of that evening in print. Yes, the UEFA Cup was only ever a consolation prize to big clubs, and yes, another 4-2-4 last half-hour came unstuck against Sevilla in the final in Eindhoven, but none of that matters to us at all.

Please forgive me for retreating to a happy place for a few paragraphs. The world is so far from a happy place right now; it's truly painful and bewildering to behold, and I'm still having to ration my exposure to it all. Even Amanda is feeling a bit low this morning and not consuming her usual level of news. The stark statistics – nearly 700 virus deaths in the UK in 24 hours, over 1,000 each in France and in the USA – are chilling enough, but it's the individual stories which have been knocking the stuffing out of us. The retired doctor who died after volunteering to go back on duty, the nurse whose daughter is expecting the first grandchild she'll now never know, the teenager whose family are having to self-isolate so can't even attend his funeral. It was all unthinkable, even earlier this year.

Amanda's mum died in January. She was 95 and had been gradually fading, but only had to leave home for her final ten days. Joan's life ended peacefully in the lovely Severn Hospice in Shrewsbury where family were welcome to come and go at any time of day or night, and where the bird and plant life outside her window prompted her to recite the verse about daffodils from Wordsworth's *I Wandered Lonely as a Cloud* as well as Keats's phrase 'A thing of beauty is a joy for ever'. A Teessider right to the very end, Joan was among a contingent from both our families in Cardiff for that League Cup triumph in 2004. She also (quite rightly) told me when I visited the hospice just how unimpressed she'd been with the two sloppy goals Boro had conceded at Spurs in their televised FA Cup replay earlier that week. The funeral was in February; the whole family were there as Joan's son, Robert, read a beautiful eulogy Amanda and her sister Liz had crafted and the two sons-in law, Harry and I, read those Keats and Wordsworth poems respectively.

Six weeks later, and none of that would have been possible. Much younger people are dying away from loved ones who then can't attend their funerals. In that respect, this country really hasn't lived through anything like this since World War Two. If there is to be a 1945 after this, it's only going to come about when this virus is finally beaten. Professor Anthony Costello, ex-director of the WHO, and the scientist whose words have resonated most with the distinctly unscientific Amanda and me, has written an article in today's *Guardian*. Until there is a vaccine – and he puts no timeframe on that, and points out that like the annual flu shot, it will have to be amended as different strains appear – we're going to live in a cycle of a slight relaxation of the lockdown at some point, followed by more outbreaks, followed by a stricter lockdown again. He once again says we need to be like the Asian countries, with mass testing and monitoring so that any outbreak can quickly be jumped upon and a chain of possible contacts tracked down and tested, and quarantined if necessary.

China have the massive advantage of being a totalitarian state, in which figures can be massaged, but also one where 40,000 medical staff from around the country can be told they're going to Wuhan to conduct house-to-house testing. South Korea and Singapore are democracies, so while their public expects them to be open and transparent about the new cases and deaths they're still seeing, the rigour of their testing to date seems to mean that very little is happening beyond the radar of the authorities, and the population trusts what it's being told. While the UK is not quite the US – Trump has parodied himself today by recommending that people wear masks, but then saying he won't – Professor Costello has for the first time, I think, specifically said that the two scientists first wheeled out to flank Boris Johnson made the wrong call. Nothing we've seen since inspires any great level of confidence, to be honest: one of the two has gone down with the virus, the other presented 'herd immunity', a theory which Professor Costello says may well be tested out inadvertently if the government and health authorities don't act quickly.

In a further attempt not to think about the implications of that bleak prognosis 24 hours a day, we've been leading a reasonably active social life. Virtually, of course. As well as the far longer and more frequent telephone calls than usual, I've downloaded at least five different methods of conducting video link-ups. Two nights ago, we hooked up with Michael and Janet in Barnes, and Lance and Lijana in South Yorkshire. Despite four of us in total having held down reasonably senior roles in TV, it took us half an hour to make Google Hangouts work satisfactorily. Last night, Microsoft Teams was given a whirl for a virtual drink with three old university friends. A larger group of us meet three times a year in a pub, but we kept it to a core four last night to keep it manageable. It was quite an interesting mix: the other three are respectively Labour, Lib Dem and Conservative, so while the Tory was somewhat on the defensive, it stayed civilised and we got into all manner of topics – concern for elderly parents, dealing with kids missing out at various stages of their education, where the line has suddenly been drawn on civil liberties and the economy vs people's welfare, the dangers of social unrest, and so on. We did also somehow manage to have a few laughs, too, not least about our collective baldness on the unforgiving screen.

We have another couple booked in for a link-up tonight, after the virtual Grand National get-together, and then the Zoom group from earlier in the week convenes again tomorrow. Margaret, who organised it, wanted to give it a name so I suggested Fat Larry's Band. Their hit single, 'Zoom' takes me right back to the upper sixth. I'll expand on that another day when I'm in need of some more escapism.

One other piece of news: for the first time in at least four years – actually it's probably five, because I put money on the seemingly ludicrous (16/1) notion that Jeremy Corbyn would be elected Labour leader in 2015 – I've lost a political flutter. I've consistently applied H.L. Mencken's theory that 'no one ever went broke underestimating the intelligence of the (American) people' and won on Trump being nominated, then winning the presidency, and transported the theory across the Atlantic to cash in on Corbyn, Brexit, Johnson becoming PM, and finally, Johnson winning a majority. I wanted to lose every one of those bets, but they have paid for a few holidays. On the same basis, I backed Rebecca Long-Bailey and Richard Burgon as the continuity Corbyn candidates to replace Magic Grandpa himself and fill the deputy role vacated by Tom Watson a while back.

I wouldn't have been able to book a holiday if I'd won in any case, but I'm relieved to discover that I underestimated the Labour membership. Keir Starmer and Angela Rayner have both won a majority on the first ballot, and assuming they quietly extricate the more intransigent members of the shadow cabinet, we might actually have an opposition worthy of the name at this crucial moment in our history. They'll have to strike a careful balance between holding the government to account and scoring openly partisan political points, but I'd trust Starmer a great deal more to achieve that than the 'Jeremy won the argument' brigade.

I still wish the decent Tories binned by Johnson and Cummings – Dominic Grieve, Heidi Allen and company – could have got together with the Lib Dems, Greens and non-Corbynistas to fill the gaping hole in the middle of British politics, but given a choice between the rabble currently in charge, and Starmer and our excellent moderate Labour MP, Tulip Siddiq, it won't be difficult to back the latter. A presence in COBRA now the Stalinists have gone might just bring some new ideas to the table. Churchill, though representing an entirely different political philosophy, was always extremely gracious about, and grateful for, the contribution of Attlee and other leading Labour figures to his national government in wartime. Maybe Churchill's biographer, once he returns to the fray, could be similarly open-minded?

Even the Johnson quarantine poses uncomfortable questions: from the outset the WHO has recommended 14 days self-isolation for those who develop symptoms, whereas the UK line has been that seven days will suffice. It's been eight days now since Johnson and his Health Secretary, Matt Hancock, first displayed symptoms. Johnson still has a temperature so hasn't reappeared, Hancock is back, but there's a worrying photo of him seemingly coughing spectacularly at yesterday's opening of the Nightingale field hospital, with the Chief Nursing Officer, Ruth May, looking distinctly alarmed two metres away. Sorry to be a doomy gloomster again, but none of this is exactly inspiring the confidence of anyone who's paying any attention.

Sunday, 5 April 2020

A really good night's sleep, for whatever reason, and I emerged on to the patio reasonably refreshed with my book, guitar, a coffee, bowl of porridge and the last fresh banana. That might have required two trips, on reflection. Spring has well and truly sprung. Amanda hadn't watched the politics shows this particular Sunday – even she's had an overdose of deflection and empty promises – and was in the middle of a 20km static cycle ride instead. I'm building up to 14km today but interspersed with an uphill setting every third km, so that's clearly far harder and more manly.

I'm about halfway through *The Road* now, and I can see why it won the Pulitzer Prize and so much acclaim. Taut and sparse, with Biblical overtones, a love story between a father and son at its core, set against an apocalyptic backdrop which makes our current situation look like it's almost under control. I've left it, for the time being, at a point where finding a years-old tin of peaches has just represented a stratospheric triumph, after a life-and-death encounter with the feral dregs of humanity on the outskirts of a burnt-out town. The Waitrose run isn't quite there yet, but give it a few more weeks.

There's a babble of noise all around: the birdsong is joined by a dog barking, the distant shrieking of children and the gentle exertions of Anthony and Louisa from Flat 7 who are exercising on the communal lawn beyond the patio. Someone's playing a piano somewhere, too – they're nowhere near the standard of the Sunday morning paternal Fats Waller renditions of my youth, but I can hardly complain given that I've already inflicted an early '80s guitar medley of 'Stray Cat Strut' and the great Roddy Frame's 'Oblivious' on the immediate neighbourhood. I glanced up during the latter and spotted Martijn and Alejandra from the flat above ours, out on their balcony. They told me to carry on, which was kind of them, but I judiciously faded it out within a few minutes. They're an absolutely lovely couple who got married last year – he's from the Netherlands, she's from Colombia, and they are exactly the type of cosmopolitan, multilingual, highly intelligent citizens of the world (and not 'Citizens of Nowhere' as Theresa May unforgivably sneered, as she tried to head Farage off at the pass) with whom you tend to rub shoulders in the 'that there Londinistan' the alt-right so despise.

I asked about their families at home: the Netherlands, surprisingly to me since I absolutely love the place and regard its people as some of the savviest I've ever met, has reacted at a not dissimilar pace to the UK with proportionally similar consequences. Many there are gazing enviously across the German border. Ale says Colombia went into lockdown early as did most of Latin America (even most Brazilian states did so, despite Bolsonaro's best efforts) and both their families seem to be okay so far.

Gareth from next door, who lives with, and looks after, his elderly father (so far, mercifully, untouched by the virus) is offering some of a batch of lemon drizzle cake he's made. I didn't ask whether he could catapult it over the wall, but it's a kind, neighbourly thought nonetheless. Anthony chipped in from the garden to ask whether we'd seen the news pictures from Primrose Hill, and we had to say with sadness that we had. That beauty spot, and viewpoint, which we visited and found uncomfortable on the very first day of this diary, appears to have been just as rammed yesterday. The hour's exercise the government has allowed everyone is one thing, and we appreciate that not every flat-dweller has any outside space, but there were groups sunbathing all over the place, to the absolute disgust of police, health workers and the 90 per cent of us who are doing what we're supposed to be doing to slow the spread.

I understand that the message from a government which seems to have infected much of itself hasn't been entirely coherent, but even so, your heart just sinks. The London death rate actually dropped slightly yesterday after a fortnight of mostly sensible behaviour; who knows what this stupidity will have done to it in a fortnight's time. This lockdown clearly can't be relaxed – and may well be ramped up – until the figures subside, so these fuckwits are just punishing everyone else. That's before you get to the poor buggers they might infect on their next supermarket run.

We Zoomed our friends Mark and Milly last night: he thinks he's had the virus as he's felt rough for a week or so, and lost his sense of taste and smell. He's back out of isolation now, but thinks the only place he could have caught it in recent weeks was their local supermarket in Acton. Milly has been left to manage their eight-year-old twin boys, one of whom is severely disabled. Jack, who goes to Watford home games with his dad (and me, occasionally) is hoping Gerard Deulofeu will be fit when the season resumes (Mark has yet to break that one to him) and is missing playing football with his friends. Joe, the sweetest, gentlest kid you'll ever meet, is missing his usual routine, and they will have both have missed their dad when he was shut away in the back bedroom. If we were South Korea and could trace that supermarket transmission to Mark back to an idiot who'd been sunbathing with his mates in a park, rather than say, a health worker or even London bus driver (five of whom have now died) you'd want to wreak a slow cold revenge sometime in the future.

Of course, we're not South Korea, so according to the ever more mutinous *Telegraph*, we're currently turning down 400,000 testing kits they're offering to send us because they won't have been 'tested to British standards'. Now, I'm no scientist, but 183 deaths in South Korea compared to 5,000 now here just might be all the proof anyone needs that their testing equipment is doing a rather better job than our pretty much non-existent testing equipment. Meanwhile, the *Mail on Sunday* has revealed that the flag-waving surge of national pride in the Excel Centre field hospital must be tempered by the fact that the government is paying millions in rent to Abu Dhabi for the venue's use. We don't even own this symbol of Great British magnificence.

Abu Dhabi's football plaything Manchester City are at least not taking advantage of Sunak's furloughing opportunity; neither (amazingly) are West Ham. A free stadium from the government seems to have sufficed. I'm not really following it, because it's too pathetic for words, but Matt Hancock appears to be trying to turn the heat once more on to Premier League footballers for no better reason, seemingly, than they're an easy target for those Tory voters who've spent this sunny afternoon drinking on an empty head. Wayne Rooney appears to have replied in his *Sunday Times* column along the lines of, 'I'll be delighted to chip in to help buy some ventilators if you can actually find any.' Marina Hyde has said, ruefully, that it was all bound to end up being Raheem Sterling's fault, since everything always is.

In a more appropriately targeted development, the *Mail on Sunday* leads with a story about Somerset Capital Management, the investment company founded by 'haunted Victorian pencil', erstwhile advocate of Third World safety standards and questioner of the common sense of Grenfell victims, Jacob Rees-Mogg. Jacob stepped back from his day-to-day role when he was appointed to Johnson's cabinet, but still holds a 15% stake which earned him an estimated £1m last year, according to the report. The firm has been telling its clients that the economic and human calamity that is COVID-19 is also a 'once or twice in a generation' opportunity to make 'supernormal returns'. Now we know this is what disaster capitalism is all about – Jacob's father William wrote its definitive handbook *Blood in the Streets: Investment Profits in a World Gone Mad* (yes, that really is the full title) – but Mogg's not just affecting events from the shadows like Crispin '£300m Brexit jackpot' Odey. Jacob is this government's actual Leader of the House of Commons, the man who went to Balmoral to reassure the Queen about the reason for proroguing Parliament. Someone, somewhere – as they have with Priti Patel – seems to have kept him locked away (in his case, in the ancestral castle in Somerset) throughout this crisis, but I hope he feels uncomfortable reading today's headlines.

Speaking of the Queen, she's doing her best by making a wartime-style appeal to the nation today. Like her Christmas broadcast, I may find an excuse not to watch it, but I do appreciate her sense of duty. I'm not so sure about her priorities on other fronts – Harry and Meghan told to do one, Andrew sitting next to her in church not so long ago – but she's in her 90s and from a different world, and to be honest, I have no strong feeling either way about the monarchy. Once she's gone anyway; she deserves to see her stint out, not least for opening her historic speech in Dublin in Gaelic a while back. Symbolism it may have been, but blimey, what a moment. That said, the monarchy's abolition would have saved me from 50 per cent of the conversations American strangers have struck up with me over the years. 'I don't give a shit', while a quite wonderful line from Rodney Bewes's midlife crisis-stricken Bob in Dick Clement's *Likely Lads* film, is just plain impolite as a response to Dolores from Des Moines, Iowa, who is merely trying to strike up a conversation at the dinner table.

Elsewhere, Bill Withers, a fine soul singer and subject of the best joke I know about putting ducks in microwaves, has sadly left us on this lovely day. Frankie Boyle is very much still around, though, and has written a column which is bleak to the point of apocalyptic, but also contains a Marina Hyde-level quotient of stupendous lines. Speaking of the dignity patients should be afforded in woefully underequipped ICUs, he says, 'It's distressing enough to be told you're being put on a ventilator. We shouldn't be adding to that by having the news broken by a doctor wearing a Superman mask and boxing gloves.' And among many barbs aimed at our leaders: 'Boris Johnson has sent a text message to every mobile phone in the UK. For a handful of children in Britain that'll have been the first contact they've had from their dad.'

And in a diatribe against the cuntraversialist Toby Young – that 'villainous kneecap' – he questions how Tobes can be keen on eugenics 'while looking like an unviable foetus'. I guess I'd disapprove if any of this vitriol was aimed at a friend or relative of mine, but at least he's giving it back there to two people who have used punching down viciously as their primary source of income for decades. Frankie's final paragraph is entirely serious, though: he asks many of the same questions most people I speak to are asking, about the world which could emerge from this nightmare. 'Surely it's time to start imagining something better?' he ends. Amen to that.

Monday, 6 April 2020

Sadly, Frankie Boyle's hope that we could all 'start imagining something better' has taken another backwards step overnight. It started well enough: the Queen delivered what I have to admit was a sensitive, adroit and surprisingly moving address to the nation. As Danny Baker said on Twitter this morning, 'Queen 1 Sex Pistols 0: turns out she is a human being.' An hour or so after that broadcast, I was on the phone to my dad when he spotted a caption on his TV saying that Boris Johnson had been taken to hospital. Neither of us have ever had a great deal of time for the man, but this is becoming Shakespearean: his pregnant partner has developed symptoms and now the job he's always wanted has made him seriously ill at a time of national crisis. And if all that wasn't chilling enough, Dominic Raab is now acting Prime Minister, and was chairing the COBRA meeting this morning.

He is a supporter of the most maniacal form of Brexit, resigning from Theresa May's cabinet over her withdrawal agreement, and as recently as 17 March this year, said that the coronavirus strengthens the case for Brexit, with or without a deal, at the end of this year. So, if he were to take permanent charge, he'd presumably keep almost all of the civil service occupied in trying to untangle that impenetrable web, and then add exponentially to the prospect of the country running short of food and medicine in the middle of winter, and in the midst of a pandemic, too.

Raab admitted during his four months as Brexit Secretary that he 'hadn't quite understood' the significance of the Dover to Calais trade route. Queen Mary I was all too aware of the importance of our narrowest route to the European continent as long ago as the 1550s, but then what are we to expect from a Foreign Secretary who thinks that Lima is the capital of the Philippines?

Raab has also dismissed feminists as 'obnoxious bigots', and written a book with other Conservative 'thinkers', including Priti Patel, which claimed that 'the British are among the worst idlers in the world'. But I really knew he was a wrong 'un when I saw him on TV responding to a disabled Scottish woman who had cited her own experiences of others dying prematurely – including by committing suicide – because of years of cuts to health and social care. I've had to Google this to check I'm not doing him a disservice. The *Victoria Derbyshire Show*, 29 May 2017: asking for extra spending in those areas was, according to Raab, 'just a childish wish list'.

In a nutshell, that approach explains why there's still far too little testing capacity, ventilator provision and protective equipment in the NHS, despite the pandemic dry run for Exercise Cygnus highlighting all those issues in 2016, the year before Raab's scarcely believable response to that disabled woman. Words you never thought you'd hear yourself say, part 94, 'Get well soon, Boris Johnson' – you may be a lazy, feckless chancer with a penchant for offensive stereotyping, but at least you finally acknowledged last week that 'there is such a thing as society'. The man standing in for you at COBRA today gives a very good impression of being a sociopath.

One reason I've seen postulated for Raab occupying that hot seat is that, according to Camilla Tominey in *The Telegraph*, the two key ministers right now – Rishi Sunak, charged with keeping the country afloat, and Matt Hancock, charged with keeping it alive – have apparently fallen out behind the scenes. Someone neutral will seemingly have to referee that contest, even if it is Raab C. Nesbitt. Sunak's financial largesse was seemingly based on Hancock and others having promised mass testing, including millions of home testing kits, which could have led to a relatively early resumption of economic activity. *The Mail* had previously reported that 'Michael Gove and Matt Hancock are "vying" to become Boris Johnson's "coronavirus chief executive".' It's very much 'Steady as she goes' in the absence of the skipper.

Then you start to picture how things will pan out if Cummings is fit for action before Johnson. Raab and Cummings: Dom and Dommer. We'd be in full-on *Book of Revelation* territory: half of our horsemen in place, death already among us, famine looming, a plague raging, Australia's been on fire this year, East Africa's had a plague of locusts and even the prophesied 'beasts of the Earth' have just added a new, and disturbing dimension to proceedings. This morning's news that two tigers at the Bronx Zoo have tested positive for the coronavirus adds yet another layer to the nightmare. Other creatures – bats and/or pangolins, possibly – passed this virus on to the human race in Wuhan, now we appear to be passing it back. I can't cope with trying to comprehend the possible ramifications of that. I think I'll take a break out on the patio and read *The Road* for a bit of light relief.

It's now a couple of hours later – Angela, who sold us this flat, has surprised us by delivering some milk and a few other bits and pieces we ordered from a local shop. Her work having been mothballed, she's volunteered to help now the shop's rushed off their feet, so there'll be no further estate agent jokes, your honour. Then I had a quick glance at the iPad: Trump has a 'gut instinct' that some completely unproven internet whisper about using malaria medication might be our universal cure. He interrupted the medics at his press conference to put that one out there; never mind that it's supported by no evidence whatsoever, and has already killed people who've tried it in the States. The other non-scientist who's been bandying that about in recent days is apparently Lady MacGove herself, Sarah Vine, who also, it seems, shares Nigel Farage's contempt for the WHO. These people are beyond help; a whole orchard's worth of apples could fall on their heads and they'd still dismiss gravity as a libtard snowflake conspiracy.

Oh, and I've finished *The Road,* against a backdrop of Anthony and Louisa's fearsome-looking, and sounding, kickboxing session out in the communal garden. It's one of those rare books whose essence will, I think, live on with me, not least because of the context in which I read it. The best and the worst of humanity came out in extremis which went far beyond even where we are now, and the conclusion was that amidst the darkness, some humans will keep the fire – or light, a candle or a torch – burning.

One thing it has solved for me is the origin of a still photo with speech bubbles coming out of it which was doing the rounds after Brexit. I've checked on Google Images now that I'm somewhat the wiser, and it comes from the apparently not-altogether-successful film adaptation of *The Road.* A father and son, dressed in rags, are pushing a trolley through an ash-covered, desolate landscape. 'Dad, that rat tasted funny,' says the boy. The adult replies, 'Just think of the blue passports, son.'

The last 24 hours have seen both Amanda and I talk more to other people than we sometimes do in a fortnight. I spoke to my brother and both my nieces last night; the younger niece, Theresa, sounds the same as ever: cheerful, matter-of-fact and pleased it's the Easter holidays so there's no more set work from school to do for a few weeks. The elder, Josie, was on the line for far longer than her sister – she's intrigued to hear that I've been writing for two or three hours every day, and says she's been writing a lot while doing her school work at home, but doesn't understand why anyone would do it if they don't have to.

J.K. Rowling is excused because she makes a living out of it. It's a fair point. I don't really want either of them to read any of this until they're older. Josie passed her 11-plus this year and is due to start at grammar school this autumn; Theresa has that to come next year, but childhood's short enough without having to know too much about what's happening in the worst situation, even of the lifetimes of their dad and me. They understand quite a lot about it, though – Mummy's a nurse on the front line,

Grandma and Grandad mustn't catch it, and it's important not to be in direct contact with them right now and to keep their hands and the house clean. They'd previously worked out for themselves – and possibly through their classmates, too – that Donald Trump is an 'orange idiot' and they're not at all happy with Bolsonaro for allowing the Amazon to be chopped down.

I've thought for a while that this young generation has been handed the most appalling of hospital passes from my generation and, even more, from the one above. We missed national service and rationing, had free education until we graduated, a far better welfare safety net than now, full pensions in the case of the older group, and a far less damaged environment. Even so, many of the over 50s have repeatedly voted to pay as little tax as possible, let public services wither, wrecked the environment and voted to take away their grandchildren's freedom to work, study and live in our 27 neighbouring countries. Unless you're Nigel Farage and you've wangled your kids German passports through your ex-wife's nationality.

Furthermore, the young are routinely branded as snowflakes who need 'safe spaces', listen too much to Greta Thunberg, and any attempt they make to do the right thing is branded as 'virtue signalling'. Of the many modern phrases that I hate – 'retail therapy', 'to die for', 'Team GB', 'staycation' – 'virtue signalling' is the worst. Anybody who ever does anything remotely decent can be conveniently dismissed as a phoney do-gooder. You might just about be able to level that accusation at a high-profile person like Bono, who does tend to trumpet worthy causes in a slightly insufferable and self-congratulatory fashion (especially given that he doesn't appear to pay any taxes anywhere) but it now seemingly extends to anyone who shows an ounce of consideration or compassion in any circumstances whatsoever. Maybe it will go out of fashion, just as paying your share of taxes for the common good comes back into vogue. We can but hope.

Anyway, it seems some young people have been calling COVID-19 'boomer remover', in that it disproportionately kills those generations who are handing over a turd-shaped baton for them to run the next, accursed-looking, leg of the human race's relay. I think the phrase is probably borne of dark humour in that most young people will, in reality, be doing their utmost to avoid infecting the older generations, but nevertheless it's been quite entertaining to see how steamed up certain right-of-centre journalists of the Baby Boomer generation have become about it all. The same people who've previously told millennials to 'suck it up, snowflakes', and lamented their alleged lack of a backbone, are now falling apart when a joke is aimed back at them. 'Don't you have a sense of humour, Grandad?' seems like a harsh, but fair, retort as these grey elders, but not necessarily betters, scuttle off to a safe space to book a preferential Ocado delivery, all the while dreaming of the Blitz and rationing they never actually experienced, but love to bang on about. None of this applies to the older people in my family, by the way, but there are plenty of them out there.

That'll do for today. As I've been typing, the UK's daily death toll appears to have gone down, though that has happened after previous weekends and is probably misleading. The daily totals for Italy, Spain and France, all of whom are ahead of us on the curve do appear to have peaked in recent days, which suggests we're still not there yet. Unlike Denmark and Austria, two smaller and highly efficient EU countries whose overall death tolls are each just over 200, there is no concrete exit strategy in any of those larger countries, least of all here, but you have to gather hope where you can find it. 'We're carrying the fire,' as they say in *The Road*.

Tuesday, 7 April 2020

Boris Johnson caused me another sleepless night last night. He's caused many over the years, both among those who know him, but also in the last four years, to millions who don't. Whatever you think of him – and you know what I think – the news that he's now been taken into intensive care at St Thomas' is deeply unsettling and destabilising for an already battered nation.

As I outlined yesterday, his stand-in is not a widely admired figure, and doesn't have any of the Johnson exuberance, which I have to admit means that even the apolitical out there know who their figurehead is. My friend Philip and I always loved the *Larry Sanders Show* in which Garry Shandling played the eponymous talk show host and Jeffrey Tambor his talentless and charisma-free sidekick, Hank Kingsley. In one episode, which Philp reminded me of last night, Larry is laid low with a bug and his producer Artie (Rip Torn) and he are working through their list of potential stand-ins, keeping in touch by phone. A few hours and various mishaps later, Artie calls Larry and admits, 'We're off the list.' 'Not Hank?' says Larry. 'I'm afraid so,' says Artie and sure enough Hank leaps into the chair and is so terrible that they can't air the show he records. You may have worked out that in likening him to Hank, Philip and I are not exactly bursting with confidence in Mr Raab. As a nation we're going to have to air whatever happens next, too.

It's a strange feeling to see someone you've mocked and, frankly, disliked for decades in this predicament. No one in any of my groups is gloating, or citing it as karma or his own fault for not following the government's guidelines. I even took down the unflattering picture of Johnson we use as an ident for the Special Measures for Eton group and replaced it with an NHS rainbow.

I think what it boils down to is that those who habitually punch down are fair game in my eyes and those of most of my friends, but now that he's stricken like this and his pregnant partner is left in isolation, basic human sympathy – and indeed empathy – instantly kick in. He really is just one of us now, and who knows, may even remain that way if and when he recovers. I stand by everything I've said about him previously – he's damaged this country badly – but now he's fighting for his life in an ICU unit, he's in a category somewhere beyond the disabled reporter Trump mocked or that Scottish lady Raab ridiculed for her 'childish wish list'. You just don't go there.

We watched the main BBC bulletin last night, and Laura Kuenssberg got it all wrong as far as I'm concerned, I'm afraid. She absolved Johnson from any blame, and even said that when she interviewed him exactly a month ago, this was a 'hypothetical' situation on the far side of the world. It really wasn't – exactly a month ago yesterday, we were visiting Jake in Newcastle. Everyone who celebrated his birthday with him knew what was coming. Amanda and I even trawled Gosforth for hand sanitiser, and finding that all shops had already sold out, bought rubbing alcohol from a hardware store and aloe vera gel from Boots to make our own when we began our isolation back in London the day after we got back.

Even so, the intolerable personal abuse Laura K receives on Twitter will doubtless be ramped up tonight and so will be the battle between anyone posting #clapforboris (yes, that's apparently trending again) and those who will be mocking his predicament. I'm told Pep Guardiola was trolled relentlessly today after announcing that his mother had died from COVID-19. Though Twitter has its glorious moments, I'm really glad not to be on there any longer.

In recent years, online fraud, cyberbullying and bots pumping out sinister misinformation have taken the online world far away from the information superhighway Tim Berners-Lee and others envisaged. In this crisis, though, Twitter excepted, it really has come into its own. If you're going to be stuck indoors, there's so much more available to keep us all connected than during any previous national crisis. I'm old enough to remember the Three-Day Week of the early 1970s when industrial strife led to electricity being rationed, meaning no TV and having to read by candlelight some evenings. There was nothing like the current threat to our lives hanging over us back then, but it was bloody boring. If you go back to World War Two – one of my dad's first memories is seeing the County Durham fells lit up as the Luftwaffe bombed Teesside – there was fear, plus very little to do. If you have access to technology now, only the former can really be excused.

I watched a glorious living room set the other night from a band of Teesside siblings, Helen, Joe and Vinny Hammill, who call themselves Cattle and Cane. We've seen them play live in London before, but they still live together in Thornaby-on-Tees, so performed an hour of originals, covers and requests from their living room. Like the Everlys, Proclaimers, the Carter family and many more, harmonising seems to come naturally to a musical family, and Helen's glorious backing of Joe's rendition of the Kinks' 'Waterloo Sunset' was as good as the original in its own way. Many other musicians are staging similar performances, though usually solo, so I'll keep searching for them.

We're finding ourselves talking on a weekly basis to friends we normally only see three or four times a year. We're also doing three online quizzes this week – tomorrow's is with a group of local friends who we often meet in the Flask pub in Hampstead for their Tuesday quiz night. Tonight's quiz, though, sees the Curry/Poncey Horse Club convene virtually. Amanda and I were double-booked with our 'Fat Larry's Band' Zoom group on the night of the first one, which Mark my old school and Spurs mate won. He gets to set the questions tonight, and because Amanda and I have a bit of a reputation for having our heads stuffed with 'useless and pointless knowledge' – Bob Dylan, 'Tombstone Blues' – Mark is hinting at a cynical manipulation of the questions. He knows our weak areas – action films, Harry Potter, music of the 21st century, most science – so I'm fully expecting an absolute stitch-up. In fact, I'd expect no less. Dylan, by the way, completely contradicted that Gove-like anti-knowledge stance elsewhere on that same seminal *Highway 61 Revisited* album. On the epic track 'Desolation Row', he warns of the Superhuman Crew who 'go out and round up everyone who knows more than they do'. Which is it, Bob? Make your mind up.

Writing about Mark and Fat Larry's Band has taken me right back to the sixth form common room at Judd, the Kentish grammar school I'd joined from Teesside at the start of the fourth form. Radio 1 was always blasting out of the music centre before and between lessons, and that was the record they seemed to play most often in the autumn of 1982. We were all studying the subjects we'd chosen (I'd ditched all forms of science) and a handful of badly behaved, but often uproariously funny, lads had left after O levels, so the sixth form was altogether less anarchic and more mellow than the two previous years had been at times. By now, we'd evolved into three basic social strata, physically divided in our sixth form common room.

I've covered my football v rugby experience in *Why Are We Always On Last?* but the rugger-buggers were the patricians in this set-up, addressed by certain teachers by their Christian names while the rest still mostly got the surname treatment, even at 18. They went off to Canada or Japan on rugby tours in the holidays, too. Even so, the rest of us no longer had to play rugby, there were free periods built in and the lessons, especially the politics ones, in our chosen A level subjects had become far more relaxed and interesting than the starchy broader curriculum of my first two years there.

On the other side of the room from the rugger lot, was an odd bunch who seemingly included every 'junior Smithers' ever to appear on *Ask the Family*. Footnote: I've used the name largely because it fits with another Weller from Woking song in 'Smithers-Jones', but there was an actual Smithers in our school. He was nicknamed 'Runt' and was the go-between for my first fleeting female encounter in the south, with Paula from the Girls' Grammar who used to get the bus in with him from Tunbridge Wells every morning. He also laughed like a drain with me and David Eastwood when we all went to see *Airplane* at the cinema, so he must have been okay, even if the school thought he wasn't and booted him out after O levels. I never heard from, or of, him again until a few years ago when Mark Bright kindly invited me into the Selhurst Park boardroom for Boro's annual defeat away to Crystal Palace, and I got chatting to a couple from west Kent who turned out to have known some of the same people I did. They'd lost track of Runt a few years later than I had after he was found guilty of insurance fraud, having driven a succession of cars into a reservoir. That admittedly rather stylish denouement might have to form the basis of the first chapter of my lockdown novel in due course.

Where was I? Ah yes, the three sixth-form groups. Along with Mark and Jan of the Curry/Poncey Horse Club and a handful of others who I can now say with certainty in my mid-50s, will be friends for life, I was one of the inbetweeners. Just not like the ones in the C4 comedy in any way, shape or form. Oh no, definitely not. Well, maybe. I was Simon with a Teesside accent, by the way. We had no interest in rugby once we didn't have to play it, followed football instead, were never going to be prefects or sign up for the after-school and distinctly weird Army Cadet Corps (guess what one of the teachers in charge of that was jailed for a few years later) but we weren't *Ask the Family* contestants, either.

I had the advantage of having been shaped in a harsher northern environment where being reasonably clever had to be hidden by playing sport, being one of the class clowns, or both. Bob Mortimer's wonderful appearance on *Desert Island Discs* last year resonated enormously with me, and not just because we sometimes run into him at Boro games. Bob lives near Tunbridge Wells now, too, strangely enough. I had one of my last restaurant meals pre-lockdown on Leap Year Day, 29 February, with most of the common room inbetweeners gang and their wives at a bustling Turkish restaurant just up the road in Tonbridge, when Tony, who now lives with his young family in New Jersey, was in town. It seemed so normal then; God knows if or when we'll be able to do it again.

As a result of thinking about all of that, and because the Queen – who actually lived through World War Two and trained as a mechanic – brought it up in her address, I've been wandering around the flat today playing 'We'll Meet Again' on the ukulele.

It's sunny again, so Amanda has escaped to the patio. Admirable though Dame Vera Lynn was – and still is, aged 103 – my range is better suited to singing it with a jaunty growl like Johnny Cash did on his *American IV: The Man Comes Around.* Of course, Dame Vera's version also accompanied the nuclear holocaust at the end of Kubrick's *Dr Strangelove,* but that's not what Her Maj meant, so let's cling on to the more positive connotations right now.

Wednesday, 8 April 2020

Fool that I am, I went straight to the Sky News website on my iPad when I woke up this morning. At 12th position in their headlines was the first non-cataclysmic item: Peter Kay is returning to our TV screens after a long absence to take part in a coronavirus charity special. I can just picture it now: ''Erd immuniteh? 'erd immuniteh? What were that all about, eh?'

I turned to Sky hoping for something sensible after I made the terrible mistake of watching the BBC's *Ten O'Clock News,* then seeing the start of Sky's newspaper review last night. On a day when the 24-hour death toll in the UK reached its highest yet, at just under 800, all the scrutiny and difficult questions seem to have evaporated, because of Johnson Watch. I say I saw the BBC bulletin, I didn't last the whole half hour, the tone being not too far short of that I'd expect from a North Korean news programme if a Dear Leader was in hospital.

Laura Kuenssberg had upset a few of my friends by saying 'now we're in a real crisis' when Johnson was first hospitalised the other day (focused as she is on the politicians, she clearly didn't mean to suggest that 6,000 deaths isn't a real crisis) but she ended her report last night with a portentous line you might hear in a funeral address given by a close friend of the deceased:

'Boris Johnson, leader, partner and father.' To be fair, I've edited sports programmes in some worrying circumstances and you're better off erring towards excessive reverence rather than face accusations of being too flip.

The papers are much worse: *The Sun* has surpassed itself with a full front-page picture of Johnson clapping outside No 10 and the headline 'He stayed at work for you...now pray at home for him'. He's not religious, you're not religious, most of us aren't religious, you insincere, cloying, phone-hacking horrors. And he stayed at work long enough seemingly to delegate the whole thing to Dom, before they failed as a group to follow their own belated advice, hence many of the staff are now infected.

Clearly this is a very sombre moment for the country, and Keir Starmer has rightly suspended a Labour mayor who said Johnson deserves to be in intensive care. However, if anyone had been paying attention at yesterday's press conference, they'd have heard Chief Medical Officer, Chris Whitty, now mercifully back in post, admit that Germany is currently in a far better place overall than we are. Guess why? They've been conducting mass testing from the very start. Boris Johnson oversaw our government response, but the fact that he's been wounded in action shouldn't detract from our 6,000 dead.

I'm not cataloguing the rest of the papers other than to relate the heading to a *Telegraph* opinion piece: 'We need you, Boris. Your health is the health of the nation.' While this sounds for all the world like something the 1980s Romanian Communist Party newspaper *Scinteia* would have said about Nicolae Ceausescu, it was actually penned by regular *Telegraph* columnist Allison Pearson. Her transformation from erstwhile rational, balanced commentator to Glenda Slagg-style *Private Eye* self-parody is a mystery on a par with Tony Blair's conversion to George W Bush's decision to topple the Iraqi regime after 9/11.

I met Allison Pearson at the France 98 World Cup when she came to Paris to interview Des Lynam. At that time, she was a witty TV reviewer for *The Independent* and the voice of sanity on BBC2's *Late Review* where she'd often be called upon to balance the more strident views of Tony Parsons and Tom Paulin. I have no idea what caused her to become a poster girl for Brexit and our PM, and regularly embroiled in social media tangles as she retweets the fringes of the internet. For example, she unquestioningly passed on a false claim that the photos of a child on the floor of a Leeds A&E ward which caused Johnson to put a reporter's mobile phone in his pocket in November, were faked. It's depressing to see a once fine journalist whose work I enjoyed change to this extent.

While these overwrought reactions appear excessive, they do highlight a legitimate problem. Most of the media can't say it, but there is now a power vacuum at the heart of the government most of them told to us elect just four months ago. This is arguably the lowest calibre cabinet of all time – Margaret Thatcher, for example, despite her reputation, had the stomach for a debate, and always had some people of experience and stature in there with her: Douglas Hurd, Ken Clarke, Chris Patten, even Nigel Lawson. The various cabinet memoirs suggest that, while fearsome and headstrong, she could occasionally be persuaded to tone things down by forthright ministers: it was only towards the end, when she pushed through the hated Poll Tax, that she stopped listening to them at all. John Major, who served as her Foreign Secretary, then Chancellor and of whom I was emphatically not a fan when he succeeded her as Prime Minister, has looked like a relative titan when he's appeared on TV in recent times.

The current government revolves around Johnson as the figurehead and Cummings working alongside him and Gove centralising control in Number 10, planning prorogation and the like, as well as root and branch reform of the civil service, BBC and the courts. The cabinet was seemingly intended only to be an echo chamber, selected as it was from those who were prepared to stomach, and sign up to, a No Deal Brexit. Dominic Raab, who didn't even make a shortlist of five candidates to succeed May as Tory leader but had resigned from her cabinet in protest at her withdrawal agreement compromise, was straight in as holder of one of the three great offices of state and de facto deputy PM.

Raab doesn't look comfortable in the role, even when he reads out the day's death toll. I wasn't convinced by him two days ago when he said Johnson was 'running the country from his bed' and I'm not convinced now when he says the PM is 'in good spirits' in an ICU. Nobody is in 'good spirits' in intensive care, surely? I'm half expecting Raab to claim that the letter we've all received today from Downing Street was typed by Boris Johnson himself from his hospital bed. If so, to quote Frankie Boyle, we'll be 'picking it up with a couple of snooker cues, like a contestant on a Japanese game show.'

But where else do we turn? The remaining two senior positions are held by Rishi Sunak, seemingly the most able cabinet minister in much the same way as I'd be the most able centre-forward in a football team of five-year-olds, but he was only promoted this year. The Home Secretary, Priti Patel – Priti Vacant, as she's known on WhatsApp in these parts – was sacked as International Development Secretary in 2017 for conducting unauthorised talks with Netanyahu and his government, while supposedly on holiday in Israel. She's been rehabilitated as a Brexit and Johnson loyalist, and law and order hardliner, but it's noticeable that she hasn't been let loose in any of the daily press conferences thus far.

The other massive problem is that this country is horribly divided. Boris Johnson, by all accounts, likes to be liked: his second, successful, run to be Oxford Union president was marked by a change in style from entitled Etonian to blokeish friend to all, and he managed to get liberal London to elect him as mayor twice by appearing to be harmless and jovial. I didn't vote for him, or even like him, but as a figurehead, both he, and those who seemed to be doing the actual work around him, pretty much carried it off. Once he played 'eenie-meenie-miney-mo' and sent in the Leave version of his two *Telegraph* articles, though, he thereby abandoned all hope of at least half the country liking him.

By contrast, division and rancour seems to spur Cummings on, and he appears to delight in riling the establishment, lefties, liberals and anyone else who's stood in the path of Brexit and then this government. You can win elections and referenda like that, but when you need the whole nation to pull together in a crisis, you may have created a huge problem for yourself. WB Yeats wrote 'Things fall apart; the centre cannot hold,' in his poem *The Second Coming*, published 100 years ago this year. He could have been writing about Britain (or America) right now.

Nuance is pretty much dead: while vehemently opposing both the holding of the EU referendum and its outcome, I grudgingly came to think that a soft Brexit with as much freedom of movement and goods as could be salvaged was the best of a bad set of options. 'Citizens of Nowhere', 'Brexit means Brexit' and other May slogans, seemingly encouraged by Nick Timothy, her own version of Cummings, killed off all that. Even then, I couldn't wholeheartedly back a second referendum, not least because I would never have held the first, so I was marooned in that untenable, and rapidly disappearing, centre ground.

After his ordeal, I really hope Johnson returns a changed and chastened man, and in an ideal world, Cummings would just go back to the bunker on his dad's farm and self-educate himself to his heart's content. Again, though, that is too nuanced a position to be held in 2020. I can only imagine what Twitter was like last night: Leave.EU, still run by Arron Banks (even though he's taking a six-month break in New Zealand) and Andy Wigmore, his fellow 'Bad Boy of Brexit' and man who looks like Bryan Ferry's gran, took to social media yesterday to pump out #clapforboris, a nationwide event, they hoped, which was scheduled for 8pm last night. Many of my friends, while hoping that Johnson pulls through, were absolutely livid about this. The papers have found one photo of a small group of NHS workers with a 'get well soon, Boris' poster, but even the man himself wouldn't expect the same minute's applause we've willingly afforded to the whole of the nation's key workers.

So, I found myself, along with the WhatsApp group from all over the country, monitoring what happened at 8pm. Here in London, there was absolute silence interrupted only by birdsong. That was everyone's experience, it seems, from Newcastle to Cornwall. Stu in Hertfordshire reported a family three doors down coming out on to their drive, realising no one was joining them, then hastily pretending to adjust their car's roof rack. But then you read Nadine Dorries's claims that she was moved to tears by the massive ovation in her Northamptonshire village and (I'm exaggerating slightly here) cries of 'Gawd bless you, Boris. You're a proper gent who knows what's good for us little people, and no mistake'; or the *Daily Express* who've put that one small well-wishing NHS group on their cover and claimed the whole country came together in an 'emotional' tribute to the stricken Father of the Nation, and you start to bristle again. I've quietly thought it for a while, but while there's much to admire about many, many individuals who live here, collectively, we really have become quite a sad country.

The incredible thing about this crisis though, is how we seem able to compartmentalise the worst situation most of us have ever known, and behave entirely normally much of the time. I guess our bodies and minds need us to do that at a time of huge stress. So, some of the same guys who have been sharing apocalyptic thoughts and articles on WhatsApp logged on at 8.30pm – just as the clapping and cheering may have been dying down in Nadine Dorries's village – to take part in a quiz. Amanda and I didn't do particularly well – horribly exposed as we were on breeds of dog, ingredients of cocktails and the works of C.J. Sansom – but it was a really good effort from Mark, and indeed Jan, who used his upgraded business Zoom account to great effect. There were a few kids present, and most partners, so the language was toned down, but otherwise the ambience was much the same as it used to be in the Wembley curry house after Spurs games.

Everyone's also trading escapist material from YouTube. Ron Chak, responding to my reference to the isolated bass playing on

Abbey Road, sent me links to two more stonkers. Keith Moon's drum track on a live performance of 'Won't Get Fooled Again' and Marvin Gaye's a capella, or at least, backing-free 'Heard It Through the Grapevine' are something else. My guitar session today comprised a giant medley of Americana, from Smokey's 'Tracks of My Tears' to Green Day's 'Wake Me Up (When September Ends)' to 'The Weight' by The Band. Technically, a majority of that last seminal group were Canadian, but Levon Helm – and most of their collective inspiration – was as American as it gets. I felt the need to remind myself how great a contribution that country has made to the sum of global culture. We have a Prime Minister who's extremely unwell and therefore unable to run the country. The US has a president who is extremely unwell in a different way and therefore shouldn't be running his country.

Trump surpassed himself overnight: the *New York Times* have obtained memos he received in January and February containing clear warnings from his own scientists, so naturally he's deflected by blaming the WHO and threatening to withdraw US funding from them. The US has already gone rogue by impounding millions of medical items bound for better-organised Canada, so it may as well opt out from another symbol of a civilised world, as it has from climate change accords and most other global initiatives. The Mango Mussolini then somehow made the plight of our PM all about himself: he told his press conference that he'd spoken to 'all of Boris's doctors' and was sending some medicines from the 'geniuses' at the US pharmaceutical companies 'to London'. He claimed that the pharma companies speak a very difficult language, but that he, presumably as a 'stable genius', could understand it. I can vaguely remember an annoying kid called Steven Broadbent who came out with stuff like that at primary school, but for Christ's sake, this man is in charge of the country upon whose alleged beneficence a 'beautiful, yuge' trade deal, and with it, our whole Brexit strategy relies.

He clearly hasn't spoken to anyone at a rather busy St Thomas', the pharma companies have said they have nothing that's been tested to offer, and even if they did, why would it not be offered to American hospitals, too? There's even a suggestion from the *Huffington Post* that Trump has a financial stake in the company which makes the malaria medication he's been peddling spuriously, and furiously, to the horror of his non-snake oil salesman scientists. If and when Johnson pulls through, Trump is clearly going to try to claim the credit. Tragically, it might work come election day in Buttfuck, Alabama. Especially, if, as seems likely, postal votes continue to be repressed in many states.

The appalling spectacle of Democrats queueing in their masks at polling stations to vote in the Wisconsin primary today appears to be a portent of things to come. Bernie Sanders has today stood down his candidacy making a Biden v Trump head-to-head now an almost done deal. Joe's getting on a bit, but seems likeable and sane, so is already infinitely preferable to the current incumbent. He also doesn't come with the Clinton baggage of Hillary or the frightening 'socialist' tag of Bernie, who though he seems to have more about him than Corbyn, might prove equally unpalatable to floating voters.

The pandemic is still going to be around in the autumn, indeed the much-feared second wave could be hitting when (or should that be if) America goes to the polls in November. Republicans are generally wealthier and own cars to a greater extent than Democrats, so will be better equipped to turn out at the polls, especially when public transport is perceived as an existential danger. Black people, despite only forming 30 per cent of the city's population, have numbered over 70 per cent of the COVID-19 death toll so far in Chicago, a horrendous reflection on their generally more crowded living conditions and lack of access to proper medical care. But then Illinois is Obama country, so of no great consequence to the president or his cheerleaders at Fox News. The electoral college system and the already extant voter suppression also work in Trump's favour. With the dice loaded to such an extent, it's no great surprise that he's still the bookies' favourite to win the presidential election.

Where America will be in the world pecking order, and how many pandemic fatalities it will have chalked up after a second term of his lunacy, is anyone's guess.

We haven't been to the US since Trump came to power, but I've had several great road trips there in the past. In an attempt to cleanse myself from having focused on this (please God) temporary roadblock to American equality and sanity, I put on my Motown playlist for my (now 20km a session) bike ride. A strange thing happened while I was out there: two robins appeared together in the Japanese magnolia tree. This might explain why what I thought was just one sometimes hovers underneath the suet cake to peck, but at other times, lands adroitly on the mesh. As a voice from the stalls once shouted at the Glasgow Empire, when Bernie Winters goofily poked his head out of the curtains during Mike's opening song, 'Ach, no. There's two of the bastards.'

I thought only male robins have the red breast, but some background reading tells me that females have a slightly more camouflaged colouring but display the red, too. It almost certainly wasn't two males given how territorial and aggressive they can be. It seems that robins often pair up during the spring breeding season – the female mostly stays on the nest, hence the greater camouflage, but they will come out together to a food source. As I may have said before, you learn something new every day, especially when you're stuck at home. I just hope there's a garden birds round in our next quiz.

Thursday, 9 April 2020

'Are we nearly there yet?'

British journalism has largely been at its most pitiful since I last sat down at the keyboard. The 24-hour death toll announced for the UK yesterday was a terrifying 938, higher than the peak in Italy, and the second-highest tally in the world yesterday, behind only the far larger US. So, naturally, this morning's headlines all express astonishment that the lockdown will be extended and the pubs won't be open for Easter after all. They've parked the thoughts and prayers for the PM, after Number 10 said he's sitting up in bed. True or not, that's seen him shoot down the running order. Other than the BBC's *News at Six,* that is, which devoted its first 12 minutes yesterday to pointless, uninformed speculation about Johnson's health, then eventually moved on to the death toll. *News at Ten* was far more all-encompassing, to be fair. I still need to stop watching quite so much of either, though.

The excellent Emily Maitlis opened BBC Two's *Newsnight* with a superb monologue about how 'fortitude', 'strength' and other macho terms currently being ascribed to the Prime Minister are trite and irrelevant in the face of this virus, and how it emphatically is not a 'great leveller', poorly paid, undervalued health, transport and supermarket workers being far more at risk than the middle and upper classes who've largely retreated into their homes. I wish more than *Newsnight*'s tiny audience could have seen it, and that rather fewer had seen the BBC's chief political correspondent describe yesterday as a 'good day' on the *Six*, because the PM is reportedly a bit better. Never mind the equivalent of ten Hillsboroughs which happened in the UK that same 'good day'. The BBC is generally performing well, though – the announcement of a record level of transmission of educational programmes, including a dedicated TV channel, while schools and colleges remain closed, being yet more public service broadcasting of a kind that we won't be seeing any time soon from Netflix or Amazon.

Much of the news media seems to be wilfully thicker than some of the public, but if someone would just explain, using a simple graph, that we currently have the highest death rate per capita in the world, perhaps the journos might ask how the hell that happened instead of simply bleating 'just make it all go away'. But then no one on the government side is going to let that fact slip at one of those press conferences, Chris Whitty, the Chief Medical Officer, having been roundly contradicted by the politicians ever since his rueful aside that we could learn a lot from Germany. Our friend Lijana, who took part in one of our Zoom link-ups, is from New Zealand, and without saying too much about her adopted country (the UK) suggested it's worth watching how the Kiwi PM conducts her daily briefings. So I did.

Dear God, what an eye-opener. If the Commonwealth really is desperate to reconnect with its old imperial overlord, as the more deluded Brexiteers would have us believe, can we please pay whatever transfer fee it takes to bring Jacinda Arden over here? She's an absolute natural who first came to international attention early last year with her magnificent handling of the massacre at a Christchurch mosque. Having witnessed Theresa May's painfully stiff post-Grenfell awkwardness not long before, Jacinda's clear, empathetic and unifying response was remarkable to behold. I particularly admired her immediate decision never to refer to the gunman by name, and to ask the media to do likewise – even though I know he recently pleaded guilty, I have no idea what he's called, so the notoriety he craved has been denied him.

Yesterday's NZ press conference was natural and calm but completely honest, possibly borne of the fact that their PM knows she's done as well as she can for her electorate. Looking from afar at news from around the world, presumably New Zealanders know it, too. 'We go hard and we go early,' she said like an All Blacks coach just over a fortnight ago, announcing a lockdown at the same time as the UK's, but before her country had suffered a single death. They've now recorded 1,000 positive tests and just one death. She and her cabinet are discussing taking a pay cut, she said yesterday, and her Health Secretary was immediately demoted when he was found to have visited his holiday cottage. Direct comparisons with the UK are probably invidious – we're both island nations but they're far more remote than we are, and Auckland is the only city that we'd class as a conurbation – but even so, bravo, Jacinda.

Back here, I'm worried that the Easter weekend, sunshine and false hope of an easing of restrictions that our less bright citizens may have derived from their newspapers, could cause another outbreak of stupidity. A full-scale adult game of cricket was broken up by the police yesterday, not far from here, in Kensal Green. That's Kensal Green in Brent, the English borough with the highest proportion of confirmed COVID-19 cases to population. And just to compound the cringe factor for the Curry Club after Daniel Levy furloughed non-playing staff, Spurs manager Jose Mourinho faces a police caution for conducting individual training sessions with members of his squad in a public park. The Really Special One. I'd imagine Mourinho has a garden, and therefore no excuse, but the way most Londoners live is not conducive to dealing with a pandemic. Fifteen public transport workers have now died here – they're now planning only to open the middle doors of buses to minimise contact with drivers – but buses and the Tube were not designed with social distancing in mind.

Then there's our accommodation. Towards the end of Boro's 11 consecutive seasons in the Premier League, so around 2008 or 2009, Amanda and I were in the away end at the Emirates for the most routine, and frankly dull, of 2-0 defeats. With their team two down and creating very little, the second half became an opportunity for our fans to air some of the more unusual items in their repertoire. When this was pretty much exhausted, anti-London/Cockney songs and all, they began making them up. 'A million pounds, and you live in a flat' rang around a quiet stadium and actually got a few smiles and thumbs-up from the surrounding Arsenal fans. A minute or two later came the cruellest of blows: 'You'll never have a garden, you'll never have a garden.'

This went down very well with the Gooner friends who contacted me after the game, and Amanda and I laughed along bitterly, too. We'd paid a fraction of a million for our Bayswater flat some years earlier, but we certainly didn't have a garden.

We're incredibly lucky to have our patio, and a communal patch of lawn now, but we were both in our 50s by the time we achieved that London milestone. If outdoor exercise were to be banned here now as some non-Londoners have been demanding on Facebook, who knows what the cost would be in terms of mental health and strained, or possibly abusive, relationships. Another call I would not want to have to make if I was in government, especially with summer on the way.

So, what else is happening? Well, Julia Hartley-Brewer has come unstuck on Twitter. I didn't see it, but Jan posted it on the Poncey Horse WhatsApp forum – my favourite shock jock had issued a rather treacly, but nevertheless understandable, condemnation of anyone who was using Twitter to be mean about our stricken PM. Understandable, that is, until someone posted her own tweeted reaction to Fidel Castro's demise in 2016. 'Delighted to hear that Fidel Castro is dead,' she chirruped. I wasn't rude enough to her that day in Waitrose. On an infinitely more pleasant note, Dick Clement forwarded an e-mail from Jeff Lynne, to whom he'd passed on this diary. Words like 'excellent' and 'clever', and a request to pass on his thanks, have left me genuinely chuffed and further inspired to carry on spending my mornings doing this. I haven't got anywhere else to be, in any case, but Jeff knows about these things, even if 'The Diary of Horace Wimp' isn't quite 'Telephone Line'.

Another welcome e-mail was from my old boss Niall. We're both great admirers of Randy Newman, who we saw live at the Royal Festival Hall a while back, and Niall forwarded Randy's delightful new lockdown song entitled 'Stay Away From Me', or possibly, 'Don't Touch Your Face'. I was very sorry to read of the coronavirus-related death of another fine American singer-songwriter, John Prine. Both his cover of Chuck Berry's 'You Never Can Tell', and his own superb compositions 'Angel From Montgomery' and 'Sam Stone', have featured on my Spotify sessions in the last few days. The latter contains some of the greatest lyrics I've ever heard – 'Sweet songs never last long on broken radios,' for example. And Alan Merrill, the man who co-wrote one of the first songs I ever learnt on the guitar, Joan Jett's 'I Love Rock and Roll', has also died of COVID-19.

The morning has nearly gone and I want to catch the sun while it's still shining on our patio table, so I'll sign off with a handy guide to freelancing from home. My ex-BBC colleague Michael left when the sports department moved to Salford, and has seen his once busy 2020 schedule, including the Invictus Games and Tokyo Olympics and Paralympics, evaporate in recent weeks.

Nine crucial steps to effective working from home:

1. Late breakfast
2. *Homes Under the Hammer*
3. Snooze
4. Check the www for funny gifs and circulate
5. Lunch
6. Snooze (duration normally dependent on what sport's on the box, so this may need some alteration)
7. Sort out any personal jobs that need doing
8. *Pointless*
9. E-mail/text client, 'Made some good progress today. Should have something to show you in a day or two.'

Good Friday, 10 April 2020

I was always much better at exams than course work, so ought to be thankful that I wasn't due to sit my A levels this year, rather than in 1983. My exam technique, such as it was, involved spending the first five minutes of answering an essay question writing down some key words and vaguely linking them in a structure. The rally driver-producers who sat next to me in TV galleries may have noticed something similar scribbled on a piece of paper, sometimes with approximate timings attached, as I attempted to navigate them, an on-screen team and the viewers through a live broadcast. I'm now writing these entries every morning, but there is a piece of paper next to the laptop on which I scribble the odd word the previous evening. Last night's handover note has a single word at the top of it, 'Resurrection'.

I've glanced at the newspaper front pages on Sky News's website and *The Sun* have done the job for me. 'BORIS IS OUT. Now that really IS a Good Friday!' Accompanied by a massive picture of him taking part in a previous Thursday's applause for the key workers. There's only room for one paragraph of text in the corner to tell us that our risen Etonian Lord and Saviour is in 'extremely good spirits' – the 'extremely' moves him up a whole notch from the merely 'good spirits' he was in, prior to rising from his intensive care unit.

No room to mention that 900 other Brits – it will have been more, only hospital deaths are appearing in the official figures – weren't so lucky yesterday. Among that 900 was Dr Abdul Chowdhury, who wrote an open letter to the Prime Minister three weeks ago asking him 'urgently' to ensure PPE for 'each and every NHS worker'. Tragically, he passed away with COVID-19 in an Essex hospital yesterday. Amanda heard Dr Chowdhury's son interviewed by Martha Kearney on R4's *Today* programme this morning. His composure and pride in his father, as a fine human being who had also set up a charitable institute in Bangladesh, had made Amanda quite emotional, even as she related it to me.

I am glad that Johnson appears to be out of danger – not least because his absence is shining a very harsh light on the vacuum at the centre of his cabinet – but I'd like, perhaps unrealistically, to hear no more about the 'strength' and 'fight' he's shown. That implies that a fine man like Dr Chowdury was somehow weaker. Who survives this virus and who doesn't is pure biological chance, as Emily Maitlis pointed out, only the truly ignorant Trumps and Bolsonaros of this world would see it otherwise.

From the ignorant to the absolutely nuts: early in my BBC Sport career I worked on quite a lot of snooker. The number two presenter to the amiable veteran David Vine was the slightly strange ex-Coventry City goalkeeper, David Icke. He'd eat his own prepared food while the rest of us tucked into sausage sandwiches, he never socialised, but was a perfectly capable anchorman, so we thought little more of it. Not very long afterwards he reinvented himself as a fully bizarre guru in a tracksuit who made an even more excruciating *Wogan* appearance than had the monosyllabic Anne Bancroft. Mrs Robinson was clearly riled by something so refused to co-operate, whereas Icke simply wouldn't shut up about a world run by conspiring lizard kings and the like.

It was genuinely sad to see what had happened to him, but nearly 30 years later, he's back with a vengeance spearheading an online campaign which is linking the coronavirus with the installation of the 5G (fifth generation) wireless network. Other than a mutual connection with China, there is no substance whatsoever to this flat-earther, 'Moon landings were faked' tosh. But somehow the simple-minded section of society now seems to have found a simple answer to a complex problem, and masts are being torn down and telecoms engineers attacked. Ofcom are currently investigating how an incendiary interview with Icke came to be broadcast on the London Live channel the other day, and YouTube have now taken it down. People have always fallen for nonsense, though: that was the central theme of one of our A level English texts, the 14th-century *Pardoner's Tale* by Geoffrey Chaucer, but it's been encouraged at the upper levels of certain governments in the 21st century by outbursts like, 'We've had enough of experts.'

I suspect Michael Gove will currently simply have 'had enough' of being at home. And not just because that means 24 hours a day spent with Sarah Vine. A family member – presumably one of his kids – showing symptoms and forcing him to self-isolate is another almost Shakespearean moment.

Gove is unable to put the teachings of Machiavelli into practice at a time when, in the absence of Johnson and Cummings, he could have been running absolute riot in there. He's only fourth in the recently announced succession list – Raab, Sunak and (God help us) Patel – all are nominally ahead of him, but a quick 'screw thy courage to the sticking place' from Lady MacGove, and some sly knife-wielding and coughing, could have seen his 'vaulting ambition' rewarded with the ultimate prize.

Meanwhile, across the Atlantic, the greatest trasher of experts of them all is still talking utter nonsense from the bridge of the Titanic. When there were 15 cases in the US, he said there'd soon be none and cried 'flu' and 'Democrat hoax'. Now there have been more than 16,000 deaths and still the drivel pours out of that tangerine face. There are various versions of this circulating, but it's been a short trip from 'the iceberg is a hoax' via 'nobody could have foreseen that Chinese iceberg' to 'I'm the greatest captain who's ever lived'.

Dick Clement, over there in LA, try as he might, is unable to prevent himself from collaborating and improving other people's tragicomic efforts, and has just sent me one of the greatest rants I've ever read. Until now, I knew little about Tommy Lee other than that he's in Motley Crue and was also in that video with Pamela Anderson. His open letter to the president has instantly elevated him to Larry David or Marina Hyde status. It begins, 'Dear Fucking Lunatic, In your recent press conference – more a word salad that had a stroke and fell downstairs …' and carries on in that vein for hundreds of words of beautiful-chosen insults and ends shortly after: 'You are a disgraceful, pustulant hot stew full of casuistry, godawful ideas, unintelligible non-sequiturs, and malignant rage. You are the perfect circus orangutan diaper.' I'm not sure I've ever given an open letter a standing ovation before, and I may not have done it full justice with those short extracts, but I can see why Pammie was attracted to the guy now. Too many tattoos or not, he's a lot more appealing than her last known crush, Julian Assange.

It's a beautiful day, with more sunshine in store for the whole Easter weekend. Please, please, everyone, don't go out and about and make this thing even worse than it is already.

Boro have just sent out their 'on this day' clip. Twenty years ago today I was at the Riverside – I must have been excused *MOTD* duties – to watch Middlesbrough 3 Manchester United 4. If you can have an enjoyable defeat, that was up there with any. United won the Premier League by 18 points that season, but Juninho and co. gave them a proper game, as they usually did back then. Paul Scholes scored one of two almost identically preposterous volleys that I saw him execute in the flesh – from outside the box when a corner was slung back to him. The other was at Villa Park, and he did it another time at Bradford when I wasn't there, as well as, I'm guessing, every day in training. Other than the fact that he couldn't tackle without conceding a free kick, Scholes was my favourite of that United team. You could watch him for 90 minutes and he would never misplace any pass, long or short. As the great Spaniard Xavi said of him, any other national team would have been built around a talent like that.

And Martijn, our Dutch neighbour, has just left us a chocolate Easter egg on our window ledge. We were supposed to be going to Amanda's sister for an extended family gathering – the first since her mum's funeral – but that small gesture of kindness will help to see us through yet another strange and secluded weekend.

WEEK FIVE

Easter Saturday, 11 April 2020

Week five of no one knows how many, least of all the UK government. I've just had a look at the word count for this, and it's passed the 75,000 mark. If I remember correctly, that's about the number I was asked to write, and delivered, for *Why Are We Always On Last?* which begs the question of how that took me far longer than a month to write. I guess the journal format means you don't take days off, plus there's a decade's worth of news per day right now.

Moreover, both the publishers and I knew I had a largely untold story to tell as the long-standing editor of *MOTD*, one which would attract at least a niche readership and get some media coverage. Gary Lineker writing the foreword and coming to the launch with the front line *MOTD* commentators, didn't hurt either. I don't suppose Adrian Chiles is going to give me half an hour of 5 Live airtime, nor will Alyson Rudd run a feature in *The Times* for these reflections on a nightmare we'll all, if we're lucky, have lived through. But it's giving me a structure to my mornings, and sparing Amanda at least some of my rants, so on I plod.

There was a sad inevitability to yesterday's news and coverage. Some 980 deaths were registered in UK hospitals, higher than any single day's toll in either Italy or Spain, despite our fortnight and eight days' extra notice respectively. The really appalling statistic for me was that of the similar-sounding 987 deaths in France yesterday, 554 were in hospital and 433 in care homes or people's own homes. We're simply not registering the latter – and we know anecdotally of people's parents in care homes through which COVID-19 has swept – so our real daily death toll is clearly well into four figures and therefore only behind the US in the entire world, with the peak apparently at least a few days away.

But never mind all that, Boris Johnson apparently watched *Lord of the Rings* and did a Sudoku in his hospital bed yesterday. What's more, he walked. Yes, he took his first steps, and naturally, like proud parents boring everyone on Facebook with the progress of their sprogs, the media relegated all other lesser, gloomier headlines and focused on our Easter miracle. Sadly, Laura Kuenssberg didn't pose the BBC's question at the press conference yesterday, so we've haven't yet found out whether or not the walk in question took place on the Thames, or merely in the hospital ward.

The Poncey Horse pre-quiz chat last night also demanded that I have a word with my ex-BBC colleagues to tell them that Stanley Johnson's relief at his son leaving the ICU shouldn't have been the main headline on every 5 Live bulletin all day. I never did have any sway with BBC News, but I thought I'd find out what was upsetting my pals, especially Tall Paul. Stanley apparently managed to pass himself off as an agreeable and harmless old duffer, when he enhanced his eldest son's 'one of the lads' reputation with his appearance on *I'm a Celebrity*. I didn't see any of it since I hold those 'voting people off' programmes responsible for a fair proportion of our current troubles. President Trump was only made possible by selective editing of *The Apprentice*, while a true great like Lincoln or Attlee would have been voted straight off every one of those shows – 'Gettysburg address? Cradle to grave? No piercings or bantz? Didn't try to shag the Made in Essex girl? Boorring.'

Worst of all, we had to endure Simon sodding Cowell on the front page of *The Sun* on election day in 2015, ordering us to vote for Cameron and avoid a 'coalition of chaos' under Ed Miliband. And the man in the street duly did as a man whose waistband is also his collar told them. That turned out well, didn't it? I've just had a quick look at Cowell's Wikipedia entry to try to work out how his arbitrary thumbs up or down saw him promoted to the Julius Caesar figure de nos jours. He's listed simply as a 'television personality', he passed two O levels at his independent school, Daddy was an executive at EMI, got him a job in the post room, and … frankly, I can't read any more. Suffice to say, Bob's your uncle, or maybe Stanley's your father.

Anyway, the 'Father of the Prime Minister', though never previously an official title to the best of my knowledge, has in the last few months filled the gap in the market left by the late Queen Mother, as the media's cuddly elderly ceremonial grandparent to the nation. Unlike the Queen Mum, who at least never expressed an opinion in public, you can't shut Stanley up. Last month, he was telling everyone who'd listen that he fully intended to go to the pub on the very evening his son finally got round to calling last orders, having previously said Boris's 'letterbox' comments about Muslim women 'didn't go far enough'. Unlike his other children, Stanley is a (belated) convert to Boris's Brexit, although he intends to take up French citizenship having been born there. He also has a novel solution to the Irish border conundrum: 'If the Irish want to shoot each other, they'll shoot each other.' Thanks, Stanley, we'll give that a go.

I guess whatever he'd said yesterday had to be cut a little slack, given that he's a parent whose son has just come out of intensive care, but frankly 'he took one for the team' is a complete misuse of a sporting metaphor. You 'take one for the team' if you fling yourself into a potentially injurious tackle or trip a goalbound opponent, accepting a yellow or red card in order to prevent your team from conceding. Boris Johnson has helped absolutely no one by failing to follow his own social distancing advice; indeed he's been part of a top-level cross-infection spree which has bewildered the rest of the world. Along with our appalling overall infection and death statistics, he has thereby removed any last scintilla of belief anywhere on the planet that the British have a clue what they're doing.

Even Isabel Oakeshott – author of the Farage/Banks hagiography, *Bad Boys of Brexit*, and current squeeze of Brexit Party chairman Richard Tice – is now saying that COVID-19 has changed everything and the transition period must be extended, but the mob in nominal charge are seemingly too paralysed by dogma to do so. They do have a real problem in that the only people who somehow think they're handling this crisis well will almost certainly be the same people who think Brexit must still happen on 31 December: *Sun* and *Express* readers, hedge fund managers, and er, that's about it, surely? Much of the rest of the country is already on to them, so four and a half more years in charge, even with a majority of 80, having in due course alienated and angered pretty much everyone – and created another dimension of seismic hardship with the supply shortages inherent in a No Deal crash-out – is not an appetising prospect for anyone with a functioning mind. And most of the herd will never be able to separate the Brexit chaos from the coronavirus chaos, so in for a penny, and all that.

And breathe. I might just go and do a mindfulness session after that. You might like to do the same if you've just read this entry. Afterwards, I'll have a light lunch with Amanda on the patio, sit in the sun (it's now shorts weather) with my new book, then do my exercises. I've discovered that Bob Mortimer and Andy Dawson are still recording *Athletico Mince* remotely. They're 35 minutes per podcast, which is pretty much how long I now take to do 20km on the exercise bike. Then we have another Zoom quiz with a different group of friends later on, and have now taken to watching *Peep Show* in bed before lights out.

Niall very generously called this diary 'Pepys Show' which reminded me of Mitchell and Webb's sordid but very funny *Odd Couple* for the 21st century. We've discovered that neither of us seems to have seen – or at least, remembered, much of series three, so that's this week's TV comedy sorted. It's strange to see the now Oscar-winning national treasure, Olivia Colman, playing David Mitchell's love interest. We've met the guy who directed the first series, and allegedly, David would have liked the on-screen relationship to spill over into real life, but, alas, Olivia saw it differently. Still, he's punching above his weight now with the *Only Connect* host and poker millionaire, so it's all ended well enough. We saw him and Victoria at the carol service at the church five doors down from us, so they must live somewhere not too far away.

The new book is *One Two Three Four: The Beatles in Time* by Craig Brown. He's the guy who writes *Private Eye*'s coruscating and extremely clever diaries, so it won't just be all the usual well-established facts. The title is a reference to Paul's shouted intro to 'I Saw Her Standing There', the first song on that first album they recorded in a day – 'Twist and Shout' sounds the way it does because it had to be recorded in one take, before John Lennon's voice completely packed up. The happiest of musical accidents.

Craig Brown also wrote *One on One,* a criminally unheralded daisy-chain of well-known people's documented encounters with each other in 101 separate, but linked, chapters. So, James Joyce meets Marcel Proust, or Ted Heath meets Terence Stamp meets Sarah Miles meets Bertrand Russell meets Lord John Russell meets Napoleon. Or, for that matter, Harry Houdini meets Tsar Nicholas meets Rasputin meets his assassin Felix Youssoupoff meets Noel Coward meets Paul McCartney. There are also 1,001 words in each chapter – not a restriction I'd like to place on myself, nor would I have fancied all the research – but bloody clever nevertheless. I can't recommend it highly enough. I hope the Beatles book is half as good, and at the very least, it will transport me to another time and place for the afternoon.

Easter Sunday, 12 April 2020

This is the morning I fully intended to walk the mile or so down to St John's Wood to watch the first gentle knockings of the cricket season. Middlesex v Worcestershire, maybe a thousand people in the ground at most, and perhaps watch a bit of Sky's live football too, in the bar high up above the immaculate green turf of my favourite sporting venue. This crossover period where the end of the football season meets the county championship – the hit and giggle T20 stuff being saved for high summer – is my favourite sporting time of the year, and the glorious weather today is taunting me as it signposts the alternative universe we could have been experiencing.

I'm a member at Surrey, too, which is also wonderful in a different way – unlike Lords, there's no dress code in the pavilion at The Oval, so you can wear shorts and a T-shirt as you sit up in the top tier and soak up the magnificent view of the city skyline. Among the many artefacts on display is a lovely tribute to Don Bradman's final Test innings in which he walked out of the now renamed Bradman door, needing to score four for a career Test average of 100. Sadly, he returned through the same doors shortly afterwards, bowled for a duck with an all-time Test average of 99.94. As a kid, I used to wonder why Australia didn't just pick him for a dead rubber at some later point and get the opposition to bowl him an underarm dolly drop, post his four, then walk off, bat aloft. I guess I didn't fully understand the nature of professional sport, especially Australian cricket.

There's also a poignant poem framed on the wall by the stairwell in the Oval pavilion about the aching longing for cricket to resume during World War Two. It'll be doubly poignant the next time I read it. The Oval was requisitioned for use as a prisoner-of-war camp back then, though it just stood empty until 1945. Lords was spared such a fate and staged exhibition matches to try to boost morale. Since I packed up regular work, I've spent a lot of time at both venues: I take in the odd Test day, and last year's World Cup final went straight into the top five sporting events I've ever attended. I have to say, though, that I've reached the age where I particularly enjoy the slow, quiet county days where there's no queue at the bar and you can take a stroll on the outfield between sessions – 'We invite you to perambulate during the luncheon interval' as they say quaintly over the PA at Lord's.

Surrey have actually been much the flasher of the two London teams in recent years: they buy up everyone else's best players and have a huge coaching entourage, because they only pay a peppercorn rent, have exclusive use of their own ground and take all the revenue from Oval Tests and t20 internationals.

Middlesex are tenants of Marylebone Cricket Club and will find themselves banished to Uxbridge or Radlett if there's a diary clash with, say, Eton v Harrow.

I'd say I now support Middlesex, even though I first watched cricket at Middlesbrough, then Scarborough. I've watched players like Eoin Morgan and Steven Finn progress from county debut to England ranks, and they remain remarkably grounded and accessible, as does their county boss Gus Fraser. They've all been on the phone in the last week to any members who want a chat – the grey pound keeps county cricket going – but more than that they're unstarry, good people. Finny and his partner regularly drove food delivery vans around London for the homelessness charity, Felix, with whom Middlesex have a partnership, long before the current crisis.

Unlike Boro, with whom I stuck, I realised fairly quickly that the Yorkshire set-up I'd first watched on our then home patch was grim and political: most of the intrigue was centred around the contentious figure, but decent run accumulator and later broadcaster, that was and is Geoffrey Boycott, but the opposing faction seemed equally unsavoury. I'll never forget Brian Close being asked in the 1980s, when he was chairman of the Yorkshire cricket committee, why the county hadn't tapped into the considerable talent in the Asian leagues of Bradford and Leeds. 'I don't ask to play for Karachi,' was the terse response.

Yorkshire cricket is unrecognisable now: hiring Sachin Tendulkar as their first non-Yorkshire-born pro was the equivalent of Rangers manager Graeme Souness signing the Catholic Mo Johnston, but I was still supporting Middlesex against Yorkshire on that incredible final County Championship afternoon in 2016, where the two teams contrived a winner takes all finish to the season. Another player I've followed from county to Test debut, Toby Roland-Jones, clinched the title and a hat-trick by clean bowling Ryan Sidebottom behind his legs with the last ball of the season. A cricketing Boro v Steaua moment: like

Boro, Middlesex have gone into this enforced hiatus languishing in the County Championship's Second Division, but it's the inevitable downs which make the sporting ups moments to be treasured.

So, in the absence of any live sport, what have we been doing? Yesterday teatime, I was indoors enjoying Craig Brown's tales of an early Beatles tour compered by the Irish comedian Dave Allen, and Amanda was engrossed in the closing stages of Hilary Mantel out on the bench, when a commotion erupted. Anthony and Louisa came tearing down the path from the communal lawn, clutching exercise mats in a passable impression of a beach scene from *Jaws.* There was no soundtrack music, though – just a volley of barking coughs reminiscent of a sea lion's mating call. It appeared to be coming from next door, to our left as we look out over our patio. Our neighbour Elaine had told us earlier in the day that Gareth next door's father had been in and out of the Royal Free Hospital this week for a suspected gastroenteritis condition, but that they were now both ill. Worrying enough already, from this building's point of view, given that Gareth and Elaine had enjoyed (socially distanced) lemon drizzle cake and tea in our communal garden last weekend.

Whether this new and horrendous-sounding coughing fit was connected to Gareth or his dad we can't say, but it was genuinely terrifying. We couldn't even say for certain whether it was coming from the garden or through an open window, but such is the confused information about the virus, everyone just ran for it. Is he covering his mouth? How far can a cough travel? Two metres, you'd presume from the social distancing policy, but I'd seen a computer simulation made by a Finnish research team showing the virus being dispersed by a cough in a supermarket over the shelves and down into the next aisle. But then, that's indoors, so who knows? We now have a situation most Brits would dread, not so much that we could die while obeying all the guidelines, though that's clearly not good, but what the hell do we say if it happens again? We have enough trouble in restaurants sending back food that isn't hot enough, so trying to shout over a fence that someone who's probably seriously ill should keep it to themselves isn't really in our DNA.

The confusion in the upper echelons of government continues apace. Priti Patel's absence from the briefings having become something of a national joke, they actually sent her out to face questions yesterday. She apologised if anyone 'feels' they don't have enough PPE – 'feelings' don't really come into it, the bald fact is that the three nurses all pictured wearing improvised bin bags some time ago have now tested positive for the virus. Then Priti tried to read out the latest testing figures. This is exactly what she said: 'Three hundred thousand, thirty four, nine hundred and seventy four thousand' have apparently been carried out so far. Unlike Diane Abbott and her mangled police figures, that doesn't make any of today's front pages. Meanwhile, in Washington, Donald Trump has been marvelling at the 'clever' virus which doesn't even respond to antibiotics. That'll be because antibiotics kill bacteria, not viruses, as anyone who's ever troubled a doctor with a cold or flu could tell you, Donnie boy.

The rest of it is unfolding, or unravelling, on a path which has been obvious for weeks. I'm sure everyone who's been screaming about it wishes they'd been shown up for being too pessimistic, but sadly, we weren't. We may well become the third country, after the US and France, to pass the 1,000-deaths-in-a-day mark shortly, and clearly already would have done so if deaths at home or in care homes weren't being omitted. Johnson has let it be known that he owes his life to the team at St Thomas'. That team was led by an Italian, incidentally; he presumably earns more than £25,600 a year, so might graciously be allowed to stay in the UK under the pretty much unaltered Immigration Act Ms Patel has sneaked out in the last couple of days. Other members of his team will seemingly be sent packing as soon as this pandemic is over. I fear that the 80 Tory majority, composed as it is now largely is of truly appalling people, is more likely to rebel if Brexit looks like being delayed than they are to stop the 'unskilled' troops of the NHS from being deported.

Meanwhile, following three more deaths of its members overnight, the Royal College of Nursing has told its members to go against every single instinct they possess and refuse to work if they're inadequately protected. Johnson has never been big on using protection, but this is heading for a dreadful, deadly stand-off. You'd assume the public would back their nurses since they've been out applauding them every Thursday evening, but the Tories still enjoy (if that's the right word) an utterly inexplicable 17 per cent lead in the opinion polls, so maybe not. Given that Greater Manchester Police have reported having to break up 500 house parties in four days, I really couldn't begin to tell you what the Great British public thinks any more, other than 'not much' in some cases.

I'm going to end on a happier note. One of my regular readers, Michael – with whom we have a Zoom link-up booked in for tomorrow – picked up on my Mike and Bernie Winters anecdote, and implored me to pass on the other classic Glasgow Empire story our old BBC colleague (and Clare Grogan's cousin) Steve McBride used to relate, so here goes. The rather flowery English singer, Dorothy Squires, was struggling with the legendary Saturday night Glaswegian audience. She paused between songs and amidst the cacophony of catcalls, one particularly loud voice cut through: 'Ach, c'mon. G'ie the old cunt a chance.' Dorothy nodded in the direction of this bellow, and said, 'Thank you, sir. I'm pleased to see there's at least one gentleman in the house.'

Easter Monday, April 13 2020

There's an unusual backdrop to this morning's diary, as Amanda is using my iPhone to have an 8am WhatsApp gathering with her friends Lynn and Vicki. I'm sitting here with my coffee, the last of my bananas, and a rather gritty cacao and hazelnut porridge pot that I clearly bought by mistake when I last dashed around Waitrose. Not recommended. The reason for the early morning pow-wow is that, while Lynn is down in Hove, Vicki lives in lovely Arrowtown on the South Island of New Zealand. We were there ourselves last April as part of a two-month break which took in the South Pacific and ended with three weeks in Java, Borneo and Bali. Thank God we did that in 2019, not 2020.

New Zealand has hit the headlines here overnight, and not because our media is comparing their two deaths so far with our 10,000 plus many more in care homes. No one is going there, especially since we had our Easter Sunday moment yesterday when Boris Johnson left hospital. Some of my more cynical friends – oh, all right, me, too – are struggling not to see the 'Good Friday at death's door, Easter Sunday resurrection' narrative as slightly, shall we say, contrived. Classic Dom has disappeared so it's more likely to have been Isaac Levido's doing. Even fewer people know who he is than are aware of Dom's malign influence, but he's the Australian 'election guru' (and pupil of the infamous dark arts practitioner Lynton Crosby) who is credited with both Scott Morrison's election win in Australia and the Tory strategy – which seemed to amount to little more than, 'Just say "Get Brexit Done" a lot and keep reminding them that you're not Corbyn,' – in December 2019. Cummings and Johnson rehired him about a fortnight ago when they realised everything was going to shit. The death toll was starting to spiral out of control, so rather than try to do anything about that, some Shane Warne-style spin was their top priority.

The New Zealand connection was in Johnson's speech, made yesterday in the suit, shirt and tie he'd somehow acquired between leaving St Thomas' and arriving at Chequers. If you didn't know who he was or anything about his history, the PM gave a fine and humble address, saying he owed his life to the NHS, and singling out Luis from Portugal and Jenny from New Zealand, the specialist ICU nurses who'd watched over him non-stop for 48 hours. Quite right, too, and it will be interesting to see whether this new Johnson will last. If he amends Priti Patel's legislation of four days ago which brands Luis and Jenny as 'low-skilled', and therefore not welcome here in future despite the 100,000 shortfall in NHS staff, or if he delays the Brexit which will have had Luis sweating on his settled status application in between saving British lives, maybe I'll believe the transformation is for real.

Former Tory MP and *Telegraph* journalist Paul Goodman described yesterday how Johnson 'always seemed to regard being ill as some form of moral weakness'; his biographer Andrew Gimson said, 'Boris never used to believe in illness.' At least that brainless macho outlook, doubtless passed on by his father and noisily shared by other 'alpha male' horrors like Trump and Bolsanaro, may have been tempered in recent days.

Johnson is the same age as me, so the sad news of the death of Tim Brooke-Taylor from COVID-19 should also have given him pause for thought, assuming he ever watched *The Goodies* or listened to *Sorry I Haven't a Clue* during his formative years. Two great sportsmen, Stirling Moss and Peter Bonetti, also left us yesterday, but both had seemingly been ill for some time. Our national COVID-19 death toll yesterday was again only behind the US on the entire planet, and was 20 times that of Germany. Professor John Ashton, a former Director of Public Health, said on TV yesterday that our actual death toll could be twice the official 10,000 if deaths in care homes, or at home, were correlated, as they are in other countries. Johnson will now recuperate for a while; he'll need to have to have dreamt up some pretty amazing excuses by the time he returns to his post.

Now that he's out of danger, his 3 March appearance with Phil and Holly on *This Morning* is doing the rounds again on Facebook. It was less an interview, more of a fluffing, but because he was relaxed and not being challenged, Johnson said a few things he's going to struggle to unsay, if anyone brings them up on his return. He may have changed his tune ten days later, but 'we're just going to have to take this on the chin' and avoiding 'draconian measures' such as banning mass gatherings, sounded for all the world like pure herd immunity theory.

He also told a press conference with a smirk that he'd visited an ICU and 'you'll be pleased to hear I shook hands with everybody' at about that time. He practised what he preached by attending the England v Wales rugby match with his pregnant fiancée on 7 March – both of them very pointedly shook hands with those around them in an 80,000 crowd. The Cheltenham Festival organisers are now using this recklessness as their excuse for going ahead with their own high-risk event the following week.

It was only when the coach of Arsenal, Mikel Arteta, tested positive on Thursday, 12 March, and the Premier League cancelled the following weekend's games, that Johnson and Cummings appeared to wake up. The countries who locked down days before that – Ireland and Denmark, for example – now have death rates in the low hundreds. We'll never know for certain, but Arteta's diagnosis may have prevented a world war-level death toll in the UK, rather than what merely looks like it will turn out to be the worst in Europe. The PM finally announced that the pubs would shut, despite the objections of Tim Martin and Stanley Johnson, and the distinct impression he gave was that this went against every fibre of his libertarian being. He generously allowed everyone time for one final giant piss-up and cross-infection session, on Friday, 20 March. This was close to eight weeks after the direct warning of a pandemic in *The Lancet,* and seems to have coincided with the release of the Imperial College data which finally persuaded Cummings that a gigantic bollock had been dropped. It's difficult to see how the new, improved Johnson would be able to work once more with the 'weirdo and misfit' who, according to *The Sunday Times,* had said 'if some pensioners die, too bad'. Time will tell.

Meanwhile, the man who brought Cummings into public consciousness, Michael Gove, has continued to take his own unique approach to life. Last heard of going into isolation a few days ago – supposedly for 14 days, because a family member had symptoms – he's been photographed jogging around a park near his home. Gove has therefore been forced to reveal that Chris Whitty gave special permission for his daughter to be tested. Quite what the front-line health and care workers who haven't been tested yet make of that is anyone's guess.

A truly beautiful afternoon here yesterday, with both of us on the patio reading our books in warm sunshine, was once more disturbed by horrendous coughing from next door to our left. I was out there when it started this time, and could tell it was coming from outdoors, and from not far away. Other voices – an American woman and kids playing – had been drifting over the wall from the same direction earlier, so the guy in question had presumably waited for an empty garden before coming outside. We let it go a couple of times – we didn't know who it was, how ill he was, or whether he felt better for some fresh air – but the third, almost impossible bark of a cough would have sounded terrifying even in normal circumstances. Putting my Britishness to one side, I shouted 'Please could you take that cough indoors?' A short pause, then the classic surly English response of, 'You talking to me?' in exactly the tone of 'You looking at me?' of pub fight cliché. It wasn't Gareth or his dad, but someone I'm pretty sure I've never met, but the best I could come up with was, 'Yes. Sorry, but that sounds bloody terrifying.'

We didn't hear any more from that direction yesterday, and it's more traditional start of the cricket season weather today, at about ten degrees colder, so we won't be on the patio, except to use the exercise bike. If it happens again, though, I'm going to point out that a cough travels at 100mph, and hope the bloke doesn't want to kill his neighbours. Mouthy though I can be, I hate real conflict, so that didn't come easily, and I sincerely hope he doesn't have the virus, for his sake as well as ours. It completely ruined the rest of yesterday for me, though.

I guess he's unlikely to still be coughing like that in a fortnight's time one way or the other, but a cursory Google of how this thing can spread was so contradictory that I've no idea whether or not he's posing a danger to us in the meantime. Either way, we've moved Amanda's bench from that side of the patio and it's now wedged in the opposite corner as far as away as it's possible to get from any more coughing, and also, sadly, out of any sunshine. If someone starts coughing from the opposite side, we'll be stuck indoors for as long as it takes.

I had another rather unnerving experience the previous evening. My ex-colleague Hannah turns 50 in a week or so, but the planned surprise party in Ipswich has bitten the dust. Instead, we've been asked to send cards to her sister who will surprise Hannah with the lot on the day. We had some cards and a stamp in the flat, so I decided to take my first walk off the premises since I last went to Waitrose, to visit the post box at about 10pm. It may partly be my state of mind, but it felt very, very weird out there. We're on the main stretch between the two hills up to Hampstead, near a cluster of small shops and the 268 bus route passes the front door, so there's decent street lighting, usually a reasonable flow of vehicles and a fair number of people walking by until pretty late in the evening.

There was a spate of kids on bikes nicking people's mobile phones a while back, but other than that, it always feels like a London neighbourhood you can walk through if you've been out or working late, even as a lone man or woman. I went to Belsize Village, posted the letter and because it was warm, took a slight detour home via Fitzjohn's Avenue, the road linking Swiss Cottage and Hampstead Village. This is normally a busier road still, but in about 15 minutes outdoors I only saw one dog-walker, an ambulance, two police cars and one private vehicle. The latter was haring up Buckland Crescent at about 60mph, so double the speed limit, followed five seconds later by one of the two police cars. The whole scene could easily have been the opening to an apocalyptic sci-fi movie. I won't be going out there again any time soon, at least not until we run out of food in a few days' time.

Tuesday, 14 April 2020

Never has the 'pleasure of small things' hit home so hard as this morning. A grim 24 hours in which I've struggled to switch off was lit up by a quite beautiful scene greeting me through our patio doors this morning. The wind got up yesterday and the lawn beyond our garden is blanketed in pink cherry blossom, dappled today by the sunshine. Then, in the foreground, a bird I've only seen here once before – and even then, only fleetingly – spent a good five minutes flitting between bird bath and suet feeder: a greater spotted woodpecker, black and white with a red underbelly and drill-like beak. The camera is stored away, but I took some half-decent snaps with the iPhone and decided to break my Facebook silence by posting one as a little beacon of spring and hope.

Prior to that, I felt as snowed under as our lawn, and not with pink blossom. To summarise: the UK's PPE shortage is now getting desperate; 2,000 care homes with largely unprotected staff now have COVID-19 cases (not included in the official statistics); and it transpires that we turned down three opportunities to join a EU procurement scheme which has left Romania and other countries stockpiling protective equipment ahead of a possible second wave. The trickle of Heath Robinson ventilators made by F1 teams from scratch, when we could have had actual proven machinery, have turned out to be ineffective against the virus. Then there's Trump, screaming 'fake' at journalists and reinventing the federal US constitution to claim he has 'absolute power' to lift any restrictions in any state. Regardless of voter suppression and the bonkers electoral college system, if he wins again in November, it's the end of the road for a once-great country and the basket case into which the UK has idiotically put all of its eggs.

Then I read that Austria, with 300 deaths in total, is reopening small shops, and shuddered at the deluded debate in the UK media that suggests we could now do likewise. *The Sun*, clearly desperate for people to buy their rag, has conducted their own online debate on reopening the economy. Two 'experts' have put the opposing cases: in the red corner is Professor Jimmy Whitworth who holds the International Public Health chair at the London School of Hygiene and Tropical Medicine. He says we can't even think about lifting restrictions for some weeks. In the blue corner is the, er (checks notes) 'associate editor at *Quilette*'. Whatever that is. A cursory glance reveals no medical, or even business, credentials. The associate editor of what appears to be a website for alt-right gobshites is none other than Toby fucking Young who, though an expert in getting his dad to get him into Oxford without the requisite A levels, and who now tweets in favour of eugenics and ogling women's breasts, appears entirely unqualified to be given equal weight in this 'debate'.

Then my friend Justin sent me a coldly factual, but nevertheless, horrendous summary of the timelines of both the UK and Germany and their respective responses to the coronavirus. It's too painful to recount in much detail – suffice to say, Angela Merkel has a Science PhD, Boris Johnson is a classics graduate who saw illness as a weakness and delegated all planning to another humanities graduate who once read a physics crammer in his bunker on Daddy's farm.

One detail did jump out at me, though. On 13 March the Bundesliga cancelled all its fixtures, chancellor Merkel having banned mass gatherings three days earlier. Here in the UK, the four-day Cheltenham Festival was in full flow. Three days later, on 16 March, Transport Minister Grant Shapps said that the UK government was making all the right calls, rather than 'just doing things that sound good'. In any other era this sneery complacency, which has now exploded in his face, would be a resigning matter, but then so would be turning down EU ventilators and PPE simply because you've blamed Brussels for everything for years. If any of them did the right thing and resigned, there'd be no one left. Shapps resigned as Conservative co-chairman in 2015 after allegations of bullying within the party. Sketch writers like John Crace have had fun at his expense since it emerged that he once operated 'get rich' internet businesses under the aliases of Michael Green and Sebastian Fox. His fellow Tory MP Michael Fabricant once said he wouldn't 'buy a used car' from him and, all in all, it seemed unlikely that he would ever return to a senior role. But he was prominent in the backbench revolt against Theresa May, and now he's a leading cabinet minister.

I'm absolutely sick of having to check the details before writing about these people – a proper free media would let the public know the calibre of people we now have in charge, but they mostly don't. I seem destined to bang my head against the wall until the glorious day when Shapps's kind are all far, far away from the levers of government. So, 2024 at the earliest.

I spoke to my poor old dad last night. The latter part of his working life – and the reason we moved south when I was 14 – was spent heading negotiations with the trade unions for ICI, Teesside's major employer. He did that job regionally, and then nationally from the late 1970s onwards. ICI at the time was an enlightened employer – they even gave me and all their employees' children who went to university an annual bursary. It was very much the 'beer and sandwiches' school of negotiations, there were never any major strikes on Dad's watch and he formed lasting friendships with some of his counterparts (there are retirement mementoes from a couple of the unions in my parents' house to this day).

Though he was probably a pro-EU Heath Conservative at the outset, the Thatcher era, with its more brutal approach to industrial relations, was very much not to his taste. But, as he lamented to me last night, echoing a point I've made here independently, there were always competent, reasonable people like Jim Prior or Willie Whitelaw around in government, and even the Iron Lady herself had a science degree and helped craft the European Single Market we're now seeing trashed. Dad watches the daily briefings, reads *The Times* and *Guardian*, and simply cannot believe the calibre of people who now make up our government. Dominic Raab and Priti Patel have greatly upset him this week, but he's no fan of any of them, to be honest.

We're still rabbiting away (virtually) to friends. Amanda had four link-ups yesterday. I teamed up with her for the last one with three ex-BBC couples, Ron and Victoria in Cheshire joining Michael, Lance and partners, and this morning I joined her for the latter part of a Zoom link-up with another TV sport producer friend, Lauren. Shortly before Christmas, Lauren's husband Bob Willis, the former England cricket great, succumbed to the prostate cancer he'd battled for some time. We first met Bob and Lauren through Michael and Lance, and our mutual friend the football journalist Paddy Barclay, who along with *Times* journalist Alyson Rudd, formed an unofficial Barnes media coterie. We often did pub quizzes together at the Sun Inn in Barnes and went to the cinema as a foursome, Lauren and Amanda in particular having bonded over an obsessive interest in the ATP tennis circuit.

Having lost Bob at the end of 2019, and taken a trip to Australia to scatter his ashes at a vineyard outside Adelaide owned by close friends of theirs, Lauren had been hoping to resume some kind of normal life after her return to the UK. She was also going to devote time to planning a memorial service for Bob at Southwark Cathedral and The Oval, scheduled for this summer. Amanda's last outing was lunch with Lauren at White City on Monday, 9 March, just after she'd got back from Australia. We went into our lockdown that afternoon.

Speaking to her this morning, Lauren is amazingly resolute, but stuck in on her own, having not even seen her parents since she got back. She's still working on a memorial book for Bob – my old BBC colleague and friend Phil Wye, who now works for Prostate Cancer UK, is involved, too – and showed us the most fantastic artwork she's been producing in isolation. I genuinely had no idea she was so talented – unlike me honing my guitar repertoire into the ether simply for my own benefit, she's creating something tangible and beautiful in extremis. Bravo, Lauren.

I'm chairing a Poncey Horse quiz tonight, having written the questions yesterday. This is my reward/punishment for Amanda and me winning the last one; having 'name the football ground' and geography as two of the five rounds rather played into our hands. The Spurs quizzers will be feeling happier about their club now it's reversed its decision to avail itself of the government's furlough scheme. Before that, Amanda's 15-year-old goddaughter and force of nature, Eliza, has set up a Zoom three-way with us, her brother Felix's godmother, Lynn in Hove, and the family home in Manchester. I talk to her dad, Andrew, quite often, but it will be lovely to link up with Anna, Felix and Eliza Clement for the first time in a while. Andrew and I will have to restrain ourselves from discussing the European Championship football archive broadcasts in June. Even if we did, 17-year-old Felix would doubtless improve on the two old farts' ideas. 'I believe that children are our future,' as Whitney Houston once sang, and those two definitely are. Put them in charge of the planet now, I say.

Wednesday, 15 April 2020

When I see that date written out, whatever's going on and wherever I am, I'm transported back to Saturday, 15 April 1989, a day as sunny as this one. As I related in by far the most difficult to write of the *Why Are We Always On Last?* chapters, a day in the videotape area at a much-anticipated FA Cup semi-final became the Hillsborough disaster. Without thinking too deeply, I can still see the bodies laid out in lines after the crowd had dispersed, upper halves covered in a makeshift fashion, legs and feet clad in jeans and trainers just like the ones I was wearing.

I'd been in a van for several hours watching the most horrific scenes imaginable unfold – close-up coverage which was rightly never broadcast, though similar stills appeared for no reason I've ever been able to discern in the following day's tabloids. By early evening, I needed a toilet break so came out of our BBC Outside Broadcast van at the corner of the Leppings Lane entrance and went to the gents beside the main stand. Suffice to say, on my return, I quietly, and without explaining further, urged that no one should go outside unless they really had to. The area surrounding our trucks was now a makeshift mortuary for dozens of the eventual, unimaginable, death toll of 96 people who'd simply gone to watch their team play football and never returned home. Decades later – and despite the best efforts of South Yorkshire Police, their friends in high places, Kelvin Mackenzie and other malign media forces – all 96 were eventually shown beyond reasonable doubt to have died through absolutely no fault of their own.

So, 31 years on, we can't say for certain how many of our current coronavirus death toll can be ascribed directly to the failure of those in authority to keep them safe. Abysmally, we can't even say to within a few thousand how many people have died of the coronavirus in the UK. The current official death toll is, as I write, 12,107, but all reputable media sources are now calling that 'the number who've died in hospital'. Unofficial estimates say several thousand more have died in care homes, and we know anecdotally of individuals who've died on their own at home. So, we're now somewhere in the vicinity of 200 Hillsboroughs, and counting.

Amanda has been looking at the worldometers.com statistics today and points out that we are the only major country in which 'N/A' populates the column for 'total recovered'. We share this distinction with South Sudan, Haiti, Yemen and a few other troubled countries who already have quite a lot on their plates. The UK has no idea who is carrying this virus, how many have died or even who's recovered from it. And yet Keir Starmer is demanding to know our government's 'exit strategy'. I had high hopes for him, especially after he cleared most of the hopeless

Corbynites out of his shadow cabinet, but I'm afraid that looks like the wrong question right now.

Care homes, where so many frail elderly people reside, are mostly reporting inadequate PPE or none at all. In the case of Park House in Stockton-on-Tees, where Amanda's Auntie Irene spent the final 18 months of her life, the wonderful staff did everything they could to make the final stages of their residents' lives as comfortable and enjoyable as possible. Since the PM has made it fashionable to name names, we're thinking of the carers at Park House, especially Tricia, Gemma, Angela and Sarah, who looked after Irene like one of their own family and always made us welcome on our visits to see her.

An outbreak there, where the communal areas for watching TV, eating meals and relaxing saw staff and patients cheerfully mingling together, would, you'd imagine, inevitably spread rapidly through the place. As well as the toll this would take on the residents, the staff would presumably be highly likely to pass it on to those at home, and the most vicious of circles would develop. That's the immediate priority for Labour and everyone else, I'd have thought.

Clueless as Britain demonstrably is, we could just belatedly copy someone else's exit strategy – preferably Germany's and not the USA's. That said, we'd need to have carried out mass testing to try to ape Germany; the daily figures of tests carried out here have now crept to just over five figures, so just 90 per cent short of where Matt Hancock assured us we'd be by the end of April.

Jake's Remoaners Messenger group contains a number of people who've worked in or around healthcare or, like us, have friends and relatives on the front line. So, when one of our number appealed to us to help her out on a Facebook thread, I'm afraid a bit of a pile-on took place. Lynne had simply, and without comment, posted a link to a *Guardian* article contrasting the early lockdown and resultant total death toll of under 100 in Greece with our own government's record. This was seized upon by Sue and Liz, two women with Stepford wife profile pictures, and an extremely pompous man called Justin, as insubordination of the highest order. 'Oh wow people hindsight is a wonderful thing,' (sic) screamed Sue. 'I don't want evidence or opinions,' said Liz as she liked Sue's comment, and 'Blame, blame, blame. Make you feel good about yourself?' said Justin.

I'm afraid our entire Messenger group descended on these people and this thread with graphs, figures, *Lancet* editorials from January, even a patient explanation of the herd immunity calamity from a senior figure at the Royal College of Nursing, who's not in our group but happens to be Lynne's friend. You might expect a partial retraction or just silence at this point, but not a bit of it. 'I don't do politics,' continued Sue, 'I'm removing all these vile people from my page,' and then, tragi-comically, 'BE KIND!!!' Liz claimed not to 'do politics either' but claimed our government 'couldn't possibly have known'. This assertion was, without a trace of irony, placed directly under an article about a government with considerably fewer resources than our own, but which somehow did know. 'I believe in resolve not attack,' cried Justin in the same actual sentence as he screamed 'condescension and arrogance' at Jake, who'd merely posted some evidence-based information. This went on until about 1am, when the know-nothing, question-nothings started unfriending or blocking us all.

The 'don't do politics' brigade turned out to be staunch Leavers and Tories, not the serial abstainers their allegedly apolitical ignorance would have suggested. Back on Messenger, Lynne expressed relief and gratitude that we'd helped her deal with what was clearly a dreadful bunch – it turned out that they were all distant relatives and in-laws who she could now cross off the Christmas card list. I don't have many friends or relatives who voted Leave or Conservative, but those who did can either construct a coherent case of sorts, or if they can't, have the sense to shut up about it in public, or on social media, especially at the moment.

The one good thing about being awake at a time long after my usual lockdown bedtime was that I went online and secured an elusive Waitrose 'click and collect' slot for Saturday morning. They don't provide that service at Finchley Road, so I'm going to take a three-mile excursion to Westfield, the shopping centre opposite BBC Television Centre, my workplace for many years. It'll be the furthest I've travelled in over a month, so I'm genuinely excited. I've even renewed my motor insurance to mark the occasion, and had a very pleasant chat with a Geordie called Mark, who's working from his dining room sorting such matters out for the AA. They're instantly on my mental list of companies who appear to be looking after their employees. Most of the ones who aren't – Sports Direct, Wetherspoons and co. – didn't number me among their clientele in the first place, and sadly, I expect their regular customers will flock back in due course, simply because they're cheap and ubiquitous and everyone's going to be skint.

Speaking, as I was, of the allegedly apolitical who are still prepared to vote for ghastliness, you really have to wonder at the 43 per cent of Americans who still approve of Trump's performance. We've watched a couple of episodes (from behind the sofa in my case) of the extraordinary and appalling *Tiger King* on Netflix, which goes some way to explaining how states like Oklahoma came to vote for the man. I doubt anyone involved would have any problem with Trump's overnight withdrawal of funding from the WHO, on which developing countries in particular rely, nor even with his delaying the issue of the measly $1,200 cheques he's sending to impoverished Americans as his equivalent of Sunak Socialism. Staggeringly, and yet all too predictably, he wants his name emblazoned on every single cheque before they're despatched. And if they're posted to the American equivalents of Sue, Liz and Justin from that Facebook thread, that display of incomprehensible egomania might even secure a few more votes for a genuine copper-bottomed monster.

There's not much else happening; the cough to our left was heard again earlier while we were out on the terrace. Not as blood-curdling as the other day, but still far from healthy-sounding. We played safe and came indoors for half an hour, but that Facebook spat has temporarily exhausted my capacity for an argument.

I hosted the latest Poncey Horse quiz last night, and self-indulgently ended with a round in which I played ten well-known guitar intros. David Brent-esque it may have been, but Jan got nine out of ten, so there must have been a semblance of 'Everybody Hurts', 'Wish You Were Here', 'Pinball Wizard' and the rest in there. Even though I've never met him, I've grown very fond of Lee's nine-year-old son Noah, who loves maps and atlases even more than I did at his age. I could see his face light up on my Celebrity Squares nine-way Zoom split, when I asked which country has Port Moresby as its capital (Papua New Guinea) and indeed he stormed the geography round with the happy outcome that he and his mum and dad won the whole quiz. Maybe Noah will be one of those dreaded experts when he's older.

In another tiny crumb of comfort, our resident robin – we haven't seen the pair together again – was perching on the seat of our exercise bike earlier. I fully expect it to have learnt to use the pedals before the week's out.

Thursday, 16 April 2020

I'm going to start today with an example of how brilliant Twitter can be. I'm not back on there, but Niall sent me this exchange which just caused me to splutter coffee out of my nose in a rather undignified manner. If you don't know who Ben Fogle is, picture a very posh Prince William lookalike who enthusiastically breezes around the planet for TV, looking all adventurous and energetic, while remaining strangely wet behind the ears. A heavily shared page from his autobiography in which he seems to have invented dialogue with a London cabbie taking him to Heathrow – 'Cor lumme, guv'nor, Tristan Da Cunha? Is that dahn near Torremelinos, gor blimey, chim chim cherroo' – hinted at something worse, but just picture him as a Tiggerish twit for the purposes of what comes next.

Overnight, Ben – who, in common with many 'celebrities' seems to be terrified of being forgotten about amidst this crisis – tweeted the following: 'It's the Queen's birthday next Tuesday. Let's throw her a surprise. At 9am 21st April, we are calling on the whole country to sing Happy Birthday from our windows and doorsteps. Let our song bring good cheer not just to Her Majesty but to the whole nation # singforthequeen'.

The first reply came from one Herdam Unity (@ DuncanBadhew), 'Hi Ben, I'm a student at Norwich University, and I'd love to reference your tweet in my dissertation about guys who were breast fed into their mid-20s. Do I have your permission?'

That's the country in a nutshell right now. Flag-waving Blitz spirit dopes versus well-informed, darkly humorous and alarmed cynics. Hancock's half-hour yesterday has had the latter category struggling to find any laughs, though. The care community is screaming out for PPE. Instead, Health Secretary Matt H is giving them all a badge with 'CARE' written on it. Yes, really. And his big pledge of the day was that old people discharged from hospitals into care homes will henceforth be tested for the virus. My expectations of this government are not high, but I would have thought most people had assumed that was happening already. If Sue, Liz and Justin from Lynne's Facebook page hadn't blocked everyone, we could perhaps have learnt why this all makes perfect sense, but I'm afraid I've been left to conclude that it's yet another absolute shambles.

Then came the journalists' questions. I was actually watching this live with Amanda for some reason, but had to leave the room when Robert Peston pompously demanded to know when the British people would have their civil liberties restored. I appreciate he's probably stung from having been suckered into trumpeting herd immunity by Classic Dom, but demanding all restrictions are dropped just as the death rate is peaking has compounded my overall impression that Peston is a bit of a prat.

If we were in South Korea, Denmark or Germany and knew who had the virus, and could trace their whereabouts and interactions, we might similarly be starting to think about restoring freedoms, but we're a hell of a long way from getting there, if indeed we ever will. Then again, Robert thinks he's had the virus, and his partner definitely has, so they're probably itching to get out there and make the most of their newly-acquired immunity. That said, the science is still far from unanimous even on that front.

Other than that, the last 24 hours has been football- and music-based escapism. I'm doing 20km on the bike, with some uphill stretches, and have developed a very trainspotter-ish tactic to see me through the closing stages. Nerd immunity, if you like. I co-produced the BBC's *Essential FA Cup Final* documentary some years ago, so from 19.46 (Derby County v Charlton Athletic) to 20.00 (Chelsea v Aston Villa) I get myself through the last half a kilometre by mentally reciting the final of each of those years.

Music sees me through the rest of it. Yesterday, I put on a random selection of old and new country music – I took a road trip with my BBC friend Ken to the Deep South in early 1991, including New Orleans, Memphis and Nashville, and we used to channel hop on the car radio and laugh at the country stations. The song titles were often half the fun: 'You're the Reason Our Children are Ugly' was one, and 'All My Exes Live in Texas (That's Why I Hang My Hat in Tennessee)' was another. The live music in bar and venues everywhere was just stunning – New Orleans jazz and Memphis blues were probably more our thing, but a good rocking country band, like the one we saw in a venue in Memphis where a waitress jumped on stage and did a pretty decent Bonnie Raitt impression, goes down well when you're there in person.

The slightly sinister backdrop to that trip was that the first Gulf War was in progress, so there were actual yellow ribbons tied around trees all over the Deep South, and it was seemingly compulsory for every band or PA system to play Lee Greenwood's saccharine 'Proud to be an American' during the course of any given evening, sometimes more than once. And it quickly became evident that you were expected to stand to attention as soon as it was played. Ben Fogle will probably re-record it as 'Proud of Boris and the Queen' in the near future.

So, a country selection it was for the half-hour or so on the bike yesterday: there were some passable songs from the old guard – Waylon Jennings, for example – and the new – Kasey Musgraves, and her great lyric about being trapped in a backwater, 'just like dust, we settle in this town'. That all had me ticking along, but then something just jumped out at me, like all American musicians of a certain age say the Beatles' appearance on the Ed Sullivan show did for them. It was Glen Campbell singing Allen Toussaint's 'Southern Nights'. I can remember this being a catchy enough 1970s UK minor chart hit, and I remember the genial blond figure who used to guest on British TV where he sometimes played the bagpipes, but I honestly hadn't realised until now just how great a record that was. Glen Campbell, along with Nina Simone and the reformed Band, are acts I should have gone to see live when they came to London in the 1980s and beyond, but I didn't fully appreciate any of them until I was much older.

I'd heard those Jimmy Webb songs Campbell sang – 'Galveston', 'By the Time I Get to Phoenix' and, greatest of all, 'Wichita Lineman' – and anyone with functioning ears can tell he had a great voice, but I fell into the trap of thinking it was music of another time and another genre. I was completely wrong – 'Wichita Lineman' is a song I now attempt to play on piano and guitar, though it's best I don't try to sing it, and it's just achingly beautiful. A fine tune and chord sequence, with a haunting lyric ('I need you more than want you, and I want you for all time') is sung by an everyman with hidden depths, out fixing telephone wires in the blazing sun. Most of all, Glen Campbell's performance makes you believe it. There's even a whole book rightly devoted to that masterpiece – *Wichita Lineman* by Dylan Jones. It was one of my birthday presents from Amanda and it's well worth a read.

Then there was the guitar playing – I dimly knew that Glen Campbell had been part of the Wrecking Crew, the best session musicians of their day, who featured on everything from Sinatra's 'Strangers in the Night' to the Beach Boys' seminal *Pet Sounds* album. Then someone – I think it might have been Harry Glasper, Boro's club historian and music buff – shared a YouTube video of Glen enthralling a gathering of country greats on a TV special, with a quite ridiculous live guitar break during his rendition of 'Gentle on My Mind'. That's one I wouldn't even bother to attempt, but having spent all yesterday evening – including a long soak in the bath – listening to his back catalogue on Spotify, I'm going to try to nail the intro to 'Southern Nights' before I host another quiz night. Even having repeatedly watched a video way past my bedtime to try to figure out what he was up to, I've not quite cracked it yet.

Then Anand Menon, my old university friend who's now a politics professor, nominated me on Facebook to post photos of the five footballers who made me fall in love with the game. Anand grew up in Wakefield, so included a bit too much Leeds United – I'll forgive him Eddie Gray – and I think it was meant to be a childhood memory exercise, but I included two players in Juninho and Lionel Messi who made the adult me feel like a big kid. Like Anand, I picked Johann Cruyff who blew me away in the first World Cup I can remember in 1974, and whom I saw score for Feyenoord at Spurs towards the end of his career. The last two were players I used to travel to watch as much as possible in my mid-teens when Curry Club Mark and I escaped school rugby to catch the train to London every Saturday. Cyrille Regis of West Brom who I once saw destroy Crystal Palace, and Glenn

Hoddle of Spurs who regularly rewarded the long train and Tube journey, then walk, from Kent to Seven Sisters

And this morning, I belatedly joined in a football challenge set on WhatsApp by the Curry/Poncey Horse Club. This was to name an XI from our lifetime, with the proviso that no two players have played for the same club or international team. So, for example, a Maradona-Messi combination is doubly disqualified since they both played for Barcelona and Argentina. The dominance of Barça and Real Madrid in recent times limits the choice greatly, but in the end, I came up with this:

Southall
Lauren Godin Van Dijk Maldini
Zidane Pelé Messi De Bruyne
Lewandowski Shearer

Eagle-eyed Matt promptly pointed out that I'd been scuppered by, of all teams, Southampton, Virgil van Dijk and Alan Shearer both having played there. So, I swapped Shearer for the not entirely dissimilar Harry Kane. Then Lee started being pedantic – 'no ball-winners' was his cry, no doubt born of watching Ossie Ardiles coaching a Spurs team of a similar ilk who generally either won, or lost, 4-3. I was thinking more Brazil 1970, but had to grudgingly admit that approach probably doesn't work in our Klopp-Guardiola era. So, I put Ngolo Kanté on the bench to come on for his fellow Frenchman Zizou should a defensive midfield boost be needed. Lee still wasn't satisfied, so figuring that I only needed one striker or maybe none at all since I was fielding three, possibly four, number 10s in midfield, I suggested that Graham Roberts (also Spurs, also England, but a bit of a thug) could come on for Kane. And if all else failed, there was no Spaniard in there since Messi, Zidane and Godin had used up the club slots of their three biggest clubs, so Goikoetxea, the legendary Butcher of Bilbao, would be my sub of last resort, detailed to hack down and mutilate the star men from Mars, or whoever it is we'll be playing.

And so, almost 24 hours have passed in almost total escapism. My friend Justin did send me a couple of interesting articles – one cautiously suggesting that London's death toll may have peaked, at least in the initial phase. I had noticed that our borough, Camden, having at one point been second in the national league table of cases per 100,000 inhabitants, is now on page five of 15 in Sky's lengthy online list of English boroughs. Eight new cases here yesterday, in a still alarming total of 443 who've presumably been tested in hospital in our small borough, does suggest there's at least been a deceleration of late.

The other excellent article, which I read yesterday afternoon, was a nuanced and detailed *Financial Times* account of what appear to have been significant disagreements behind the scenes among our government's scientists. I may have been over-simplifying in some previous diary entries when I laid all the blame at the feet of Dominic Cummings. Then again, he created a self-image of the vengeful loose cannon who would 'whack' the BBC, civil service and judges, and through whom all decisions were to be made – and he brought in the behavioural scientists who appear to have usurped the medics at one point – so frankly, bollocks to the nasty little freak.

He's back in Downing Street, by the way. There's a photo of him predictably failing to observe social distancing as he swaggered in with an aide, that poor woman who always seems to have to accompany him, and as if by magic, 'a Number 10 spokesman' is saying that the coronavirus makes it even more imperative that we Brexit on 31 December, even if the EU requests an extension. We're told that the Prime Minister is not working while recuperating at Chequers, so this is an unelected misfit and weirdo inventing the government's latest stance on the hoof. He's clearly learnt absolutely nothing while sitting at home, so maybe it's stupid to expect a remotely improved Johnson to return in due course. To be fair, almost all the cabinet he hand-picked are as demented in their pursuit of the No Deal cliff-edge as Dom is, so almost certainly would have signed it off if they'd been consulted. Quite why the EU would beg us to stay, especially given the extraordinary mess we're making of this crisis, is anyone's guess.

Our official death rate of 880 today, nowhere near the real figure, is still miles higher than any other in the EU (Germany had 52 deaths today, for example). We're the small and increasingly insignificant mirror image of the US in Europe: I'd have nothing more to do with us if I were the EU. Shut the Channel Tunnel at Calais and leave us to it. Meanwhile, we can hide the appalling economic damage Brexit was already going to cause, wrapped up as it will be in the unimaginable wreckage of the coronavirus, and I honestly don't think most people in this country will even notice. Just as they seemingly haven't noticed how badly we've dealt with both Brexit and the virus to date.

And there we have it: by thinking about Cummings, how a small dose of this virus will doubtless have left him feeling even more invulnerable, and the irreparable damage he's caused our country, all the escapism of the last 24 hours has abruptly ended. Thanks, Dom. I'd love to meet you, don't know where, don't know when, on the other side of this. That said, I'd probably just scream incoherently in your face, and you'd chalk it down as another victory.

Friday, 17 April 2020

The madness continues apace. I still can't watch Piers Morgan, though I'm told his loud contrarianism on *Good Morning Britain* is, for once, being deployed appropriately. *BBC Breakfast* is pitched somewhere around a *John Craven's Newsround* level, so I rationed myself to the first 15 minutes of a Sky News hour. Alex Crawford, who's normally to be found in the same war zones as my friend Christina Lamb from the *Sunday Times*, reported from some Liverpool care homes. It's actually an appropriate redeployment, the staff and patients there being in the sort of danger Alex normally sees in Yemen or DR Congo. No PPE to speak of, but the staff still provide the personal care and attention we saw Auntie Irene receive, and they just scoffed at Matt Hancock's claim that testing has been rolled out to care homes. Not one such test seems to have been carried out on Merseyside.

Hancock appears to be the fall guy for the austerity implemented by his predecessor, and some weak NHS leadership, but perhaps it would be better if he stopped making wilder and wilder claims which consistently fail to stand up to scrutiny. *The Telegraph,* meanwhile, reveals that herd immunity was utter bollocks on at least two fronts: South Korea has found 100 cases of people testing positive again weeks after being discharged, so seemingly not immune at all, and in any case, to get close to the mooted 60 per cent of the population being infected would apparently take eight to ten waves of viral spread like the one we're having now. Good luck selling that to the British public, most of whom probably don't realise yet that this isn't the one and only wave anticipated. The WHO have advised countries not to set store by antibody tests, after the UK had bought 3.5 million of them. None of ours, seemingly acquired from a Chinese Del Boy, have been found to work satisfactorily, in any case. Hey-ho.

Some really sad news among the impersonal statistics this morning: Norman Hunter, that legendary hard man, but also a gifted England international footballer, from the great Don Revie Leeds United team of the 1960s and '70s, has died of coronavirus. If anyone would still like to imply that our PM survived because he's 'strong' and a 'fighter', Norman's passing really does show that they don't know what they're talking about.

All of this may explain why Captain Herd Immunity, Classic Dom, threw that Brexit dead cat on the table yesterday. He needn't have bothered – the media had already found another distraction to focus on: the story of Captain Tom Moore, a 99-year-old World War Two veteran, raising £14m for the NHS with a sponsored walk around his garden. A noble effort, undoubtedly, but it sends a shiver down my spine. Too many things which should be publicly funded aren't: lifeboats, Amanda's Witness Support service for victims testifying against often violent offenders in court, to name but two. Passing round a bucket for the NHS is not how it's supposed to work. Nor are many other fine things which are currently happening: teams of students making face masks on 3D printers, Barbour's Tyneside production line turning its hand to manufacturing hospital gowns, or the various attempts to produce home-made ventilators.

If Crispin Odey, or Jacob Rees-Mogg, or Amazon or Starbucks, paid more tax, the fifth-richest nation in the world (as of a month ago, anyway) might just have a health service to match the magnificence of its staff. Mike Ashley's personal fortune is £2bn; that £14m Captain Tom has raised is 0.7 per cent of the Ashley stash. And that's before he sells Newcastle United to the Saudi Arabian government, as has been reported. That should work out well – at least until the next Rainbow Laces Day, when the entire first XI will have to be publicly beheaded for promoting homosexuality.

That's just reminded me of a late-night exchange I heard on Radio 5 Live when I was driving back from work in Salford a few years ago. The discussion topic was homophobia, and how it was more prevalent in some regions than others. A survey had suggested that north-east England was in this respect the least liberal area of the country, with some archaic views still firmly entrenched. A caller with a Geordie accent eventually came on the line: 'I've been listening to this debate and I think you're being very unfair on us all up here. There's nee problem whatsoever – the gays have their own area where they're never bothered and everything's just fine. [Pause] It's called Sunderland.'

The other companion story comes from my time working on the BBC's *Look North* in Newcastle in the late 1980s. The BBC's patch in the NE also included Cumbria and one of our news stories this particular day was a serious assault on a gay man in Carlisle. A police chief inspector was wheeled out to address the media and appeal for witnesses, then said this: 'We appreciate that the gay community here in Carlisle may be reluctant to speak to the police, but I'm happy to meet them at their own convenience.'

Not much else to report: we panicked slightly when our neighbour Elaine didn't appear outside for the lusty Thursday 8pm applause for our key workers. Fortunately, this seems to have been unconnected to the sonic-boom coughing from next door's garden. Elaine's broadband had packed up as she was writing a report (she's a surveyor), so she'd driven to her office at the other end of Hampstead Heath to finish it off.

Speaking of the minute's applause, I simply can't believe the footage I'm seeing today from Westminster Bridge, shot at 8pm yesterday. Dozens of police cars were lined up between Parliament and St Thomas', officers – not properly socially distanced, were out applauding, and among them, the Met commissioner Cressida Dick. Even worse, considering the fines the police have been dishing out to joggers who stop for a breather and the like, they turned a blind eye to dozens of civilians, many with children in their arms, who were crowded at either end of the cop convoy for a 'look how much I care' selfie they could then post on social media. I suspect St Thomas' was chosen because most of these people voted for the blond chap who recently emerged from there after having his life saved by the foreigners they also voted to chuck out. I suppose it's good of them all to applaud the people who'll be treating them in a week or so, after the virus has taken advantage of this irresistible opportunity to spread.

In other news, the greater spotted woodpecker – who I presume has strayed from the same Heath, where they can often be heard, but are rarely seen – is now visiting daily, but his favourite suet cake is almost finished, and the hardware store where I buy it is still closed. It would be opening again next week if it was in Denmark or Austria, but … let's not go there again.

We rounded off the evening watching a play that we'd missed at the theatre – *Cyprus Avenue* by David Ireland, starring

Stephen Rea. The Royal Court Theatre, like many others, is currently streaming recordings in full on YouTube. Rea was characteristically brilliant and it was a fine tale of deep-set bigotry – set in Northern Ireland, but the themes are universal – until the last 20 minutes when it became inexpressibly violent and grim. Not quite the escapism we'd had in mind.

For some reason I was reminded of the scene in *This Is Spinal Tap* where the band are in Memphis paying their respects at Elvis Presley's Graceland grave (incidentally one of the stops on that 1991 road trip Ken and I took). Having tried, and failed, to harmonise on a rendition of 'Heartbreak Hotel', the following exchange takes place between the magnificently gormless band members. Nigel Tufnell: 'It really puts things in perspective, though,' and David St Hubbins: 'Yeah. Too much fucking perspective.'

WEEK SIX

Saturday, 18 April 2020

Author's note: a re-reading of today's entry reveals that the first few paragraphs appear to have been written in a similar frame of mind to that in which Edvard Munch found himself when he painted *The Scream*. More delicate readers, or those who prefer to avoid a sarcasm-infused rant, may prefer to join at the paragraph which begins, 'Bandsintown have been in touch again.'

I'm still struggling to compute the stupidity of those who crowded on to Westminster Bridge with their families for their 'look at me, look at me' selfies during the Thursday evening applause for key workers. Even worse, it took place under the indulgent gaze of massed, at best semi-socially distanced ranks of police including the Met commissioner herself. In a normal country, or even here pre-2016, that might have been a resigning matter, but there are dozens and dozens of public officials who could be facing far graver charges right now, so that was small beer.

Maybe those of us who haven't seen our families or friends in many weeks should just arrange to meet them at the street party any given Thursday evening on the bridge, just by the Miracle of St Thomas' makeshift memorial. There's bound to be one by now, doubtless strewn with balloons, teddy bears, football shirts, and handmade signs and cards to the effect of, 'Well chuffed the angles didn't take you, Boris. PM of all our hearts. Buy you a pint soon. Hur-hur. You da man. Get Brexit Dun. LOL XX.'

Even the good things this country does are inevitably trashed all too soon. We took from Italy and Spain the admirable idea of applauding health workers at a given hour, but a few weeks later appear to be stripping that fine gesture of all its dignity. My sources beyond Westminster Bridge talk of fireworks, fancy dress, communal drinking in the street, and boy racers tooting car horns, as having variously infested their local versions. By tomorrow, I expect to read that Simon Cowell – currently overshadowed by whatever it is the radio told me earlier that Michael Ball has taken to number one in the charts for the NHS – has signed Captain Tom Moore to re-record Clive Dunn's 'Grandad' with Gary Barlow. All proceeds to go to an NHS 'charidee', so as not to interfere with Simon and Gary's offshore tax arrangements. 'Number 10' is already letting it be known that Captain Tom is in line for a knighthood; Classic Dom knows a distraction technique … sorry, hero, when he sees one.

But instead of fuming about this absurd country which I may never be able to leave again, I'm simply going to list some bald statistics from yesterday's respective official figures, as listed on Worldometer:

Total population: Germany 83 million; UK 68 million; South Korea 51 million

New COVID-19 cases recorded today: Germany 575; UK 5,599; South Korea 22

New COVID-19 deaths today: Germany 53 (includes deaths in care homes); UK 847 (does not include deaths in care homes); South Korea 4

Overall COVID-19 deaths to date: Germany 4,105 (including those in care homes); UK 14,577 (not including those in care homes); South Korea 229

Overall deaths per million people to date: Germany 43 (care homes included); UK 190 (care homes to be added later); South Korea 4

Life goes on pretty much as normal in South Korea, with social distancing and mask wearing where possible, and Germany has now cautiously announced that it thinks the epidemic is currently under control there. The sound of tumbleweed is the response from Whitehall. Still, as Sue, Liz and Justin on Lynne's Facebook page told us, we 'don't want to hear evidence and arguments' and, frankly, who needs statistics or indeed protective equipment when you can simply wrap yourself in the Union Flag? Two world wars and one World Cup, Fritz. Your strain of the virus, and the one in South Korea, is bound to be boring and regimented, and therefore far easier to control than our feisty British bulldog strain. Stands to reason.

In any case, our protective equipment is so good you get to wear it at least twice, UK government guidelines having been amended accordingly overnight. We swerved the pan-EU procurement exercises not once but three times, so we've run out, yes, but that's just a coincidence; we're taking back control and eliminating all annoying foreign red tape, even before 31 December. The WHO, 'clever people telling us what to do' (N. Farage), was wrong about 'test, test, test' – 105,000 airline passengers flew into the UK last week, including a large number on flights from New York, Madrid and other hotspots, but naturally we didn't test or quarantine any of them on arrival – so the WHO is bound to be wrong about disposing of PPE after use, too. We say use it as many times as possible, sharing is caring, and feed that elusive herd immunity. The WHO even dared to say today that there's no evidence that those who recover from the virus have any extra immunity. We could have proved that for you by letting 80 per cent of Brits catch the thing, but the bloody evidence and experts meddled and we eventually bottled it.

Still, we're not just 'matching Indian health and safety standards', as Jacob Rees-Mogg demanded, but going further – and lower – by the day. NHS staff wearing aprons because there are no gowns left, and hospitals running out of oxygen (this morning's *Telegraph*) are a good thing; it concentrates doctors' minds wonderfully. Hurrah for us. No guidelines please, we're British.

Bandsintown have been in touch again. You may remember that this is the website which tells you when artistes you listen to are touring. I'm glad they're still employing some of their staff, even in the absence of any live music, but it has gone ever so slightly weird. Following on from the recent 'Jimi Hendrix has sent you a message' e-mail, came one today which said, 'Hello Paul! Bob Marley is going to be live-streaming a show.' Perhaps all the bizarre stuff about 5G masts causing the virus has made me over-sceptical, but I'm really not sure that's going to happen, Bandsintown.

I'm back at the keyboard now after an interlude of Homer's *Odyssey* proportions. I actually went out of the front door, then the side gate, walked to my car and – you're not going to believe this – got in it and drove to a supermarket. And not even the nearest supermarket, they don't do click and collect, so get this: I drove to a whole other London borough! Man, it's incredible out there. There are streets, the odd car and a few buses, some boarded-up shops, the odd socially distanced queue outside a convenience store, a jogger or two and someone walking their dog and then, when you get a bit further into town, you turn right on to something called a dual carriageway. Apparently, it's the actual Westway that The Clash sang about 40 years ago, and it turns out it's still there. Once on it, I drove past a big covered-up tower block with a green heart emblazoned on it. Turns out that's called Grenfell Tower, and dozens of Londoners died there a while back because of years of corner-cutting, inept management and indifference from the authorities. Those were different times, though – can you imagine something like that happening now?

And so to the massive Westfield Centre, currently abandoned bar Marks & Spencer and Waitrose. The click and collect order duly collected, I got back in the car and drove home via the scenic route. The latest (still utterly muddled) advice issued yesterday suggested you can, after all, now drive somewhere to do your daily exercise, and that the police are no longer entitled to rifle through your shopping bags to make a judgement on whether what you've bought is essential. So, I went straight down the Bayswater Road through Notting Hill Gate, turned right at Marble Arch, left at Hyde Park Corner and again at Trafalgar Square, then meandered north all the way home. My first impression is that London has more or less become a reverse image of itself: there was one person at Piccadilly Circus – he had a camera on a tripod and was presumably taking an eerie Eros photo which may appear in a publication in due course.

Trafalgar Square had a solitary jogger running through by the lion statues and one couple taking a walk in front of the National Gallery, and that was it. The place you'd normally go to escape the crowds – the park – was, by contrast, comparatively busy. We used to visit Hyde Park and Kensington Gardens most days when we lived in Bayswater and it looked fairly normal in there today – loads of joggers, a few people on bikes and families wandering around. The cafes will be shut, but it could have been any spring Saturday otherwise.

The shopping streets are similarly back to front. Charing Cross Road and Tottenham Court Road, which would normally be heaving on a Saturday, were so empty you could have walked their entire length without having to swerve around anyone. I only saw one branch of Boots and one Korean grocery store open, in that entire stretch of what must be two or three hundred shops and restaurants. Meanwhile, in the places where people actually live – Shepherd's Bush, St John's Wood – there are orderly, socially distanced queues outside the food shops. One or two of the smaller food outlets – the odd kebab shop and Albertine's wine bar on Wood Lane, scene of many a BBC leaving do back in the day – seem to be preparing takeaway food to keep themselves ticking over as best they can. I actually felt slightly emotional driving around; as far I could see, the people of this city really are trying their best to keep up their side of the social contract. The billboards, presumably because no one is buying advertising space for the usual consumer goods and cinema releases, are full of quaint, and rather touching, messages asking people to look out for one another, saying we're all Londoners regardless of where you were born, and thanking nurses and doctors.

I sincerely hope that Westminster Bridge shambles was a one-off of over-excited social media-obsessed selfie halfwits, who may feel slightly ashamed of themselves now. I doubt we'll see the police doing that again – next time just applaud wherever you happen to find yourselves, please, rather than replicating a Formula One grid on a major London bridge. Speaking of selfies, for the last stretch of my homeward journey, instead of retracing my steps and driving by the depressingly locked-up Lord's – even in winter, the Grace Gates are normally open if you want to take a tour or visit the museum or shop – I went straight on at the junction of Lissom Grove and St John's Wood Road. For the first time in the four years we've lived in NW3, I didn't have to stop at the Abbey Road zebra crossing to allow a never-ending stream of visitors to replicate that album cover.

To be fair, that's one selfie I can forgive, having variously sought out the village in Sicily, Palazzo Adriano, where *Cinema Paradiso* was shot, the bar in Rio where 'The Girl from Ipanema' was written and the house in which Stan Laurel was born in Ulverston, Cumbria.

Not that I took selfies at any of those places, but I'd rather any future visitors to London wanted to walk in the footsteps of the Beatles than sneak into St Thomas' to try to find the exact spot where Boris Johnson took those first baby elephant steps back to health.

Sunday, 19 April 2020

I have something set up on my iPad which I can't remember installing, or paying for, called Apple News. At various points, I've told it I don't want any more articles from the *Daily Express* or about *The X Factor*, so it tends to give me headlines I might be tempted to investigate further. Last night, after the latest Poncey Horse Quiz (we won, largely thanks to my having been subjected to question master Jan's esoteric music tastes for nearly 40 years) the following popped up:

'*CORONAVIRUS|INSIGHT*
Coronavirus: 38 days when Britain sleepwalked into disaster
Boris Johnson skipped the first five Cobra meetings on the virus, calls to order protective gear were ignored and scientists' warnings

fell on deaf ears. Failings in February have cost thousands of lives.'

I clicked on the article, actually more of an in-depth investigation, discovered it was from the *Sunday Times*'s Insight team, and read on. It's effectively the full jigsaw puzzle of some of the fragments I've been speculatively firing from this keyboard for more than a month. There are attributed lines from scientists, some unattributed ones from within government and, if anything, the whole mess has been even worse than I, or my better-informed friends, had previously thought.

If you'd asked me who'd chaired the first five COBRA meetings on the virus, I'd have assumed it was the Prime Minister. I'd have been perfectly prepared to believe that he was disengaged or had interjected some 'Operation Last Gasp' inappropriateness, but he would have been there, surely? Thinking back to my own career, it was inconceivable that the person at the top of an organisation wouldn't chair a crisis meeting, at least up to the point where they'd succumbed to a virus by ignoring their own advice.

Not a bit of it: Johnson was in Mustique as the WHO raised the alarm; then, while swathes of the country were under flood water, he disappeared to Chevening for 13 days in February (I'd forgotten that). According to the article, this was to sort out the mess left by his divorce, announce his engagement and break the news to his children that he was bringing yet another baby into the world. Classic Dom was indeed, as I'd always suspected, left holding the other baby, that is, running the actual country. There are dozens and dozens of damning lines in the investigation, but this one from a senior adviser jumps out: 'Preparations for a No Deal Brexit had sucked all the blood out of planning for a pandemic.'

Credit where it's due, it's an amazing and all too credible piece of journalism. I posted the non-paywall version on Facebook and logged on to Twitter for long enough to do likewise. I know from experience that 20 people will engage with something like that, whereas a hundred plus of my extended family and friends will like a picture of our goldfinches, but frankly, if any lazy apolitical Tories out there are offended and think 'now is not the time', then tough.

The first person to 'like' the post on Twitter was the reliably sound-as-a-pound Peter Reid, he of the hairdryer treatment to Johnson at that charity football match. I then saw that Emma Tucker was following me, so I followed her back and exchanged messages. She's only been editing the *Sunday Times* since late January, and I doubt she'll ever publish a more important piece of journalism, so I thought I'd tell her so. I've always been told – particularly by Christina Lamb – that Rupert Murdoch is not particularly hands-on with the journalists at Times Newspapers, regarding them as the fig leaf of quality behind which he can hide the rest of his unsavoury tat (those are my words, not those of the *Sunday Times*'s chief foreign correspondent). Even so, that's a hell of a way to make an impact as a new editor in extraordinary times.

One final, miserable note on that investigation. I was dimly aware of Amanda shouting in the living room as I stirred in bed this morning. She'd watched Sophy Ridge, excellent as ever for her tiny Sky News audience, then switched to Marr on the BBC. The *Sunday Times* story featured prominently in Marr's newspaper review (which I've since forced myself to watch) during which Hugh Pym, the BBC's health correspondent, dismissed it with an airy 'hindsight is a wonderful thing' to the accompaniment of furious nodding from Marr. 'It's not hindsight, that's the point,' is what Amanda and anyone else who'd actually read the thing was shouting at the screen.

I simply don't understand BBC News any more – I've always said there couldn't have been an editorial edict from on high, for example, never to question Brexit; I never received one, beyond the universal editorial guidelines, in my whole career. And yet, BBC News and the *Sunday Express,* with its risible 'The

Hard Work Is Paying Off' front page are the only media outlets seemingly failing to question the government today. Robert Peston, in particular, has today expressed his dismay with some of the government's previous messaging.

Having that exchange of messages with Emma reminded me of a point my friend Justin made the other day. 'It's ironic,' he said, 'that for years cabinet ministers have been associated with PPE. People have wondered whether a degree in PPE is a good preparation for a career in politics. It certainly doesn't seem to equip them with the skills necessary to manage PPE.' Tens of thousands of words ago, I explained that to some of us, PPE had always meant Philosophy, Politics and Economics, whereas it now stands for the altogether more urgent Personal Protective Equipment.

When I went to University College, Oxford, to study PPE, I was aware that prime ministers like Heath and Wilson had studied the subject, and I chose it primarily because I'd enjoyed my politics A level course. I knew that Univ had been the alma mater of Percy Bysshe Shelley, Clement Attlee and Ernest Beveridge, author of the report which led to the creation of the welfare state. I'm not sure I knew who Stephen Hawking or Bill Clinton were in 1984, but they're now also celebrated in college literature as having studied there for their first degrees.

The primary reason for choosing Univ was that it was billed as having a high state school to private school intake (true) and supposedly a 7:5 male:female ratio (false, hence plenty of socialising with secretarial colleges and trainee nurses) but it was, as I've said before, a very down-to-earth place. The tutors were ahead of the curve back then in terms of encouraging state school applicants, and I already had a place on a course at Manchester University, so I found the interview process relaxed and friendly.

An undoubted advantage of the Oxbridge system is that small groups of students – 12, I think, in my year started out studying PPE – had individual or paired tuition with in-house academics for each of the three subjects. We had just two private school pupils in our set of 12, but less satisfactorily, no women whatsoever. That improved somewhat after a year when both Christina and Philippa Thomas (now a presenter at BBC World) changed courses from chemistry and English respectively to join us.

My friend Justin also moved across from English but had a bit of a falling-out with the tutors and eventually completed his degree at UCL in London. Justin and I have remained a tad unimpressed with the course we took. He's also still distinctly unimpressed with my alleged failure to bring him breakfast after he'd queued overnight at the Oxford Apollo in the spring of 1985 for tickets for Live Aid. I still think he's misremembered, or that we got our wires crossed – I was never up in time for breakfast – though I will be forever grateful that his sacrifice allowed us to attend such an historic event.

I struggled with economics in the first year, having not taken it at A level, so although I eventually got my head around a small proportion of the syllabus, I dropped it like the proverbial after the first-year exams. I actually got my best mark in economics, but it had a mathematical and pseudo-scientific element which meant you could just as easily fail it. I honestly don't think anyone reading this could fail politics, in particular, or even philosophy, even if you sat some of my finals papers this evening. You needed to have worked hard and read reasonably widely to get a first, but a middling second in something like British politics – 'The British electoral system is unfair to smaller parties. Discuss' just requires a reasonable grasp of what's going on in the world.

I sat that paper and answered that question the morning after the 1987 General Election, when as usual, the Tories had secured a big majority with 40 per cent of the votes and the centrist SDP/Liberal Alliance were absolutely diddled – 22 per cent of the vote, just 22 seats. Moral philosophy wasn't a lot more difficult: 'Is killing ever justified?' is something we could all discuss over dinner or a beer. You might get a first if you quoted Kant, Mill and Rawls, but you'd struggle to fail altogether. And indeed, I didn't.

Thereafter, whenever I saw Nick Robinson or Robert Peston interviewing Ed Miliband or David Cameron on TV, I thought 'PPEists', not 'look at those clever people'. Cameron got a first – something which has bugged Boris Johnson ever since, to the point where he described Cameron as 'a girly swot' in a note to an adviser more than 30 years later. But if you watched Cameron in action, it could have been any of us reading a half-arsed 4am essay in a tutorial and giving off an air of knowing what we were talking about. It took me a year to realise I could do that, and I never remotely thought it qualified me to run the country, but then Cameron went to Eton with Johnson, so thought he should be Prime Minister because, quote, he'd 'be rather good at it'. So, as I joined meritocratic BBC Sport, where there have never been any other PPEists as far as I know, they all went off to play politics, or to write or broadcast about it.

Rupert Murdoch did PPE, as did Evan Davis and Simon Jenkins, Michael Crick and David Dimbleby, Krishnan Guru-Murthy and even Julia sodding Hartley-bloody-Brewer and Toby bastard Young. So naturally, they tend to understand, or even know personally, the people they're interviewing: whether it's Yvette Cooper or Edwina Currie or William Hague or Philip Hammond (ex-Univ) or Lord Mandelson or Rishi Sunak or Liz Truss, they probably did PPE too. All of those politicians definitely did, by the way. Even in the foreign news, Bill Clinton, Bob Hawke, Malcolm Fraser, Benazir Bhutto and Aung San Suu Kyi are former PPEists. Nobel Peace Prize winner Malala Yousafzal, whose autobiography Chris Lamb co-wrote with her, is currently in the third year of her PPE course. A quick quiz question for you: the two Health Secretaries who will appear before chair Tim Martin at the whitewash at the end of this, sorry, that should read, before the probing no-holds barred inquiry – Jeremy Hunt and Matt Hancock – both read which degree at which university? Yep, you've guessed it. And they'd both have gone into that ministerial post knowing about as much about running the NHS as I do, but unlike me, they thought they had the credentials and bluster to carry it off.

Of the 14 of us who ended up reading PPE at Univ in my year, half ended up in the media. As well as Chris, Philippa and me, John Ridding is a senior figure at the *Financial Times*, Ed Crooks broadcast on the BBC then wrote for the *FT*, Andy Baker was at Guardian Online and still works in the world of websites, and Alex Kershaw wrote articles for *GQ* among other publications, then acclaimed biographies of Jack London and Robert Capa as well as a number of books about World War Two. And in the years above and below us, there were Nick Robinson, Emma Tucker and the, shall we say unusual, Nick Denton who founded Gawker.com.

No one, bar Stewart Wood, who entered the House of Lords having been a senior political adviser to Gordon Brown, went into politics itself. I thought Nick Robinson might have done, but it seems that none of these bright people took the plunge, and most of the ones from elsewhere who did would probably not have been friends of mine. In addition to sightings from afar of Johnson and the Bullingdon Club, I've recently had it pointed out to me that an odd little Scottish bloke who occasionally came across from Lady Margaret Hall to our beer cellar to meet his Univ ex-schoolmate Duncan Grey, was none other than Michael Gove. He didn't pick up any bad habits from us, honestly.

Fundamentally, the difference between the two forms of PPE is that one involves undergraduates waffling on about the meaning of life for three years, while the other is a matter of life and death and is happening now.

Monday, 20 April 2020

You know that old trees just grow stronger
And old rivers grow wilder every day

Old people just grow lonesome
Waiting for someone to say, 'Hello in there, hello'

I could have copied the whole lyric out, but that extract is taken from 'Hello in There' by the late John Prine. Thanks to Philip for pointing me towards a beautifully poignant version the Australian singer Emily Barker performed from lockdown on this weekend's *Loose Ends* on Radio 4. Amanda had raved about it, too, but I'd forgotten to check it out until Philip also mentioned it in an e-mail exchange. I worked out earlier that the last time I physically touched a fellow human being other than Amanda, was five weeks ago tomorrow when a helpful lady swapped a £1 coin for two 50p's with me outside Sainsbury's so I could take a trolley. Even so, we're probably communicating more than ever before with our friends and family. Being old and lonely right now is almost unimaginable, but as so often, a Prine song makes you think about it.

Cover versions of songs was last night's theme, too. I still think healthcare is a fundamental right, and needs to be funded from taxation not charity, but BBC1's *One World: Together at Home,* a fundraising celebration of key workers to which some of the world's most celebrated musicians contributed from their homes, mostly struck the right note. One of my most striking memories of Live Aid was relatively low-key: Elvis Costello walking on stage with just an acoustic guitar and playing what he called 'an old Northern folk tune' for 80,000 people to sing along to – 'All You Need is Love' – was exactly in the spirit intended. The two-hour pull-together on BBC One last night – I understand the original was of Live Aid proportions – was genuinely uplifting, we thought. I get Elton John choosing 'I'm Still Standing' (though, to be honest, his voice has gone) and even the four remaining Stones collaborating on 'You Can't Always Get What You Want' was darkly humorous, though not to the extent of the scene where it's played at a suicide victim's funeral in the excellent 1980s movie *The Big Chill.*

Billie Joe Armstrong's stripped back 'Wake Me Up When September Ends' and Taylor Swift's 'Soon You'll Get Better' were personal songs, each about a parent as it happens, which worked more universally in this context. The cover versions stood out for me, though – Lady Gaga singing Charlie Chaplin's 'Smile', Shawn Mendes and Camila Cabello duetting on 'What a Wonderful World', Stevie Wonder paying tribute to Bill Withers on 'Lean On Me' and even the oft-derided Michael Buble's version of one of the greatest songs ever written, Brian Wilson's 'God Only Knows', were all carefully chosen and appropriate.

Tom Jones had really thought his contribution through: standing in front of a painting of his childhood home, he explained how he owed his life to the NHS, having spent two years in isolation there with tuberculosis. He then covered just about my favourite song to play on the guitar, Big Bill Broonzy's 'Glory of Love'. And the closing perfectly illustrated what even as a Dylan fan, I tend to hold to be true: you often don't realise the full greatness of his songwriting until you hear a cover version. The Kingdom Choir, all 17 of them, joined in from 17 separate locations, on an ethereal version of 'Make You Feel My Love'.

We may get used to lo-fi television; indeed we may have to get used to it. Despite some stupidly premature headlines screaming 'A Cure By September' last week, my limited scientific understanding is that there's never been a successful vaccine for any of the coronavirus incarnations, stretching back to SARS and beyond. Every pharmaceutical company and research institute in the world is pulling out every stop to try to develop one – let's hope it's not found in the States where Trump would probably ban its export – but it's certainly not a given that there'll ever be one, and putting a timescale on it is pretty much pointless. Look at HIV/AIDs – it took 30 years or more of very gradual progress and trial and error – the development of antivirals, and ways to manage rather than cure the symptoms, to reduce that virus to where it is now. Clearly the sum of collective learning gets greater every year, or even every week in the case of the novel COVID-19, but if ever the world needed to pull together and pool its knowledge and resources, it's now. Even Michael Gove secretly knows now that we really haven't had enough of experts after all.

Donald Trump continues to plough his own furrow though. The dictionary definition of solipsism is, 'The view or theory that the self is all that can be known to exist.' That is Trump's world view in a nutshell. The US elected a solipsist. So did the UK in December, to an extent, but Johnson does have his limits. It doesn't look like Trump has: he sent out a series of capitalised tweets over the weekend, picking out certain states and screaming 'LIBERATE MINNESOTA/VIRGINIA/MICHIGAN'. Each of those states has a Democrat governor he's taken exception to, and in all three – and many other states – gun-toting weirdos flying flags and Trump banners from pickup trucks, or resembling rejected extras from *Easy Rider* on motorbikes, are rallying menacingly in state capitals to demand that coronavirus restrictions are lifted. There was something approaching a Tiananmen Square stand-off in Denver, Colorado, where two brave medics in protective gear stood in the road to face the jeers and Neanderthal idiocy of what I've seen described as the Flu Klux Klan.

It's difficult to understand how a great democracy has found itself – and its venerable old constitution – reduced to this in the middle of a pandemic. My brother John the lawyer says it's because Trump knows if he either loses or fails to delay the election, he's going to jail. I was discussing this earlier on the phone to my friend Phil who worked in Atlanta for some years: guns, the bizarre philosophy that public provision of medical care is tantamount to communism and now this, make us both glad to live here, not over there at the moment, for all our faults. We may have a beleaguered public health service, behave dopily on Westminster Bridge and panic-buy toilet roll, but we don't have to pay to go to hospital, nor do we panic buy ammunition and swagger around state capitals waving guns. I love the States, and firmly believe that the UK government is our least competent in at least two centuries, but even so.

We watched another online stream of a play from the archives last night. Howard Brenton's *Drawing the Line* told the story of Cyril Radcliffe, a British High Court judge who was sent to India in 1947, five weeks before that country was to be partitioned, and the nation of Pakistan created. He was given just over a month to draw arbitrary boundaries between what would be Hindu-majority India and the largely Muslim Pakistan. As he met the various entrenched and hostile parties, he realised this was pretty much an impossible task: in disputed areas like Kashmir and the Punjab, the border he drew led to violence and distrust which lasts to this day. Up to two million people were killed and 14 million displaced in the mayhem which followed the British withdrawal in August 1947, but you still felt sorry for Radcliffe, who became increasingly distraught as he realised there would be bloodshed, however he redrew the map.

I couldn't help but be reminded of current Health Secretary Matt Hancock: towards the end of the play, actor Tom Beard gave Radcliffe a hangdog look and mannerisms similar to those we're seeing from Hancock in the press conferences. Hancock has been in the role for under two years while Jeremy Hunt, now the chairman of the Commons Health Select Committee which is supposed to scrutinise Hancock, held the job for the previous six years. Under Hancock's tenure, until a month or so ago, the NHS was firmly on the back-burner, more or less relegated to a bargaining chip in the US trade talks which will follow the all-consuming Brexit that he, almost uniquely in the current cabinet, voted against. Clearly, you have to be a bit of a careerist weasel to have hung around in those circumstances when almost all the decent Tories have run for the hills, and even the far from spotless Hunt opted for the back benches. Even so, I suspect the long nights looking at testing and PPE figures (protective equipment, not his somewhat tarnished degree) have reduced him to a Cyril Radcliffe-style tormented figure as the death toll mounts.

Or he could read *The Sun*'s latest editorial and bask in a warm glow. News International must be a very strange place to work – in the past, there was a party line, albeit *The Sun* would scream 'Gotcha' and 'Hurrah for Maggie' while *The Times* would just say she was 'simply marvellous', but once Blair had gone on his hands and knees to Hayman Island, Australia for a private audience with Rupert Murdoch, all the latter's publications gave him the green light to govern. As ever, Old Scrotum Face knew Tone was way ahead in the polls, so merely backed a winner, but it meant there was a perceived favour done and that his media dominance would go unchecked despite the change of government. Right now, we have the *Sunday Times* poleaxing the government and *The Sun* picking it up and dusting it down.

I must point out that I've only seen today's Currant Bun editorial because Remoaner group member Stel, who lives in Bulgaria, had been sent it by a relative who says he's had enough of Stel's social media negativity about Johnson and co. Regardless of what Stel's relative thinks it adds to his argument, it's not even *The Sun*'s finest hour.

'Let's cut the backseat driving and let Boris and his team get on with it!' cries the headline, and it doesn't get any better or less obsequious in the text beneath. Politicians can't be 'at the top of their game' when everyone is carping, apparently, according to the never-carped-at-anyone *Sun*. As far as I can see, the problem is that they are at the top of their game, it's just that their game is Snap while the universe is playing chess.

The line which floored me, though, is the seemingly serious assertion that there is no need for 'a massively expensive public inquiry afterwards'. This immediately put me in mind of Peter Cook's skit on the Jeremy Thorpe trial in the *Secret Policeman's Ball*. One of Peter Cook's many great lines as Justice Cocklecarrot was, 'The defendants have very wisely chosen to exercise their right not to go into the witness box to answer a lot of impertinent questions. You are not to infer from this anything, other than that they consider the evidence against them so flimsy that it was scarcely worth their while to rise from their seats and waste their breath denying these ludicrous charges.' That, along with the release of the *Life of Brian* the same year, and my dad starting to bring *Private Eye* home on the train, changed my outlook to that of the cynical, sceptical figure I am today.

I suspect Rebekah Brooks and Rupert himself – if he's communicating from the airtight lair inside a volcano to which he has presumably retreated to stroke a white cat during this pandemic – feel that if there's a proper inquiry, then maybe there'd be a renewed appetite for Leveson II. That would never do.

As I've said before, despite my issues with so much about this country, its ability to be cantankerous and darkly humorous in the face of absolutely anything is a constant source of joy. Following on from Ben Fogle's backfiring attempt to start a #clapforthequeen, it became known over the weekend that, given the current circumstances, the Queen has asked that the traditional 21-gun salute to mark her birthday tomorrow be cancelled. Poncey Horse club immediately concluded that 'the old girl's done Fogle up like a kipper there', then 'of course, Ben F. will still be out in his garden shouting "Bang"'.

Then there's dear old 99-year-old Captain Tom raising millions for the NHS with his laps of his garden. Who could be cynical about that? Answer: Britain could. Someone posted a 'Space Oddity' parody in which 'Ground Control to Captain Tom' in vaguely Bowie tones started ordering him to do more and more bizarre things. There's a Newsthump story doing the rounds which suggests that the Department of Work and Pensions has now pronounced him fit to work. And finally, I was sent a carefully mocked-up Breaking News still of the old boy waving cheerily, with accompanying headline, 'Captain Disappears with £20m – last seen boarding jet with two strippers, shouting "Laters, motherfuckers"'.

Tuesday, 21 April 2020

Before the BBC covered the 2014 World Cup in Brazil, I made contact with the UK's ambassador in the South American country. Although I'd never met him, he was the younger brother of my university friend Katherine, with whom I've kept in touch. Alex had previously been posted to Lisbon, married a Portuguese woman and spoke the language fluently. We exchanged a couple of e-mails and I put his team in touch with our people who were in the process of planning the BBC's logistics. He clearly couldn't believe his luck as a sports fan to be posted there for both the World Cup and then Olympics two years later, and it seemed to make sense from the UK's point of view to have a bright, youngish bloke who spoke the language representing our interests out there. We met Katherine and her husband for dinner a couple of years later. 'How's Alex getting on in Brazil?' I asked. 'Ah,' she said, 'he's been brought back to London to help David Davis with Brexit.'

I'm telling that story to illustrate what seems to have happened all across the civil service in the last four years. It's the only explanation I can find for the staggering and continuing PPE acquisition scandal. It's over a month since I wrote about the companies who had tried to offer our government protective equipment, but had eventually given up and sent it abroad. This morning Sky are reporting that this is still going on to a massive extent; millions and millions of items produced here are currently in transit around Europe and beyond. Hugh Pym on the BBC has said that three companies contacted him direct after he asked a question about PPE in a press conference last week, saying the government had still not got back to them.

Robert Jenrick/Generic triumphantly announced on Saturday that a huge supply of PPE had been sourced in Turkey and would arrive the following day. A few small snags have since emerged: 1) no one had contacted anyone in Turkey at that point; 2) the consignment would last the NHS just three days, and contained fewer items than just one planeload we breezily sent to China a while back; and 3) despite RAF jets being scrambled to collect it, it still hasn't arrived. That *Sunday Times* line keeps coming back to me: 'Preparations for a No Deal Brexit had sucked all the blood out of planning for a pandemic.'

The only plausible explanation I can find for this criminal inability to liaise with British firms, act collectively with the EU as we were invited to do, or even speak to other countries before blithely making promises, is that the whole of Whitehall is still diverted to chucking us off a cliff on 31 December. 'Taking back control' is already showing us just how little clout we have on the world stage, now that we're a small and not very competent country acting outside the orbit of the world's largest trading bloc.

Meanwhile, our friend Margaret's neighbour is a consultant at St Thomas' Hospital. Johnson was indeed treated there, contrary to some of the wilder conspiracy theories, but he was kept in a high dependency unit, and never transferred to intensive care. It's a bit of a grey area because he does seem to have received the dedicated one-to-one nursing supervision associated with ICU treatment, while not ever going on a ventilator, so contrary to some suggestions was clearly seriously ill. It shows you how desperate everything has become when you are relieved at the possibility that his condition was, at worst, exaggerated for political purposes, not invented altogether.

Elsewhere, something unprecedented in the whole of economic history occurred yesterday: for a while, the price of oil was negative. Yes, demand has fallen so low that storage facilities are full and oil producers were briefly prepared to pay to have it taken off their hands. And yet more is emerging about the scandal that was the Cheltenham Festival. There have been 125 COVID-19 deaths so far within the Cheltenham NHS trust, more than twice as many as in any other trust in the South West England health region. The chairman of Lancashire County Cricket Club has, sadly, died of the virus having attended the Festival, as have an unusually high number of people in Worcester, a city which supplies many of the agency workers for the four-day meet. Others who attended – Charlie Austin, the footballer, the comedian Lee Mack and Camilla Parker Bowles's ex-husband, Andrew, among them – fell ill with the coronavirus after their outing to the races, but have survived. Who knows who else they've then infected?

If we were carrying out tracking and testing like South Korea and Germany are, I'd place a large wager on thousands of cases and a number of deaths having resulted, directly or indirectly, from an accumulative quarter of a million people gathering that week. But then wagers seem to be part of the problem: it's estimated that a third of all donations to the election funds of Conservative MPs come from the gambling industry. *The Daily Mirror* reported that Conservative MPs Caroline Nokes and former bookmaker, Philip Davies had accepted free Cheltenham 2020 VIP tickets from the bookies. When Tracey Crouch resigned as sports minister in 2018, she claimed that Davies had successfully gone over her head to secure a delay to the curbs on fixed odds betting terminals that she'd promised. Davies also faced a Parliamentary Standards investigation in 2013, and was forced to issue an apology after failing to declare hospitality he'd received from Ladbrokes. And Matt Hancock is the MP for racing's HQ, Newmarket.

On a happier note, last night's final of *University Challenge* was terrific. Now a BBC show with Jeremy Paxman asking the questions, the last series of the previous incarnation, presented by Bamber Gascoigne for ITV, was in 1987 when I was an undergraduate. At that time, Univ had an established and excellent quiz team which always ranked highly in the inter-collegiate league. My friend Nick from the Fat Larry's Band Zoom group was, and still is, a great quizzer; Robin Darwell-Smith, now the college's historian and archivist, could name any piece of classical music in a nanosecond and had a ridiculous knowledge of ancient history; John Authers, now of the *Financial*

Times, wasn't too shabby either, nor was Roger Mortimore, who became a pollster at Gallup (as a PPEist in the year above me, who stayed on as a post-graduate, Roger very kindly let me borrow the essays which helped him towards a first, when it came to revising for my finals).

There wasn't a scientist among them, which seems strange now, but they were a very good collective. Once they'd been selected to appear on the programme, they were invited to Granada Studios for a night in a hotel and a TV appearance with Bamber. In case anyone was indisposed on the night, they were told to bring a reserve, so set a general knowledge quiz for anyone in college who fancied making up the numbers. I was very much up for it, not least because I'd applied to the BBC by then, and was duly nominated. In the end, I made several trips to Manchester, visited the *Coronation Street* set, rubbed shoulders with most of the cast in the Granada canteen, and was given some great advice by Bamber and his production team about my prospective career in the media.

The Univ team all stayed in rude health, so didn't need me, and notched an all-time record score, which still stands, of 520 as they trounced Reading en route to a final clash with Keble, Oxford. Keble had an extraordinary captain in Steven Brindle – I've just googled him and he is now the Inspector of Ancient Monuments for English Heritage – who kept just beating our lot to the buzzer for a 325-250 win. I still have the commemorative Finalist glassware I received for never getting on the air.

So, naturally, I still follow the show avidly. This year, the final two were teams from Corpus Christi, Cambridge and that font of COVID-19 research, Imperial College, London. Vying to be this year's Brindle were the two outstanding competitors of the series: Ian Wang of Corpus and Brandon Blackwell of Imperial. The latter comfortably prevailed – his team-mates, including Richard Brooks from our hometown of Stockton-on-Tees, were also strong, but Brandon must have some kind of photographic memory. How else does a guy from Jamaica in Queens, New

York City, who's doing a Masters in Computer Science, know that Oakham is the county town of Rutland?

I couldn't help but hope that our Prime Minister was watching. He has been known to describe black people as 'picaninnies with watermelon smiles' and his chief adviser's first appointment to his Downing Street team was a eugenicist with a propensity for claiming that black people are intrinsically less clever. Brandon Blackwell is the intellectual equivalent of Jesse Owens, disproving grotesque theories through sheer brilliance. He was quite intense, as anyone might well be with that much knowledge bursting out of them, but he classily applauded his opponents and encouraged his own team-mates throughout. If the US can ever countenance another black president, they could do a lot worse.

Wednesday, 22 April 2020

As I've previously mentioned, Armando Iannucci used to stage an end-of-term revue at our college. The ingenious wordplay later seen by a wider audience in *The Day Today, The Thick of It* and *Veep* was already evident, fully formed in the young Armando. He's recently said he couldn't make political satire any more, because reality in both the US and UK started to ape, then surpassed, even the wildest creative imagination. Two of the phrases he's left us for posterity, via perma-angry spin doctor Malcolm Tucker, sprang to mind this morning: the governance of the United Kingdom of Great Britain and Northern Ireland is now both an omnishambles and a clusterfuck.

Tall Paul was up early posting to the Poncey Horse political sub-group, Special Measures for Eton. He's already restored its icon, a picture of Boris Johnson casting a giant shadow of a penis – this was felt to be inappropriate when the PM was in hospital – and today Paul posted possibly the most damning headline and article in the history of the usually staid and sober *Financial Times*: 'UK government's coronavirus strategy in chaos.'

The daily Covid-19 media conference cum Kraftwerk gig, March 2020. Dominic Cummings was still working on his three-word slogans at this point.

Dominic Cummings, Britain's very own Top Cat.

Johnson and Cummings behind bars. One can but hope.

The UK calls last orders long after most of Europe. Fathers Dougal and Jack in Wetherspoons.

The 2020 Cheltenham Festival. 'The best way to accelerate the Covid-19 spread' – Professor Sir David King, ex-chair of the government's scientific committee, SAGE

How Cheltenham should have looked. Trafalgar Square, after lockdown is belatedly imposed.

Not the wartime Prime Minister he had in mind.

Bolsonaro and Trump – the two global kings of Covid-19 by June 2020, remembering just in time to bend their elbows.

Angela Merkel and Jacinda Arden – leaders with no y chromosomes, and, at the time of going to press, remarkably low Covid-19 death tolls.

Barnard Castle, a celebrated County Durham market town. The perfect place to test your eyesight.

Heroic NHS workers briefly leave the front line to send No.10 a message.

The puppet show continues. So does the anger.

The government's own messaging rebounds, and unravels. A street in Kentish Town, London.

Happier times. The morning after they won the 2016 referendum. Cheer up, lads.

A landlord leaves his property after checking on his tenant.

'Just say fantastic effort, ramping up testing, world-beating app, clap for carers, send the virus packing. Anything to fob them off.' 'Right-ho, Dom.'

The Premier League returns after 100 days away, and reflects.

Real leadership and vision from Number 10 at last – Marcus Rashford returns to action.

Nearly 2,000km cycled without leaving the garden. (Photo: Amanda Armstrong)

Our greater spotted woodpecker. (Both photos by the author)

Our patio oasis of calm is shattered – it's even kicking off amongst the goldfinches.

Yesterday's utter farce to surpass anything in *The Thick of It* saw Sir Simon MacDonald, the most senior civil servant at the Foreign Office, tell the House of Commons Foreign Affairs Select Committee that it had been a political decision not to take part in the EU's medical supplies procurement initiative. This seemingly just confirmed what a 'Number 10 spokesman' said at the time – in short, we're not getting involved because 'we've left the EU'. A couple of hours later a risible letter, supposedly from Sir Simon, said he'd misspoken and that everything he'd just told the committee was wrong.

The *FT* has also run some projections, based on the latest care home figures which suggested an extra 1,000 deaths at the end of March/start of April, and they estimate there may have actually been around 41,000 COVID-19 deaths in the UK, rather than the 17,000 being officially declared. Per population, that would make us the most-hit sizeable country in the world – our daily death toll having been behind only the US for some time now. And yet certain cabinet ministers – Liz Truss, Rishi Sunak and Michael Gove – are seemingly demanding the lifting of restrictions. While his stock is understandably high right now, Sunak knows some potentially horrendous economic conditions lie ahead.

I'm dismayed, but not in the least surprised, to see that Toby Young has set up a website calling for the economy and civil rights to be put first. Herd immunity minus the immunity, in other words. See ya on the Tube next week, eh, Tobes? Yeah, right. His partner Caroline Bundy has given the game away in this week's *Spectator*: 'Toby spent the first week of lockdown in bed convinced he had coronavirus. He didn't. He is a complete hypochondriac at the best of times ... anxiety levels through the roof ... started taking hydroxychloroquine, vitamin C and anything he'd read about' ad nauseum for a whole article.

And when it comes to PPE, we've been Del Boyed again – the RAF plane sitting on a Turkish runway has been fobbed off with just a fraction of the PPE promised by our contact down the Nag's Head, Istanbul. Meanwhile, every single person in France is about to be issued with a washable face mask by the government, Tall Paul tells us his brother living in Singapore has a new one delivered to his door every week, as does every single other person there. And that's civilians; many of our doctors and nurses can't even get them. I'm afraid I've become a bit of a coward when it comes to facing individual stories. The mounting figures are horrifying enough. You may know the cold statistics connected to, say, the Christchurch earthquake or the Rwandan genocide, but as we discovered on our travels, visiting either the genocide memorial in Kigali or the museum in Christchurch, where footage and individual stories of victims are shown, is when it hits you. The story on *Channel 4 News* of Dr Yusuf Patel, a much-loved GP in East London who had been scouring eBay for a protective mask prior to catching the virus and ultimately dying of it, was close to unbearable. If he'd lived in Singapore, Dr Patel would have had a new mask delivered to his door every week, regardless of what he did for a living, but not in Brexit Britain.

I wish Toby Young could have taken part in the FaceTime conversation we had this morning with Amanda's niece Emma and her husband, Tom. Tom manages a ward in a Shropshire hospital; he says it's harrowing, but they're coping with hospitalisation rates which are lower than in the cities. It sounds like he had the virus a month or so ago himself, and he says they've seen so many false negative tests – this aspect I find understandable given the newness of a rapidly mutating virus – that they're being ultra-cautious and treating everyone with respiratory problems as potential COVID-19 patients. That presumably hasn't been possible in besieged city hospitals. His huge fear is a second spike when restrictions are lifted and, for example, grandparents are reunited with grandkids (social media, presumably egged on by people like Toby Young, is apparently already planning freedom parties).

Tom knows all of that means the workload and death toll will shoot up for a second time in his hospital in leafy Shropshire, let alone what it will do in Birmingham or London. Emma, an optometrist who now co-owns and runs a branch of Specsavers, was full of admiration for her 30 staff. Prior to Sunak's rescue package which saw them all furloughed, they'd all volunteered to take a pay cut. One chap even took Emma to one side, and said he'd go without pay and dip into his savings. The social contract writ large. Bravo to the Specsavers staff in Wellington: your boss is very proud and grateful.

As a tiny contribution to the social contract, we've decided not to add to the strain in London's open spaces, and stick to our patio and exercise bike. We thought we'd have an outing yesterday – Amanda hadn't been out of the front gate for three weeks, so we drove to the pay car park at Hampstead Heath. Quite rightly, it's been requisitioned so that as many NHS staff as possible working at the Royal Free Hospital can stay off the Tube. The streets were busy around there, not least because of the hospital, so we decided to drive a mile to Primrose Hill where our parking permit gets us closer to a green space.

We may have even walked for more than our permitted hour, because we went down to the adjoining Regent's Park. We avoided the narrow bridge which features in one of Amanda's favourite films, *Brief Encounter* – Trevor Howard rows into the bridge, then falls into the lake, to the accompaniment of Celia Johnson's cut-glass chortles. We've also made a detour on our way to the Lake District to visit Carnforth railway station in Lancashire, where the emotional goodbye scenes take place, to the swell of Rachmaninov's *Piano Concerto No 2*. The station clock is still there, for anyone who's seen the film.

The park looks absolutely beautiful in what is apparently the warmest April for over 300 years, and bar a couple of small gaggles of young men and the odd jogger refusing to alter course while snorting like a warthog, everyone was clearly observing social distancing. A young mother apologised profusely when her very small daughter toddled towards us, and we actually ended up thanking her for even being aware of it. It just goes to show there's still a vestige of *Brief Encounter* about Britain; it's always tickled me that the film to this day remains a huge favourite in Japan, where apparently they think that we are still like that – faultless manners, fortitude and a sense of morality, with passion smouldering under the refined surface, but always kept in check. A trip to the away end at the New Den would put them straight. Amanda loves that, too, bizarrely enough.

My Facebook friend Mihir has a young family, and not a great deal of outside space, so he's in London's parks every day. In a recent post, he divided the public into four categories. We saw all of them in Regent's Park yesterday:

The Majority: *tremendously polite and cross the road as soon as they see me trundling down the pavement. Being brown and often sporting a backpack, I've been used to this behaviour for decades. But never really appreciated it until now.*

The Lovey-Dovey Couples: *on no account can they let go of each other's hands, let alone go single file. This would clearly cause their relationship to self-combust. I hate them. And only partly because I'm jealous.*

The Joggers: *forget all the other coronavirus conspiracy theories. It's clearly all part of a mission by joggers to rid the world of non-joggers.*

The French: *usually loudly on the phone to their beleaguered countrymen back in Paris. Proudly gloating that the parks of London are still open, but baffled as to why boulangers are not classified as key workers. Oblivious to all others and determined to hold the centre-ground pavement-wise, even if it means sending a three-year-old head first into traffic. Or maybe especially so.*
Am I right? Or am I right?'

We love all things French in this household, so I ummed and aahed before including that final category, but there were several such types (and Americans, too) bellowing into mobiles as we walked around, and we also had to swerve between two French father and son pairs who were shouting at each other from the opposite railings on a bridge, so Mihir may not be exaggerating his experience by much. He's spot on about joggers – absolute homicidal maniacs, the lot of them.

A famous Frenchman once said, 'L'enfer, c'est les autres,' which translates as 'hell is other people'. I've always thought it was a tad harsh to dismiss the entire human race like that, but now that an unknown proportion of strangers have the capacity to kill you, maybe Sartre was like Martin Peters and simply ahead of his time.

And there's more. My ex-BBC colleague, Graham, fellow fan of early Genesis, (though he doesn't share my view that the *Lamb Lies Down on Broadway* could have been an excellent EP, rather than a self-indulgent double album. I also think that about Pink Floyd's *The Wall*: Roger Waters, like Peter Gabriel on the *Lamb*, had got lost up his own fundament by then) has his own take on 'les autres'.

Here's what he had to say about his neighbour in a recent group e-mail: 'Particularly amused by Armo's coughing neighbour anecdote. Apparently the ONS reports a rise in community cohesion since the outbreak and more than half of adults in the UK say they feel an increased sense of belonging with their neighbours. We have been living next door to a madman for the last 15 years – to call him eccentric would be to describe Maradona as a half decent footballer. Lockdown is not suiting him well and he has spent the last 3 weeks prospecting for oil, or so we assume, in his front garden. This has come at the expense of a severed Virgin Media cable (ours) and a fractured water main (Thames Water). Their van is currently outside the house … I've been putting out the washing.'

An appeal to my distribution list: Amanda isn't writing me handover notes any more, although she regularly sorts out my errant punctuation and syntax, so if you have anything you'd like to share more widely, I'm very happy for you to ease my workload. Including two contributions from friends means I've finished half an hour early, at 11.30am this morning. Thanks Graham and Mihir for giving me even more time to fritter away on this gloriously sunny day.

Thursday, 23 April 2020

Scene: Border control at Heathrow Airport a year from now. A swarthy-looking man is being interrogated by a uniformed member of the UK Border Force.

Official: 'I'm sorry, sir. Your passport says you were born in Cappadocia, Turkey, and the stamps in it suggest you've moved around the Middle East a good deal. Have you ever visited Britain before?'

Swarthy man, 'No, but I'm a very important figure here.'

Official, 'That seems doubtful. Do you have proof of a job here at a salary in excess of £25,600?'

Swarthy man: 'I have a role here, but it's unpaid.'

Official: 'Well I'm sorry, but the home secretary has been very clear that unless you earn £25,600 per annum, you are unskilled and therefore not welcome in Britain.'

Swarthy man: 'I don't want to enter the whole of Britain, my role is confined to England only.'

Official: 'This is UK Border Force, our rules apply to all four nations. In any case, why would your role be confined to England only? Are you planning to play football or rugby or cricket for us? You'd need to be resident for several years to qualify, and we're not letting you in anyway.'

Swarthy man: 'Well, that's a shame. Particularly given today's date.'

Official: 'What do you mean, today's date?'

Swarthy man: 'It's me. St George. Your patron saint.'

Happy St George's Day, one and all. Yes, the old boy lived his entire life in the vicinity of the eastern Mediterranean; whisper it quietly but the slaying of a dragon may well be a myth, and he was executed outside the Greek city of Nicomedia, in modern-day Turkey, for his Christian beliefs in the year 303. He is also the patron saint of Valencia, Catalonia, Beirut, Freiburg, Genoa, Gozo and of soldiers and syphilis (separately, apparently) as well as of the countries of Georgia and Ethiopia, and his saints' day is a public holiday from Bulgaria to Kerala. Even so, you just know he would have wanted to be English, really.

Speaking of immigration, a YouGov survey has found that only five per cent of the British population now think it's one of the most important issues facing the country. That grim Vote Leave campaign team which now runs Downing Street, the tabloids, and the excessive airtime afforded to Farage pushed that up to 40 per cent in time for the EU referendum, but it's been dwindling ever since. The same survey suggests that just under 70 per cent now think Brexit should be delayed while 90 per cent think lockdown and people's lives should be prioritised over the economy. Unfortunately, the UK recently elected a majority of MPs who disagree on all three fronts.

Yesterday marked the return of Parliament – with a few key figures in the chamber, but most joining by video link. For some reason best known to himself, septuagenarian Jeremy Corbyn turned up in person to watch on as his successor, Keir Starmer, showed what's been missing for five years. An opposition, basically. Boris Johnson is not going to enjoy this new set-up any more than Dominic Raab did yesterday. A leading QC calmly and forensically revealing weaknesses in the government's case (such as it is) and crucially, no backdrop of order paper-waving, braying halfwits to drown out any decent points made. It's more like the courtroom in which Starmer once excelled, and a good deal less like Eton Pop or the Oxford Union where Johnson first played to the gallery.

In direct contrast to the YouGov survey findings, it turns out that yesterday's virtual meeting of the Tory backbenchers' 1922 Committee was unanimous in demanding a lifting of the current restrictions. The new intake in particular is dominated by get-rich-quick, or always-have-been-rich, types and in the absence of all voices of moderation like Rory Stewart or Ken Clarke, it's little wonder the collective thinking is positively Jungian … sorry. Toby Youngian, 'Get the serfs on the Tubes and buses and into their workplaces while I sit at home Zooming my backbench chums, otherwise my investment portfolio's going to be looking distinctly ropey' seems to be the gist of it.

I adapted a line from World War One *Blackadder,* in the trenches just ahead of the Big Push, to describe senior BBC management's approach to sending us all to Salford, but it's far more appropriate now. General Melchett (by phone): 'Good luck, chaps. We're right behind you.' Captain Blackadder: 'Yes. About 200 miles behind us.' Chris Whitty, the Chief Medical Officer, made sure that he got it on public record yesterday that he thinks severe restrictions will be needed for another year. I'm pretty sure that was in response to Raab's earlier claim in the Commons that the government's inept response thus far has been guided by the scientists. Let's hope Whitty's painted them into a corner this time.

Everyone connected to government seems to be operating now with one eye on a future inquiry. As for those backbenchers and people like Toby Young, these are the very same people who argued that economic damage was a worthwhile price to pay for blue passports. They're now arguing that lots more lives lost is a worthwhile price to pay to protect the economy. Applying simple logic gives us this league table of priorities: 1) Brexit; 2) the economy; 3) people's lives. At least we know where we are now. The tragedy is that we're stuck with these maniacs until 2024, just as we've found an opposition leader who looks like a Prime Minister.

Not that I've spent the whole of the last 24 hours thinking about all that. Most of yesterday was given over to another Poncey Horse quiz and general group silliness. Amanda had a diary clash, so I didn't win this time. Family Garner – Lee, Jo and young

Noah – won for a record third time, and would get to keep the trophy if there was one. The biology round and too many modern album covers in the picture round didn't play to my strengths.

Then there was a long and extremely funny e-mail group discussion within my ex-BBC Sport distribution group about some of our more ridiculous collective experiences, many of which centred on our ex-boss, Brian Barwick. I wrote extensively about Brian – and toned him down a bit – in *Why Are We Always On Last?* Suffice to say, modesty and tact weren't high on his list of attributes, but a CV which includes head of BBC Sport, head of ITV Sport then chief executive of the FA, showed he had an uncanny ability to walk into any room and hold court. And he provided us with some great anecdotes.

The collective account of how, as programme editor, he first booked and then dropped one of the Three Tenors from the live coverage of the 1994 World Cup Final in LA reached the following crescendo, as related by Michael:

'I believe [floor manager] Dave Bowden was the man escorting Placido Domingo. As it was told to me, the talkback dialogue went like this:

'DB (walking upstairs to our studio): "Dave Bowden for Brian. I am nearly at the studio with Placido."

'BB: "Thanks, Dave. Dessie – Placido Domingo will be with you shortly."

'Des Lynam (raised eyebrow. Look down the lens): "What am I going to talk to him about, Brian?"

(Pause)

'BB: "Fair point, Des. Brian to Dave Bowden. Let's stand Placido down, thanks."

'DB: "We're right outside the studio, Brian. What shall I tell him?"

'BB: "Give him a badge, Dave."'

Those official BBC badges were useful currency in international broadcast centres, if you liked another broadcaster's World Cup issue T-shirt, but Placido's probably doesn't rank among his most treasured career mementos. As Ron pointed out, though, 'give them a badge' is uncannily similar to Matt Hancock's attempts to pacify care professionals 26 years on.

Then there was the time Brian decided that *Sportsnight*'s iconic Tony Hatch theme tune needed a revamp. Bizarrely enough, I sat next to Tony at Ron's wedding and told him how I associated his composition with the sheer terror of trying to cobble together a midweek football edit. Brian had previously commissioned a music producer he knew to rearrange the *Match of the Day* theme: this lasted through the first and second rounds of that season's FA Cup before the papers and a backbench question in the House of Commons persuaded him to change it back. Undaunted, he commissioned Jan Hammer, at the time very much in vogue for his compositions for films and the hit TV series *Miami Vice*, to come up with something for our midweek sports flagship.

I was working on *Sportsnight* at the time, and can remember the suppressed chuckles at the back of our weekly meeting (suppressed because Brian wasn't a man who took kindly to mockery, unless he was dishing it out) as this became a long-running soap opera. The boy Hammer wasn't providing anything on a par with Tony Hatch's breakneck rollercoaster anthem, and his laid-back efforts were more in keeping with his time as keyboard player in the Mahavishnu Orchestra than an adrenaline-fuelled invitation to stay up late to watch some boxing and FA Cup replays. If you were in the vicinity of the *Sportsnight* office in the late afternoon back then, it was worth your while listening outside Brian's door, or barging in on some spurious pretext, to witness his exasperated end of a regular phone conversation with the music maestro in the States. Two of the better lines we collectively claim to recall were, 'It just needs, like we say in this country, more bollocks,' and 'Look, just throw the fucking kitchen sink at it, Jan.'

Sharing these stories sustained us all for most of yesterday. Another was Brian introducing himself to the great Kenyan athlete Kip Keino over hotel breakfast at a World Athletics

Championships. 'Bloody good bloke, Kip,' was his subsequent verdict. As Brian left programme making and entered management, he became increasingly pompous. He had a few moments at the FA, especially when he tried to appoint Felipe Scolari as England manager, but was arguably at his worst in a series of interviews he gave at around the time of 'Snatch of the Day', when ITV outbid the BBC for the Premier League highlights. Before this turned into a ratings and critical disaster, he told a queue of journalists that *Match of the Day* was 'tired' and that his ITV would revamp and reinvigorate it, having 'sneaked in under the radar' to acquire the rights. Brian was now Douglas Bader, not just the man waving the bigger cheque.

He later got completely carried away, and started discussing his 'legacy'. One particular *Independent* feature on the great man back then seemed to have been terminated just before he burst into a rendition of 'My Way'. Instead, it ended like this, and I quote: 'The most fun I've had is touching the ermine of the cloak of fame – and I've had a good laugh.' He gave us a good laugh, too, albeit sometimes unintentionally. I've promised the BBC Sport group that I'll have that quotation printed on a T-shirt for each of us if we all emerge out of the other side of this. Failing that, it would still entertain the rest of us as a potential epitaph for any of our number.

Friday, 24 April 2020

There's been a slightly dangerous sense of expectation building up in our neighbourhood in the last day or so. From having the second most cases per population of any borough in the country early on in this pandemic, Camden has slipped down to page six of 15 on Sky's chart. Of the bottom five in the table I mentioned a month ago yesterday, Gateshead and Middlesbrough – each of which had registered just a single case then – are now in the top ten most affected boroughs. Half of that ten are still London boroughs: Brent, which starts about a mile away from here in Kilburn, has the most cases per head in the whole country, although Sunderland is rapidly catching up.

The long and the short of it is that people have seen from the daily briefings that London's figures have been the first to plateau – almost 5,000 COVID-19 cases in hospital in the capital earlier this month are now down to under 4,000, and there were only six new cases registered in Camden yesterday – so the talk over the fences last night after the applause for key workers was what restrictions will be lifted and when.

This seems alarmingly premature to me, although Scotland's first minister Nicola Sturgeon – as usual, embarrassing Whitehall into action with her competence and directness with her public – has laid out a tentative, and very cautious, plan for her country. This will see flexible and gentle freeing up of businesses and institutions which can enforce social distancing, and may vary by area. Looking at the stats, the Western Isles has had six cases – no new ones in over a week – and no deaths, so you can imagine that Hebridean schools and businesses may be open before those in Glasgow or Edinburgh. Although London seems to be over the worst right now, that's very much temporary – open up most businesses and fill the Tube, and there'll soon be a rapid regression.

What does seem clear is that mass gatherings will not be happening for maybe a year or more. If Tim Martin hadn't insisted that pubs were safe, or the Cheltenham Festival hadn't opened its doors, or we'd tested anyone entering the country six weeks ago, we might have seen a fraction of the cases and deaths, and normality might have been restored more quickly, but that ship has sailed. At least we're trying to roll out testing to key workers – the numbers are still far too low, but the intent seems to be there. Even so, all too predictably, the Department of Health website has crashed under the weight of applications on its first morning. Meanwhile in the States, the Mango Mussolini appears to have plumbed new depths overnight with his suggestion that people should inject themselves with disinfectant. If Trump would like to take part in a clinical trial in which he alone participates, it could be seen as a good plan, but otherwise it's stark, staring bonkers.

I had a chat to Elaine in the adjoining flat from a few metres away, and she confirms that both Gareth and his dad in the next-door building have had COVID-19. Gareth's okay now but his father, John, is back in the Royal Free. He seems to be breathing fine, but a cut on his leg has turned very nasty. Apparently, that's another possible side-effect of which we were previously unaware, as are the gastro problems which originally saw him admitted.

Then I went, amateurishly masked and gloved, to two of our local shops about 200 yards away in Belsize Village. I picked up a prescription, some soap and shampoo and a pair of haircutting scissors from the excellent chemist, where only two at a time are admitted and the staff seem to be fully kitted out. Then into the Late Store for a few bits and pieces, including *Private Eye* – a magazine so Luddite you can't even subscribe to an online edition. Even *Viz* and the *Big Issue* have managed that, so pull your finger out, Hislop.

The lovely Afghan family who run that small, extremely convenient shop – mass lobbying by local residents drove away a Co-op which tried to take over a vacant restaurant, and might have put them out of business – are all kitted out, too. The woman behind the counter was as friendly as ever, and says her husband has been driving her to work from Enfield some days, but that she's dreading the Tube becoming crowded again. Like many families in outer London, three generations of hers are under one roof. The particular prevalence of this arrangement among British Asian families, plus a high population density, have been cited as a key factor in the very high COVID-19 figures in Brent. Something similar also seems to have applied in Italy and Spain – grandchild goes to school, adult children go to work, they become unwell but recover, grandparent dies, is all too common a pattern. So, whatever the 1922 Committee agrees via Zoom, or Toby Young says online while cowering under his duvet, let's err on the side of caution, shall we? As Nicola Sturgeon put it: in time, we can do things to try to revive the economy, but we can't bring people back to life.

Safely back at home after my outing, I spent the rest of yesterday reading more of Craig Brown's Beatles book. As you'd expect from the satirist who has produced a magnificent send-up of Mail Online in the current *Private Eye* – 'Celebrities in Lockdown – 'Attish-Who! Former Doctor Who star contracts virus'; 'Onlookers shocked as callous Meghan Markle is spotted grinning in LA park just three days after Italy announces 20,000th corona victim'' – Brown is at his best when skewering the absurd people who surrounded the Fab Four. The Maharishi Yogi, Allen Klein and Yoko Ono, to name but three.

The music he finds unimpeachable, but they do seem to have been a very gullible foursome. A guy called Magic Alex, of whom I'd vaguely heard, seems to have sponged off John Lennon for years while spreading all sorts of discord. But then, a bit like Maradona or other brilliant sports people, they were ridiculously young and not very worldly. George Harrison was only 22 when they recorded *Revolver* – I still can't get over how they recorded 'Eleanor Rigby' or 'Tomorrow Never Knows' less than three years after they made 'She Loves You'. Just the most ridiculous arc of development. You can understand what is often cited as the ludicrous fact that the now seminal 'Strawberry Fields Forever/ Penny Lane' double A-side single was kept off the UK number one slot by Engelbert Humperdink. More remarkable, arguably, is that the British public had kept up with them through the previous 11 rapidly evolving releases which had all topped the charts.

In the evening, Amanda decided to mark Shakespeare's birthday – unlike St George, he actually was English – by watching a YouTube broadcast of the gender-bending National Theatre production of *Twelfth Night* with Tamsin Greig as Malvolia. I'm happy to accompany my Eng Lit graduate wife to the Globe or elsewhere to see anything by the Bard, but I've seen *Twelfth Night* at least twice on stage, so I drifted off a bit.

Instead, I read a draft of a biography of Bob Willis which Lauren has e-mailed to me. It will form part of the book (whose chapter headings, ingeniously, will be Bob Dylan songs) to accompany Bob's memorial service, which is now expected to take place in 2021. As this will be the 40th anniversary of Bob's 8-43 spell at Headingley, which turned a legendary Ashes series on its head, it will work particularly well, especially for Prostate Cancer UK with whom Lauren and Bob's brother David, are liaising. Lauren has just recorded a long interview with my ex-BBC colleague Phil Wye, who works for the charity, to help raise public awareness. She is determined that some good comes out of Bob's untimely death.

I've kept up my daily ration of music and sport. My 'On this Day' reminders on Facebook have been awash with Boro memories in recent days: two injury-time winners in four days – at home to Reading and away at Bolton – which I attended towards the end of our 2016 promotion season, and a rare iPhone photo I took at Derby County of a pile of celebrating Boro players in front of the away end two years later. We pretty much clinched a play-off place that day, though we lost the semi timidly to Aston Villa, and then lost the creator of that goal (Adama Traore) and scorer (Mo Besic) that summer to Wolves and Sheffield United respectively. It was probably the last Boro away day I unequivocally enjoyed, so I watched an edit on YouTube and marvelled at how Traore ever lit up the Championship for us, before he completed his transformation from what appeared to be a rugby league player in the wrong sport to Premier League danger man at Wolves.

I'm coping without sport – though frankly the prospect of the World Snooker Championship being played in the summer has given me a boost. It's the one sport (other than darts) that I can see working (minus a crowd, of course) under social distancing restrictions, so I'm primed to watch far more of it than at any time since the 1980s. I still think the more optimistic projections for football and cricket may not come to pass this calendar year.

But as Tavares sang, 'Don't Take Away the Music'. I'm twiddling away on my two stringed instruments and keyboard as ever, but the Spotify session on the exercise bike (20km in under 32 minutes now) has become ever more eclectic. Two days ago, I gave Beethoven's *Pastoral Symphony* a blast, although I'd misjudged its length and finished before the Classic FM's Greatest Hits closing movement. Yesterday, I went with *101 of Motown's Greatest* on random shuffle. Not a duff track among the Marvin Gaye/Supremes/Four Tops stuff, but I was absolutely flabbergasted when 'Build Me Up, Buttercup' by The Foundations came on. It's a good song, but I had it down as one of those well-produced catchy, but slightly derivative, British singles of the late 1960s like 'Jesamine' by The Casuals or 'Baby Come Back' by The Equals.

Back in the day, when I was editor of *MOTD*, I often found myself dealing with letters which required a diplomatic answer. On one occasion, the South Korean Embassy complained about the closing sequence after David Beckham's free kick against Greece had taken England to the 2002 World Cup. Our producer Steve Boulton had flown solo with a small DV camera to Japan and shot some material which we interspersed with match action. The South Koreans, perfectly reasonably, pointed out that they were co-hosts, too, so I sent a very diplomatic reply of explanation. The next thing we knew, producer Ian Finch and I were on a paid-for media tour of South Korean venues which helped provide a balanced set of tournament titles.

A slightly more awkward moment came when we got the FA Cup contract back and one Mike D'Abo wrote to us. He'd penned an entirely new set of lyrics to his aforementioned composition 'Build Me Up, Buttercup' and was now calling it 'Build Me Up, FA Cup'. I didn't know he'd written the song, but I did know that he'd been the lead singer of Manfred Mann, succeeding Paul Jones in the era of 'Mighty Quinn', but also, more recently, the victim of a cruel but hilarious Chris Morris prank on Radio 4's *On the Hour*.

Mike was by now a DJ somewhere in the West Country and Morris conducted an almost unlistenably cheesy Smashy and Nicey-style interview with him about the importance of local radio for 'lissners in the communidy'. So, when the poor bloke sent in his new lyric – I've not kept it, but 'From Yeovil to Hull, we'll cheer every goal' might have featured – I had to let him down very gently. I was relieved on his behalf when another fine song I had no idea he'd written, but which Rod Stewart, then the Stereophonics covered – 'Handbags and Gladrags' – became the theme music to *The Office*. A much better fit on a proper TV classic, and the royalties should still be keeping the boy D'Abo ticking over.

WEEK SEVEN

Saturday, 25 April 2020

'While Toilet Duck and Dettol are trending, here's a reminder of the word "ultracrepidarian": one who consistently offers opinions and advice on subjects way beyond their understanding.'

I'm not back on Twitter, but someone posted a screenshot of that tweet elsewhere, from one of the accounts I miss. Susie Dent is a lexicographer from the Oxford English Dictionary who has for a number of years explained the etymology of unusual words on C4's *Countdown*. I talked to her at length a few years ago at a Christmas party given by Jane Morgan – Des Lynam and John Motson's agent – during Des's stint as presenter of the show, and she was just great. Clever (obviously), much funnier than I would have expected and an *MOTD* fan. Susie's tweets aren't always topical, but when they are, they manage to be withering without being too nasty, which is an achievement in itself.

Donald Trump is, of course, the ultracrepidarian she had in mind. His scarcely believable recommendation that people should inject themselves with disinfectant has drawn warnings from the manufacturers of Dettol and Domestos and a string of inventive memes and social media posts in the last day or so. Dean Gordon, the ex-Boro player who lives in Sunderland, has had his share of run-ins with the alt-right in those parts, so simply asked anyone who still wants to defend the guy to defriend him. I came late to the thread below Dean's, by which time there were dozens of replies seemingly unanimous in their anger and despair. I congratulated him on finally uniting his friends, and he told me he'd had to block two people who still wanted a barney on behalf of the Wearside branch of the Tangerine Tyrant's supporters' club.

Even so, very few in the UK would defend Trump's irresponsible and borderline psychotic intervention. Trump has even blocked erstwhile sycophant Piers Morgan, and Nigel

Farage has been noticeably less vociferous in his defence of late. Even Trump's US supporters, though they tend to lack a formal education according to surveys, would know better than to ingest disinfectant, surely? The problem will be that they may not even find out that he said it – Fox News are not reporting it, and everything else was long ago dismissed as 'fake news'.

Not that this country can sneer too much: Trump's the only world leader our PM's spoken to during his recuperation and a YouGov survey published yesterday says that Johnson is trusted by the public to a far greater extent than are newspaper or TV journalists. I don't trust some journalists either, but Bojo was sacked from *The Times* for fabricating a quote from his own godfather and, during his stint as *Telegraph* Brussels correspondent, was described by Chris Patten as one of 'the greatest exponents of fake journalism' for his tales of 'bendy bananas' and the like. He was later sacked from the shadow cabinet for misleading Tory leader Michael Howard. And then there was the NHS red bus and Turkey claim during the Leave campaign. Most of the British public simply seem to see him as the funny fat man on TV. And now that will doubtless be the funny fat man who nearly died so that we could live. The simple fact that even our hospital death figures show we've had more than ten per cent of the global deaths from this virus, despite having less than one per cent of the world's total population, seems to be completely lost on them. The *Financial Times* projection is that the real UK death toll, including those in care homes, is now over 40,000. London has now lost more people than it did in the Blitz. Unfortunately, it seems that a huge chunk of our population thinks that's just one of those things, and not to be blamed in any way on those who supposedly govern us.

This applies especially to Brexiteers, 79 per cent of whom told YouGov that they think the UK government is 'doing a good job' in its handling of the coronavirus, even as they're visibly in total disarray. Those splits in society seem to be irreversible, whatever the circumstances. The latest outrage – that humanities graduate

Dominic Cummings and the Leave campaign's stats guru have been sitting on the supposedly independent SAGE science group which advises the government – will be lost on 95 per cent of the country, just as the non-appearance of the Russia report and the Cambridge Analytica scandal were. So will the fact that Sir Patrick Vallance, the government scientist seemingly closest to Cummings, and chair of SAGE, withheld details of these extra members of his group.

Just as outrageous, we now know that government ministers were alerted last year to the risk of a coronavirus pandemic. A leaked confidential Cabinet Office briefing, the 2019 National Security Risk Assessment, warned that the UK must have a robust plan to deal with a pandemic virus of potentially catastrophic social and economic consequences, not to mention the potential damage of any lack of preparedness. The 600-plus-page report was signed off by, amongst others, Sir Patrick Vallance. I'm now in agreement with Pete, my statistically driven friend from Facebook that Sir Patrick – he of the herd immunity presentation – should 'go, go, go. Right now.' He won't, of course. These people never do these days.

When the government – or more specifically Kuenssberg and Peston's 'Number 10 spokesman' – has repeatedly deflected by saying it's 'following the science', it's effectively been Classic Dom and cronies saying, 'It's not our fault, we're doing as advised by … er, a committee which includes Classic Dom and his cronies.'

Looking at the above, the only sensible contribution to today's entry thus far comes from Susie Dent, the only woman who's featured prominently. The world leaders who are showing empathy and common sense in this crisis, as well as achieving results, are Angela Merkel, Jacinda Arden, Nicola Sturgeon and the female prime ministers of Denmark and Finland. Rachel Johnson has pointedly praised Sturgeon today for her open handling of the lockdown and the grown-up conversation she's having with the Scottish people. 'By stark contrast, my brother's government,' remained unsaid. Trump and Bolsonaro see vulgar machismo as the answer to everything and our own PM isn't much better, with 'take it on the chin' messaging and his cavalier refusal to believe in illness until it struck him. Testosterone is not the antidote to this virus. I'm coming to the conclusion that men are mostly next to useless in these circumstances: I couldn't stand Margaret Thatcher, but even she was a scientist who would have chaired every COBRA meeting, asked some searching questions and acted decisively early on in a process like this.

Our working lives at BBC Sport often illustrated this gender divide. There's a female head of sport now, and women working at every level, but back in the day, the producers and editors were almost all men and the PAs and production managers were all women. It was a bit less macho by the time my generation started to run the programmes, but I still used to liken myself to Hong Kong Phooey. He was a cartoon character from the 1970s who'd convinced himself he was a crime solver and a Bruce Lee-style martial arts exponent to boot. He'd posture in front of the mirror, making a huge scene and crying 'ha-so', but would then completely balls up his quest and, more than likely, knock himself unconscious. Phooey's silent assistant was a cat, who would trip up the bad guy with an outstretched paw, tie him up in half a second, raise an eyebrow and let his boss think he was the hero when he eventually came round.

We had a string of production managers like that – Kay Satterley was the first I likened to Phooey's cat, then Hannah, whose 50th birthday it is today, Anne Somerset and more recently, Mel and Nicola – who calmly kept the show on the road while the men postured and pontificated. I may be exaggerating slightly, and I'm not even sure of the cat's gender or name, but all BBC Sport veterans will recognise that there was some truth in that description. We need more cats called Jacinda and Angela in charge of the world and less of the alpha male Y chromosome-fuelled decision-making.

Okay, I've wrested control of the keyboard back from Amanda now, and … no, actually, I really wrote that. It's another lovely

Saturday; this is generally the hardest day of the week to be in lockdown. Weekdays still feel like a bit of a skive, but I know I would have spent today watching sport. I probably wouldn't have trudged up to Boro v Cardiff, not least because I would have been at Reading v Boro last week for a desperate relegation battle, but looking at my calendar, I would have been at Middlesex v Derbyshire at Lords (it's 11am right now, so the first ball of the match would be about to be bowled) then would probably have found a football match in the afternoon. I can't remember the rest of the fixture list, but there'd have been a meaningful match somewhere in the London area as the season reached its climax. As it is, Saturday brings some of the rest of this building out on to the communal lawn. Most people here seem to be replicating office hours working from home, so I can see Anthony and Louisa doing their kick boxing routine beyond our bird bath as I write this. Amanda's on the exercise bike – I put that off until teatime every day, essay crisis-style, in yet another male/female divergence.

The one bonus is that, since it's the weekend, she won't tell me to keep my music-playing quiet in case I disturb the workforce. I'm doing another Beat the Intro round in a quiz tomorrow so I need to break off now to work on The La's 'There She Goes' and other happening tunes of the late 20th century.

Sunday, 26 April 2020

I'm tempted to issue a *Private Eye*-style apology: yesterday's diary entry may have given the impression that the conduct of the female gender during this crisis was in some way superior to that of their testosterone-fuelled opposite numbers. I now realise, in the light of the past day's events, that there was not a jot or scintilla of truth in these assertions.

Dear old Allison Pearson appears to have embroiled herself in a terrible Twitter tangle yesterday. Various highlights/lowlights were reposted on Facebook. In the continued absence from 10 Downing Street of the man 'whose health is the health of the nation' and whom we 'love – really love', her infantile outlook on life has turned to, 'Are we nearly there yet?'

'Two friends have told me they are unilaterally leaving lockdown today,' she harrumphed. 'They are furious with the government.' It degenerated from there: these friends are women in their 30s and 40s apparently, so more likely to die in a plane crash, and they won't come into contact with anyone vulnerable, so what's the problem? From what I saw of subsequent exchanges, poor Allison has a Trumpian understanding of the virus – my nine-year-old niece understands that it's highly contagious and that even if she feels okay and doesn't go near Grandma, she could give it to someone in a supermarket, or once she's back at school, who could then give it to an old person. In any case, people are dying at all ages, but having belatedly caught up with the repeat idiocy on Westminster Bridge at 8pm on Thursday just gone, there seems to be an urgent need for some *Janet and John* COVID-19 books to be distributed to every household, especially Allison's.

Then there was Radio 4's *Today* yesterday morning giving over a segment of its airtime to Mary Wakefield, the deputy editor of *The Spectator*. When she's not freeing up pages for the latest cuntrarian outburst from Toby Young, Taki or Rod Liddle, she's Mrs Dominic Cummings. So yesterday evening, when one of the WhatsApp group posted a link to her homily, I felt obliged to listen. Toe-curling would be an understatement: this was body-curling. Dom, contrary to his reputation, is an 'extremely kind man' and when he was stricken with the virus, their four-year-old son Ceddy (as Alan Hansen would have said, 'That's never been a name') put on his doctor's outfit and brought hot Ribena to Daddy's sickbed. Mary, a devout Catholic apparently, prayed on her knees for Dom and Boris, and this supplication paid dividends.

I'm not going to get on my high horse about organised religion, but in the same way as Norman Hunter didn't die of

COVID-19 because he wasn't 'strong' enough, I'm not having it that the praying power of loved ones determines who lives and who dies. I'm also suspicious of rotten people seeking refuge in religion, especially Catholicism – from the mafia to the IRA to post-Iraq Tony Blair, the culture of the confessional provides all too easy a cop-out.

Sadly, I allowed myself to be misinformed. The person posting the clip, who shall remain nameless, claimed it was broadcast in *Today*'s 'Thought for the Day' religious/spiritual slot, normally reserved for the Rev. J.C. Flannel or Rabbi Lionel Blue. This ignited me like a Chinese New Year firework display, and I fired off an e-mail to the soon-to-depart *Today* editor, Sarah Sands. I had a lengthy e-mail exchange with her a while back about John Humphrys who, prior to his long-overdue departure, had made the show unlistenable, in this household at least. As an ex-editor myself, who'd often had to answer complaints about pundits and presenters with whom I had varying levels of sympathy, I managed to have a perfectly civilised online conversation with Sarah and I appreciated her taking the time to reply. So, I felt somewhat chastened this morning to receive another polite and friendly reply from her which told me it hadn't been broadcast in the 'Thought for the Day' slot at all. They're running a series of essays on the coronavirus at the end of each day's programme, and I must have missed the anti-government one from playwright David Hare the previous day, but she's glad I'm finding the show more listenable now John Humphrys is no longer in the chair.

I'm quite annoyed with myself; it's very satisfying as an editor to be able to correct an angry viewer or listener, as I once did when the director-general of the BBC was made aware of co-commentator Mark Lawrenson demanding that England give the ball to the 'white players'. I dug out the match recording, discovered that Lawro had been talking about 'wide players', and replied accordingly. Lesson learnt: always check the context of a clip. Even more annoyingly, my complaint should have been that this nauseating paean to Classic Dom was broadcast on the very morning when he was under fire for simultaneously serving on the allegedly independent committee dishing out the 'science' and running the government which supposedly follows that science. Hey-ho.

Since I didn't watch yesterday's press conference, I'd better not lump Priti Patel in with Allison Pearson and Mary Wakefield and draw a contrived *Macbeth*-inspired portrait of the three of them crowded around a cauldron on the 'blasted heath'. I have seen the clip in which Priti celebrates the current decrease in shoplifting figures, though. I imagine pub fights and fare-dodging are at an all-time low, too, but she's too easy a target.

The significant, and truly depressing, figure to emerge from that press conference is that 813 deaths in hospitals were recorded in hospitals in the UK in the previous 24 hours, along with 4,900 new cases. We've now passed the 20,000 death mark government scientists said they hoped to avoid, with unofficial estimates now somewhere well beyond 40,000. For some time now, we've only been behind the much more populous United States in these grim daily league tables. Even more worryingly, we've stayed at a similar level for around three weeks now. Italy and Spain, whose statistics we appeared to be following early in this outbreak, only peaked for a week and have dipped ever since. Italy, which was a fortnight ahead of us in every aspect throughout the growth phase of the statistics, last saw figures to compare with ours of yesterday at the end of March, so almost four weeks ago.

We are literally what, prior to joining the EU, we were described as figuratively, 'The sick man of Europe'. And yet, the first question from the journalists at every government press conference – and sadly, the BBC goes first every day – appears always to be, 'When are you lifting the restrictions? Are we nearly there yet, Dad?'

Stories abound today of Tory donors, ministers and back-benchers wanting to send the workforce back into the danger zone and taking the inevitable casualty figures on the chin. A check of the Worldometers website yesterday afternoon sent me into the worst gloom I've suffered throughout this whole saga. By contrast to our 813 deaths and 4,900 new cases in 24 hours, Germany had 45 deaths and 419 new cases. Greece, a country at which the rest of Europe has done nothing but sneer in recent years, had zero deaths and 16 new cases yesterday and has only registered 130 deaths in total. That's a sixth of our daily total, over a month into our half-arsed lockdown.

Amanda copped the brunt of my ranting yesterday, and once I'd shut up, I fired off some further furious observations in an e-mail exchange with Niall, who'd contacted me with a TV box set recommendation. As he said, maybe it's the Irish in him (and me – three of my eight great-grandparents emigrated to County Durham, and there's some Spanish further back) but neither of us understand why there isn't more widespread anger at our government's utterly appalling handling of an admittedly dreadful situation. Greece just locked down – properly, presumably, so no unchecked flight arrivals, mass gatherings to applaud (then overload) health workers from Westminster Bridge, or shambolic PPE provision – and they can now start to think about lifting restrictions in a responsible manner. We look set to lift them and watch a second, potentially even worse, wave hit us.

I saw an article yesterday which actually placed Johnson, Cummings and even Grant Shapps's multiple identities among the 'doves': those who are cautious about lifting restrictions. Not one of them isn't seemingly hell-bent on a No Deal Brexit to multiply our problems, but we now have a situation where they find themselves the relative voice of moderation, urged as they are to be even less cautious by the ghastly people who fund, support and surround them. Allison Pearson, and everyone else at *The Telegraph*, has presumably had a 'release the hounds' message passed down from those twin Mr Burns, the Barclay Brothers. All's safe on the island of Brecqhou, not least from any EU tax scrutiny, so the health of their share portfolio trumps the health of their readership, and the usual frenzied arse-licking of Johnson, every time.

I ended up in a bad place yesterday teatime, but forced myself to do some exercise. At the age of 55, it's not healthy to feel that level of violent anger towards anyone, so I translated it into my fastest 20km on the exercise bike so far, at under 31 and a half minutes. 'Extremely kind man' though his wife claims he is, I treated the pedals as if they were Cummings's Mekon head, to the strains of a proper live heavy rock album of my youth, UFO's *Strangers in the Night*. 'Doctor Doctor' and 'Rock Bottom' seemed like an appropriate headbanging soundtrack to my mood.

Then I got up this beautifully sunny morning, apologised to Amanda for yesterday's gloom and ranting, and cheered myself up with the latest Randy Rainbow song which my brother has sent to me. Randy's eviscerated Trump again, this time with a ridiculously breezy rewrite of 'A Spoonful of Sugar' from *Mary Poppins*. Whether lines such as 'There's no vaccine, so try some Mr Clean' and 'He diatribes and recklessly prescribes, that some Pledge on your pancakes makes coronavirus pass' will ever reach the core Trump support is questionable, but the thin-skinned orange maniac is currently refusing to conduct any more press conferences with what he's now branding the 'lamestream media'. Sorry, but Randy is smarter and funnier than you are, Donnie boy. Bigly.

I then treated this writing session as anger management therapy, interrupted only by my lovely nieces FaceTiming us from Kent. They're so sensible and philosophical about their school and holiday plans being up in the air, and about spending every day under a roof with two octogenarians rather than their school friends. They've also been working hard at their studies and finding time to cycle round the neighbourhood, develop an interest in sewing and our family history, and to make bird feeders. After half an hour of their sunniness, you can't help but feel a glimmer of hope for our collective futures. I just wish they were able to vote, lobby the powers-that-be, or seize control of Allison Pearson's Twitter feed.

Monday, 27 April 2020

Yesterday was a better day. It had to be, to be honest. I can't afford to let slip all the progress I've made since the worst of my dizziness and associated anxiety and gloom of five years ago. We were involved in a record three quizzes yesterday: Amanda's sister and her husband threw one for the extended family, then we hosted the Fat Larry's quiz – I chucked in my intros round again, slightly adjusted for us all being pretty much the same age – and finally we did Neil's esoteric Poncey Horse quiz. Neil lives very near BT Tower and set a fantastic London photographs round gleaned from the walks he's been taking around the deserted centre of town. In a borderline non-PC round, he also gave the women ten questions on the offside law – Amanda did passably well – and the men ten yoga positions to name – I was hopeless. We did predictably poorly on Neil's round about the late DJ Avicii and associated acts, so didn't win, but it was good fun nevertheless.

It's the most British thing ever to want to socialise remotely with friends and family but to be unable to say that. A quiz provides the perfect cover – everyone's getting more and more creative with their questions, but it's effectively just a virtual pub or barbecue with all the usual running jokes and affectionate insults. And a David Brent-style prat like me who wants to get his guitar out at the drop of a hat.

I read an interview over the weekend with Brandon Blackwell, the New York whizz-kid who dominated this year's *University Challenge*. He'd already won quite a lot of money on shows like *Jeopardy* in the States, but came to Imperial College to study for his post-grad specifically so he could get involved in the quizzing in this country, which is apparently far more developed than it is anywhere else in the English-speaking world. Brandon became heavily involved in the London pub quiz scene and thought about applying for *Mastermind*, but realised he'd be at a huge disadvantage having not grown up with our popular culture, so *University Challenge* it was. Even then, he watched lots of old *Newsnight* episodes on YouTube so that his split-second reaction time wouldn't be slowed by trying to fathom Jeremy Paxman's posh accent and drawling delivery.

Speaking of David Brent, now we have Netflix we've decided to catch up with Ricky Gervais's *After Life*. I met Ricky years ago when we got him to do a Brent pep-talk for FA Cup final day – 'Yes, Mr Seaman, moustaches are still acceptable. In the north,' was one memorable line. With the honourable exception of the David Bowie cameo in *Extras*, he's arguably never again quite hit the heights of *The Office*, but he has an interesting mind. *After Life,* about a middle-aged journalist who's recently lost his wife to cancer, has very much divided those friends who've watched it. The first episode seemed almost designed to repel, but we've watched the first three now and will persevere.

The locations particularly interested us: we're used to cinematic liberties being taken with London – a walk across Tower Bridge taking us straight to Buckingham Palace or similar. This takes it a stage further: Gervais's character Tony leaves an office on a Home Counties high street (Beaconsfield, apparently) then walks straight into various parts of Hampstead. Gervais's home in the series is recognisably on the Vale of Health, a cul-de-sac enclave on Hampstead Heath where some friends of ours have a cottage. Rowan Atkinson lives in the big house next door, and keeps a very low profile at their summer party. We saw some location filming going on with Joe Wilkinson and Roisin Conaty outside the nearby pub, the Flask. Ricky Gervais lives in Hampstead, too – he and his partner Jane can often be seen walking their dog on the Heath – so has presumably moved as much of the production as possible to his backyard.

Funnily enough, the *MOTD* presentational team are doing much the same now. Alan Hansen's dream would have been to lie on his sofa in Southport watching any matches involving the big five, while grunting 'log that' by video link to some poor sap who was preparing his analysis. I've not previously watched any of the home-made archive shows they've been running in the *MOTD* slot since lockdown, but that may well have been a mistake. I watched this weekend's episode on the iPlayer yesterday, and it was just great. Ten bonkers Premier League moments were discussed, from the Cantona kung-fu kick to the Keegan 'I would love it' rant, and freed from the time constraints imposed on a day when actual matches have been played, you saw the real off-duty Lineker, Wright and Shearer, linked by video from their living rooms. There are glimpses of their personalities in any programme they make together, but this was more like the chat we used to hear in the production office or when they have a meal together, and I found it compulsive viewing.

Wrighty is a big, lovable kid in many ways, but he nailed the mixture of horror and glee any of us feel when something goes spectacularly awry. As the editor, I always made sure there was some official BBC tut-tutting within our show when, for example, Paulo Di Canio pushed over referee Paul Alcock, but it was always an objectively funny episode: from Alcock's Laurel and Hardy pratfall to Nigel Winterburn getting in Di Canio's face, then exaggeratedly cowering out of the way. Wrighty shared dressing rooms with Di Canio and Winterburn and provided some background and a great comic narrative. Likewise, Shearer was on the pitch when his team-mates Lee Bowyer and Kieran Dyer were sent off for fighting each other. I've heard him relate that and other crazy tales of that Newcastle era in private, but enough time has elapsed for a wider audience to hear about it as well.

Finally, the Cantona kung-fu kick prompted Wrighty into a heartfelt examination of how it feels to take excessive abuse from the crowd. Once I found out about the far-right past of Matthew Simmonds, the man who claimed in court that he'd merely shouted, 'It's an early bath for you, Eric,' I have to say I always felt a sneaking admiration for what Cantona did. Obviously, it could have prompted a riot and he had to be banned, and even Wrighty wasn't really condoning it and never did anything quite like that himself. However, having been on the end of the racist abuse I know he suffered, especially in the 1980s, he mounted a coherent partial defence of Cantona's instinctive reaction. It was a bit like a much more interesting version of the moral philosophy tutorials I attended at university – Lineker and Shearer are empathetic men and consummate professionals, so managed to bring a rather profound discussion back around to a hope that the togetherness we're currently seeing in society may persist once life's back to normal. Just a great piece of TV; when I started this journal on that first football-free Saturday, I wouldn't have foreseen that I'd be enjoying a show made like that six weeks later.

Boris Johnson is now back in Downing Street. He has a job on his hands keeping that fragile societal togetherness on the rails. Incredibly – to me anyway – he's now facing as much, if not more, pressure from those who want a bonfire of restrictions, as he is over the failures in testing and protective equipment and our appalling casualty statistics. I've banged on about this before, so will try not to repeat myself, but Catherine Bennett has pulled together some of the current right-wing thinking today for *The Guardian*, and it's truly alarming.

To start with the darkly comical, Toby Young, having been outed by his wife for his hypochondria, is now telling *Spectator* readers that, as a veteran of the virus (your wife says otherwise, Tobes) his 'death would have been acceptable collateral damage' and that prolonging 'the lives of a few hundred thousand mostly elderly people is an irresponsible use of taxpayers' money'. Actually, that's not comical at all, is it? It does, however, help to explain a previous *Spectator* article in which he lamented that six of the ten invitees to his stag do didn't turn up, including his best friend. And yet Boris Johnson's supposedly more sensible younger brother, Jo, appointed Young to an education committee a while back. This decision had to be reversed when, despite deleting most of his back catalogue of 56,000 tweets, some extremely lewd ones had already been screenshot; Young became too embarrassing even for a modern Tory government.

Elsewhere, the Govester seems to be on manoeuvres. I doubt many people who've lost loved ones to this virus will agree with Michael Gove's apparent desire to 'run things quite hot', ie, shift the balance away from lockdown in the direction of firing up the economy. You can see what's driving his thinking – the UK is accruing staggering levels of debt each passing week – but sadly, any reopening of the economy carries huge risks, especially since we haven't suppressed the virus sufficiently in these early weeks. *Private Eye* used to cite a generic fictitious Tory backbencher called Sir Bufton Tufton. The real life Sir Geoffrey Clifton-Brown, MP for the Cotswolds, says, 'We have to accept a bit of risk.' There will be 'more and more coronavirus cases', but 'we just have to accept that'. That probably looks like a more appealing theory when viewed from the Cotswolds than it does here in London NW3.

It really has come to something when we're relying on Johnson and Cummings – the pair who caused that referendum result, buried the Russia report, sacked all moderates and appointed a eugenicist – to be the voices of reason. Having actually experienced some of the horrors of this illness themselves, we just have to hope that they'll listen to the scientists, and don't cave in or do anything reckless. Dom is uniquely placed in this regard since his history degree has somehow earned him a seat on the science advisory panel, SAGE.

One final piece of information which has come to light – though only in *The Guardian* and on Sky News, naturally – illustrates perfectly why I have little confidence in this government. It was reported that the Vote Leave data modelling man who has been sitting on the SAGE committee along with Classic Dom is called Ben Warner; unlike Cummings, he has at least studied science formally, even if physics seems to be the wrong discipline to entitle him to a view on a pandemic. By sheer coincidence, Ben's brother Marc – who also worked on the Vote

Leave campaign – runs a company called Faculty A1 which was awarded a £250m NHS data contract shortly after Cummings entered Downing Street to work with Johnson. And now the lucrative contract for the much-vaunted NHS tracking app has been awarded to … Faculty A1. Our collective futures are in the hands of this cabal, racket, call it what you will. To quote *Private Eye* again: isn't life grandy and dandy?

Tuesday, 28 April 2020

Boris Johnson returned to Downing Street yesterday. We were relieved to hear that he doesn't appear minded to give in to the libertarian maniacs, and is aware of the dangers of a second spike in cases. Shame he went round shaking hands in hospitals and at the rugby during the first one, but at least he may understand it now, albeit the hard way. 'Many people will look at our apparent success' was either horribly deluded, though, or yet another whopper and he still couldn't resist applying dodgy analogies. I'm not at all sure the virus really is a 'mugger', but if it is, then our PM walked down a dark alley at midnight waving a stuffed wallet in the air, shouting, 'What-ho, mugger chappies.'

In truly sobering news, it's been revealed that the actual death figure for the first week of April, once care home and other community deaths are factored in, is 35 per cent higher than the previous hospital figures. So, the current death toll is not really 21,000 or so, but actually somewhere well above 25,000. This revised tally sees us go into the same territory as the recent much-slowed figures for Italy and Spain, and will soon put us second in the world behind the USA.

The scientist who's impressed us most – Professor Anthony Costello – has reacted today to *The Guardian*'s unearthing of the identities of 23 of the people who sit on the SAGE committee, whose science the government claims to have followed throughout. He confirms my unscientific observation that

Dominic Cummings and his stats man should be nowhere near it, but also points out that 13 of the 23 work directly to two of the others – committee chair, Professors Patrick 'herd immunity presentation' Vallance, and Chris Whitty – and therefore this 'may well influence their ability to speak freely'. Professor Costello is appalled by the complete absence of epidemiologists, molecular virologists and intensive care experts. His conclusion is that SAGE is not fit for purpose in current circumstances. Doubtless there are professional rivalries involved, but it really isn't a verdict anyone wants to hear from an eminent scientist, or which will have been reached lightly.

As I've been typing this, Amanda has been listening to a very graphic Radio 4 programme detailing life on the NHS front line at the moment. It's audio only, of course, but is conjuring up visual images of a Hieronymus Bosch painting or grainy photos from the Somme. Truly horrible and disturbing. I've also seen quite a few mentions of last night's *Panorama*, which seemingly exposed further dismal details of the government's PPE failings. I say 'mentions' – Sky, some of the newspaper websites and various friends thought it merited coverage, but I'm told it didn't make the main BBC bulletins or the Twitter feed of the BBC's chief political correspondent. It's now some way down the BBC News website's agenda, below 'the weekly shop is back in fashion, says Tesco's chief', to name but one major scoop.

This may be wrong – I've pretty much stopped watching for the sake of my blood pressure – but I have serious scholarly friends who feel there's now a two-tier BBC News system in place: journalism for grown-ups around the margins; digestible baby food for the herd on the main bulletins. Amanda often remarks on how worked up I get about BBC coverage. The best I can come up with in my defence is that, having worked there for 30 years and watched and listened to it avidly for 55 years, the BBC is almost like family. I want it to match my admittedly high expectations under the most trying of circumstances. Ninety-five per cent of its output, outside of news, has been tremendous of late, and may even have kept the Cummings wrecking ball at bay. My ever-diminishing exposure to the main news bulletins in particular, though, feels like I'm watching on helplessly as one of my close relatives shacks up with a known con man.

By contrast, I've just received one of those 'let's get this message VIRAL' reposts from a Facebook friend. I won't name her, because she's a well-meaning but rather sheltered individual, but I will name the originator since he's so keen to go viral (unfortunate word in the circumstances, but then it's an unfortunate post). One Dan Baldwin names individual members of the 'Negative UK Press' – his capitalisation – who are actually all TV, not press, journalists. They are apparently missing 'the mood in this great country of ours – the United Kingdom'. Claiming to speak for an entire nation is rarely a good look, but he carries on, saying that the government are 'doing their very best' and that we need 'hope, optimism and faith'. I assume that Dan actually exists and isn't another of Grant Shapps's alter egos. Either way, I've defriended people for less, but I know that the person who reposted it has no malign intent, just an entirely apolitical outlook and innocent desire for everything to be okay. Unfortunately, things aren't all okay, and Dan Baldwin – I'd take odds of 100/1 on that he's a Tory Leaver – doesn't want anyone asking inconvenient questions of our politicians, as long as he voted for them.

His entire timeline for late 2019 seems to have consisted of catching fish and simplistic abuse of the Labour Party, so I doubt he'd be as acquiescent if Johnson had lost the election. And just to cap it all, he signs off with seven Union Jack emojis. I'm not sure what the flag-to-truth exchange rate is at the moment, but seven sends out a clear message that he's very, very patriotic, and that anyone who doesn't see everything his way is not really British. He's also dopey enough to allow anyone, not just friends, to read and reply to his posts, so Dan has just had both barrels from me. And quite a few other people, to be fair.

Meanwhile, Michael Gove really does seem to be on manoeuvres. He had me shouting at the TV again yesterday with a claim that the Brexit negotiations are on course. It looks to an outsider very much like they're heading for the No Deal iceberg, so who knows what's going on there, or whether he'd ever mount another leadership challenge somewhere down the line. *The Sunday Times* is now banned (outrageously) from the Downing Street press conferences for running that article the weekend before last, but Gove and Murdoch are very close – Rupert was in the room when the Govester interviewed Trump for *The Times* – so only time will tell.

Radio 4's *Dead Ringers* used to portray Gove as a cross between a gossipy Scottish fishwife and Matt Lucas's teenage delinquent, Vicky Pollard. 'I'm not one to gossip yeah, but no, but yeah, you should have heard what Theresa said about Boris,' and so on.

For our own lockdown amusement, Amanda and I have recast that scene in *Some Like It Hot* when Little Bonaparte, head of the Chicago mafia ('Friends of Italian Opera') plans to 'rub out' Spats Columbo (played by real-life gangster George Raft) by hiding an assassin in a birthday cake. But not before he's remonstrated with Spats for carelessly allowing witnesses of a mafia shoot-out to escape.

Here's our re-imagined version:

'Some people might say shaking hands with everyone in da hospital and sitting huddled up together on da front bench was a little careless, but I say … to err is human, to forgive divine.'

'Some people might say that missing da first five COBRA meetings was kinda sloppy (bangs fist on table) but I say … ya can't keep a good man down.'

Who knows whether Michael Gove will ever run for the Conservative leadership again, like he did in 2016. I may well be wrong, but I think he could be destined never to land the top job. Tory MPs choose a final two candidates and the dwindling band of elderly members get the final say. I can't say I have a hotline to that particular electorate, but if the vote was held now, I'd expect Rishi Sunak to get the nod.

I made a rare foray on to my own Facebook page at the weekend, and as sometimes happens when I don't post about politics, there were something like 100 replies from all manner of people I rarely hear from – for the first time in five years in the case of my university friend Becky, who's lived in France for nearly three decades. I simply posted my Johnny Cash and ukulele version of 'We'll Meet Again'; I'd recorded it for Hannah's birthday video, but decided to inflict it on everyone else, too. The message in the lyrics is appropriate right now, as the Queen rightly pointed out, and frankly, who cares about inhibitions during lockdown?

I'd like Howard Goodall to make one of his musicology for the masses documentaries about those old-fashioned songs which seem to me to work better on the ukulele than guitar. They all have similar chord structures – ones you almost never hear in modern songs: C or G is often followed by E7 or A7, effectively in a different major key – and there's usually a certain jauntiness, even when the lyrics aren't upbeat.

I sometimes play blues songs on the ukulele, usually out of Amanda's earshot, but objectively that's not really appropriate. 'Sunny Side of the Street' is a song which does work, imho; it's a standard, credited to McHugh and Fields, but which was actually sold to a publishing house by my dad's hero Fats Waller for a fixed fee, believed to be $200, when he was destitute before he became famous. And, naff though they and their mostly novelty songs were deemed to be by some of my peers in the 1980s, Chas and Dave's 'Ain't No Pleasing You' would have been a huge 1920s hit. Chas Hodges was a terrific pianist, and there's a fine orchestral arrangement on their original version, but I love playing it on the ukulele, too.

My favourite of all songs of that ilk though, comes from Laurel and Hardy's classic four-reeler *Way Out West*. That glorious dance outside a saloon bar is accompanied by the song

'At the Ball, That's All' by the Avalon Brothers. That scene was painstakingly recreated by Steve Coogan and John C. Reilly for the fine and very moving film, *Stan and Ollie*, recently, and immediately reminds me of both my grandads. They'd known each other for years through work, long before my parents married – that 'friends shaking hands, saying "how do you do"' line in Louis Armstrong's 'What a Wonderful World' has always made me think of them for more than 50 years – but they were quite different in other respects.

My Grandad Armstrong was a rather courtly churchgoer who kept meticulous accounts for a living in a County Durham pit office, whereas my Grandad Allen eventually managed a fleet of coal lorries in the same area, and was a more voluble, extrovert figure who cracked daft jokes and took foreign holidays with Grandma Alice, before either became the norm. But I can remember watching the BBC's incessant daytime repeats of Laurel and Hardy with both of them when I was a kid, and sharing the sheer joy of beautifully constructed silliness with two men who were both born in 1908, nine years before that great on-screen pairing had first worked together.

So, 'At the Ball, That's All' (fortunately Amanda shares my love for that song, and especially the dance) gets a ukulele outing pretty much every time I pick the instrument up, and the original soundtrack recording would probably be the one disc I'd save from the waves in the unlikely event that I'm invited on to *Desert Island Discs*. In the meantime (picks up uke), 'Diddly-bo – commence your dancing, commence your prancing.'

Wednesday, 29 April 2020

The conflict between wanting to be well informed and needing to stay sane raged before I'd even got out of bed this morning. I sleepily glanced at my iPad and a couple of Facebook posts led me to feel that, as a trained journalist of sorts, I needed to know more. Firstly, there was a massive piss-take of Nigel Farage who'd apparently made a non-essential journey, along with someone to film him (who may well not live in his household) down to the south coast to stand on an empty beach and bleat about illegal immigration. As someone who has nailed his colours to Trump's mast, always wanted to sell off the NHS and is even more laissez-faire than Boris Johnson, he has nothing to offer on the subject of COVID-19, but even so, this was almost comically needy. The clip I saw was of a completely deserted beach with only Farage's lurid description of imagined hordes from far-flung lands to fill the void, but given my 'Thought for the Day' mishap, I decided I'd better check the context.

Then, more importantly, my stats friend Pete referred to the latest Office of National Statistics data which revealed 3,000 deaths from COVID-19 in care homes in Easter week, but still showed 6,000 further unexplained deaths above and beyond the figure for a normal year. The overall UK death toll that week was the highest since records began. Certain experts, cited by Pete, think these excess unexplained deaths must be COVID-related too and that, by now, care home death numbers are probably outstripping those in hospitals, since the latter are finally receding a little this week. Pete projects that our actual number of COVID deaths may well be more than 50,000 by now.

Thinking back to our visits to Auntie Irene's care home, doctors, nurses, physios, hairdressers, chiropodists, cooking and cleaning staff, friends and family of the residents as well as the carers troop in and out all day. They then go back to their homes, and you start to understand why our new infection figures are so far ahead even of the other hotspots in Europe. I really should immerse myself in Pete's sources, I thought, before I further alarm anyone else.

So I warily opened the overhead cupboard that is Twitter, and sure enough, all manner of forgotten junk fell on my head. The first object to land on me was that someone masquerading as Jennifer Saunders had defended the government and branded dissident NHS staff as liars. By the time the real Jennifer Saunders had disowned this, it had been passed on thousands of times over. Then there was widespread fury among people followed by my dormant account that Lord Sugar had added 'I agree with every word' to that asinine Facebook post claiming that inquiring journalists were 'missing the public mood'.

Elsewhere, Anand has retweeted an added angle to the award of the NHS tracker app to Classic Dom's accomplices. I didn't understand all the technicalities and the fears about invasions of privacy and the speculative technology potentially failing, to be honest. The geek community, though, seems united in its opposition to Ben and Marc Warner, Cummings's favourite Warner Brothers (maybe their COVID-19 app can be called 'What's Up, Doc?') and their selection ahead of what a non-geek might imagine would be the more tried and trusted route of a Google/Apple joint development.

Eventually I found Farage's empty beach post: it was indeed as tiny-minded, pitiful and attention-seeking as the clip had made it seem, and most of the replies underneath absolutely trashed him. Just above that was a post from Lewis Goodall, a campaigning Sky journalist who along with the excellent Faisal Islam moved to the BBC a few months ago. Sadly, not to frighten the horses on the main bulletins, but to join that other troublemaker Emily Maitlis on the virtually unwatched fig leaf of editorial freedom that is *Newsnight*. Following on from the previous evening's *Panorama*, Goodall had spoken to some front line NHS workers about the continuing PPE debacle, and posted a link to his *Newsnight* piece on Twitter. Unfortunately, the first reply, from an account festooned with Union and St George's flags and called 'Make Britain Great Again', had unearthed evidence that, while a student, Lewis had been a member of the Labour Party. MGBA also claimed that one of the doctors interviewed by *Panorama* was a Labour member, so aided by a pile-on by no-follower accounts seemingly straight from a bot factory in Moscow, all criticism of the government was summarily dismissed as lefty libtard fake news.

Pretty much every other tweet, whether about Mike Pence refusing to wear a mask in a clinic where they are compulsory, or Carole Cadwalladr's incredulity at Matt Hancock praising the *Daily Mail* for buying and flying in a planeload of PPE from China (it was supposed to embarrass you, Matt) was accompanied by default spleen from the other side. I'm usually with Lewis, Carole and probing journalism, which is why I followed them in the first place, but in the end, what's the point? Absolutely nobody is changing anyone's mind in the Twittersphere and it's just an unedifying cacophony. I'm afraid I didn't even do too much more number-crunching on the death toll conundrum. When I was paid to get things right for an audience of millions, I double- and triple-checked everything, and will endeavour to continue to do so here on other days, but by now, my head was exploding. I rammed the overhead Twitter cupboard firmly shut and got up and made myself some breakfast as the goldfinches flitted about outside.

As I type, it's been announced that Carrie Symonds has given birth to Boris Johnson's latest son. That'll buy him and his government a few more days' grace from predictable quarters and spleen from others. I wish the new mother and her blameless offspring well. For the country's sake, though, I hope the royal baby-style circus that will now accompany every moment of the poor little bugger's young life doesn't become another 'let's all pull together, dissent is treason' saga which outweighs tens of thousands of avoidable deaths. The Remoaners' Messenger group has just posted the following Twitter exchange: Robert Peston tweeted, 'Having babies changes us …' James Felton replied, 'The first 7–9 kids didn't do it, but I've got a good feeling about this one.'

I feared we might witness a conflict like that last night. Our latest get-together via WhatsApp involved Doctor Liz and two couples from our NW3 area, who we met through Liz and now meet sometimes for dinner. An inveterate traveller, Liz celebrated her 50th birthday a few years ago by hiring a small ship to sail round the Galapagos and inviting 35 or so of her friends along. I managed to extract an unheard-of three weeks' leave during the football season, and Amanda and I travelled to Peru and Bolivia before everyone gathered in Quito and flew out to the Galapagos. Probably the greatest holiday we've ever had, and the private cruise with umpteen doctors and assorted friends was an absolutely incredible experience.

So, last night, we, Doctor Liz and the two other couples, one moderately left wing, the other all-female and default non-nasty, but unquestioning, Tories, all linked up. It would probably horrify 'Make Britain Great Again' man to hear this, but there are few Conservatives on the NHS front line, and Dr Liz definitely isn't one of them. The Tory duo launched into a well-meaning and upbeat 'we're all in it together, the virus is a great leveller' spiel. I could see leftish Martin bristling on our split screen, but he restricted himself to relating a cartoon he'd seen of a man in a deckchair in a big garden swigging a cocktail using exactly that 'leveller' line, as hundreds of people burst out of the windows of a high rise behind him. Good point, well made.

Then Liz related her latest front-line experiences, in particular of the PPE fiasco. She's refusing to wear the clearly risible cooks' aprons that have now been issued in lieu of gowns at her hospital, but being the dedicated professional she is, she's soldiering on and is just taking the risk. But because she has that gallows humour of the wisecracking surgeons in *M*A*S*H*, she just made everyone laugh instead of directly pointing out that she and her staff are hardly on the same 'level playing field' as most of the rest of us.

I also chucked in the *Panorama* revelation that the government has been counting every pair of gloves as two separate PPE items for the purposes of massaging their figures. Sounds like a Classic Dom ruse to me, but I made it darkly comical too, since that's how Dr Liz was playing it. It was actually a thoroughly affable conversation, and I think the two default Tories learnt a lot more than 'Make Britain Great Again' man is ever likely to do on Twitter. And their basic old-fashioned British decency of 'we're all in it together' and hoping everything is going to be okay isn't the worst way to live, so maybe I learnt something, too.

At the very least, it reminded me of something I first realised during the early days of my relationship with Amanda. Back then, she worked as a House of Commons researcher. As I met the three MPs she worked for at various times, I realised that the two Tories she worked for were thoroughly decent men, whereas the Labour man was an absolute expenses-fiddling, copper-bottomed rotter. This did not accord with my preconceived notions of either party. Admittedly, neither Tory – one of whom was Ken Clarke's close friend, the other had been recorded saying of Margaret Thatcher, 'I wish that cow would resign' – would have survived the Cummings cull, but there are lifelong Tory voters out there who don't know that any of that has happened and think they're still voting for the steady old One Nation Conservative Party of financial prudence. There are a couple of ageing examples in our extended families, too, and though I have been known to despair of them on the quiet or to post things on Facebook which I hope will rattle them, they aren't bad people. I'd hazard a guess that 'Make Britain Great Again' man on Twitter probably is a bad person, though.

In other news, the weather has turned nasty. Yesterday would have been the fourth day of Middlesex v Derbyshire at Lord's, and for the first time this spring I'd rather have been here than there. There is little worse in the sporting world than watching the covers go on, off, then on again just as play is about to resume, with the result that a decent run chase finish peters out into a bore draw. My own pitch inspection of the patio was appallingly misjudged – four minutes into my thirty-one and half on the exercise bike, the heavens opened. I ploughed on, urged forward by a random shuffle of Spotify's 'Classic Rock Workout' playout. This was mostly okay-ish, but not really classic fare: Van Halen, Guns N Roses and the like. Then Free came on – not my favourite of theirs ('Wishing Well') but the decent, if more hackneyed 'All Right Now'. This was fine for a couple of minutes, until abomination of abominations, the gradual build of bass and guitar in the middle section was butchered. This was the horribly edited single version.

Paul Rodgers has one of the great rock and roll voices – Tony Blair was right about that, at least – and you can't help but marvel at how even a boy from the dodgy end of Middlesbrough came up with those cocksure lyrics, aged just nineteen. Even so, using that truncated version is like showing the Carlos Alberto goal v Italy or Gareth Edwards's try v the Barbarians, but only joining for the final pass. I also recalled how I first developed an adolescent dislike for Radio 1's Smashy and Nicey brigade in 1978 as they repeatedly chuntered over, and faded out, two of the greatest guitar breaks in chart single history – at the end of Gerry Rafferty's 'Baker Street' and Kate Bush's 'Wuthering Heights'.

It was probably the cold rain beating down, but I'd worked myself up into a fury and was preparing to cancel my Spotify subscription when with four kilometres to go, a moment to rival 'Southern Nights' leaping out of that humdrum country compilation occurred. One of the greatest intros in rock history – Mick Taylor's brooding apocalyptic guitar then those explosive four beats from Charlie Watts and we're into 'Gimme Shelter'. I can keep time, but as with that other masterpiece of the Rolling Stones' Mick Taylor era, 'Tumbling Dice', I have no idea how a quiet gentleman drummer manages to inject so much swagger into those tracks. It's one of those recordings which is pretty much perfect and despite the soaking I was still receiving, I flew through the last part of my bike session.

A while back, we watched an excellent film called *Twenty Feet from Stardom* which won that year's Best Documentary Oscar. This was a celebration of the contribution to popular music of the backing singer – Darlene Love, who was in constant demand throughout the 1960s to appear on Sam Cooke, Elvis and especially Phil Spector records, featured heavily; so too did Merry Clayton, who along with Taylor and Watts, sent 'Gimme Shelter' into the stratosphere 51 years ago with her studio vocals.

Bruce Springsteen, Stevie Wonder and other celebrated lead vocalists heaped praise on these often-overlooked contributors. The chief beneficiary of Merry Clayton's extraordinary role in 'Gimme Shelter' was characteristically less generous, though. ''Oo'd wanna be a backing singer?' leered one Mick Jagger.

The apocalyptic outlook in 'Gimme Shelter' was informed by the Vietnam War. Coincidentally, yesterday saw the USA's official coronavirus death toll pass that for American soldiers serving in the Vietnam War. When you think of the lasting effect that nightmare has had on the American psyche, you can't help but wonder why this current catastrophe, overseen not by LBJ and Nixon, but a lunatic who urges the injection of disinfectant then claims like a lying child that he was being 'sarcastic', doesn't seem to have provided a similar tipping point.

Trump's popularity ratings are roughly where they were before he oversaw the current mess. I guess MAGA people and my MGBA friend on Twitter have waded in so far in their unswerving adoration for their respective blond figureheads, and their 'Lock Her Up/Build The Wall/Take Back Control/Get Brexit Done' sloganeering, that nothing – not even the two worst sets of COVID-19 statistics in the world – will ever change their minds. It's like trying to reason with members of a religious cult.

Meanwhile, what of the hapless, slant-eyed gooks the GIs left behind after the airlift from Saigon? Well, Vietnam, having employed tracking and testing from the very first, has registered 270 COVID-19 cases and no (zero) deaths. Normal life has completely resumed, other than in their previously booming tourist industry. No way are they allowing foreigners from shitholes like Britain and the States to enter until we sort ourselves out.

I'm going to end for the day on a lighter note. The ex-BBC distribution list continues to entertain – Graham provided us with an update on his next-door neighbour, with an accompanying photograph of a large wooden structure. 'Turns out he wasn't digging for oil after all,' Graham wrote. 'He was instead constructing some kind of rustic bus shelter; strange, as we live at the end of a cul-de-sac far removed from any of the local routes.'

World War Two's prisoners of war built model battleships out of matchsticks: in the absence of a vaccine, potentially for years or possibly ever, or radical Vietnam or South Korea-style solutions, Graham's neighbour may have built a life-size Titanic which blocks all sunlight from the entire street before this is over.

Thursday, 30 April 2020

I had a vivid dream last night in which I was watching cricket in an indeterminate hot country with people I knew when I was a kid in Teesside, and no social distancing or virus in sight. Waking up to this morning's headlines felt a good deal less real than the dream. 'Concern over training at emergency morgues run by UK festival firms' sounds like black humour along the lines of the Monty Python 'Holiday Home for Pets Pie Company', but it's for real.

As a new father once more, Spaffer Johnson is afforded celebratory photographs on every front page. Most have also found room for the fact that our official COVID-19 death toll is now 26,000 and poised to overtake Italy as the highest in Europe. *The Sun* swerves this news and divides its front page between Johnson and Captain Tom who's going to be made an honorary colonel today on his 100th birthday. *Sun* readers' cups and pint glasses really will be overflowing this morning: their website features the following story: 'Beer We Go: Wetherspoons plans to reopen pubs in June.' I hope that's Father Jack being overoptimistic, but we'll see.

We finished the first series of Ricky Gervais's *After Life* yesterday – I found a couple of moments in the last two episodes quite moving, though the whole series, while ultimately life-affirming, was an interesting exercise in challenging the viewer to stay with it. I may well not have done so had an unknown made the first episode in particular, but I guess you earn that right as you build up a body of work. The Beatles couldn't have started their career with most songs on the *White Album* – I argued only recently with Bob Fisher, a Teesside radio presenter friend of mine that it would have made an incredible single, not double album and that, even so, the master recording of their longest-ever track, 'Revolution No 9', should have been fired beyond the stratosphere on one of NASA's Mars probes.

The Office was innovative in British comedy, but Garry Shandling's *Larry Sanders Show* had already paved the way in the US by dispensing with a studio audience and conventional camera shots, and *This Is Spinal Tap* was a towering early-'80s mockumentary landmark. The technique of reacting into the camera wasn't new, either – as Ricky is the first to acknowledge, it was pure Oliver Hardy. But what *The Office* had from the outset was an Everyman and Everywoman in the romantic subplot featuring Tim and Dawn. They represented the audience as the monstrous Brent, Gareth and Finchy did their worst. The first four episodes of *After Life* had very little to counter-balance the initially nihilistic lead performance, but it was worth our while persisting. We'll take a break, then watch the second series which is now on Netflix.

The weather is still ropey, though the colour scape in our garden has changed once more and there are white and yellow roses in bloom. I still have plenty of nyjer seed, so the goldfinches are very active, but the suet cake is no more (at least until our online order arrives) so the woodpecker isn't bothering with us for the time being.

I was feeling lethargic yesterday – like Lord Sugar's treacherous journalists it's possible that I 'misjudged the national mood' by not having an extra spring in my step after that joyous baby announcement – but I did force myself to spend half an hour (and a bit) out on the exercise bike. Again, mid-random shuffle on Spotify, a song just leapt out. Having praised Merry

Clayton's contribution to 'Gimme Shelter', the music gods sent me something arguably even more sublime this time: 'Tin Soldier' by the Small Faces. This is more of a duet than singer and backing singer combination, and frankly Steve Marriott was more of a singer than Mick Jagger in any case. According to Ronnie Wood's autobiography, Keith Richards wanted Marriott to join the Stones when Mick Taylor left in 1975. Apparently, Jagger felt upstaged by Marriott at his audition. Hardly surprising, since Steve was possibly the greatest white vocalist of that or any era, and was joined by his then girlfriend P.P. Arnold on the chorus of this masterpiece. Paul Weller, not unreasonably, picked 'Tin Soldier' as his one disc to rescue from the waves on *Desert Island Discs*, and I think I'd pick the footage of Steve and P.P. singing it live on French TV as the most stylish thing bar none I've ever seen on YouTube. I've just watched it again, and it's so cool I had to leave the room to put on an overcoat.

I've seen both Marriott and Arnold perform 'Tin Soldier' separately live – Marriott belted it out with his Packet of Three in an Oxford pub venue in the mid-'80s. He had lost all his 1960s suaveness, and cut a dishevelled figure in his dungarees, but by God, the voice hadn't gone. Joe Brown joined him for an encore, and we were told later that the landlord had to pay Steve in cash because his finances were in an absolute mess and the Inland Revenue were after him. He died a few years later in a house fire, aged just 44.

P.P. Arnold, who now lives in Spain, played the 227 Club on Great Portland Street a couple of years ago. Amanda and I bought tickets, but didn't really know what to expect. We needn't have worried – she looked and sounded incredible, and worked her way through her own solo career (the original hit version of Cat Stevens's 'First Cut Is the Deepest', for one) and some well-chosen covers, all backed by Steve Craddock's band. Craddock was Paul Weller's guitarist for a while, and a member of Ocean Colour Scene, so she was in safe hands. The set was interspersed with highly entertaining anecdotes about all manner of musical greats: Mick Jagger, unsurprisingly, was among the first Brits to slobber over her when she arrived in the UK after a stint backing Ike and Tina Turner. Then Steve Marriott wrote the magnificent 'Afterglow of Your Love' for her to sing, before snatching it back, having decided it was too good not to include on the Small Faces' classic *Ogden's Nut Gone Flake* album. So, P.P. (Pat, to her friends) had to make do with sharing vocals on the finale of her set – one of Craddock's band achieved a manful 75 per cent of Marriott's vocal on this occasion – a barnstorming 'Tin Soldier'. If there's a better ending to a gig, or indeed any song, than the urgent, ascending chord coda to that number, I'm struggling to think of it. I'd have given anything to see the original duo perform it together, but the two halves separately in one lifetime will have to do.

A further wave of nostalgia has just swept over me, with a text Amanda received from my Auntie Christine. Apparently, it's a quarter of a century to the day since Ayresome Park saw its last competitive football action. While Christine, Amanda and my cousin Laura spent the sunny afternoon on a long walk, my Uncle Michael, cousin Alison and I secured three very hot tickets to the match, and took lots of photos of the ground to mark the occasion. Bryan Robson's Boro team took a giant step towards promotion to the Premier League with a scrappy 2-1 win over Luton Town. Naturally, Boro missed a penalty, then let Luton equalise, before John Hendrie scored the final goal at what had been the club's home since 1903, and the young lad with Down's Syndrome in the row in front jumped into my arms to celebrate.

I'd only been going there since 1971, but players like Wilf Mannion who'd straddled World War Two were paraded pre-match and old-time fans who were present when George Camsell scored 59 league goals in one season in 1926/27 lingered at full-time to bid a final farewell to the old place. In typical Boro fashion, Dixie Dean scored one more goal the following season for Everton to set the all-time record, but he took penalties and Camsell hadn't joined from Durham City until mid-September, so it's all just another example of history diddling the Boro.

Along with Highbury and many other fine, and not so fine, old grounds, a modern club had to leave the past behind and move on in the all-seater world. However, going first (at the time, the Riverside was the biggest British stadium to be built since World War Two) means that countless other clubs have since either emulated or surpassed our new ground.

I'm really not sure when – or under what circumstances – I'll be able to watch football at the Riverside or anywhere else again. The football there with Juninho et al. went up to another level for a decade or so from 1995, but Ayresome Park will always be the place where I watched my first – and for several years only – football matches. I haven't bought a football programme for decades, but I have one from the first game I went to with my dad, on 6 February 1971: the editorial 'Ayresome Airs' contained quaint phrases like 'we must make reference to Frank Spraggon's injury'; 'it will be a mystery forever how we did not come away from Millwall as handsome winners'; and 'we must redouble our efforts to attain our goal'. Only Boris Johnson still talks like that, and he's usually lying.

Among those companies advertising in this gloriously flimsy and dated publication were Newbould's Pies, Jack Hatfield's famous Sports Shop with its 'largest stocks in the North', the greyhound racing at Cleveland Park, building firm CW Athey of Linthorpe Road (CW Athey Junior was later to play cricket for Yorkshire and England) and poignantly, the shipbuilders Swan Hunter who were advertising a host of new jobs as part of an 'Expansion on Teesside'. A certain Elvis Costello song from the Thatcher era immediately springs to mind. The game finished Middlesbrough 5 'Downing (Derek, not Stuart), Hickton (2), McLimoyle, Laidlaw', Norwich 0 – as it turns out, the biggest win I would ever see at Ayresome Park. Much as I loved the place, it was (mostly) downhill ever after.

Friday, 1 May 2020

May Day. More like mayday, mayday this morning. At no previous point in my 55 years on this planet have I woken up with a start thinking about what someone I dislike is going to call his child. Tom, maybe? Colonel Tom's valiant laps around his garden to raise money for the NHS for treating his broken hip and skin cancer should be, in all honesty, unspeakably embarrassing for what was the world's fifth-biggest economy, and wouldn't be necessary if we hadn't had ten years of Boris Johnson and co. in charge. He should therefore be forgiven for telling *BBC Breakfast* that Johnson is doing a 'great job' on the occasion of his own 100th birthday.

Even so, Dominic Cummings may well already be working out the perfect time to reveal that the Johnson sprog will be named after both the nation's new mascot and St Thomas' Hospital. The day we officially pass Italy's death toll to become the most deadly place on Earth other than Trump-ton is probably Classic Dom's best bet for an optimal dead cat effect. So, in a few days' time, then (Amanda isn't with me on this. She thinks Tom is far too prosaic a name for a Johnson child when you consider the other monikers some of his kids have been saddled with: Peaches, Lettice and Apollo).

In the meantime, if the clip I've seen of Keir Starmer handing Dominic Raab his own arse in a sealed evidence bag the other day is anything to go by, it may be best for Johnson to take his paternity leave an hour at a time i.e. every Wednesday at noon, so as to continue to avoid Prime Minister's Questions. Not that it will matter, having said that: Starmer could – and almost certainly will – politely tear Piffle-Paffle Wiff-Waff to pieces simply by reminding him of the sloppy and downright stupid things he says on a daily basis.

Johnson's first, quite ridiculous, pronouncement on leaving hospital was that 'many people would be looking on at our apparent success'. He could get away with such arrant nonsense when opposed by the equally useless Jeremy Corbyn, but a leading QC is inevitably going to pounce on such a gift. Johnson having rushed to his girlfriend's hospital bedside (the first person ever to wangle annual, sick and paternity leave in the same month?), Raab had to try to explain this indefensible tosh from his boss, and naturally couldn't even begin to do so. But only the usual politically minded five per cent of us will ever know as and when Johnson is duly eviscerated. The same people who watch *Channel 4 News* or read a broadsheet, or write 100,000 plus futile words like these.

The other 95 per cent can seemingly be fobbed off by the cynical exploitation of Colonel Tom, Tim Martin talking about reopening 'Spoons pubs in June, the iffy prospect of football doing likewise and the utter rubbish from a 'TV insider' that 'ITV are certain lockdown will be well over by the time *I'm a Celebrity* starts in November'. This is bollocks on several levels – November is when the second wave of the virus is likely to be in full flow; even if air travel has resumed, there will be temperatures taken prior to boarding and all manner of other restrictions; and thirdly, the UK will be the last country whose citizens are going to be welcomed overseas, let alone by Australia which has got away very lightly, in relative terms, with the first wave of infections. British exceptionalism is simply not going to cut it, even with Ant and Dec on board, and even in the former colonies.

The tabloids and their websites, though, will just keep pumping out 'Corrie's Bev Callard for Jungle 2020' and similar bilge, and will largely be believed. No one will remember the 'it's all over. Everyone to be vaccinated by September' nonsense they peddled a fortnight ago, let alone *The Sun*'s editorial back in 2016 which shrieked 'Sack the Docs'. Health secretary Jeremy Hunt had apparently 'bent over backwards' for the 'infantile hard-left militants' hell-bent on 'swelling their bank balances' while maintaining 'the fiction of "saving" patients'. I bet Johnson's erstwhile jogging partner Tony Gallagher who wrote that, the blessed Rebekah and all the rest, went outside last night, and ostentatiously clapped the NHS like performing seals.

They see their readership and a sizeable proportion of the British public much as *The Simpsons* depicts Homer, as he's driving along looking at roadside advertising hoardings. He hypnotically repeats every line he reads, laughs or drools (if it's food) at the idiotic slogans and completely forgets each one once he reaches the next. That Mencken slogan – 'No one ever lost money underestimating the intelligence of the public' – is, sadly, at least partly true, as far as I can see.

I'm feeling particularly cynical today having discovered that yesterday was the tenth anniversary of what could be seen as a *Sliding Doors* moment in British politics. Gordon Brown, having 18 months earlier led a concerted global response to the banking crisis, left a Sky News microphone switched on as he got into a car and described a Labour voter he'd just met, Gillian Duffy from Rochdale, as 'some bigoted woman'. That unfortunate phrase sparked uproar: on reflection, her question 'Where have all these Eastern Europeans come from?' could have been answered with two words: 'Eastern Europe', but the UK had chosen not to cap immigration numbers after EU expansion in 2004, which resulted in a sizeable and sudden influx of people into some areas. Brown's perceived dismissive and aloof snobbery – albeit not intended for public consumption – set off an El Niño effect which has so far lasted a decade.

From then on, the media took every opportunity to interview Farage at least a couple of times a day, most politicians felt the need to pander to the 'legitimate concerns' of racists and bigots who in turn felt emboldened to express views 'you're not allowed to say any more'. From being a topic of little interest to the vast majority (just five per cent saw it as important in 2010 surveys) immigration increasingly dominated the UK's newspapers and airwaves for the next six years, before miraculously slipping away again once the damage was done. Being allowed to say the supposedly unsayable ad nauseam became the new norm and we ended up where we are now – adrift from Europe and with a psychotic new best friend.

Back to our current reality and yesterday was the day by which Matt Hancock had promised us we'd reach the magic 100,000 tests a day. A figure which would mean we could test everyone in the UK in just over two years, as long as they didn't push their luck and want to be tested more than once. Hancock will doubtless be pushed out red-eyed before today's press conference – Johnson having done his first for some weeks yesterday and (probably) muttered 'sod this for a game of soldiers' afterwards. It could well be that Hancock found a thousand people yesterday to volunteer to each have a swab shoved up their nose 100 times, so that spurious target may just about have been reached. Either way, one more puddle of failure probably wouldn't be noticed amidst this sea of incompetence.

I am finding that anger works a treat on the exercise bike, though. I judged the weather better yesterday early evening: not only did I avoid the intermittent downpours, but I witnessed a full semi-circle of a rainbow surround the house beyond our communal lawn. Feeling strangely competitive as well as aggressive, I decided to go flat out, and became the Roger Bannister of the patio as I pedalled my usual 20km in 29 minutes 59 seconds. I then staggered in and watched the first complete *Channel 4 News* I've seen in some time.

It was an astonishing piece of TV: I've been struggling to watch the individual stories everyone's been showing, but these were so beautifully and sensitively put together – plus the bike ride had left me unable to move – that we couldn't help but stay glued to the screen. I had a good cry on more than one occasion – firstly, they showed two tales from hospital ward to recovery at home of two COVID-19 survivors and their spouses. One of the recovered patients, Peter, woke from a coma to croakily inform the doctor bending over him, 'Farage is a nutter.' Then there was a very moving account of an old lady whose dementia-suffering husband had died along with eight others from COVID-19 in a care home.

Finally, the fantastic 97-year-old Elizabeth, one of the original team at the World War Two Bletchley Park codebreaking centre, linked up with Jon Snow from a care home in Hampshire. She sounded like Celia Johnson in *Brief Encounter*, but by God, was she sharp – in the course of three minutes, she pointedly referred to the hasty rebranding of her carers from 'unskilled' to 'key workers' in recent times but doubted that their salaries would reflect their new status, and said the government had been 'too slow off the mark'. I think I may ask Elizabeth to write this journal for me from now on.

WEEK EIGHT

Saturday, 2 May 2020

I owe Matt Hancock a small apology. Yesterday, I suggested that the target of 100,000 tests in a day by the end of April, with some jiggery-pokery, 'might just about be met'. The daily figure only rose above 20,000 earlier this week, but somehow more than 122,000 tests were duly registered on 30 April. My thoughts immediately turned to the Chinese swimmers who were taking whole minutes off world distance records before they were banned for taking performance-enhancing drugs. Then it occurred to me that the figure could simply have been Priti Patel trying to say 'one thousand, two hundred and twenty'.

Amanda tells me that the Home Secretary wasn't on press conference duty yesterday, so it wasn't that, after all. I'm waiting expectantly for the day that she joins the Chief Medical Officer and the Prime Minister behind the three podiums. At that point, we'll have Priti, Whitty and Shitty. Thank you, I'm here all week. Literally.

It turns out that the new figures don't entirely stand up to scrutiny, since they include home testing kits despatched by post that day as well as thousands of second tests done when the first ones haven't worked. We'll find out in due course whether there was anything medical in the 40,000 envelopes the Hancock family (probably) addressed and posted on Thursday, but to be fair, it is all a step in the right direction.

It needs to be, because the increased testing is giving us new infection statistics still exceeded only by those in the United States. Now we're finally including care home deaths, our toll of 739 announced yesterday is way, way out of kilter with the other big European countries – Italy registered 269, Spain 281, France 218 and Germany 39. Bojo can bang on about the NHS not having collapsed, which is both true and a relief, but his claim that 'many people would be looking on at our apparent success' left out the words 'very stupid' between 'many' and 'people'. As the surprise sage of our times, Piers Morgan, apparently put it rather brutally yesterday, 'The stats don't lie, especially when the stats are corpses.'

The confusion is rather summed up by Johnson having begun to suggest that wearing masks in public may after all be beneficial, a move described as having 'no scientific benefit' by his Health Secretary earlier in the week. For what it's worth, for weeks now I've been wearing a rather flimsy oven-cleaning affair, which I'm having to wash and re-use, every time I've been to the shops. In much the same way, we locked down a fortnight before that official decision was painfully extracted from our instinctively libertarian leader.

As for masks, they were clearly worried about the shortage of all PPE for front line workers, and should have come clean and simply said that nurses, doctors and care workers come first, we'll deal with masks for the general public later. That would have been the grown-up approach. I'm no scientist, but wearing masks in public is common in the Far East and among people of east Asian origin on their travels. They're better at pretty much everything than the crumbling West these days, as a glance at Worldometers tells you, so I'll follow their lead, given the choice.

Or you can believe Donald Trump. Among the conspiracy theories doing the rounds, the one which suggests that COVID-19 was man-made in a Wuhan laboratory, whilst completely unsubstantiated as far as I know, has a degree of plausibility greater than, say, the caveman thinking which is seeing 5G pylons torn down. A Japanese Nobel science laureate has argued in favour of that man-made theory; others have said it definitely originated in animals. However, for the president of the United States to throw that in as a dead cat China-baiting fact at one of his press conferences would have been reckless beyond belief if we weren't talking about this particular president of the United States. As with his 'inject disinfectant' lunacy earlier in the week, he's seen something somewhere on Fox News or while skim-reading a briefing document he doesn't understand and just blurted it out in public.

I know a couple of mental health practitioners, and that profession seriously think Trump has been unwell for some time. He wasn't very likeable as a younger man, but old recordings show him to be far sharper than he is now. He even once had something approaching a crudely self-deprecating sense of humour. Sadly, the 25th Amendment to the US Constitution requires either the vice-president and a majority of executive officers, or a majority of both houses of Congress, to declare the incapacity of a president. Neither will be happening any time soon.

There are some pretty awful people in charge of countries all over the world, but the other notable one providing Trump-like cause for concern right now is one Jair Bolsonaro of Brazil. He's dismissed COVID-19 all along as 'a little flu', and told his vast nation to 'man up'. When Brazil's death rate surpassed that of China this week, he said to reporters, 'So what? What do you want me to do?' He subsequently claimed that he was ignoring all WHO advice because they 'promote masturbation'. Takes one to know one.

Sky News showed aerial footage yesterday of 13,000 rudimentary graves being prepared for the poor of São Paulo; and state governors, as with Trump, are desperately trying to circumvent the callous maniac at the national helm. Given Brazil's history, you'd wonder if the army might intervene. This tends only to have happened in Latin America, though, when leftist governments have been elected – Bolsonaro is a fascist in the true meaning of the word, a full-on racist, homophobic anti-intellectual and most of the other things juntas tend to like.

He's declared his intent to seize back the 14 per cent of the country currently reserved for indigenous tribes who 'don't speak our language'. This has given the green light to a startling acceleration in the destruction of the Amazon rainforest. Sadly, given its size, over-crowded cities, lack of public healthcare and a madman at the helm, Brazil looks like it's the next disaster-in-waiting. When Bolsonaro becomes a baffling figure in the history books, I hope it's noted that he exempted our UK government from the withering criticism he heaped on Emmanuel Macron (in an all-encompassing tirade, he even mocked the physical appearance of the French president's wife) and Angela Merkel among others. Their crime was to express alarm at the forecast that the entire Amazonian ecosystem, which provides 20 per cent of the world's oxygen, will disappear altogether within 50 years.

Trump and the UK government were singled out for praise by Bolsonaro for their alternative stance, best summarised as, 'On you go, mate – fill your boots. Don't listen to the Frogs and Krauts.' Taking back control, and the special relationship. Makes you proud, doesn't it?

Away from such horrors, I've finally finished Craig Brown's Beatles book, and a fine read it was too. He ends with the saga of Brian Epstein's sadly truncated life, and you can't help but think how much easier it would have been for the Beatles' manager, as a tormented homosexual, in more recent times. Especially since he was British and not Brazilian. I intended to start Hilary Mantel's *The Mirror and the Light* next, but its length (900-plus pages) the fact that I know how it ends (spoiler alert: Cromwell is separated from his head) and Amanda's curate's egg review is putting me off. That said, I've read the first two in the trilogy, and I'm not exactly going anywhere for a while, so I'll take the plunge at some point.

We're now four episodes out of six into Ricky Gervais's second series of *After Life*, and it's becoming quite compelling. For some reason, I'm attracted to his miserable sod cracking dark jokes, loving some aspects of life, but raging at arseholes, persona. And, with his track record, he attracts outstanding cameos and co-starring roles from fine actors like Penelope Wilton, David Bradley and Annette Crosby.

Having had 'Tin Soldier' seared on my brain all of yesterday – and then played it on the guitar (I know better than to try and sing it) the bike ride in the evening was accompanied by

Spotify's Small Faces radio. These playlists tend to be very well chosen: in the vein, and from approximately the era, of the named band. I pedalled away to tracks such 'Alone Again Or' by Love and 'Dear Mr Fantasy' by Traffic and a couple by the band themselves, the vaudeville psychedelia of 'Lazy Sunday' and then the barnstorming 1966 UK number one, 'All or Nothing'. That song is always tinged with a little sadness for me: when I saw Steve Marriott and his Packet of Three live in that Oxford pub about five years before he died, a recognisable but dishevelled figure turned at least one of the choruses into 'All or Fuck All'.

I've seen Bob Dylan live a number of times, and often defended his esoteric reworking of his back catalogue – they're his songs and he can do what he wants with them, in essence. More importantly, Dylan has never really been able to sing in any conventional sense, whereas Marriott still had the gift of that stunning voice, even as the once immaculate barnet was in disarray, and the Carnaby Street dandy clothes had become a saggy pair of dungarees. Marriott didn't actually play much of his back catalogue – his band were set up for blues and heavy soul re-workings, but I felt uncomfortable even at the time at his turning a truly great song he'd written into a cheap, sweary laugh.

I remember talking to Dick Clement during our all-nighter after Chelsea won the Cup Winners' Cup in Stockholm. His take on Derek and Clive was largely one of sadness: having produced Cook and Moore at the height of their powers in *Not Only but Also*, he didn't enjoy hearing them swearing and celebrating bad taste as their partnership disintegrated. My adolescent generation saw it differently: it was a liberating and secret pleasure to indulge in such filth, which I saw largely as a parody of the sort of cretins I occasionally found myself next to on London's football terraces. I guess Dick felt, like I did with 'All or Fuck All', a sense of sadness that they were somewhat cheapening and indeed wasting an immense talent.

Talking of performers in their dotage, I went to see the aforementioned Bob Dylan at British Summer Time in Hyde

Park last year, topping a bill which also included Neil Young. When I've seen him a number of times previously in smaller venues, the audience has generally been entirely on Dylan's side: they know he's slightly weird, probably won't talk to them, and that it might be a few bars in before they know what song he's playing. This sometimes applies to his quite brilliant band, too. As with Ricky Gervais, an orderly queue will form to play with the great man, but until the last two or three years where he's tended to have a more predictable set, Dylan could start playing anything in any key and the band were expected to join in.

Part of the joy for people like the late Bob Willis and me was that the set list, and even the style in which any given song would be played, was never remotely the same from one night to the next. Bob W would sometimes go to several concerts on the same tour. I only did that once: two successive evenings at the House of Blues during the Atlanta Olympics, on which I think only three songs were played both nights. Given the extent of his back catalogue, Dylan could completely change his set every night for weeks on end if he felt like it. This approach went badly wrong at Live Aid, though, where on the spur of the moment he decided to play an obscure early track of his, 'When the Ship Comes In', but hadn't told his guest accompanying guitarists Keith Richard and Ron Wood.

In Hyde Park last year, a more diverse crowd having watched Neil Young play conventionally and superbly shortly beforehand were initially a little lost during Dylan's set. There was respect for who he is and was, but a weird country two-step was about a minute in before some mumbled lyrics led to a murmur of, 'This is "Like A Rolling Stone".' But then out of nowhere, and for the first time on English soil in many years, he did the most achingly stripped back, sincere and careful 'Girl from the North Country', which I'm not embarrassed to say, left me with something in my eye. That wonderful ballad, with the same English folk song origin as Simon and Garfunkel's 'Scarborough Fair', was written right at the start of the then Bobby Zimmerman's song writing career for his first serious Minnesota girlfriend, Echo Hallstrom. I happened to have read that Echo had died earlier in 2019, and though he naturally wouldn't tell his audience any of this, Bob had brought her song back into his set list after many years' absence the previous week, in Stockholm, in the country of Echo's ancestry. There was a hushed silence throughout what even those who didn't know the background could tell was a heartfelt moment.

My own Girl from the North Country hadn't accompanied me on this particular Hyde Park outing, but if I never see Bob Dylan play live again – and I'd say the odds are that I probably won't – I'm going to carry that memory around with me for the rest of my life.

Sunday, 3 May 2020

A week on from my correspondence with the editor of the *Today* programme, I thought I'd try it again. Long shot, but I tried to be polite and play the Team BBC card and drop Ms Kuenssberg a line:

Hi Laura
Ex-BBC Editor here. Thank you as a licence payer for your hard work and dedication, but I hope I can pass on my thoughts from the very close attention I'm paying to the scientific chatter in particular.

Reporters are about to be briefed that 'the science has changed', just as you all were on herd immunity. 2m social distancing will miraculously become 1m, to get people back to work. And masks, previously bad, will now be good. The latter has always been true, as you'll know if you've been to Japan or Korea in the winter, but the government has been concerned about the public getting supplies before front line workers. If they were prepared to treat us like adults, they could have simply told us that, but spin and obfuscation are their default setting. OK for winning a referendum or election, not so good during a pandemic.

And I'm sure you have already, but have a look at the opinion polls this morning which suggest that the vast majority do not want to go back to work at the moment. And they're right – especially here in London – our figures are comfortably the worst in Europe, because of that fatal two-week dither before lockdown. The Cheltenham Festival – as you correctly pointed out the other day – and pubs remaining open long after even those in Ireland, were disastrous mistakes. Just as the bookies and Tim Martin were influential in that laissez-faire thinking, so are Conservative Party donors and tax-exile newspaper proprietors in this clamour to get back to work. Most people who will have to get on the Tube, to work in a classroom or warehouse, are far less keen.

This really is not a level playing field. The Downing St team has been an exception to the ONS findings that the poor, BAME and urban are much the most likely to contact this dreadful virus. And a second spike would be worse here than, say in Germany, because our base figures and geographical spread start from a far worse place.

Best of luck, and stay safe.

Paul Armstrong

I won't hold my breath for a reply. I hadn't looked at Saturday's front pages when I wrote yesterday's entry – as I've said before, I think they're given far too much weight everywhere, from the BBC boardroom to Whitehall. However, the vanguard led by so-called libertarians like Toby Young has now made it into the mainstream. Yesterday's *Sun* led with 'Red Better Days' – despite our quite appalling new infection and death figures, we'll all apparently be back at work by 26 May and renewing our Super Soaraway Sky Sports subscriptions in time to watch Premier League football by 12 June.

Could be wishful thinking via Rebekah, from Rupert whose share price needs a boost, but it was written by their usually un-hysterical and well-connected political correspondent, Tom

Newton-Dunn. We've met Tom's sister a few times through mutual friends, and she's a Lib Dem who campaigned harder against Brexit than anyone we know. I've never felt I should ask her about her brother's job, but he always comes over as moderate and reasonable whenever he appears on TV. Nevertheless, imagine doing that job for a living. In return, today's *Sun on Sunday*, that rebrand of the phone-hacking cesspit that was the *News of the World*, has been granted an exclusive interview with Johnson which I won't be reading. 'Cripes, I thought I was a goner' will be the gist of it.

Newton-Dunn's source – probably Classic Dom – clearly wants this out there in order to test the water, set the agenda and soften up the public, and sure enough it's worked, in the sense that it seems to be flagged up on every other news website. And superficially, the uninformed and the greedy will doubtless see it as good news, along the lines of Bozza's rallying cry that 'we're over the peak', which despite not exactly being borne out by the evidence, made most front pages on Friday.

I alluded to the new Office for National Statistics findings, but the detail is very stark. Multicultural and poor Newham in east London had registered 144 deaths per 100,000 inhabitants by Easter, while Jacob Rees-Mogg's North Somerset had just six deaths per 100,000. So, that's one 24th of the likelihood of catching COVID-19 and dying from it, if you live in his constituency and not inner London. It's not really a level playing field after all, is it? Jacob himself has been keeping fairly quiet, which given his history of unfortunate comments, may be no bad thing.

Plenty of other Tory backbenchers and donors have been piping up, though – they're extremely keen that the undeserving poor, dusky or otherwise, get back on the Tube, into warehouses (and up chimneys, for all they care) to make them a profit. 'Take it on the chin, serfs, or if you don't fancy it, we've got you on zero hours: you can sod off home, and we'll wheel in some other poor sap whose family have run out of money and food.'

As for the polls I alluded to: *The Observer* is reporting that four out of five of us don't want the lockdown lifted, while Emma Tucker's *Sunday Times* may have incurred the wrath of Rupe and a further Classic Dom ban by daring to suggest that just one in four adults would currently feel safe at work and a clear majority don't want schools to reopen. Who are these wimpish adults, eh? I bet they aren't risk-taking entrepreneurs with money stashed away in a tax haven. In which case, who gives a toss what they think, particularly with no election until 2024?

I always thought that Nye Bevan's description of Tories as 'lower than vermin' was over the top. Indeed, I've always had a minority of Conservative friends and relatives even if, at times, it means agreeing to disagree, or an awkward changing of the subject. When it comes to the Tory Party we now see in front of us, though – the one which, since Ken Clarke, Rory Stewart and co. were kicked out, has been denuded of anyone capable of individual thought or compassion – I'm beginning to think Nye may have had a point.

The few non-loons who remain in the Conservative Party look for all the world like complete sell-outs. Amanda and I watched a Channel 4 'year in the life' documentary about the parliamentary party a while back. The person we thought came out of it worst wasn't one of the die-hard Brexiteers – they are what they are – it was the supposedly moderate Remainer Nicky Morgan. Having shared fellow contributor Anna Soubry's despair on camera throughout the year, and especially during the Johnson/Cummings takeover, she eventually performed a remarkable volte-face and accepted the role of Culture Secretary and a life peerage from the duo. She has since retired from ministerial life but kept the peerage. The best defence Nicky could muster at the end of the documentary was 'Well, I'm a big fan of *Hamilton* and as the song says, "I want to be in the room where it happens."'

Regardless of what's announced at the three-week review on Thursday, I am truly sick of Cummings and Johnson torturing decent people with fishing expedition leaks to papers, using EU citizens as bargaining chips, tormenting fine professionals who happen to be lawyers or civil servants or work for the BBC, and now this. The last four years have been horrible, and this is now becoming too much for many people's mental health. How dare they just continue to piss around with our lives like this, even during a pandemic? 'Ooh if you're good, you might get some football to watch – we know you like that, don't you, little people?' Fuck off. And when you come back, fuck off again.

I got on the bike yesterday teatime, quite wound up, and put on a random selection of songs I'd apparently listened to a lot on Spotify in 2019. Before the end, I was in tears. I'm not particularly proud of that fact, but there you go.

My nostalgia for Teesside is a bit like the feelings many Brexiteers claim to have for Britain. The difference is that my Teesside actually existed and still does, to some extent. I know the rundown high streets of pound shops, bookies, drug addicts and cheap pubs are depressing, but I also know how proud, defiant, warm and funny the people always were, and mostly still are.

I haven't lived there since 1979, and most of my trips back since have been to visit Amanda's Auntie Irene, watch Boro, or both. As well as the well-known Teessiders like Bob Mortimer and various football players and managers, there are some talented young musicians we follow. I've mentioned Cattle and Cane before, but there's also a superb, increasingly well-known folk group from the area. They're called the Young'uns, because that's what the other regulars of Stockton Folk Club used to call them when they shyly began to demonstrate some stunning three-part harmonies and instrumental prowess at their open mic sessions.

They also write great songs – we saw their remarkable stage show *The Ballad of Johnny Longstaff* in London last year. This tells the true story of a young man from Stockton-on-Tees, whose anti-fascist activism in the 1930s led him first to protest against Oswald Mosley's blackshirts when they held a rally in Stockton, then to fight alongside George Orwell and other idealistic internationalists against Franco in the Spanish Civil War.

The song which stopped me in my tracks wasn't from that show, but it is related, in that it's about the East End of London standing firm against Mosley's fascists in 1936, at a time when thousands were attending his rallies and the *Daily Mail* ran its infamous 'Hurrah for the Blackshirts' front page. It's called 'Cable Street' and is sung a cappella.

This is the last verse:

And yes, there was violence, and yes, there was blood, and I saw things a lad shouldn't see
But I'll not regret the day I stood, and London stood with me
And when the news spread the day had been won, and Mosley was limping away
There were shouts, there were cheers, there was songs, there was tears, and aye, they're borne to this day
And we all swore then, we'd stand up again, for as long as our legs could,
And that when we were gone, our daughters and sons would stand where we stood.
Was the first time I'd heard two tiny words said by every woman and man
Now I'll say them still, and I always will: No pasarán!

It's difficult to explain exactly what got to me. I know a bit about the political and social history of that era, and how important the resistance both in Stockton and at Cable Street was in foiling the incipient British Fascist movement. We've also been in recent years to the unexpectedly magnificent Museo del Memoria in Santiago, Chile which graphically depicts the murderous overthrow of a democratically elected regime by General Pinochet's fascists.

There were two British angles to the outrage – firstly, Margaret Thatcher's later unforgivable protection of, and reverence for, the general himself; and secondly, the brave and principled stance of the Rolls Royce aircraft workers of East Kilbride who, from 1974 to 1978, refused to allow their factories to be used to repair the aircraft which had bombed and killed the elected president Allende and many Chilean civilians. Instead, they impounded their engines, severely hamstringing the regime, and provided hope and solidarity for the beleaguered Chilean resistance movement. I made a donation to the crowdfunding of a documentary made by a Chilean director, Felipe Bustos Sierra, about these spirited, funny but principled Scots who took that stance. Two years ago, we met a couple of them, in their 80s by now, at a London screening. *Nae Pasaran* was the title of the stirring film – a Scottish twist on that Spanish Civil War cry, 'No pasarán' – 'None shall pass.'

Scotland is still largely sound when it comes to the far-right, Nigel Farage having been made particularly unwelcome in Edinburgh a couple of years ago, and both Brexit, and UKIP then the Brexit Party, having been trounced at the ballot box north of the border. Heartbreakingly, though – for me, at least – my native north-east, birthplace of the Jarrow marchers and home to the young trio singing that tale of Cable Street has lost its way quite horribly of late. My dad and I are both convinced that it's not just the misted-up lens of nostalgia that makes us believe that both Johnson and Farage would have been run out of the Teesside we knew in the 1970s. Most of my former school friends and the Boro fans I know loathe both those supremely posh charlatans, but somehow they conned many other people who lost their steelworks, chemical factories, mines and shipbuilding into thinking that rampant disaster capitalism and blaming of 'the other' is the answer to anything, let alone the north-east's woes.

Cameron fronting Remain and Corbyn's Labour didn't resonate up there either, and I can entirely understand that, but every statistical analysis ever conducted shows that Brexit will disproportionately cripple the region, and yet it comfortably won the day in the north-east. Not only that, but three years later, the region chose to absolve the party which inflicted a decade of austerity which again hit them harder than any other part of the country. Towns like Redcar and Blyth returned a Tory MP for the first time in 80 years, or ever, in the case of my parents' home area of Bishop Auckland. Their new MP is a 26-year-old woman who has been photographed with some unsavoury far-right types. And now three of the top four boroughs for COVID-19 cases per population in the country are from the north-east. Yet, such is the collapse of identity and self-esteem up there, they seemingly just keep asking to be kicked a bit harder. Somewhere amidst the confusion, though, there is a soul and a core of decency. Those three Teesside voices harmonising on a hymn of anti-fascism just seemed unbearably poignant, and I completely – as opposed to partially – lost it for the first time in this entire lockdown.

Fortunately, Amanda was in the bedroom watching the NT production of *Frankenstein* when I came indoors, so I'd just about recovered some dignity by the time she came back into the living room. We then watched the last two episodes of *After Life,* which managed to combine the uproarious – a *Phoenix Nights*-style local talent night containing a very obvious side swipe at James Corden – with the profoundly sad, then some unrepentant schmaltz and soppiness to finish. It was clearly intended as a wistful celebration of life, love and human decency, and as such, it was exactly what I needed at that very moment. Thanks, Ricky. I'm still running scared of Hilary Mantel, though – maybe today's the day.

I ended the day wallowing in football nostalgia. Twenty-eight years ago this weekend, Boro won promotion to the inaugural Premier League season by coming back from a goal and a man down to win at Wolves with our only two shots. The winner was a stooping header from Paul Wilkinson which bounced 17 times before rolling against a post, then trickling over the line. A marvellous Dick Turpin day out. It also led to one of the great trivia questions when Sky assembled all 22 PL captains for a promo and group photo shoot later that summer. Who's that alongside Gordon Strachan and Peter Beardsley? Why, it's only Alan Kernaghan. No wonder we went straight back down.

Then I watched a recording I'd made of ITV's classic match reprise from the afternoon. Coventry v Spurs in the 1987 FA Cup Final. I was at that game – my Uncle Barry having somehow landed two tickets from the Durham FA. I always loved Cyrille Regis who by now had left West Brom for Coventry, and even though the equally marvellous Glenn Hoddle lined up for the opposition, I was firmly behind the underdogs. Spurs had won lots of FA Cups, the Sky Blues weren't likely to get there again. And Keith Houchen of Middlesbrough (his nephew is now the mayor of Tees Valley) had featured in a particularly epic mud and thunder derby, playing up front for Hartlepool at Darlington, in one of the last games I went to before moving south. It was an amazingly open game – I'd completely forgotten all manner of big chances and that big Cyrille had a goal ludicrously chalked off for an alleged Houchen push – and it was strange to see extended highlights, voiced by Brian Moore and pre-disgrace Ron Atkinson. The short clips I've seen since have always featured John Motson for the BBC.

I say clips, there really is only one clip from that game. I've seen better technical finishes in the flesh – Zidane for Real Madrid in that 2002 Champions League Final at Hampden, James Rodriguez's volley in front of 50,000-plus Colombians in the Maracana at the last World Cup I worked on – but for sheer hairy-chested Boy's Own journeyman's finest hour goose pimples, Keith Houchen's diving header takes some beating. I hadn't registered quite how good the build-up was, either. A towering flick-on header from big Cyrille, first time trap, turn and lay-off to the wing from the eventual scorer, and a beautiful whipped cross from Dave Bennett. Trevor Peake, another journeyman about to snatch the cup from Hoddle, Waddle and Ardiles, claims he was shouting 'fly and you'll get there' behind Houchen, and fly the boy did. I was right behind it, sheer poetry.

Like Keith, I'd scuffed myself more than once in a Teesside playground trying to emulate Allan Clarke's winning diving header in the 1972 FA Cup Final, but that was a controlled finish from a top-drawer international-class forward. This was a bloke just launching himself; a bloke previously only known nationally for rolling in a penalty for York which had put Arsenal out of the cup, and who was soon on his way to Hibs, then Port Vale and back to Hartlepool.

Forget all that 'it's only a consolation prize' tosh you kept seeing on Arsenal Fan TV as serial failure Arsène Wenger merely came back with FA Cup after FA Cup. If you support Ipswich, Wigan or Coventry, then Roger Osborne, Ben Watson, or especially Keith Houchen, gave you your moment of a lifetime.

Monday, 4 May 2020

I crawled out of bed at 9am, after a night disturbed by bizarre dreams about being on holiday somewhere with no social distancing and, for reasons best known to myself, waking up at 4am suddenly recalling the long-forgotten Jennifer Arcuri scandal (London Mayor Boris Johnson, a frequent visitor to her flat for 'technology lessons', allegedly facilitated foreign trips for her and funnelled a sum of money from a mayoral fund the way of her business) and wondering whether we'll ever hear about that, or the Russia report into possible interference in our referendum and elections, ever again.

I became aware of strange noises outside the bedroom window, and discovered Amanda vigorously brushing something into the surface of our patio. The difference between the two of us is illustrated by the fact that I only did something about our mossy patio when I went arse over tit on a wet day in February, when trying to top up the bird feed. I went out to a hardware shop and bought some Acme Die-You-Mossy-Bastard and chucked it around angrily, to reasonable effect. It still didn't look great but I could now stand up in wet weather, so that was enough for me. Amanda has researched and ordered something which will apparently provide us with the aesthetic joy of a lighter, pinkish tinge to our outside space, and spent two hours early this morning diligently and carefully applying it.

I was rather hoping the UK's virus response had entered a holding pattern stage. The planted whispers are reverberating out there, and we'll have to wait until Johnson's address later in the week for confirmation, by which time our British exceptionalism will have seen our death toll overtake Italy's. At least, in the absence of the Eurovision Song Contest and Euro 2020, we can claim to have outgunned the Continent on one front this year. Then Pete, my stats friend, said on Facebook that Ben Wallace, our anonymous Defence Secretary, had been on *Today* and said precisely what I'd told him a couple of days ago that the government would start saying – masks were bad, but are now good, and one, not two, metre social distancing will be fine. Cummings, Ben Warner and Professor Vallance will doubtless come up with some 'new science' via SAGE in due course for the government to 'follow'.

Jake's Messenger group is alight with the news that Professor Sir David King, former Chief Scientific Adviser to the Brown and Blair governments is setting up an alternative SAGE, including our favourite non-jargon scientist, Professor Anthony Costello, which will meet live on YouTube and intends to present the government with 'robust, unbiased advice'. Professor King has previously said that he 'could not recall a COBRA meeting not attended by the PM of the time', and that the Cheltenham Festival was 'the best way to accelerate the COVID-19 spread'. I really wish I'd been wrong about all of this and especially the next bit, but his prime issue is the 'lack of transparency' which sees plainly political decisions like the U-turn on face masks defended as 'following the science'.

Professor King has clearly talked to exasperated scientists on the SAGE committee and singled out one all too predictable fly in the ointment. 'Dominic Cummings has the ear of the Prime Minister, so who is informing the Prime Minister about science?' he asks. That self-taught physics in Daddy's bunker isn't seen by some eminent scientists as a good basis on which to fight a pandemic. It clearly isn't good news that leading scientists have felt the need to break away like this, but I hope their open meetings are well reported and not just by *The Guardian* and *Channel 4 News*, and that they very quickly examine the bizarre decision to give the contract for the NHS app to Cummings's stats man's brother. Right-wing website Guido Fawkes has launched a smear campaign based on Professor King having worked for Brown and Blair and Prof. Costello having, horror of horrors, once attended a Labour Party conference. This tends to suggest that someone, somewhere is rattled, but also sadly that even scientific arguments are likely to descend into the same left-right, Remain-Leave abyss as everything else in British public life.

I'm no computer geek, but Jake's Messenger group is particularly unsettled by the Cambridge Analytica-style data gathering which will seemingly accompany the new NHS app. The Google/Apple proposal was for the data to be anonymised, so you'd know when you'd been in the vicinity of a registered COVID-19 sufferer but the database wouldn't know either person's details. The combination of Cummings, personal information and, it's now being suggested, facial biometrics, and the need for a 'digital certificate' before you can work has the potential to become ever so slightly sinister, especially now there's a growing body of evidence to suggest that BAME communities are more susceptible to the virus. Remember that Cummings's first appointment to Downing Street was Sabisky the eugenicist, and also that the whole Cambridge Analytica electioneering apparatus united openly white supremacists like Bannon, Salvini and Bolsonaro, and the whole thing becomes slightly unnerving. We may all be over-reacting, but I'd say it's better-founded paranoia than that which is driving the ripping down of 5G masts or the injection of disinfectant.

Right, enough politics. I expected today to be a holding pattern day of just a few times the Hillsborough death toll, and more spin – the baby having already been named something or other, not Thomas, but something to do with two of the doctors who treated the PM. Sorry, I do know the poor little sod's first name is Wilfred, and probably not as a tribute to Mannion of the Boro. Or Brambell of *Steptoe and Son* and the *Hard Day's Night* movie. I genuinely can't be bothered to research what the rest of the string of names actually was. There were lots of them, naturally – you don't get on the waiting list for Eton without four or five monikers to prove your superior breeding. Speaking of Eton, I've discovered that today is the fifth anniversary of a zinger from one of that school's illustrious alumni: David Cameron's prescient observation, 'Britain faces a simple and inescapable choice – stability and strong Government with me, or chaos with Ed Miliband.' Phew. Thank goodness a bacon sandwich put paid to that alternative Britain, eh?

My geeky research gene led me to profound disappointment yesterday – inspired by watching that Coventry City FA Cup win, I read a long form article by Daniel Harris of *The Guardian,* published in 2017 on the 30th anniversary of that classic final. It was all going well until this line: 'At the following month's general election, Houchen and Ogrizovic would exploit their fame to campaign for their local Tory MP.'

In 1987, when the Iron Lady was at her absolute worst? Well, thanks for ruining that rose-tinted memory of the journeyman from the Boro, Daniel. I'll have to file that memory away with other things I once loved, but which are now tainted: *Annie Hall*, Botham's Ashes and the music of the Who, for example. The last of those is nothing to do with Pete Townshend's ill-advised computer research some years ago. I was just depressed by Roger Daltrey's more recent bellicose pro-Brexit outburst on Sky News.

I've finally started the Hilary Mantel opus. It's superbly written and atmospheric of course, and I'm trying hard not to picture capricious, venal Henry VIII and cunning, arch manipulator Cromwell as Johnson and Cummings. Cromwell was pro-European and from genuinely humble origins, for one thing. You just can't read her work quickly, though, and 70 pages in, with 834 to go, I already know this is going to be a long haul. However, as the Durham miner who used to wear boots which were two sizes too small every day said, it'll be a hell of a relief once they're off/it's finished. That's a bit harsh. I'll enjoy reading it, but it does look daunting at the moment.

Covering the athletics circuit for BBC Sport way back when, I got slightly tired of British athletes who were knocked out in the first round of a competition but were still thrilled to have broken their 'PB' or personal best, and there are few things more dull than old farts who've taken up jogging, posting their routes and times on Facebook. So, I won't dwell on the fact that I did 20km on the bike in under 29 minutes yesterday – even though it represents a Chinese swimmer level of record destruction – I'll concentrate on the inspirational, motivational soundtrack instead. I opted for what were apparently my most listened-to songs of 2017 on Spotify's random shuffle: Teenage Fanclub, the wrily comical Young'uns song, 'A Place called England', and the only Jimi Hendrix cover I know which is better than the original. While his own version of Dylan's 'All Along the Watchtower' may be the best cover ever recorded, as Bob himself has acknowledged, Jimi's 'Little Wing' is uncharacteristically understated and all too short. It fades out at 2'21' for some reason, just as it's getting going. It took Steve Ray Vaughan to send it into orbit.

Then on came T Rex's 'Get it On'. I can't hear that without laughing and thinking back to Rick Wakeman's one-man show at the Union Chapel a year or so ago. Before he joined Yes, Rick was a session man responsible for elevating David Bowie's 'Life on Mars' and Cat Stevens's 'Morning Has Broken' with his piano virtuosity. He played both songs that evening, but also told the story of the easiest session payment he ever earned. Rick showed up at the T Rex session for 'Get It On', only to discover that it was a straightforward raunchy guitar number. Marc Bolan, worried that his pal would be out of pocket if he wasn't used, just got Rick to run his hands right along the piano – glissando is the technical word – at three or four suitable junctures during the track. There's no other piano whatsoever on the finished recording.

By contrast, the piano part on the song which was playing as I reached 20km is sublime. When Art Garfunkel launched his solo career in 1973, there was one obvious problem: Paul Simon had written pretty much every song he'd ever recorded. He'd have to go down the Sinatra route and tap into the best songwriters out there to provide vehicles for his extraordinary voice. Randy Newman ('Old Man') and Van Morrison ('I Shall Sing') songs duly appeared on his debut solo album *Angel Clare,* as did two by Sinatra's favourite modern songwriter, Jimmy Webb.

Though Webb is no mean pianist himself, the Wrecking Crew's Larry Knechtel played on 'All I Know'. Larry had done a reasonable job of tickling the ivories on a previous minor hit on which Artie had sung – 'Bridge Over Troubled Water' – so he was drafted in once more by Roy Halee, who had also produced that final Simon and Garfunkel album. It sounds as if they were trying to recreate the feel of that track with a simple voice plus gospel piano and tender lyrics, gradually building to a crescendo with strings and a fully unleashed vocal of choirboy purity. It unfailingly makes me think of how I feel about Amanda. If you hate 'Bridge Over Troubled Water' – and I know some people do, just as I don't like 'Imagine' all that much – you may not enjoy 'All I Know', but I'd recommend it to the rest of the world.

Tuesday, 5 May 2020

It takes something special for phlegmatic, reasonable Amanda to quietly say, 'That's one of the worst things I've ever heard,' but Sir Graham Brady, chair of the Conservatives' backbench 1922 Committee, pulled something out of the bag yesterday. In a Commons debate where one after another of the members for rural golf clubs raged about the continuing restrictions,

Sir Graham firstly urged the removal of 'arbitrary rules and limitations on freedom as quickly as possible', then suggested the public had been 'a little too willing to stay at home'. A contender for Jacob Rees-Mogg's crown as Victorian Mill Owner of the Year.

I thought I'd Google what I presumed was a self-made businessman gobshite to rival Josiah Bounderby in Dickens's *Hard Times*. I don't mean to get personal, but alongside a picture of a horsey man in a suit was a CV of Durham University, PR consultant, Centre for Policy Studies and safe Cheshire seat, all by the age of 29. So, his disdain for workers was along the lines of that book co-authored by the distinctly unworldly Liz Truss, Dominic Raab and Priti Patel which described the British workforce as 'among the worst idlers in the world'. And we're relying on that horny-handed son of toil, Boris Johnson to rein in their slave-owner instincts. Remind me again why Redcar, Blyth and Middlesbrough South elected this lot?

A more amusing story emerged last night about that other right-wing nightmare, Nigel Farage. Following his futile trip to Sussex the other day, he turned up in Dover yesterday, once more trying to seize back the attention he's been missing with a rambling diatribe recorded by a camera crew. Thirty thousand mostly poor or elderly people dying from a virus seems to have passed him by – the news should all be about illegal immigration, apparently. Kent Constabulary turned up at his door last night to question his claim that he was carrying out 'essential work', and he subsequently launched a pompous and nonsensical civil liberties defence on Twitter. The first response, from Elliot Eastwick, was pithy and to the point: 'Rules are rules, you mustard-panted *****.'

This was a reference to last week's attempt to get himself noticed: that ghastly rictus grin plastered all over his face, and wearing a plum-coloured jumper and mustard cords, Farage had ostentatiously banged a saucepan to camera during the Thursday night applause for key workers. Never mind that he told a meeting in East Sussex that 'I think we are going to have to move to an insurance-based system of healthcare.' The only good which came out of that little exhibition was a quite brilliant montage by the genius that is Cold War Steve (I don't see as many of his montages as I should now I'm off Twitter) in which Farage and his saucepan have been inserted into a welcoming party for Hitler and Mussolini. The video image of Nige's pan-banging has also been edited into that great Blue Oyster Cult *Saturday Night Live* sketch in which Christopher Walken demands 'more cowbell' on 'Don't Fear the Reaper'. If only we were as good at managing reality as we are at satirising it.

Amanda and I even found the funny side of this NHS app being trialled on the Isle of Wight. Much as the self-appointed experts on the British workforce have clearly never been within two metres of the average workplace, Dom's cronies may have chosen the wrong trial venue. The Isle of Wight is the very definition of both meanings of 'insular'. My last trip there was for Esther Rantzen's *Hearts of Gold* – we filmed a supposedly warm-hearted bus driver, who turned out to have relocated from Birmingham to 'get away from the Pakis', and his decrepit and ancient passengers. Unless it's changed a lot, it's the sort of place where they throw spears at Ceefax. Even if the three people there who own smartphones install this thing, 'track and test' isn't going to reveal much while everyone's confined to their houses. Call me a cynic, but a micromap tracking twenty-three and a half hours of occasional movement from bedroom to living room to bathroom, with a half-mile circuit in the early evening to take the dog for a walk, probably isn't going to produce the required technological breakthrough.

I honestly think we'll be on our hands and knees pleading with Google and Apple within weeks, but I'd really love to be proved wrong. In the last 24 hours on Facebook and elsewhere I've seen a piece in the *Sydney Morning Herald* entitled 'Biggest Failure in a Generation: Where did Britain go wrong?'; a *New York Times* editorial headlined, 'The UK needs a Real Government, not Boris Johnson's Puppet Cabinet'; and Professor Menon, possibly showing off a little, posted an untranslated piece from *Le Monde*. It referred to an appearance on Sunday's *Andrew Marr Show* by the Minister for Transport, Grant Shapps, or one of his alter egos. I saw a clip of this, in which he preposterously claimed that our statistics were simply more honest than those for other countries. Like one of those itinerant footballers who whinges to the press back home and thinks no one at the club will find out, Grant/Michael Green/Sebastian Fox hasn't worked out that forrins will find out what's been said on the BBC. I understood the gist of the article but, in any case the final line, 'Le tragique exceptionalisme GB' requires no translation.

And as if to prove that conclusion, I became embroiled in a farcical exchange on Facebook last night. I signed up a while back to a page called North London Coronavirus Updates which is run by a group of local papers in these parts. A young, and probably very stretched, journalist called Lucas Cumiskey had posted a link to a report he'd written for the *Islington Gazette* which marked the 100th COVID-19 death at the local Whittington Hospital. The first reply came from Maggi: 'What about numbers for survivors?' Lucas immediately posted another article of his which explained that 233 COVID patients from the Whittington have recovered and been sent home. Next contribution from Peter Beattie: '100 per cent right, Maggi, doesn't fit the left-wing bias of this paper.' I felt for Lucas, a young lad probably being paid next to nothing on a pared-back local paper, and pointed out in a reply that his reporting had been perfectly balanced and that statistics don't have a political affiliation. I then posted a screen grab of the upper echelons of the Worldometers COVID-19 statistics chart as an illustration. We are the only country of any size which still has N/A in the 'numbers recovered' column, so Lucas had done as much as he could by reporting the Whittington's tally.

This seemed to be akin to asking about Peter's grandmother's sexual preferences and he and some enraged others leapt in.

'That's just your opinion,' shrieked one, clearly thinking I invent the global statistics on a daily basis. Like Shapps/Green/Fox on *Marr*, the next allegation was that other countries are massaging their figures. I pointed out that unlike Germany and France, to name but two, we weren't even including deaths outside hospitals until last week, but on and on it went. 'It is what it is' was one retort from a David Wilkey who felt the government weren't in any way to blame – not the swimmer unless he can't spell his own name, which is perfectly possible. Yes, 'it is what it is' was our government's approach, David, but have a look at the German figures: no Cheltenham Festival, lots of early testing, about a fifth of our death toll, a tenth of our current daily new cases. Should they have just said 'it is what it is', too? I gave up in the end, but this is liberal, diverse north London which lies right in the eye of this first spike and subsequent ones. If they're thinking like that, imagine the Cheshire golf club bores who surround Sir Graham Brady?

I'm plodding on with Hilary Mantel – more than ten per cent of the way there now, and the only TV I watched yesterday was the latest home-made *Match of the Day*. This time it was a top ten of PL players who never played for one of the 'big six'. Much as I love listening to Lineker, Shearer and Wright interact, I chiefly watched this one to check that Juninho was included. Had he not been, my e-mails to the *Today* editor and the BBC's chief political correspondent would have been well and truly surpassed. He was, of course, and the top three was Gary Speed, Jamie Vardy and Matt Le Tissier. I wouldn't argue with that, and it was another really good watch. I think I'd rather watch a show like that in perpetuity, with lots of wonderful archive, than a repulsive Saudi-owned Newcastle starting to win things when actual football returns. What would we Boro fans do with our post-Carling Cup glory ditty 'have you ever seen a Geordie with a cup? Have you fuck', or indeed that banner with a huge arrow pointing to the away end at Tees-Tyne derbies, which simply reads 'Trophy Virgins'?

I know what my cycling music will be today: a Stranglers compilation to mark the sad COVID-19 death of keyboardist Dave Greenfield. I saw them live in the early '80s, and although they came under the punk/new wave umbrella they were slightly older than most of their rivals, and were accomplished musicians under the swagger. Dave Greenfield in particular was the natural successor to Ray Manzarek of the Doors: he could do mellow, as his composition 'Golden Brown' demonstrates, but he could also produce as good a swirly and aggressive keyboard part as you'll ever hear. I'm thinking in particular of 'No More Heroes', which I struggled for years to try to play.

I can do a watered-down version of the main riff, but the solo is 'I'll get my coat' time, and for far better musicians than me. One of the great tracks of that or any other era, it came out when I was 13, and unlike some of the raw punk that was around, it blew me away then and now. When we visited the room in which Leon Trotsky was murdered in Mexico City – just around the corner from his lover Frida Kahlo's studio – it was as much as I could do not to break the respectful hush with 'he got an ice pick that made his ears burn'. The rest of the lyrics – 'No more Shakespeare-os', and so on – ring more true than ever these days, too. There's certainly one fewer hero now that Dave Greenfield is no longer with us.

Wednesday, 6 May 2020

Well, we did it. In a year when our hopes of Eurovision Song Contest and Euro 2020 glory have been cruelly snatched away from us, we've still shown that shabby nearby Continent what's what. Yes, despite giving them several weeks' head start, we've raced past the hapless Italians to register the highest COVID-19 death total in Europe. And we're certainly not finished yet. We've found a few thousands care home deaths from April that we'd forgotten to include, so we'll have a clear lead of several thousand once they're factored in.

The UK and USA are now way out in front, blazing a trail ahead of all lesser nations – the 'tremendous, yuuuge' trade talks, to give us access to chlorinated chicken in return for our souls, are back up and running in the safe hands of Liz Truss. We're even in tandem with our former colony and fellow linguaphobes in not installing the same COVID-19 smartphone app system as much of the rest of the world. The Warner Brothers app has today been reported by the *Health Service Journal* to have failed every single test of 'clinical safety and cyber security' to date. Even Dominic Raab C. Nesbitt, pushed out to face the music instead of Bojo yesterday, was unable to wriggle his way out of the inconvertible fact that our app, even if it does ever work, won't be compatible with any other country's, so we probably won't be able to travel anywhere for some time. Except possibly to sell our organs across the Atlantic, once Liz Truss has done her worst.

To cap it all, *I'm a Celebrity* veteran Nadine Dorries, arch Brexiteer and pair of short planks – she had to beg the ERG WhatsApp group for help when some sixth-formers asked her some rudimentary questions about tariffs and the Single Market – has been promoted to Minister of State at the Department of Health. I've been alerted to a Twitter exchange which followed this announcement: Sean tweeted, 'The bottom has been scraped,' to which Karen P. replied, 'Careful, Nadine might think that's the new way to test for COVID-19.' I might have to reinstall Twitter at some point to have a gallows laugh while I'm trapped on this ridiculous, mossy, virus-riddled rock.

Topping the European charts hasn't made the lead story of any paper other than the *Daily Mirror* and *The Guardian*, though. At about 8pm yesterday, *The Telegraph* suddenly remembered a story they – or possibly someone in Downing Street – have been sitting on since 30 March, and where they led, *The Sun* and *Mail* followed. Professor Neil Ferguson (remember him?), the man whose Imperial College projections led to the hasty abandonment of herd immunity, self-isolated in March when he developed COVID-19 symptoms. A fortnight later, he foolishly invited his 'married lover' (copyright: the papers) to visit him at his house. This was a clear breach of government guidelines, and once it became public yesterday, he resigned from SAGE.

The Telegraph's revelation, though, was clearly timed to distract from reaching the highest death toll in Europe, and to add fuel to their 'lift the lockdown' fire, which has become their entire editorial focus in the days leading up to Bojo's big speech, which has now been moved to Sunday. 'Sleazy old professor, how dare he take away our inalienable right to send other people's children up chimneys?' appears to be the thrust of today's argument.

An unholy mess awaits on all fronts. A friend who I shan't name is senior enough in a large organisation to have been included in the tentative plans to lift the lockdown at a big company's London HQ. He says the proposals he's seen are totally unworkable, and predicts that much of the workforce will either stay away, or try it for a couple of days, get stuck in a kilometre-long queue from the company's lifts stretching back to the Tube platform, and give up. People who are running out of money won't have the choice, though. The lovely Afghan family running our local convenience store have to get here from Enfield every day. That's just about okay when the Tube is running at ten per cent of its usual numbers; it's emphatically not okay if those numbers multiply, whatever the government says about staggered working times. Maybe their shop can reverse its usual hours and they can open up at midnight and go home at 6am.

Tory MP after Tory MP is being wheeled out to advocate a grand reopening of the economy. Sir Iain Duncan Smith had his verdict ready within seconds of Professor Ferguson's resignation – given the speed at which IDS's brain usually processes information, it looked like he'd already been tipped off and primed. He represents an Essex constituency, as do many hardliners past and present (Tebbit, Sir Teddy Taylor, Theresa Gorman, Francois, Jenkin, Patel) so it's possible that some of his constituents are acquainted with London, just as one or two of

Sir Graham Brady's may occasionally have to visit Manchester, but those in Dorset and rural Yorkshire are far removed from city dwellers. It seems the same pattern is emerging here as in the States – if they didn't vote for us, fuck 'em: New York, London, Chicago, Manchester, LA and Glasgow didn't vote for the blond populists, so let's make policy for Somerset and Alabama, who did.

Blimey, even by my standards, that's got cynical. Yesterday would have marked the end of Cameron's second five-year term as PM, had he stuck to the plan once he got his majority and we'd avoided chaos under Miliband. Of course, since then we've had two elections, that referendum and the disaster that was Corbynism instead.

I've treated the last five years in politics like a rather more important version of supporting Middlesbrough, or indeed making television programmes: 'Expect the worst, and you may get a pleasant surprise.' In terms of my relationship with the bookies that's been, 'Back the worst possible outcome: you'll make money every time, but still feel sick to the stomach.' I never foresaw being unable to spend any of that money, though. Having managed to be out of the country for every Brexit deadline to date, a grand trip to Argentina then Antarctica was in the pipeline for New Year 2021, and the supply chain catastrophe that would follow a No Deal Brexit. That this government is still ploughing on with that amidst a pandemic almost upsets me more than their inept handling of that pandemic. They buggered around for two or three weeks before lockdown as the virus arrived, this No Deal iceberg is visible from seven months and more away, but their exceptionalism means that we still expect the iceberg to change course.

The first exception, and glimmer of hope, in those five years of remorselessly cashing in on things I didn't want to happen, was Keir Starmer's election as Labour leader. Later today, that eminent QC takes on Piffle-Paffle Wiff-Waff De Pfeffel Johnson at PMQs, a first prime ministerial appearance in Parliament for six weeks. The Speaker of the House has already registered his anger that the new lockdown measures will be announced on TV on Sunday, rather than face scrutiny in the Commons. There will be no baying backbench arseholes to buoy the Eton Pop veteran, since they can mostly only join by video link. I confidently predict that today will see the debating equivalent of Arbroath 36 Bon Accord 0, which will be satisfactory in one way, but simply won't matter in the end. Even if Starmer left Bojo in tears, screaming for Nanny and confessing to manslaughter, embezzlement and treason, *The Telegraph* will doubtless have another bonking scientist story up its sleeve, and no one will ever be any the wiser.

Right, it's gloriously sunny out there. I am completely out of lighter material at the moment, so I'll have to hope that page 160 onwards of the Mantel saga of Tudor machinations and beheadings throws up something frivolous for me to report back on tomorrow. Peter Kay would be able to base a whole stand-up routine on it, so why can't I? 'T' Reformation? What were that all about, eh? Eh? 'Enry just wanted to gerris leg over din't ee, eh? Eh? Dirty old bugger. And d'ya remember all that hey nonny nonny stuff? Yer grandad wearing one of them daft ruffs and eating roast swan. Eh? Eh? Yer laughing, madam – yer laughing cos it's true. Eh? Eh?'

Thursday, 7 May 2020

When Al Gore made his film about climate change, I remember seeing a cartoon depicting two adjacent cinemas. There was no queue outside the venue showing *An Inconvenient Truth*, but the one next door, for *A Reassuring Lie*, stretched around the block. So it is with today's newspapers. I'm not going to read the details for the sake of my sanity but suffice to say the *Daily Mail* is screaming 'Hurrah! Lockdown Freedom Beckons'; '"Stay Home" Advice Scrapped' shrieks *The Telegraph*, though their elderly proprietors presumably won't be straying from their private island; and 'Happy Monday!' bellows *The Sun.* The dead cat strikes again – not a mention of the UK's official death toll passing 30,000 yesterday, because Monday is going to be Freedom Day. 'Stay Home' is no more, and not because the insertion of the word 'at' is going to make it grammatical. No, we can just get out there and exercise our inalienable right to spread any virus we want, wherever we want.

We had 6,111 new COVID-19 cases yesterday, our third-highest daily tally so far, and from only 67,000 tests (that 100,000 figure was a one-day-only publicity stunt). Germany had 365 new cases yesterday and even they are treading slowly and carefully. We also registered 649 deaths yesterday, way more than any other European country – that tally is still two-thirds of what it was at its peak, so unless it's lost its collective mind, as it may well have done, the government should have almost no wriggle room.

How Bojo the Clown satisfies the expectation of normality those headlines will have created among the poorly-informed, while not sending us hurtling towards a second spike, is anyone's guess. As for the testing, South Korea never needed more than 20,000 a day at any point because they never let it get out of hand. Given where we are at the moment, 67,000 tests a day – nearly ten per cent of which are positive – is scarcely scratching the surface. Whatever he announces on Sunday – and please let it be cosmetic adjustments only – this household will be changing nothing about its daily routine. We're very fortunate to be able largely to sit this out; on the other hand, we're unfortunately bang in the middle of the city which will once more be hit first and worst. That applies to almost any non-Tory seat in England, but especially in London.

If Prime Minister's Questions decided anything, Boris Johnson would now have left office. I watched it in full for the first time in a long time, and it was, as we expected, as great a mismatch as you will ever see. For a fleeting moment, I felt sorry for Johnson. Every lame defence he mounted had been anticipated by Starmer.

'We shouldn't make international comparisons' was countered by Starmer producing the diagram which has been shown daily at every government press briefing for almost two months. This charts, er, international comparisons and is accompanied by analysis from the scientist on duty. Initially, it was to reassure us that we were lagging well behind Italy, then Spain. In recent days, you simply can't spin it, unless you're Robert Peston and want to know when the line on the graph of cumulative deaths will go down. Dr Jenny Harries tried, as politely as she could, to explain that was physically impossible unless we were expecting some resurrections. She'd clearly forgotten about the Easter miracle of Boris our Saviour.

Johnson looked distinctly un-miraculous yesterday in the face of several short and polite factual dismantlings from Starmer. Unlike the Corbyn era, Piffle-Paffle just can't get away with waffle and idiocy like his 'apparent success' line. Starmer will simply do what he used to do so effectively in court: note self-incrimination, then deploy it to devastating effect. Johnson's spectacular loucheness usually sufficed against the non-forensic Corbyn, who would allow himself to be riled, then baited and jeered by the government benches. There's none of that in an empty chamber now – Johnson looked like he was back at school facing a firm but fair teacher who was picking apart the abysmal essay he'd scribbled in ten minutes.

What I found shocking was just how inarticulate our PM, the man who would be Churchill, is when he's under pressure. It was as if someone had edited together every 'um', 'er', 'hmm' and hair ruffle from every Hugh Grant/Richard Curtis collaboration into one long, unwatchable sequence. As Max Hastings, Dominic Grieve and many other former colleagues said long before he got the job, Boris Johnson is manifestly unequipped to be Prime Minister. He just wanted the job, not actually to do it. He's probably still not fully physically recovered, he has his new baby keeping him awake and has surrounded himself with appalling advisers and an utterly useless cabinet.

And next Wednesday, if he hasn't put in some paternity leave, he will once again have to face Starmer who'll be armed with the newly emerging details of the latest and greatest PPE fiasco so far. After that 'will they, won't they?' cliffhanger which dominated the headlines for days, with RAF planes scrambled across the continent for a dashing dawn raid, the entire consignment of 400,000 gowns sourced from Turkey has turned out to be unusable.

The British Medical Association's survey of doctors suggests 50 per cent of them have had to source at least some of their own PPE. One of Jake's Messenger group provided a harrowing update from the world of community trust rehab units yesterday. With care homes now refusing to take elderly COVID-19 patients from hospitals, her workforce is collapsing physically and mentally, both with hopelessly inadequate PPE and many staff now absent either because of the virus or stress. Her summary, 'If they lift lockdown, the NHS will be overpowered within a few days,' is truly alarming. Or you can believe the 'Hurrah! Happy Monday' front pages of the *Mail*, *Telegraph* and *Sun* instead, if you so wish.

The latter stages of PMQs, once Starmer had sat down, were rather less traumatic for Johnson. I'd forgotten how parochial this part can be: amidst a few further barbs from Labour and SNP backbenchers, shire Tories queued up to namecheck something local, dressed up in the form of a sycophantic question. The MP for Aylesbury invited his Right Honourable Friend to join him in congratulating Bertie the Bus for a sterling contribution to the war effort. Johnson was delighted to do so, especially since it involved alliterative use of his favourite letter of the alphabet.

Yet again, though, just as you think one over-promoted blond buffoon is having a dreadful day, the other upstages him. While I still hope against hope that any relaxation of our lockdown is going to be cosmetic, Donald Trump has, within the space of two days, both declared the lockdown over and that this is the 'worst crisis America has ever faced'. He's also back on a half-baked campaign trail. Yesterday, this involved possibly the most surreal outing of his already impossibly bizarre political career. He went to Arizona and refused to wear a face mask while visiting an actual face mask factory. Meanwhile the PA system, you'd hope satirically, blasted out 'Live and Let Die'.

Having finished my bike ride early, I caught the end of the UK government's press conference. Amanda tries to watch them all, and usually comes away grimacing and shaking her head. Yesterday's was very much the B-team: lead scientists Whitty and Vallance were off somewhere, possibly checking that *The Telegraph* has no dirt on their private lives. I didn't know either of their replacements and, at first, I didn't recognise the besuited man behind the middle lectern reserved for the day's short-straw drawing cabinet minister. Until he spoke, it looked like this was a waxwork of George Osborne borrowed from that inadvertently comical sub-Tussauds joint in Great Yarmouth. It turns out it was in fact the Housing Minister, Robert 'Generic' Jenrick, luckily for him facing the media before his trumpeted Turkish PPE haul had been revealed as a complete dud.

Generic was pitted against the might of the regional press, seemingly determined to make the Bertie the Bus of Aylesbury question look like the Spanish Inquisition. A Cornish journalist asked about support for their tourism industry, then used his follow-up question to seek assurances that outsiders would be prevented from spreading the virus in a so far relatively unaffected area. I'm afraid I may have lapsed into unseemly anti-Cornish bigotry at that point, as I reminded anyone within earshot that this was the same 'cake and eat it' county which voted overwhelmingly for Brexit, then asked the very next day whether Westminster would compensate them for the enormous subsidy (c. €700 million over ten years) they'd no longer be receiving from the EU.

Amidst all the noise and chatter, one piece of sporting news did cut through. The French and Dutch football authorities have called an end to their domestic seasons, but Germany is now planning to finish the Bundesliga campaign, with a resumption in late May. Dominic Raab did his best *Fast Show* 'Soccer!' impression the other day by feigning excitement at the possibility of the Premier League also resuming. With the 75th anniversary of VE Day being commemorated tomorrow, and more lashings of freedom coming up on 'Hurrah! Happy Monday', we certainly won't want Jerry to spoil the party and upstage us on the soccer front.

Much as I'd love some live football to watch on TV, and understand the desire of my TV colleagues to make themselves useful again, especially the freelancers for whom this has been an especially worrying time, I fear the worst. A total of 6,111 new infections here yesterday vs 365 in Germany tells its own story. If it goes ahead, it will all be off again as soon as we have another Mikel Arteta or Callum Hudson-Odoi-style infection. Even before that, there are players and club doctors already expressing misgivings and the clubs themselves seem bitterly divided.

As with all other Premier League decisions, a resumption requires 14 of the 20 clubs to vote in favour. Aston Villa and – surprise, surprise – Lady Brady's West Ham have already said they'd prefer to swerve an awkward relegation battle, thanks very much. Other clubs are panicking about losing TV revenue, and some apparently are weighing that up against the bonuses they won't have to pay if the season is declared null and void. Relegation being cancelled would, almost certainly, lead to legal action from Football League clubs if, as a consequence, three of them aren't promoted. Expect an absolute mess, with the worst-case scenario being a fudge of no relegation and three promotions, with six extra fixtures being added on to next season. That will, you'd assume, at best be played behind closed doors, and at worst could be ruined completely by further virus outbreaks.

There is one further, almost totally inconsequential, ramification of this morass. I can't keep on writing this forever – it's giving my mornings some much-needed structure, but diminishing returns will set in, not least if I have to keep tabs on so many casualties and such government ineptitude for much longer. My tentative plan, having begun to write on that ominous day when *Match of the Day* was replaced by *Mrs Brown's Boys*, is to knock this on the head once some kind of normal football service is resumed. So, if they don't get their act together, Lady Brady and co. could turn this into the *War and Peace* of rambling and ranting.

Friday, 8 May 2020

There's a scene in *The Young Ones* where a Cockney geezer character called Brian Damage, played by Alexei Sayle, waves a gun around and rants dementedly about whether or not the sky's blue, then accuses Neil the hippie of 'being sar-carstic'. When a terrified Neil mutters that he was 'y'know, not being sar-carstic', Damage instantly pipes down and cheerily says, 'Well, forget everything I just said then, all right?'

So it is with this morning's newspapers. The reckless barrage of 'Happy Monday' and 'Hurrah, Lockdown Freedom Begins' caused mayhem yesterday. My friends, on Facebook and elsewhere, were shocked and angry, while some simpler souls around the country seemingly caused a traffic and social gathering spike not seen since before this all started.

Today, by contrast, no retractions or apologies. Simply no reference at all – nothing, nada, it never happened. A couple of the tabloids have lamely put 'oh, look over there, everyone. It's the 75th anniversary of VE Day' on their front page instead. *The Sun* has found a twin unifying distraction – something nice about Colonel Tom, something horrible about a Premier League footballer. In the absence of any scandal connected to Raheem Sterling (though I'm sure they tried), Kyle Walker visited his sister, so that'll do. The *Daily Mail* has retreated altogether, into familiar right royal territory, with some guff about Prince Andrew being sued over an unpaid ski chalet bill, and pictures of 'Harry and Meghan's £15m LA hideaway'.

I've loathed *The Sun* and *Mail* for decades, even before their coverage of the Hillsborough tragedy, but what they did yesterday was nuts, and should – but won't – be called out for its recklessness by our politicians. Dangling freedom in front of their poorly informed readers one day, completely failing to mention it the next. There is also the question of who the hell had briefed the press late on Wednesday, before we woke up yesterday to discover that pub gardens, picnics and most of the rest of an Englishman's birthright were seemingly to be available to all our bulldog breed once more from Monday. I say 'Englishman' advisedly: Scottish First Minister Nicola Sturgeon made it abundantly clear that she'd opt out of the UK-wide approach if any of this was even vaguely true, and non-Scot Dominic Raab C. Nesbitt subsequently told the daily press conference that there would in fact only be limited tweaks.

Another 'the science has changed' excuse was duly wheeled out to explain the discrepancy – the cabinet was, unlike many of the rest of us, apparently shocked to discover that PPE-free care homes were bucking the trend of the reinfection rate coming down. You can imagine their faces as some of them finally worked out that sending untested old people from hospital to care homes meant that other old people were dying and care workers were duly passing the virus on to their families. R between 0.5 and 1, is the Pi R squared of our times. Mildly comical though it is to hear our Prime Minister talk about keeping the reproductive rate down, R is the measure of how many others a person with the virus has infected. More than 1 means exponential growth, which is why the Cheltenham Festival went ahead. Ah …

The *Mail* in particular, came in for some serious flak from my Facebook friends. Mike McGeary, who used to work for the Boro, and rarely posts about the news or politics, pointed out that 'hurrah' was an unfortunate word for them to have splashed on their front page. He simply posted the 'Hurrah for the Blackshirts!' Rothermere front page of the 1930s next to yesterday's offering. In a less noticed development (though Jake's

Messenger group spotted it) the Mail Online ran a bizarre pre-VE Day article, headed as follows: 'Germans don't use World War Two rhetoric to describe the pandemic response because they associate it with loss – but Britain and the US are happy to invoke the "Blitz".' Translated from Basil Fawlty speak, this suggests that the Germans are adult enough to associate the pandemic response with 'loss', which should therefore be minimised; whereas, if you're not careful, invoking the Blitz can easily be accompanied by 'losing' 30,000 or more people. Or 70,000 and counting, in the case of the other large Anglophone World War Two victor.

I understand why winning World War Two has such historical significance – though VE Day was Victory IN, not over Europe – but sadly, it's also pretty much the last major decision of its kind that either the UK or US has got right. From Suez to Iraq, we've seen where that swagger has led us, while the 'losers' – particularly Germany and Japan – have quietly rebuilt highly advanced and civilised societies.

It's probably the height of treachery to type that on VE Day. I'll honour the silence for those who served in both our families, but I'm sick of the sanctity now attached to being able to shut up for a minute or two, or indeed how big a poppy you wear. I've never been more ashamed to be a Boro fan than at Stoke in November 2018 when James McLean, a young man from Derry (where the British army shot 26 peaceful protesters in 1972) from the home team chose not to wear a poppy for the umpteenth year in a row. He has explained repeatedly that he fully respects the dead of both world wars, and honours the minute's silence, but won't wear a poppy which also symbolises the British army's casualties in Northern Ireland. This nuanced, personal decision led McLean to have death threats screamed at him, right through the supposed silence and for the next 90 minutes, by an alarmingly large minority of proud patriots in the away end (most of whom weren't wearing a poppy either and who, statistics suggest, cheerfully voted for the Brexit which may still wreck the Northern Irish peace process).

There's a growing danger of similar half-witted nonsense being attached to the weekly applause for care workers. As well as the stupidity of the mass gatherings on Westminster Bridge, which have badly misrepresented a largely disciplined capital, I read the appalling story of a woman in Manchester who was tending to her poorly child at 8pm, so didn't clap in the street as mandated, and was subjected to a hate campaign by her neighbours on social media.

The latest opinion poll shows a still solid 50 per cent support for the Conservative Party. Any one of those people who still claps for an NHS which has been undermined and underfunded by their party for the last decade is a raging hypocrite for thinking they can simply clap away the years of wilful negligence. Even so, I still wouldn't orchestrate a pile-on on social media. I stopped wearing a poppy after that Stoke experience, I'm afraid, but I will keep turning out at 8pm on a Thursday, with the Royal Free within earshot and few Tories (as far I'm aware) in the neighbourhood, but I am beginning to wonder about it all. I know for a fact that our friends and relatives on the NHS front line would much rather have PPE and other resources than applause.

I also fear that social pressure – and inversely proportional social distancing – will be applied to get whole communities to join in the VE Day street parties which are being planned for today. The weather is beautiful, the papers have declared that lockdown is over, the booze will flow, and it's possible that the ICUs will be fully deployed again in two or three weeks' time. Living in a multinational community should spare us from that kind of forced, and downright dangerous, jollity in these parts.

In recent years, Amanda and I have occasionally talked about going to live abroad. Two of our respective preferred options are the countries which, along with Germany, seem to enrage Englishmen more than any other. Perhaps it's because I'm married to someone who's lived there (twice) and is bilingual, but I have never understood the antipathy so many English people profess to feel towards France. Even when I'm there without Amanda – five weeks during the 1998 World Cup and three visits during the 2016 Euros – my O level French is more than enough to get by. I love their lifestyle and have never once encountered the snottiness which is alleged to characterise French people.

That option, which Amanda would have pursued at the drop of a chapeau, is probably lost to us now, since I dithered while we were still EU members, hoping that things would improve here. The other country in which I'd happily live, if it wasn't for the weather, is Scotland. Again, this would provoke outrage in some quarters, but I think it's objectively now a far better country than England.

Despite having a tenth of the population of England, Scotland more than pulls its weight culturally – from Burns to Livingstone to the films of Bill Forsyth to Aztec Camera and Teenage Fanclub and – intellectually – from John Logie Baird to Alexander Graham Bell to James Watt to my favourite philosopher, David Hume. Edinburgh was the world's most advanced city during the Age of the Enlightenment of the late 18th century and, if you can escape the festival crowds, is still arguably the most pleasant city in the UK.

The one area which matters much to me and in which Scotland probably does lag behind now – though not historically – is sport. I'm not talking about the Calcutta Cup, that total mismatch in which a country with more rugby players than the rest of the world put together usually beats the alumni of two Scottish public schools plus a few Borders sheep farmers. In the team sports I'm bothered about, there's not much cricket in Scotland and the football has suffered from a lull in the formerly remarkable stream of home-grown talent, as well as from the total dominance of the two Glasgow giants. Their outmoded sectarianism and virtual monopoly of media coverage hide a fabulously esoteric sporting scene beneath.

Over the years – and especially once I was Salford-based, and Saturday 3pm kick-offs were no longer a given – I visited all but one of the 42 league grounds in Scotland, Cove Rangers replacing Berwick Rangers last season having spoiled my complete set. In recent times, BBC Alba have moved lower division games to Friday or Saturday evenings, so I even managed to be at Kilmarnock one afternoon and Ayr United the same evening, then at a Sky live game at St Johnstone in Perth next day.

It's proper old-fashioned stuff, with football of variable quality, cheap admission, Bovril and hearty pies, hilarious songs and exasperated lone cries of anguish. Many of the grounds (Morton, Queen of the South) are Ayresome Park era relics, others are quirky (Brechin City, with a hedge down one touchline) or beautifully situated by the sea (East Fife, Arbroath). Over a number of years, I've been all over Scotland nerdishly accumulating grounds; it's a glorious country and if it wasn't for the fact that you need to wear long johns for four or five months every year, I'd be happy to live there.

In 2014, though it was none of my business, I was relieved when Scotland rejected independence, as much as anything because it's such a good influence on the rest of the UK. It's seen right through every right winger from Thatcher to Johnson, didn't take to Corbyn either, realised how awful an idea Brexit was, and continued to be funny, sardonic and yet still, somehow, perfectly affable to any English person who doesn't behave like a numpty on its soil. In retrospect, that great Teessider Bob Mortimer called it right in 2014. In the only political tweet I've ever seen from him, he posted that horrendous picture of Cameron and Johnson posing in their Bullingdon Club finery. His accompanying caption was simply, 'Scotland: this is your chance to get rid of this filth.' They didn't in the end, though, older people, and those who understandably didn't warm to Alex Salmond, winning the day. David Cameron, who then preened near a microphone that 'Her Majesty purred' when told the result, sadly thought he could achieve much the same with his EU referendum and so we find ourselves where we are now.

Much as I'd hate to lose them, I can see almost no reason why the Scots wouldn't now opt for independence under Nicola Sturgeon, given half a chance. Even what previously seemed like valid economic arguments no longer wash: a No Deal or even Awful Deal Brexit is set to further ruin all of us, so they may as well just cut their losses and get off this sinking ship as soon as they can, then hope they can rejoin the EU.

We've heard Nicola referred to in certain circles as 'a wee gobshite'. A very successful gobshite, I would say. Her leadership throughout this crisis has appeared exemplary from afar, and in stark contrast to what we've seen from Westminster. Even yesterday, she made it clear that she wouldn't criticise any lockdown decision made in London, but that Scotland simply wasn't ready to change anything substantial, and would opt out if she and her team saw fit.

I actually think she did Boris Johnson a favour there: within the current heartless and brainless Conservative Party, and amidst the clamour from our grotesque tabloid press, my current impression is that Johnson, Hancock and even Raab may be voices of relative caution in Whitehall. They may even be realising, possibly for the first time, that some of the people urging them on are true sociopaths, not just flirting with it to upset the liberals. There was even a recent *Bloomberg* article which suggested that Cummings muscled in on SAGE because, once he saw the light on herd immunity, he wanted that body to advocate the initial lockdown more urgently and unequivocally. The one recent thing I can make no sense of, though, is the briefing the newspapers must have received this week before most of them announced that the lockdown was over. Unless a Machiavellian strategy of unfathomable complexity is in play, how did that help anyone?

These are strange times indeed: unless it turns out that they briefed the 'hurrah!' madness which has set everyone's cause back even further, I think I now find myself, albeit temporarily, on the same side as Johnson and Cummings. They simply have to hold firm against those voices who are still openly advocating tens of thousands more deaths as an acceptable by-product of opening things up/making money. It's just extraordinary, and all too similar to the USA and Brazil, except that in each of those cases, the leader is firmly on the side of the sociopaths and will have to be thwarted and overruled by sane people every sorry step of the way. It could be too much to hope that they're not re-elected, either.

I hope this won't be misconstrued as a Homer Simpson response to the tabloids dangling 'hurrah, freedom beckons' in front of me, but I'm in between two successive journeys in two days beyond the neighbourhood. Today, Amanda is accompanying me for her first car ride in some weeks, whereas yesterday I ventured out on my own.

The vagaries of click and collect slots led me to a fifth different Waitrose in seven weeks. This time, I drove to Markham Street in Belgravia, three miles or so from here. The streets looked halfway back to normal, with several cafes now serving takeaway food along the Edgware Road, although the numbers thinned out considerably as I went down Park Lane, passing pretty much every venue in which I ever attended a football or TV awards do. Round Hyde Park Corner and into Belgravia, that strange, but attractive,. quarter dedicated to embassies and upper crust apartments. The Portuguese Embassy, where we attended a function prior to Euro 2004, lies about 100 yards from this previously unknown (to me, at least) Waitrose. It was civilised and orderly, like all the others, but nevertheless slightly eerie, with maybe half the customers and most of the staff in makeshift PPE.

Just as I pulled in to park at the end of the return journey, a song which evokes very specific memories came on my random shuffle. Just under a decade ago, Cheshire-based singer-songwriter Thea Gilmore was given the lyrics to several unfinished songs by the late Sandy Denny. Sandy was a founder member of Fairport Convention and the only vocalist ever allowed to share a Led

Zeppelin track with Robert Plant, namely 'Battle of Evermore' from *Led Zeppelin IV.* She died in the 1970s, but Thea wrote an entire 2011 album of songs called *Don't Stop Singing*, using the words she'd left behind. One of them, an excellent jig called 'London' became a reasonably big hit, and the assistant editor of our Olympic coverage, Ron Chakraborty, duly clocked it.

Ron is the man who keeps sending me extraordinary music videos, the latest of which is a ukulele version of Radiohead's 'Creep' which I'm still struggling to comprehend as physically possible, let alone try to play. The refrain to Thea's song, 'I wish I was in London, that's where I want to be' and lots of upbeat fiddle-based instrumental breaks almost screamed out to be a music montage at London 2012, and so it became. I ran it at the end of the last show I had the privilege to edit at that joyous and momentous event, and it was given several further airings.

Thereafter, back in Salford, it became a happy 'our tune' for Amanda and I, and Ron and his wife Victoria, when we met up for our regular Thai meals in Wilmslow or visited each other's homes. We all liked Cheshire – Ron and Vic are still there, in Knutsford – but much as I love so many places I've visited, I'd still say London and New York are the only truly international cities on the planet, in as much as they're more global than national. This is precisely what some people hate about both, and the two cities have come horribly unstuck in the face of COVID-19. Welcoming the world, having hundreds of languages spoken and every imaginable cuisine eaten, also means you'll probably be right in the eye of a global pandemic, and won't necessarily receive much sympathy from certain quarters, even within your own country. I didn't burst into tears this time, but hearing that wonderfully optimistic ditty, dedicated to my home city, ringing out as I drove past the huddled masked masses was extremely poignant.

So naturally, I picked up the guitar afterwards and played what is a jaunty but relatively straightforward number, based around four chords. Nothing wrong with that, the same applies to many classic songs down the years – 'Stand By Me' and all but the middle eight of 'Back for Good', for example.

But the other Sandy Denny song I love to play is quite a complex number, especially given the almost unbelievable fact that she wrote it as a teenager. It's in the key of E, but the second chord is one I couldn't have named, but which I worked out by watching someone play it on YouTube. It's described on a chord site where I've just looked it up as F#m11/E – I'll take their word for it – and the same initial progression features on the title track of George Harrison's masterpiece *All Things Must Pass*, or at least it does when I play it. From there on, the two songs depart – so, unlike 'My Sweet Lord' and the Chiffons, I don't think George was sued for plagiarism – but the sense of wistfulness remains as further unusual chords come into play.

Sandy's original recording with Fairport Convention formed the centrepiece of one of the greatest plays and individual performances I've ever seen – Mark Rylance as the charismatic yob Rooster Byron in Jez Butterworth's lament for a lost England, *Jerusalem*. Heresy though it probably is, among the many fine cover versions – Judy Collins, Nina Simone, Eva Cassidy – is one which I would contend is even better than the original: the sublime version by Susanna Hoffs of the Bangles on her stupendous collaboration with Matthew Sweet of song covers from different decades, *Under the Covers*.

Give it a whirl. The song selection and execution on the sixties edition in particular is almost faultless. And if you listen and don't agree, you're either very young or a cloth-eared idiot. Either way, if it's possible, the incredible song in question is even more poignant during lockdown than ever before. 'Who Knows Where the Time Goes?', indeed.

WEEK NINE

Saturday, 9 May 2020

Last November, I took my clapped-out 2009 Renault Clio to our local garage for its MOT. Given how little I'd been using it, and the fact that I'd piled on the miles during the four years I'd commuted from Cheshire to Salford, I did a mental calculation that if the bill went beyond £500, I'd be straight on the phone to Webuyanycar.com. I could always hire a car on the rare occasions I needed to get off the public transport grid. The repairs needed to get the battered old heap through its test came to about £400 in the end, so I gave it one final year. I have no idea how we would have made the last two months work if I hadn't.

All home delivery services in these parts have, not unreasonably, been allocated to key workers and the vulnerable, or, if you're lucky, long-established repeat customers. If I'd walked to do the shopping in either Belsize Park or on the Finchley Road, as both Amanda and I always have until recently, I'd be restricted to what I could carry, so would have joined the socially distanced queue every couple of days and developed significantly longer arms by now. As it is, having ventured to Waitrose in Belgravia on Thursday, I treated Amanda to a drive to IKEA in Wembley yesterday.

Sadly, we only visited the car park – Swedish meatballs and a chest of drawers I'd still be assembling at 5am being off the menu for the foreseeable future. Several weeks ago, our friend Margaret from the Fat Larry's Band Zoom group circulated an e-mail from King's College, London asking people to take part, via an app, in an independent study they are conducting into COVID-19. The research is being led by the college's Professor of Genetic Epidemiology, Tim Spector. All it involves is putting aside a minute a day to give them a health update, and they now have three million people across the country reporting to them, a tally I suspect the Classic Dom crony app currently being trialled/ tried for witchcraft in the Isle of Wight may never achieve.

Ninety per cent of the time, I've simply ticked 'feeling normal' and 'haven't had a test' and moved on. Several weeks ago, I had a couple of days where I ticked the 'sore throat' box. I had ear issues too, but I was fairly sure it was just one of my ENT flare-ups, which fortunately subsided before I had to decide whether to chance an appointment with a consultant. Something similar happened a few days ago, exacerbated, I suspect, by a very high pollen count and the fact that we've spent a lot of time in the garden recently. Amanda's had a bout of hay fever too, which suggests that's what's behind my symptoms, but I ticked the 'sore throat' box and thought nothing more of it.

On Thursday evening I received an e-mail inviting me and other members of my household to have a COVID-19 test. King's have the Department of Health's agreement that their reportees are classed as volunteers and should be tested if they have any of a long list of symptoms. I was given instructions to log into the essential workers' portal, describe myself as a volunteer (as generous assessment of a minute a day on a research app) and book a slot. Wembley was our easiest option and, to my surprise, more than 500 slots were available yesterday, so I clearly wouldn't be taking one from an NHS or care worker. I assume this doesn't apply to every testing centre.

It's drive-in only at IKEA, so off we toddled. I plugged in the iPhone to use GPS to make sure I took the right exit off the North Circular and my music downloads went into random shuffle mode. As we pulled into IKEA, that happy feedback accident which precedes the first Beatles single of my lifetime gave us a moment of dark laughter, 'I Feel Fine', then a swab down the throat and up the nose from two guys in full protective gear, and we were out again. The results will be texted to us in the next couple of days. It was an impressive operation, and while it's encouraging that so much testing capacity has been jacked up, there were only three or four other cars there. I hope we have done our tiny bit to help King's College's research. We'll also have taken the government nearer (by two) to the

100,000 tests a day target which has eluded them every day since last weekend.

I'm typing this as the birdsong and sunlight stream through our open French windows. Amanda has failed to make me the coffee she promised 20 minutes ago, but on the other hand, she's just researched this next paragraph or two on her iPad, so all is forgiven. She says that, once more, she can hear the sound of thundering hooves. Followed, presumably, by the creak of a stable door.

Just a month or so after pretty much every other nation on the planet, it's rumoured that the centrepiece of Bojo the Clown's sad face-squirty flower address to the nation tomorrow will be 14 days' quarantine for all arrivals into the UK. In the first three months of this year, of the 18.1 million arrivals into the UK, only 273 entered quarantine. Almost all had arrived on those three flights from Wuhan in that brief period before herd immunity seemingly replaced testing and tracking.

By the end of April, even with most flights cancelled, we still had 105,000 passengers a week arriving untested in the UK. There were 17 unchecked flights a day coming in from Milan the weekend after Lombardy entered a lockdown which was far stricter than ours has ever been. It was only when airlines began to see them as economically unviable that those flights began to dry up. The industry body Airlines UK, which represents the likes of Virgin and Ryanair, have reacted to the proposed 14-day quarantine with horror, saying that such a move will 'kill international travel'. I'm genuinely sorry for their employees, but that seems preferable to killing many more people.

Even Robocop Home Secretary Priti Patel has (apparently) been advocating some form of quarantine for weeks, which would at least have been consistent with the 'Take Back Control' mantra she has parroted for four years. Having said that, she still managed to charter a plane to throw out some Poles earlier this week – no screening or social distancing for them or the 40 Home Office escorts accompanying them.

Elsewhere, three neighbouring EU countries with a shared modern history and combined COVID-19 death toll in the hundreds – Latvia, Lithuania and Estonia – have tentatively announced that their citizens can begin to travel between the three in the coming days. Unlike our fellow island nation, New Zealand, which simply closed its borders on 10 April, and has registered one solitary new case in the last three days, we would seem to have placed the livelihoods of Branson, O'Leary and their unfortunate employees ahead of the lives of people.

Doubtless Bojo will tell us tomorrow that, once more, 'the science has changed', but it really hasn't. In a different, non-profit driven sector, unions representing the teaching profession and ancillary staff – cleaners, caterers, admin, etc. – are strongly resisting the notion of pupils returning to school until there is clear, written scientific evidence that it would be safe for everyone to do so. Even Classic Dom and his SAGE committee will struggle to cook that up.

This is a proper omnishambles, clusterfuck or anything else you'd like to call it. Jake has posted a very simple and stark graphical analysis which has been conducted based on the correlated figures provided by Johns Hopkins University. The nations of the world are divided into three categories: the first is entitled 'Countries beating COVID-19' – the graph of their daily new cases looks like a child's drawing of a steep mountain with a diagonal line up and down again. New Zealand falls into this category, of course, as do Norway and Iceland, but also some less wealthy nations like Vietnam and Cambodia. The next category is 'Nearly there' with a steep upwards slope followed by a significant if slightly bumpy down slope. This includes all those countries we were feeling sorry for a few weeks ago – Italy, Spain and Iran. The third category is 'Countries which need to take action': steep upwards slope, little or no sign of a corresponding rate in the down slope, if there even is a down slope. We and the US are rubbing shoulders with Iraq, Bangladesh, Brazil and Somalia in this group of nations.

Every day, more and more condemnation is poured on the UK's handling of this crisis. Some of it comes from the non-toadying fringes of our media, but there are whole dung heaps of disapprobation from around the globe. Justin sent me a fascinating interview with Larry Brilliant, the veteran American epidemiologist who spearheaded the final stages of the successful global struggle to eliminate smallpox. Having discussed America's approach and tried his best to assess Trump rationally, he was asked about the response in other countries. Unprompted, he cited the UK as the one standout failure to date. 'You can't make a bigger mistake than they did,' was his verdict.

Italy's *Corriere della Sera*, meanwhile, describes our situation as 'like a nightmare from which you cannot awake'; Christoph Mayer, London correspondent for Germany's DPA news agency, describes us as 'Europe's problem child' and the Greek daily *Ethnos* laments 'incompetent leaders' and describes Johnson as 'more dangerous than coronavirus'. Derek Jameson's old TV series *Do They Mean Us?* which compiled clips of quirky overseas perceptions of Blighty, would be a rather more sombre affair if it was revived right now.

Back home, though, the messages have been so mixed that they may as well have been pulped in a blender. 'Hurrah!' and the promise of a 'Happy Monday' from the worst of our press may have been frantically rowed back since by cabinet ministers, but they appear to have helped give the green light to a gigantic outdoor party yesterday. I don't quite get how a two-minute silence and address from the Queen on the 75th anniversary of VE Day morphed into some of the scenes I've seen online.

Amanda and I kept quiet for two minutes at 11am, went off to IKEA for our tests and returned to a day pretty much like any other. By the evening, though, I started to see some extraordinary posts. The *Evening Gazette*, whose headlines I'm offered by Google because I source their Boro updates, posted video footage of a shambolic Teesside attempt to ape the recently cancelled Notting Hill Carnival. Bunting and flags were everywhere, there was loud music, dancing, drinking and hundreds of people cavorting all over the streets of Grove Hill in Middlesbrough, the English borough currently third on the list of COVID-19 cases to population. Many of the posts from locals underneath suggested that these clowns wallowing in a British military victory from long before even their parents' time were, in many cases, the very same people who'd been out boisterously applauding the NHS the previous evening.

There seem to have been similar scenes in various other parts of the country, and long into the night, if the eyewitness accounts of my various groups are anything to go by. Sky News went live to a mass singsong in the street in Wimbledon: 'We'll meet again' – yes, perhaps in an intensive care unit in two or three weeks' time. A quite imbecilic conga – perfect for breathing in the person in front's slipstream – on a street in Warrington was cheerily broadcast by *BBC NW Tonight* and trumpeted on its official Twitter account. As the author Jonathan Coe put it, 'We can die happy now we've done the conga for our war dead.'

Curiously, it's all gone unreported by the same tabloids who'd breezily told their readers that lockdown was almost over. There wasn't a hint of any of it in this multinational neighbourhood and I watched no TV at all yesterday, but there's a short clip doing the rounds on Facebook of Fiona Bruce in the BBC News studio handing over to a reporter in Cosham, Portsmouth. He was standing cheerily addressing a camera in front of a scrum of dozens of people partying on down in their street amidst a sea of red, white and blue. Rather than suggesting they might like to get back on to their own premises, or at least make a vague attempt to socially distance, this reporter was happy to soak up the special atmosphere on this special day.

For once, some vox pops would have been interesting: 'Do you have any idea what VE Day was?' for example. And moreover, 'What the hell are you doing, you lunatics?' Not a bit of it – even actual service people and Blitz veterans on the streets of London on the actual VE Day in 1945 would have been hard pushed to match the reckless revelry BBC News were tacitly endorsing in the middle of a pandemic.

Up in Middlesbrough, it might well have inspired cooped-up Teessiders to copy the scenes being relayed from Portsmouth. I have a horrible feeling we'll be seeing a lot more of that footage in the months and years to come. It could even become the successor to Neville Chamberlain and his piece of paper, though I suspect Johnson's various 'shook hands with everybody', 'take this on the chin' and 'our apparent success' moments may pip it to the post in the historical misjudgement stakes.

It seems ludicrously unimportant in the scheme of things, but by doing most of the uphill 5km early on and saving some of the downhill 5km for later, I recorded a new PB of 28 minutes 35 seconds in the 20km personal cycling Olympics. I was aided by Aztec Camera radio on Spotify which threw up 'French Navy' by Camera Obscura as a rhythm track to which I could pedal the closing stages. Another fine band I could have added to my 'wonderful Scottish things' list yesterday. With the exception of the odd rogue Rangers supporters' club gathering, I bet there wasn't too much Union Jack madness on the streets of Scotland yesterday.

Speaking of musical matters, I had a lovely e-mail this morning from Daz, an ex-BBC colleague of mine, whose soundness on many matters on Facebook and marriage to an EU citizen earned him an invitation to Jake's 'Just for the Remoaners' group. He's also on my weekly mailing list, and a keen musician. Daz got in touch to tell me on the quiet that Sandy Denny wasn't in fact a founder member of Fairport Convention. Apparently, a woman called Judy Dyble was the original lead female vocalist alongside Ian Matthews, later of Matthews Southern Comfort, who had a UK number one with Joni Mitchell's 'Woodstock'. I'm delighted to stand corrected: on the grounds of authenticity, though, I'll leave my original mistake where it was. Just as I will when Dom's cronies' app eliminates COVID-19 from the Isle of Wight, then the planet, and becomes the penicillin equivalent of its day, with Alexander Fleming-style knighthoods to follow for Cummings and the Warner Brothers. Fleming was Scottish, too, come to think of it. Another one for the list.

In the meantime, since he tells me he can play Dave Pegg's melodious bass part (I assume it was Dave Pegg, Daz will tell me next week if it wasn't), Daz and I are going to get together, if and when we ever emerge from lockdown, to duet on 'Who Knows Where the Time Goes?' Neither of us are exactly Sandy Denny, though: I haven't told her yet, but Amanda might have to be our singer.

Sunday, 10 May 2020

In two days' time, my mum turns 80. She's getting through this awful time okay, with the help of her wonderful visiting carer Tracey and my doting dad. It must be very strange to have her son (my brother John) and her two grandchildren in the house, but not within touching distance – I'm not sure exactly how they're managing all the logistics, but they're all at least able to congregate at a distance in the garden now that the weather is warmer.

Our latest FaceTime with my nieces revealed that they're working on baking a cake for the big day, having smartly kept some currently unobtainable flour stashed away. Amanda and I would really like to join them on Tuesday, rather than simply posting a card and arranging for a present to be delivered, but we can't take even the slightest risk of taking anything down to Kent from Virus Central. And having been disgusted with Nigel Farage when he drove all over south-east England for non-essential purposes, I'd be a hypocrite if I did likewise.

Dad and I had a lengthy chat last night, which inevitably moved on to our mutual despair with the government. As a former manager of a large team of people himself, he feels the buck stops at the top and continues to be utterly exasperated with Johnson.

Having watched his post-hospital performances, he's concluded that our Churchill tribute act (a shit Elvis in a tragic Blackpool restaurant, not Bjorn Again or the Bootleg Beatles) actually isn't very bright. I think that may well be true, notwithstanding the occasional deployment of an unusual word from his thesaurus and a limited ability to conjugate Latin verbs. He can't have been all that good even at that, given his lifelong resentment of the firsts attained by both his own brother and David Cameron. Dad had clocked a moment in a press conference when Johnson expressed pride that the peak of the virus had coincided with the lockdown, as if that was the result of brilliant planning and timing. In fact, it was a product of basic cause and effect – a peak would inevitably occur once a lockdown was in place. Producing a tangible down slope, having finally implemented a half-arsed and belated lockdown, is proving to be the real problem.

He may not advocate the injection of disinfectant, or express surprise that antibiotics don't kill a virus, but Johnson seems to understand even elementary science little better than Trump does. Hence his reliance on Cummings at SAGE meetings and in the commissioning of NHS apps. Only someone who's pretty clueless, as well as lazy, would rely on an allegedly self-taught humanities graduate to interpret this grave situation for him. Angela Merkel actually is an academic scientist, and it shows.

The latest overnight strategic/chaotic media leak is the new government slogan. Gone is the 'Stay Home' of the last six weeks, in comes 'Stay Alert. Control the Virus. Save Lives'. This is framed in green, not the previous red. Amanda thinks this frankly dire messaging is subtly saying 'over to you', the light having already been switched to green with that incompetently planted 'Hurrah, Happy Monday' disgrace. We're sticking rigidly to our arrangements, as are our friends and neighbours, but after the 'catch the virus for our fallen' debacle of the VE Day anniversary, Hackney police tweeted with sadness that they were 'fighting a losing battle' yesterday, as London Fields became overwhelmed with huge groups lying around on the grass.

Tall Paul took a walk down by Richmond Bridge, and sent Poncey Horse Club a photo of what appeared to be a normal summer scene. An ice cream van was doing brisk business, and there were even groups of people sitting out with pints of beer bought from an enterprising/reckless 'essential' food shop. Okay, so some of those people won't understand that, even if they're young and healthy, they can transmit the virus to someone like my dad in a supermarket who'll then take it home to potentially deadly effect, but what an absolute mess it all is. The Scottish, Welsh and Northern Irish governments are pointedly keeping the 'Stay Home' message, and ignoring this bizarre new messaging from England. I'm afraid I think that's the right call. The Scots have even pointedly made the slogan grammatical, by inserting an 'at' between 'stay' and 'home'.

I still lean towards my gut feeling that this continues to be caused by ineptitude as it has from Day One, but what if it is now a deliberate passing of the buck? If you catch it, it'll be your fault, because you didn't 'stay alert' or manage to 'control the virus'. Back when Bojo caught it, he was technically 'staying home', assuming he caught it in a Downing Street gathering and not from shaking hands, either during a hospital visit or at the jolly old rugger. So, in the spirit of 'stay alert', I've treated the virus the way I normally would my car keys and searched high and low for it around the flat this morning. My conclusion is that I couldn't see it, therefore it's not here and I've done my bit to 'control the virus'. I can now put my Union Jack bowler hat back on with pride, and rejoin the street party.

Honestly, it's all so pathetic I could weep, and yet I'm obliged to watch that idiot's address tonight and go along with whatever rearrangement of the deckchairs on the Titanic he – sorry, 'the science' – has decreed. Half of those who'll watch him will think, 'Funny blond man can be serious with an autocue, too,' and would therefore vote for him every day until the crack of doom if they could. More worryingly still, three-quarters of the nation won't watch him at all, will continue to have no idea what they're supposed to be doing or why, and the whole miserable downward spiral will continue.

I had a chat from about five metres away yesterday with Martijn, our Dutch neighbour, who was exercising in our communal garden. He's told me that Google, where he works, have told their staff to work at home for the rest of the year. With a pregnant wife who's also doing some work from home, he's relieved not to have to work out how to get to their office behind Kings Cross, or indeed try to achieve social distancing in their lifts.

He's also worked out, as has the EU's trade commissioner Phil Hogan, and most other well-informed people across the continent, that the UK government seems to be hell-bent on No Deal with a further eight-to-ten per cent hit to GDP (the 2008 global banking crisis caused a two per cent dip) and will try to hide it amidst the chaos of the coronavirus fall-out. Knowing where I used to work, he asked me if I'd seen that the BBC website's main headline was 'Italy passes the 30,000 mark for highest death toll in the EU'. The fact that Britain, I guess technically not an EU member any more, had raced past that figure while the papers were screaming 'Hurrah!' for Happy Monday was tucked away in paragraph three. Martijn's a very bright, media-savvy man, so simply asked me, 'What's going on there?'

I could only sigh and shrug, but Rob from Jake's Messenger group has posted an article from *The Economist* examining the UK's media coverage, and how, unlike the rest of the world's media, it's largely let the inept British government off the hook. This line from 'a senior BBC journalist' alarmed him (and me) in particular: 'The bosses are keen that we come out of this with the sense that we looked after the interests of the nation, not just our journalistic values.' Not only does that fly in the face of everything I was ever taught on training courses, or while doing my job, or when consulting the handbook of BBC editorial guidelines, it's completely self-contradictory. Looking 'after the interests of the nation' surely involves pointing out when the

Prime Minister gets something wrong – admittedly that would be someone's full-time job – or at very least, raising the alarm about PPE and the NHS sending the infected into care homes. It also should mean not asking 'when will lockdown be lifted?' at every press conference, or framing chaotic street parties and congas as Auntie's reassuring daily dose of good news.

Much as I want to be across everything to inform both myself and this journal, I'm only seeing clips of BBC News second-hand now. I've stopped watching it entirely in real time because I don't need my news sugar-coated. This isn't World War Two where we don't want to provide succour to a sentient enemy. Also, I love the rest of the corporation too much to put myself through the misery of watching its compromised main news output any more.

The BBC drama *Normal People*, set in Ireland, has drawn me in. Various people we know have raved about it – Amanda started to read the book by Sally Rooney on holiday last year, but didn't like it. She's given up on the serialisation, too. The lead female character, Marianne, initially behaves like a snotty, superior cow to her sixth-form teachers. Amanda is very strict about that kind of thing and wants no more to do with her; I want to know why she behaved like that, and am now finding out. Plus, Marianne's fumbling relationship with the male lead Connell is really well drawn, the whole thing's beautifully acted and shot, and moreover I wish one of my grandparents and not just their various parents had actually been born in Ireland, so I could get myself a passport. We went to the West Coast last year for the Galway Races and visited Sligo where *Normal People* is set, and Boyle, Roscommon where there's still a pub bearing my grandmother's distinctive, and very local, surname, Mattimoe. An absolutely lovely part of the world.

Both in terms of the setting and the normality of the socialising and other scenes, it really feels like a case of, 'Look what you could have won.' Amanda, meanwhile, is immersed in an Icelandic Scandi Noir drama called *Trapped*. Much as I enjoyed what now feels like a long-lost dream – our week in

Arctic Norway across Brexit Independence Day three and a half months ago – the snowy wastes and bizarre/unhinged characters of *Trapped* weren't really doing it for me, so we now have a 'his and hers' TV drama hour each evening.

I had a good afternoon on the bench (now moved back to its original place in the absence of any further barking coughs from next door) with Hilary Mantel yesterday and have now finished the first section of the *Mirror and the Light*. I'm 255 pages in, a mere 650 to go. Cromwell and Henry are still regularly reminding me of Cummings and Johnson – maybe there are some deliberate but subtle allusions, given it was written so recently – and I won't complain if Cummings is taken to the Tower before I reach the point where Cromwell is.

Meanwhile, football is slowly resuming in some countries. It never stopped in Belarus, where president Lukashenko is in complete denial. He held a full military parade for VE Day just as, according to an alarming Sky News report, the virus is spiralling out of control in his country. South Korea has just become the first football stronghold to resume the professional game. That country has produced some fine players: Park Ji-sung at Manchester United and in particular, Son Heung-min who is not only a favourite of the Spurs Curry Club, but was top of the class in the military service he's just completed back home.

'Top of the class' would not be the phrase any Middlesbrough fan would associate with our South Korean import of a decade or so ago. Alleged striker Lee Dong Gook scored precisely zero goals for Middlesbrough in 23 Premier League appearances between 2007 and 2008. Yet he played 105 games between 1998 and 2017 for his country, reaching a decent tally of 33 goals. While some of the Asian qualifiers may distort the figures – though, let's face it, Wayne Rooney also benefited from playing in the era of qualifiers against Liechtenstein and Andorra – South Korea have consistently performed creditably at the World Cup itself, and not just the one they co-hosted, so that 100-plus caps must say something for his ability as well as longevity.

The only time I've seen South Korea play in the flesh, as far as I can recall, was at, of all places, QPR. In the run-up to the 2010 World Cup, they played the Ivory Coast at Loftus Road at 2.30pm one Wednesday. The kick-off time was set to suit the TV audience back in Asia, but it suited me, too. BBC Sport was still based at Television Centre round the corner at that point, and a choice between an afternoon in the office and a spot of research into two teams we'd be covering in the summer wasn't a difficult one. We knew the people at QPR quite well, so though it looked like good fun among the two diasporas – the Ivorians were outnumbered by huge numbers of Koreans, but made plenty of noise, too – I went into the directors' box, for a decent view as much as the prawn sandwiches.

I remember the then Brazilian coach and former World Cup-winning captain Dunga was there (they'd been drawn against the Ivorians in the finals) as was Roy Hodgson, who subsequently spent that summer working with us. Sitting right next to me was my old mate Peter Reid, also on a scouting mission. We looked at the team sheet together – Didier Drogba and Park Ji-sung were among the familiar Premier League names. 'Lee Dong Gook,' said Reidy. 'Isn't he the one who played for your mob?' 'God, yeah,' I replied. 'Absolutely useless. Couldn't hit a barn door.' Four minutes in (I've just checked that – no shoddy journalism here) a sublime Korean half-volley from outside the box flew into the top corner. The rest of the directors' box may have wondered why two of their number were wiping away tears of laughter as the PA announced that our first goalscorer of the afternoon was one Lee Dong Gook.

He's been at it again, ten years on – aged a remarkable 41, he came off the bench to score the only goal of the game with a glancing header for Jeonbuk Motors against Suwon Bluewings in the K-League's grand reopening fixture. This was seen all over the world, including a live streaming by BBC Sport. The game was played behind closed doors and group celebrations are out, even in a country with a death toll of just 256, so instead

Lee made hand gestures to express his support for the country's health workers. Top man, as Reidy would say. It may have been misplaced and distinctly un-PC, but it's good to see that at least the first part of one of Teesside's dodgier ditties came true in the end: 'He shoots, he scores, he eats your labradors – Lee Dong Gook, Lee Dong Gook.'

Nothing dodgy about the music of the man who managed to break into the COVID headlines yesterday, albeit for very sad reasons. The great Little Richard died yesterday at the age of 87. As Stewart Wood said on Facebook: the young Bob Dylan's ambition was 'to join Little Richard'; Jimi Hendrix said, 'I want to do with my guitar what Little Richard did with his voice;' while John Lennon added, 'When I first heard "Long Tall Sally", it was so great I couldn't speak.' And, Stewart added, 'Just listen to early McCartney,' especially the Beatles' cover of the aforementioned 'Long Tall Sally'.

Yesterday's cycling soundtrack picked itself – Rolling Stone listed 'Tutti Frutti' as number one in its list of the most influential records of the rock era, so that was my starting point, with a playlist of his greatest hits to follow. I had no idea he'd returned the favour by covering McCartney's 'I Saw Her Standing There', but that was good as you'd expect, too. The sheer exuberance and pounding piano of the great man actually drove me to smash my personal best for 20km by over a minute. I could scarcely walk afterwards, so 27 minutes 35 seconds is probably going to stand as my own tiny permanent memorial to the utterly marvellous Little Richard. Until tomorrow, I bid you a fond 'A-wop-bop, a-loo-bop, a-lop-bam-boo.'

Monday, 11 May 2020

It's 5am and I've had as much sleep as I'm likely to get. I cannot remember witnessing anything quite as disturbing in my five and a half decades of living in this country as that prime ministerial address last night. Not Margaret Thatcher at her worst, nor Tony Blair falling under the spell of George Bush, not even the morning after the Brexit vote.

I assume that everyone who's reading this in 2020 will have watched it, but just in case this is ever read by anyone in the future – maybe my nieces when they're older – I'll try to articulate something beyond 'aaaarrrrrghh'.

The address achieved something I would have previously thought impossible: a combination of too little, too late and too much, too soon. Despite being pre-recorded, the whole thing looked off the cuff and amateurish: a besuited, coiffed, but still fist-pumping Prime Minister said pretty much nothing of substance in the entire 15 minutes, yet as Amanda predicted, appeared to throw the ball firmly back into our court.

Go to work if you can't work from home, but try to avoid public transport, was the bewildering headline. The smallest children – the ones who insert anything they find into their mouths, sneeze and cough all over the place and have no concept of social distancing – will be the first back to school. You can go out for as long as you like, but you can't come within two metres of anyone from outside your household. Around 280,000 people have died across the globe so far from the coronavirus, 32,000 of them here in the UK – officially, at least. Those figures were, naturally, not mentioned at all, but Johnson started his ramble by congratulating himself for managing to swerve a potential final death toll of 500,000. That figure was mooted by Imperial College on 12 March as the likely outcome if we took no restrictive measures whatsoever, and actually forced the abandonment of 'herd immunity' the very next day, but he threw it in there anyway. He'd previously seemingly signed herd immunity off before he disappeared to Chevening for 13 days to sort out his myriad family issues, so perhaps we should be profoundly grateful to only have an eighth of the world's death toll with under one per cent of its population.

For a student of languages – albeit dead ones – Johnson has an extraordinary, almost Trumpian, ability to render words meaningless, but at the same time, sinister. The lyrics are gibberish, but the tune and body language are geared to show how a clever person should sound and look. You know what, hypothetical person reading this in the future? Those of us who lived through that waffling abdication of responsibility last night really don't need to relive the whole thing. Just watch it on YouTube or whatever you have now, while I try to get my head round what it might all have meant – other than, 'I'm stuck between the demands of the rich maniacs in my party, and the reality of how badly I've messed this up. Over to you, and I hope saying "Be Alert" and "Control the Virus" (England only) means it's now entirely up to you if you choose to put your life at risk.'

Even Petronella Wyatt, posh and privileged daughter of right-wing journalist Baron Woodrow, and erstwhile paramour of Johnson (Michael Howard sacked Bojo from his shadow cabinet for misleading him about Ms Wyatt having a termination and a miscarriage during their affair) tweeted the following: 'How are lower-paid workers supposed to get to work without using public transport? In their Rolls Royces? What sort of world does the PM live in?'

Let's assume for a minute that what I believe was initially stupendous incompetence has now mutated into a more sinister strategy. I'm about to posit something which may or may not be/come true. It's a possible explanation of what certain deeply unpleasant and, at this point, desperate people could be thinking. I would categorically not share this more widely at a time like this, but I think my readership can cope with a few apocalyptic hypotheticals. If it doesn't happen, we need never speak of it again, but there are signs that at least some of what follows is already under way.

English society continues to divide almost precisely along the lines of Brexit. I would guess that many of the 48 per cent who voted Remain are comparing the UK data with that from overseas, and realise that we are now a rogue nation, with only the US, Brazil and Belarus for company (well, maybe Sweden, but at least theirs is a strategy they've shared with their public). The 52 per cent will either not compare us with other countries (the people they respect are telling them not to do so) and be unaware that the daily 4,000 new cases we are still seeing seven weeks into a lockdown is a catastrophe, or, worst of all, they do know, and refuse to renege on the blind faith they place in politicians who tell them that our innate national superiority will win the day, when all evidence points to the contrary. Just a continuation of Brexit in other words.

That supportive proportion may not stay at 52 per cent, but they're hanging on in there if the polls are to be believed, so many will not budge even when we can't travel anywhere while others can, or even if we start 2021 with food and medicine shortages. I suspect many can't be shifted, even if our graph starts to look like the one I saw this morning of the 1918–1919 flu pandemic. That returned after a first summer spike and subsequent small dip, with a far worse second one the following winter.

As indicated by the increase in fines Johnson announced yesterday for those who flout the yet to be published 60 pages of new rules, the forces of law and order – and possibly the army in due course – will be authorised to clamp down heavily and visibly on those who step out of line. You can go to work, drive anywhere, get on public transport, still fly in and out without being quarantined (he didn't close that stable door despite all the media talk) but they're going to have your guts for garters if you do anything which might spread the virus. Yes, I know that makes no sense whatsoever. Hefty fines will, you suspect, mostly be doled out to city dwellers, not white middle-class people in the shires: *The Daily Mail* and *Telegraph* care about the rights and lives of the latter. I can't see even this government asking the army to force people to take their kids to school or to get on to public transport to go to work – although financial pressures might make them.

Essentially, this is being treated as a battle: having failed woefully to defeat the invisible enemy, they're not above turning to that old favourite, the enemy within. If you think all of this is inconceivable now, or it hasn't entirely to come to pass in a year's time, feel free to let me know.

In the meantime, I've temporarily rejoined Twitter. I remember that Tory charlatan of a previous era, Jeffrey Archer, making an excruciating appearance on the Dame Edna Everage show. 'You have to be able to laugh at yourself,' he said feebly at one point. 'Well if you didn't,' Dame Edna fired back, 'you'd be missing out on the biggest joke in history.' Unsurprisingly, in the aftermath of Johnson's Nightmare on Downing Street, social media was brimming with cogent anger and depressing trending topics ('Should I go to work tomorrow?' is plain heartbreaking) but British inventiveness is still rampant and the gallows humour was impressive. That collective ingenuity should be diverted to trying to find a way of socially distancing workplaces and transport now that the government has passed the parcel bomb back to the public. In the meantime, I'll confine myself to just a few of the hundreds of parodies now circulating after the red-bordered 'Stay Home. Save Lives. Protect the NHS' message board switched to the less panic-inducing green-bordered 'Stay Alert. Control the Virus. Save Lives' yesterday. Not in Scotland, Wales or Northern Ireland, however. Given our descent down the mountain is so slow and perilous, they would like to leave things the way they are.

Incidentally, it's some achievement to unite the SNP, the Labour government in Wales and the Union Jack, sash and bowler hat 'Come On, Arlene' brigade in Norn Iron and turn yourself into the Prime Minister of England only. Anyway, those slogans: take your pick from 'Meaningless Slogan. Three-word Platitude. Invoke Heroism'; 'Be Vague. Cover Our Backs. Shirk Responsibility'; 'Eat Chips. Clap Louder. Save Yourself'; and 'Hot Dog. Jumping Frog, Albuquerque'. There's even a random government slogan generator doing the rounds: my first three spins threw up 'Lose Control. Do Do Do the Conga. Don't Eat Bats'; 'Drink More. Sod the Poor. No Tongues'; and 'Get a Gun. Shoot the Virus. Yeeehaaw.'

In the interests of balance, I should highlight a couple of counter currents that are competing with this tidal wave of cynicism. *The Telegraph* has, for reasons best known to itself, rebranded Johnson as Nelson Mandela on its front page. Emblazoned above the most dignified picture they could find of the PM is the headline 'Long Road to Freedom'. Oh, and the BBC 2019 Sports Personality of the Year, Ben Stokes, tweeted, 'I felt like I was in the room and he was talking to me … what a brilliant speech @BorisJohnson well done (clapping emojis)'; 27.1K likes, and counting for that mind belch – a tally of twats which may well overhaul the UK's official COVID-19 death toll later today. I've never been comfortable with him becoming a national hero, but as far I'm concerned, he's taken it a stage further and ruined both the Cricket World Cup Final I attended last July and that subsequent Headingley Ashes miracle. I watched the latter on TV in the Antwerp Arms, Tottenham, taking my seat 15 minutes into the Spurs v Newcastle game. I now wish Jack Leach had run out the Cro-Magnon yob on 99 and that Steve Smith and David Warner had danced a jig on his prostrate, heavily tattooed form. Not really.

As I've been typing, we've both received texts telling us that our COVID-19 tests have, mercifully, come back negative. The biggest nightmare for us would have been just one of us having the virus. We have one bed, one bathroom and a small kitchen, so we had no idea how self-isolation would have been achieved. There has been some pleasure taken in small things in the last 24 hours. A wren hopped into the birdbath while we were having lunch yesterday, and a birdsong app I've installed points to a nightingale and red kite having been somewhere in the vicinity. I hope the former successfully avoided the latter.

I've watched two more episodes of *Normal People*: they're now at Trinity College, Dublin and many of the scenes are uncannily reminiscent of my time at Oxford. Except Marianne has seen sense and ditched the arrogant and pretentious debating society smoothie for whom she'd initially fallen. That didn't happen often enough in my experience. We won Justin's extremely challenging Fat Larry's Band quiz, largely thanks to Amanda's extensive knowledge of cinema history.

Speaking of movies and indeed Ireland, the man who co-wrote the BAFTA-winning screenplay for *The Commitments*, Mr Dick Clement, has been in touch. He rightly assumed that I would have written something about the late, great Little Richard's demise, so offered the following anecdote which I have his permission to reproduce here, not least because it's great craic, as they say in *Commitments* country:

'Ian and I wrote a screenplay about Sam Cooke a few years ago based on Dream Boogie *by Peter Guralnik. Sam's first tour of the UK was in 1962. He turned up for a gig in Doncaster and was met by the promoter (the appalling Don Arden), who desperately needed his help because Little Richard, who was top of the bill, refused to sing anything except gospel songs.*

'Sam found him in his dressing room, clutching an enormous bible, eyes closed in prayer. It was October, at the height of the Cuban Missile Crisis, and Little Richard was convinced it was all his fault that the world was about to end because he had turned his back on God and chosen instead to play the Devil's music. "The Apocalypse! Fire and Brimstone! The Seven-headed Dragon!"

'Sam did his best to convince him that other factors were involved and they were there to do what they did best: take people's minds off fear and anxiety. But when the headline attraction walked onstage, he gave no clue whether he was going to rock or preach. He sat at the piano stool, flexed his fingers and raised his hands. Everyone held their breath. Then the hands came crashing down and they heard "Good Golly, Miss Molly". (I'm smiling as I type the words.)

'A footnote to the story – I can't remember whether this was in the book or not – is that Sam found the key to that enormous bible. When he unlocked it he found it full of gay porn.'

I can't top that. See you tomorrow.

Tuesday, 12 May 2020

On this day in 1940, Adolf Hitler ordered the invasion of France, and within six days his forces had reached the English Channel. Later in the month, 'Operation Dynamo' would begin evacuating 330,000 allied troops. Meanwhile in West Auckland, County Durham, the second child of Tommy and Alice Allen entered the world. In peacetime, Margaret Helena Allen followed her older brother Barry to grammar school in Bishop Auckland. The girls' school was next door to the boys' grammar (once attended by Stan Laurel while his father managed the local theatre) and at the age of 14, she met Brian Armstrong at a school dance.

They've been together ever since: she continued to be a teacher while he switched jobs and became a manager at ICI. And they had two sons in the 1960s: Paul and John, reasonably enough 'stopping before we had a Ringo', as she's been known to say. And today she'll be in a garden in Sevenoaks, Kent a social distance away from one of those sons and her two granddaughters. All being well, the cake her granddaughters have baked for her, and their bouquet of flowers, will be accompanied by champagne and chocolates ordered by us from London. Happy birthday, Mum.

We FaceTimed her this morning via my brother. John was in his suit, preparing to represent a client in a remote court later this morning, and passed the phone to Mum and Dad who spend the morning in the kitchen once John and his daughters have finished breakfast. It seems to be fairly chaotic but cheerful down there; my mum assures us it's not her fault that Hitler invaded France and has noted that Burt Bacharach turns 92 today, while our Chancellor of the Exchequer also celebrates his birthday today and is precisely half her age. How can the only vaguely impressive member of the government have been born in 1980, by the way? She likes the new Leader of the Opposition and, like us, wishes he'd been in place a year ago. Despite not being very mobile, Mum insists on sweeping the kitchen from her wheelchair every day after the younger battalion have done their worst. The girls had attached a red ribbon to her brush this morning, and as we spoke, were in the dining room applying finishing touches to the cake she hasn't yet been allowed to see.

We'll try to arrange some kind of garden visit before too long, assuming London's virus tally isn't about to start spiking again. I'm increasingly wondering why I'm bothering to adhere to the government's muddled guidelines, since no one else seems to be, but as it stands, driving for an hour to sit outside someone else's house isn't allowed. Glancing at the front pages this morning I was intrigued by *Metro*'s headline, 'You just see Mum as Dad waits in the car then you see him as she waits in the car.' This is a hybrid of the garbled advice given by the Prime Minister and his de facto deputy Dominic Raab during the course of yesterday.

I was steered by a couple of friends towards BBC Sounds last night to listen to Mishal Hussein's Radio 4 *Today* interview with Raab. Mishal worked with us at the 2012 Olympics and while she's delightful company, she's also fiercely intelligent. She eschews both of John Humphrys's default settings – chummy fireside chat (David Davis, Lord Lawson) and foaming, interrupting hostility (moderate Remainer Tories and all points left thereof) – but gently skewered Raab, much as Starmer did with Johnson at PMQs. Until I reminded myself who he is and what he stands for, I felt slightly sorry for Raab yesterday. By all accounts, Johnson and Cummings didn't even consult the inner cabinet circle before recording Sunday's gibberish. Raab was sent out to defend something about which he hadn't been consulted and which made little sense to anyone other than Ben Stokes, so no wonder he floundered.

As I've been typing, the worst journalistic take I've seen during the lockdown so far (some achievement) has been sent to me by Justin. With a covering note simply reading 'Enjoy', he forwarded a link to an article by Trevor Kavanagh in today's *Sun*. I've just read it to Amanda and she urged me, in all sincerity, to check that it's not a spoof. I've checked and it isn't. The headline is 'Lockdown will turn out to be a terrible mistake and now we're being held to ransom by the bug'. The first sentence is a complete misrepresentation of 'hard-left showbiz luvvie Miriam Margolyes' – the actress has revealed that she had the same momentarily mixed feelings many of us had when Boris Johnson was in hospital, but decided she had to be better than that and was relieved that he recovered. Probably best not shared on TV, but a lot more nuanced than Trevor's representation of her thought process: 'If they can't dance on his grave, the Dementors will do everything possible to kill his political career.' This was just the warm-up. 'Downing Street is now hostage to the health-and-safety mafia, whipped into line by opportunistic public sector unions'; 'draconian social distancing'; 'bonking Professor Neil Ferguson's crackpot forecasts of half a million dead without lockdown'. On and on he foamed for a dozen more paragraphs, but you get the gist.

Where Sir Graham Brady MP had merely hinted that 'the public are a little too willing to stay at home', Trev has let the entire litter of cats out of the bag. He sees it as utterly monstrous to have felt a certain ambivalence about the fate of 'Boris' – you'll notice I generally refuse to use the PM's Christian (actually middle) name on its own, since he's not remotely lovable or my mate – but millions of public sector workers are work-shy, eminently disposable units fit only to be corralled into the virus's path. There is not one qualifying note of empathy or compassion for say, nurses or care workers, in the entire article.

Trevor is 77, and was *The Sun*'s political correspondent from the later Thatcher years onwards under Kelvin MacKenzie, at a time when they could boast 'It was *The Sun* what won it' about any given election, with some justification. He and Kelvin ranted to telling effect at a time when much of the country read, and was influenced by, their rag. I'm afraid I'm left feeling unclean having read his latest article (thanks, Justin) and now see Trevor Kavanagh rather as Miriam Margolyes did Boris Johnson. I'd never say that someone deserves to catch the coronavirus, but he comes close. Still, he almost certainly retired long ago to a big house in a leafy safe Tory seat to which the little people can deliver his food and bile medication, so I'm sure he'll be fine. The rest of us can just rely on the 'good old British common sense' Johnson (sorry, Trevor, I'm using his surname again) claims will win the day. This will be the same British common sense which led Johnson, Hancock, Cummings and Professor Whitty to catch the virus from each other.

We're in a holding pattern once again in terms of what happens next. It will take two or three weeks before the statistics tell us what material effect the last week of next-level chaos has had. *The Sun* and most other tax exile-owned papers are trying to hold the 'back to work you go, serfs' line, but everyone we've spoken to – Amanda's school friends, her largely apolitical sister, the Fat Larry's crowd of differing party political persuasions, my two old football mates Mark and Javier (TV producer Mark is currently furloughed; sports photographer Javier recently took redundancy) – are a mixture of bewildered, scared and incandescent right now.

The new pictures of crowded Tube platforms, the tangible rise in traffic levels, big groups of teenagers hanging around unchecked and the uncertainty about their kids' schooling are all provoking dismay. Johnson's suggestion that you just talk to your boss if you have childcare issues with the schools still closed suggests he's never worked in a regular workplace. Maybe my next Zoom meeting needs to be with Ben Stokes.

A further public display of anger came from a most unexpected quarter yesterday and has been doing the rounds on social media. I've previously described ITV's *This Morning* as the 'oh no, not the comfy chair' of political interviews. To be fair, it doesn't pretend to be *Panorama* or *Newsnight*. Perhaps Philip Schofield and Holly Willoughby were stung by the criticism of their pre-election selfie-taking with Johnson, or more likely, Schofield in particular had reached his Middle England tipping point yesterday. Either way, they opened their show by describing the previous evening's address as something which they would have found unbelievable in a drama, and then Philip uttered what may have been the rudest thing he's ever said on camera: 'He arsed it up.'

In all the excitement, I've forgotten to relay the most dramatic episode of the last 24 hours. At 4am, I became vaguely aware of rustling noises outside on the patio. I was about to dismiss it as the wind whistling, or a cat or fox on the prowl, but in the nick of time, I remembered the English government's new messaging, 'Stay Alert'. I put on the patio light and tiptoed outside. Sure enough there, skulking in a corner, was the coronavirus. Summoning all my strength, I wrestled it to the ground and after a long struggle I managed to subdue and 'Control the Virus'. Inattentive and unworthy citizen that I am, I temporarily struggled to remember the third part of this game-changing advice, but now that I've recovered my composure, I'm signing off for the day to 'Push pineapple, grind coffee.'

Wednesday, 13 May 2020

Mum's birthday appears to have gone about as well as it could have done. My brother sent us a photo of the birthday cake the girls had made, which was almost impossibly impressive. All in white with a piano motif – I guess because they know she loves music – surrounded by pink flowers. Absolutely extraordinary from an 11- and a 9-year-old stuck in a house for weeks, but then so are most of their creative endeavours. It reminded me somewhat of the Rolling Stones' *Beggars Banquet* album cover, except I'm pretty sure they won't be aware of that, let alone that it was made by a professional: a very young Delia Smith. The Fortnum and Mason champagne and chocolates from us duly arrived, and Mum left us a sweet message to say she'd like to be 80 again tomorrow.

Other than that decidedly bitter-sweet good news, it's all a bit grim, to be honest. The exercise bike's gear system has failed so you can only pedal at one not very firm tension. I blame Little Richard. I doubt that'll be repaired during lockdown, but I guess it's better than it breaking down altogether. I've failed to read anything – other than the latest *Private Eye.* They've mixed up the same reproduction rate/super-spreader/Boris Johnson lines I premiered here, adding 'with appropriate social distancing measures it's feasible the PM can get the reproduction rate down to 1 woman this year'. There's a good MADD red baseball cap joke ('Make America Drink Disinfectant') and a funny section on home schooling which suggests that, for the time being, weaker children will have to inflict their own Chinese burns. I particularly enjoyed this Downing Street press conference exchange, though:

Priti Patel: 'Though shoplifting figures are down, the Prime Minister reports that he's been mugged by a Mr COVID, who's invisible.'

Reporter: 'The mugger was a metaphor, Home Secretary.'

Patel: 'Well, when we catch him we'll send him back to Metaphoria.'

Normal People has reached what I hope is a nadir. Badly damaged Marianne is studying in Sweden away from Connell, the only non-dreadful bloke in this particular Sally Rooney universe, and is making a succession of increasingly awful boyfriend choices. Again, it's all too reminiscent of student days: my movie soundtrack of that set of memoirs would have to include Joe Jackson's 'Is She Really Going Out with Him?' The fact that I'm persevering with *Normal People*, despite it frequently making me squirm, is a testament to the quality of the film-making and especially the two lead performances from Paul Mescal and Daisy Edgar-Jones. I was genuinely astonished to discover that Daisy is from London; authentic dialect training has moved on a long way from Dick Van Dyke in *Mary Poppins* and Sean Connery in *The Untouchables*, though it probably helps that Daisy's mother is Irish.

Meanwhile, in Amanda's Icelandic drama in the other room, a Lithuanian mafioso sex-trafficker has succumbed to hypothermia, two people have burned to death (separate fires) and a beheaded and dismembered corpse turns out to have been fatally stabbed before the chainsaw was activated. You can't say this household conforms to traditional gender stereotypes.

The news continues to be unremittingly grim. We English have been asked to stay away from Scotland, Wales and even the Lake District. No one – councils, police, National Park authorities, mountain rescue teams – was consulted in Cumbria before Johnson blithely told us to drive and exercise anywhere we want last Sunday, and they say they will not be able to cope with visitors right now. The UK's daily death toll was yet again the second-highest in the world and yet again above 600, and the new cases were close to 4,000 yet again, from just over 60,000 people tested. We've had the second-worst death figures in the world for the whole of May, but the government's response is to launch an attack on Keir Starmer for annihilating Johnson at PMQs again, and simply to drop the international death statistic comparisons from the daily media briefings, in the hope that no one notices. That might well work outside the politics and media bubble, as it tends to do for Trump. That supposedly all-important target of 100,000 tests a day by the end of April hasn't been met again since the end of the last month.

The Guardian printed another digest of the reactions from a universally dumbfounded foreign press – to put it bluntly, the UK is now the world's barometer of abject failure. Each country's media is warning that if their own lockdown isn't lifted carefully enough, their nation may end up a few steps down the road to the chaos in the UK. We're a global warning sign, just as many of us sink further into VE Day and Brexit-fuelled national delusion. Even Trump can't touch us for atrocious per population COVID-19 figures. And yet much of this country hasn't even noticed. The two top trends on Google in the UK right now are the possibility of McDonald's drive-throughs, and Subway sandwich shops reopening. It doesn't get more John Bull than that.

We'd been advised by friends to watch *Hospital,* two one-hour programmes about our local hospital, the Royal Free, and its response to the pandemic. We watched the first part last night – it was too emotionally draining to watch both programmes back-to-back – but, as I felt with what should have been the warning footage from Italy several weeks ago, it ought to be shown in small chunks between programmes on BBC One and during advertising breaks on commercial TV. That way, the truth avoiders and non-social distancers, as well as those who want to put the economy first or just get back in the pub, might understand the reality of what we're putting the simply magnificent staff of the NHS through. Instead, it was tucked away on BBC Two, meaning that a relatively small audience will have seen a full hour's rebuttal of Trevor Kavanagh's assault on the 'opportunistic public sector'.

It would be impossible, even for a veteran *Sun* hack, not to be moved by the story of Nancy, 50 years an NHS community nurse, as she recovered from the brink of death to walk out of the hospital three weeks later. The ovation Nancy received from everyone on duty, and her speech to them about her pride in the NHS, reaffirmed my commitment to the somewhat tarnished Thursday evening round of applause. Even if the governing party and the worst of the VE Day party animals are utter hypocrites for joining in, the applause from around here in NW3 can, it seems, be heard in the Royal Free, so that's more than enough reason to keep it going.

Thursday, 14 May 2020

We really ought to clap long and hard for the Royal Free tonight. That second wave of the sick and dying may well have deluged them in due course. Yesterday's pictures of public transport in London were simply obscene. One nurse described her journey to work as a 'COVID party bus'. Sky News showed more people pouring off one bus at its terminus than you would have thought physically possible, and even where masks were being worn, they looked very much as if a microorganism 0.001 millimetres in diameter might just work its way through the gaps. Still, the news that golf courses are open and that deer stalking resumed yesterday will doubtless have put a spring back in the urban workforce's collective step.

In the rural v urban, England v the rest of the UK, comfortably off v poor workers, low tax v public spending and white v diverse schisms that our government has found itself indulging, I'm with the latter each time, despite being English, white and comfortable financially. Boris Johnson is finding himself under the cosh from his backbenchers and traditionally supportive newspapers for his perceived equivocation on some of those fronts. In recent years the Conservative Party has turned on its leaders every time they've wavered from the full rabid policy package. Cameron lost the sympathy of many party members over gay marriage and for not being a fully-fledged Europhobe, May, despite her agreeable lack of human empathy, was never forgiven for having voted Remain and for not fancying No Deal very much thereafter. Now Johnson is upsetting some of them for trying (and admittedly failing) to steer a course between a proper lockdown and the out and out Darwinist 'survival of the fittest' approach the true Right crave.

We had our first visitor to the house in two months this morning. A local company called Silver Saints organises handymen (and women, I guess) to visit for a whole range of household repairs. With the exercise bike not functioning properly, and our living room lights having blown a while back, we bit the bullet and summoned help. A friendly Italian chap called Giovanni turned up in a mask, and established that an internal tension belt had snapped on the bike. He retrieved it from inside the mechanism but, as I'd suspected would be the case, said that only the manufacturer could fix it. We'll just have to carry on with it half-cocked until we can sort something out. He sorted out our electrics, though, his company charged us online for a half an hour of his time and off he went.

We'd also run out of milk, and Amanda needed a prescription picking up, so I went across to Belsize Village where the multinational staff at the chemist's shop were their usual slick selves and the lovely people at the Late, Late Shop not only had milk but had sourced the first flour I'd seen in weeks. The packaging was in Romanian, the staff are mostly Afghan; the masked lady on the till assured me that her journey from Enfield was, while busier than previously, not too scary at the moment. The Belsize Shuffle was in full force on the pavements, the Portuguese café/deli is selling takeaway food and has reconfigured itself with an entry door, and a separate exit door around the corner, and is allowing two people in at a time. Other than the fact that most people are wearing masks, some of which look enviably professional, it's the sort of London neighbourhood scene which led to that advert with Harvey Keitel being shot there. And the 'British common sense' to which Johnson appealed while passing the buck back to the public on Sunday was very much in evidence. The only snag being that I suspect not one of those people would be seen as really British in the eyes of many shire Tories.

As for the latest on Boris Johnson, I'm conscious that I'm in danger of exhausting my vocabulary and that, unlike our esteemed Prime Minister, I don't have five or more years of school Latin and Ancient Greek (and a mediocre second-class degree after three more) upon which to fall back. I think I'll let Marina Hyde's latest masterpiece do it better: 'You miss one universal credit meeting and your benefits are stopped; you miss five Cobra meetings and you get to address the nation on its working responsibilities from a drawing room so vast you'd need a hansom cab to traverse it.

'Tell you what might look nice: a stable. Let's get some plans drawn up. I feel like a door might be an idea? We could put it over there – where that horse we used to have used to be.

'"We will be governed entirely by the science," he kept gibbering on Monday. We will be governed entirely by you, more's the pity.'

It's surprising, given his history, that Johnson has seemingly never faced a QC before. I likened the previous PMQs to Arbroath 36 Bon Accord 0: this one was an international class dismantling comparable, let's say, to Australia 31 Western Samoa 0 (World Cup qualifier, 2001). My Boro mate Geoff texted to say 'he's looking behind him for non-existent support and assurance – reminds me of (centre half) Derek Whyte playing for us in 1996/7.' Johnson got in a complete tangle with his timeline of the government advice which saw untested elderly people sent into care homes from hospitals for the first six weeks of this crisis. Starmer, typically, had all the information to hand, and firmly put him straight – Johnson/Cummings later sent a hurt letter talking about maintaining a consensus (tell that to Dominic Grieve and Ken Clarke, chaps) and I've broken my rule by watching the iPlayer to see how Laura Kuenssberg handled the spat. Veteran *Telegraph* columnist Peter Oborne claimed last year that senior BBC executives had told him that 'it's wrong to expose lies told by a British prime minister because it undermines trust in British politics'. I get that to a certain extent – Laura rightly said that the 'lawyer' had got the better of the 'showman', but used verbal gymnastics of Simone Biles quality to avoid saying directly that the latter may have inadvertently or deliberately misled the House.

Another moment of careless Johnson bluster has also returned to haunt him today. Last year, he'd told a gathering of Northern

Irish business people that they could throw all EU paperwork 'in the bin', post-transition. It now emerges that there will of course be checks on goods crossing the Irish Sea after all. Johnson's turning on Starmer for 'breaking the consensus' yesterday worked, though, as virtually every reply to Tom Newton-Dunn's painstakingly factual Twitter thread accused both Newton-Dunn and Starmer of wartime-style treachery. I guess that comes with the territory if your followers include *Sun* readers, but it's still pretty depressing that default cries of 'fake news' and 'unpatriotic' are now par for the course here, just as they are for Trump supporters.

John Crace's latest political sketch summed it up:

'In other times, it might have been uplifting for the opposition benches to see the prime minister so comprehensively dismantled. But there was little cheering or a sense of satisfaction, because in a time of crisis you rather hope the country would have a leader in whom you could believe. Someone you could trust to make at least some of the right decisions. But we have Boris. Incompetent, unprepared, selfish, lazy, amoral, and just not that bright. And no matter how many times Starmer batters him with an indefensible charge sheet at PMQs, Boris will remain prime minister for the duration.'

Rather than write any more today, I'm just going to reproduce a simple timeline I posted on Facebook a couple of days ago. A chap called Ben Claimant put together a thread on Twitter, which I've crosschecked (from 14 March onwards) against this journal, and altered somewhat. When I started writing this journal, two months ago today, the primary aim was to give me something to do and I hoped it might also provide a bit of entertainment for like-minded friends and family. I never thought for a moment that I would be setting out what follows. It makes stark reading:

31 December 2019: China alerts WHO to new virus.

21 January 2020: An editorial in The Lancet *warns of the likely arrival of a pandemic in the UK.*

23 January: Study reveals a third of China's patients require intensive care.

24 January: Boris Johnson misses first COBRA meeting.

29 January: Boris Johnson misses second COBRA meeting.

31 January: The NHS declares first ever 'Level 4 critical incident'. Meanwhile, the government declines to join European scheme to source PPE.

5 February: Boris Johnson misses third COBRA meeting.

12 February: Boris Johnson misses fourth COBRA meeting. Exeter University publishes study warning the coronavirus could infect 45 million people in the UK if left unchallenged.

13 February: Boris Johnson misses conference call with European leaders.

14 February: Boris Johnson goes away on holiday. Aides are told to keep Johnson's briefing notes short or he will not read them.

18 February: Johnson misses fifth COBRA meeting.

26 February: Boris Johnson press conference discusses 'herd immunity' strategy, the PM announcing that many people will lose loved ones. Government document is leaked, predicting half a million Brits could die in 'worst case scenario'.

29 February: Boris Johnson retreats to Chevening, his country manor. NHS warns of 'PPE shortage nightmare' – stockpiles have dwindled or expired after years of austerity cuts.

2 March: Boris Johnson attends his FIRST COBRA meeting, declining another opportunity to join the European PPE scheme. Government's own scientists say over half a million Brits could die if virus left unrestrained. Johnson tells the country, 'We are very, very well prepared.'

3 March: Scientists urge the government to advise the public not to shake hands. Boris Johnson brags about shaking hands with coronavirus patients.

4 March: Government stops providing daily updates on the virus following a 70 per cent spike in UK cases. They will later U-turn on this amid accusations they are withholding vital information.

5 March: Boris Johnson tells public to 'wash their hands' and says it's 'business as usual'.

7 March: Boris Johnson joins 82,000 people at the England v Wales Six Nations rugby match.
9 March: After Ireland cancels St Patrick's Day parades, the UK government says there's 'no rationale' for cancelling sporting events.
10–13 March: The Cheltenham Festival takes place, more than a quarter of a million people attend.
11 March: 3,000 Atlético Madrid fans fly to Liverpool.
12 March: Boris Johnson states banning events such as Cheltenham will have little effect. The Imperial College study finds that the government's plan is projected to kill half a million people.
13 March: The FA suspends the Premier League, after Arsenal's coach and a Chelsea player test positive for COVID-19, citing an absence of government guidance. Britain is invited to join the European scheme for joint purchase of ventilators, and refuses. Boris Johnson lifts restrictions for those arriving from coronavirus hotspots.
14 March: The government is still allowing mass gatherings, as Stereophonics play to 5,000 people two nights running in Cardiff.
16 March: Boris Johnson asks Britons not to go to pubs, but allows them to stay open. During a conference call, Johnson jokes that the push to build new ventilators should be called 'Operation Last Gasp'.
19 March: Hospital patients with coronavirus are returned to care homes in a bid to free up hospital space. What follows is exponential growth of virus cases in care homes.
20 March: The government states that the PPE shortage crisis is 'completely resolved'. Less than two weeks later, the British Medical Association reports an acute shortage of PPE.
23 March: The UK finally goes into lockdown.
26 March: Boris Johnson is accused of putting 'Brexit over breathing' by not joining the EU ventilator scheme. The government then state they had not joined the scheme because they had 'missed the e-mail'.
27 March: Boris Johnson tests positive for the coronavirus.
1 April: The Evening Standard *reports that just 0.17 per cent of NHS staff have been tested for the virus.*

2 April: The PM says, 'We will have turned the tide within 12 weeks.'

3 April: The UK death toll overtakes that of China.

5 April: 17.5m antibody tests, ordered by the government and described by Boris Johnson as a 'game changer', are found to be a failure.

7 April: Boris Johnson is moved to intensive care with coronavirus.

11 April: Boris Johnson leaves hospital. Dr Abdul Chowdury, who wrote to the PM three weeks ago about the PPE shortage, dies of the coronavirus.

16 April: Flights continue to bring 15,000 people a day into the UK – without virus testing.

17 April: Health Secretary Matt Hancock says, 'I would love to be able to wave a magic wand and have PPE fall from the sky.' The UK has now missed four opportunities to join the EU's PPE scheme.

21 April: The government fails to reach its target of face masks for the NHS, as it is revealed that manufacturers' offers of help were met with silence. Instead millions of pieces of PPE are being shipped from the UK to Europe.

23–24 April: The government announces testing kits for ten million key workers. Orders run out within minutes as only 5,000 are made available.

25 April: The UK's death toll from coronavirus overtakes that of the Blitz.

30 April: Boris Johnson announces that the UK has succeeded in avoiding a tragedy that had engulfed other parts of the world. At this point, the UK has the third-highest death toll in the world.

1 May: The government announces it has reached its target of 100,000 tests a day – they haven't conducted all of the tests, but have posted testing kits. This is also the last date at the time of writing (13 May) on which the 100,000 target is even claimed to have been met.

4 May: The number of NHS staff who have died from coronavirus overtakes the number of British military personnel who died during the Iraq War.

5 May: The UK's death toll becomes the highest in Europe.

6 May: Boris Johnson announces that the UK could lift restrictions by next week. The newspapers trumpet this. 'Hurrah' and 'Happy Monday' shriek the headlines.

7 May: The anniversary of VE Day is used by many in the country as an opportunity to abandon the adherence to guidelines.

10 May: Boris Johnson makes a divisive, confusing and vague announcement, which drops both the NHS and 'staying at home' from future messaging, instead merely asking the public to 'stay alert'.

Friday, 15 May 2020

Month three of spending every morning at the keyboard begins today, as week nine comes to a close. Unless my pessimism is misplaced, I may have about two or three weeks of relative calm now in which to try to find some light and shade. We have reached an uneasy plateau in the UK of a mere four or five times the Hillsborough death toll per day with something like the average attendance at a League Two match testing positive every 24 hours. After that, I suspect we may be unravelling again, with an increasingly desperate government lashing out at sections of the public, the opposition, scientists, the BBC, the EU, Raheem Sterling – pretty much anyone.

Still, we're steadily getting rid of those Europeans 52 per cent of us voted to chuck out four years ago. There were many EU-born staff featured in part two of *Hospital*, the BBC documentary about the Royal Free. Maybe they'll be able to stay permanently, as long as they know which monarch succeeded Edward V. Others will miss out on taking their citizenship tests, having unfortunately died of the virus, and the Italian Embassy says at least 30,000 of their nationals have gone back to Italy during the pandemic. That's back to Italy, the European country first ravaged by this, but which now has it under far better control than it looks like we ever will.

Spain, already disconcerted by British ex-pats (we're never immigrants) flouting the lockdown in their Union Jack pub and HP sauce enclaves, is hoping to invite pretty much every European nationality to holiday there this summer – albeit with screening and social distancing in place. All the Schengen Zone nationalities, that is. Healthy Croatians, Cypriots and citizens of the Irish Republic will most likely find themselves in the same bracket as the infectious Brits. The UK provides 22 per cent of all tourism to Spain, but it seems they don't much fancy a second spike in Magaluf and elsewhere. Unlike the STDs, Sambuca shots and awful food we usually like to share among ourselves, there's no guarantee that we wouldn't pass on COVID-19 to the locals. It will be quite difficult for the main UK news bulletins to sugar coat that news should it ever reach the masses. 'Their loss, we'll go to Skegness instead,' will doubtless be the tabloid war cry. Or, maybe, 'Up yours, Señors.'

International comparison graphs may have been dropped from the government's press conferences this week at just the wrong moment. While we still trail only the US in our overall death toll and will do for some time to come, Brazil is now exceeding our daily death toll figures and Russia has more new cases. Johnson, Trump, Bolsonaro, Putin – we have a much smaller population than the others, but it's proving to be an interesting global lesson in what nationalist, testosterone-fuelled leadership can do for a country. And indeed, in the extent to which populism actually values people.

Our new relaxed guidelines say we can now drive anywhere we want and can view properties again. If only I'd thought it through, I could have visited Mum on her 80th birthday if my parents had just put the house up for sale for the day. There'd have been an estate agent there, too, but there was apparently enough cake to go round. Or Dad could have put a brush in the car boot and driven Mum up here, and I could have employed her as our cleaner for the day. We just need to 'stay alert', and anything's possible in common-sense England.

This morning's papers are reporting the surprising claim that there are currently just 24 new COVID cases a day being confirmed in London and the reproductive rate is down to 0.4. However, there are supposedly 4,000 new cases a day in the north-east and Yorkshire with an R of 0.8, perilously close to that disastrous 1 beyond which growth becomes exponential. While I'm highly sceptical of these figure as, reportedly, is SAGE – we know that for every confirmed case, there are many, many more out there with non-life-threatening symptoms – I've been following the graphs of confirmed cases per borough throughout the last two months, and it's certainly true that, of late, London boroughs have been swept from the top of the charts.

Total case statistics are going to be skewed towards recent infections because initially, when London was bearing the brunt, only hospitals were testing. All the people we know of in London who've had the virus, went untested, bar a couple of elderly people who ended up in hospital, one (the neighbour of friends) sadly died, the other – John next door to us – has now been discharged. Now that far more people are being tested, the top four English boroughs are currently in the north-east. Two of them – Gateshead and Middlesbrough – were near the bottom of the table some weeks ago when Camden was ranked second in the country. Camden is now recording very small numbers of new cases – just two yesterday – and is down to page 9 of 15 on Sky's chart, while Hull, which was rock bottom for weeks, has now overtaken us.

I'm still taking all this with a pinch of salt – we watched the second part of *Hospital* last night and it made the Royal Free look like a field hospital. Oxygen in the wards was having to be rationed to cope with the rapid influx of COVID-19 patients; a month's supply was running out after only two to three days. However, that was a few weeks ago and we understand from Doctor Liz and others that there is a lull now in the COVID intake in London hospitals. They're all braced for that second spike, though, and we just have to hope and pray that the scenes on public transport this week don't send the virus back out of control.

We're taking more encouragement from this news than we have from anything in weeks, and are about to take a PPE-clad walk in celebration. I still think the government has relaxed lockdown too soon, and undoubtedly so in NE England if those figures are even close to being correct, but it shows that a lockdown can, and did, have a mitigating effect on the death toll. I just don't trust our government to make the right calls at the right time.

The other, more sinister, development in today's papers, and elsewhere in the media, including this morning's *Today* on Radio 4, is summarised by a classically awful *Daily Mail* front page. A stock photo – from which, it now turns out, a black girl has been airbrushed – shows a smiling white woman and child reading a book together. 'Let Our Teachers Be Heroes' barfs the headline. The teaching unions, in seeking scientific evidence to reassure them that it's safe to go back to the classroom next month, are this week's 'Enemy of the People'.

Apparently 'Britons are bonding together in a spirit of compassion and generosity', all of which is under threat because Sir and Miss aren't altogether convinced that being near 30 snotty-nosed kids in an enclosed space is necessarily a good idea, especially given this government's track record. Being concerned about your own safety, and that of your young charges and their families, makes you a 'militant' who's 'playing petty politics', apparently. Gavin 'Why the long face?' Williamson is the Secretary of State for Education who will deal with this standoff. Williamson is the former fireplace salesman who, as Tory Chief Whip, menaced uncooperative backbenchers with a tarantula called Cronus which he kept on his office desk (I wish I was making this up). He was sacked by Theresa May from his next job as Defence Secretary, in May 2019, for the relatively minor crime (these days) of leaking confidential information after a National Security Council meeting. If I were the teaching unions,

I'd be only too happy to take Gav's word as his bond, and do as the *Daily Mail* tells me.

We've just been for that walk, and didn't actually have to use the PPE. We drove up towards Bishop's Avenue – home to absurdly rich people like Richard Desmond and Laksmi Mittal and parked on equally posh Ingram Avenue. Several mansions were having building work done (Lee from the Curry Club is driving to a nearby road every morning to supervise a project) and we spotted a Maserati and Aston Martin on the same drive. We walked down to the Hampstead Heath extension, a large grassy open space which backs on to Hampstead Garden Suburb, the early 20th century residential development planned around a Sir Edwin Lutyens-designed square. A whole host of creative types – Sir Ralph Richardson, Evelyn Waugh, Tony Hancock – lived there, and Tom Hiddleston, Hugh Laurie and Harry Styles do so now, apparently.

Only a few dog walkers were in the woods and open spaces. Given that we were happy to change paths if anyone approached, we didn't come within several metres of anyone in over an hour. It was easily the most pleasant outing we've had in the whole lockdown period – we won't risk it on a weekend, but it's definitely an option from now on.

So, the Hampstead Heath extension is a goer, but the Brexit extension appears to be a goner. I'm back at the keyboard and will try to summarise all the dismal political developments in a paragraph, rather than destroy my post-walk buzz.

Michael Gove is blaming the EU for anything and everything, Trade Secretary Liz Truss seems poised to remove or reduce tariffs on food imports from the US – chlorinated chicken and hormone-injected beef, yum, yum – and with no EU regulations to follow, we probably won't even have a country of origin label to help us to know what horrors to avoid. Even Gove thinks Truss has gone too far with her concessions, apparently, so there must be something seriously unhinged in the pipeline.

Meanwhile, 'May and Johnson hung civil servants out to dry,' according to an Institute for Government report; Health Minister

Nadine Dorries and two other Tory MPs have retweeted a false claim from a far-right website that Keir Starmer had protected paedophile gangs when he was Director of Public Prosecutions. They've since deleted those tweets but not before they were shared tens of thousands of times.

Classic Dom has a new project – four non-executive directors have been appointed to the Cabinet Office, two of whom worked with Dom on the election law-flouting Vote Leave campaign. A third, Bernard Hogan-Howe, was head of the Metropolitan Police when it decided not to press charges against Vote Leave, despite the Electoral Commission having deemed it guilty of electoral malpractice. A new Joint Biosecurity Unit is to be set up in this new-look cabinet office. A secret selection process has put this unit in the hands of Tom Hurd who just happens to have been at Eton and Oxford with Boris Johnson. What a happy coincidence.

As with the US, this barrage of dreadful developments, and list of people who would have resigned or faced the sack in previous times, is too overwhelming for the average mortal to process. We're now becoming numb, and impervious to several things happening every day, any one of which would once have been an era-defining outrage. Watergate, the Profumo affair and all the rest would struggle to be included five items down the running order in any current news bulletin.

Even I can't face rummaging around to try to work out how this sinister-sounding Biosecurity Unit under Boris's soggy biscuit club compadre will cooperate with/undermine SAGE, or why Dom's Vote Leave cabal will now be running the Cabinet Office, as well as most other branches of government. Fortunately, Carole Cadwalladr is on to it. Unfortunately, whatever she unearths, even if it's of Cambridge Analytica/Facebook proportions, her only reward will be another Pulitzer nomination, the admiration of a small percentage of the public and the tag 'crazy cat lady' from Arron Banks, Andrew Neil (quite shamefully in his case, although he deleted his tweet the next morning) and every alt-right man sitting at a computer in Mummy's basement. The rot's too far gone now; it will only cease to spread if the entire building collapses. Oh, and BBC Four, the best channel on British TV or at least the one we watch most often, seemingly faces the axe.

A busy social day or two has seen me chair another Poncey Horse quiz (self-indulgent music intros round on keyboards this time) and then being actually asked to fetch the ukulele during a Zoom gathering of BBC and ex-BBC friends. Laurel and Hardy's 'At the Ball, That's All' rounded off an evening of some very funny TV anecdotes, a few of which I'd never heard before. I won't name the chap we all felt was BBC Sport's worst-ever assistant producer, but I wasn't previously aware that he'd added the Cheltenham Gold Cup to his showreel: not because he'd directed it, edited the programme or contributed any content, but because he'd 'logged it at Television Centre'. And a famous story I'd forgotten was retold: a 1970s *Match of the Day* edit in which a close-up of Eddie Gray taking a throw-in cut to a wide angle of the ball arriving at the feet of ... Eddie Gray.

On the TV drama front, Amanda has finished *Trapped* – all the murders were solved and everyone in any position of power in a small Icelandic town was found to be up to their necks in criminality. But only because the banking crisis had left the country destitute.

I've now finished *Normal People*, and touching though parts of the series were, the ending didn't fill me with emotion as many others seem to have found. Spoiler alert. Opting to 'fulfil' your dream where a career (almost always as a writer, actor or musician) wins out over your personal life is a bit of an American movie cliché, in the over-rated (sorry) *La La Land*, for example. My job seemed like a dream job to many people (mostly men) and I often felt inextricably linked to it. Until my ears packed up and I wasn't any more, but that's turned out okay in the end.

The overriding thing which resonated from *Normal People* was how much of a pain in the bum students can be. We take ourselves, and the ebb and flow of relationships, far too seriously at that age when we're still finding our way in the world. Admittedly, I'm saying that from the comfortable position of late middle-age and having got the embarrassing stuff out of the way before I eventually found my soulmate, while still remaining friends (as is Amanda) with the only serious long-term girlfriend I'd had before that.

Enough of chick-lit adaptations. A major European football league is live on the box again from tomorrow. I've been to a few matches in Germany – Champions League ties at Bayern and Borussia (I much preferred the latter) the Porto v Monaco final in Gelsenkirchen in 2004, and a World Cup 2006 group game in each of Berlin and Leipzig, but never a Bundesliga match. Since that league seems to be as much about vast crowds and great ambience as what happens on the pitch, it will be weird seeing it played behind closed doors, but it will undoubtedly add to the pressure on this country and our Premier League to try to follow suit.

As with most other leagues, there are certain teams whose results I follow. My German friend Markus is from Middlesbrough's twin town, Oberhausen, and is a massive Anglophile who became a Boro regular when he studied in Teesside for a year in the 1980s. I caught up with him after our 97th-minute equaliser at Millwall last season (we'd only pulled it back to 2-1 in the 89th minute). He'd been in the family stand with his young son, so I had to push my way through the police horses by the away end, and into the unhappy home throng beyond, in order to find them. That hairy experience notwithstanding, I look out for his team Schalke 04's results, and I'll watch them live on BT Sport tomorrow, although I might have to support their opponents in what's normally a huge derby.

Second-placed Borussia Dortmund, just four points off the top of the table, are the team most likely to catch the tedious, unlovable behemoth that is Bayern Munich. I also have a sneaking admiration for FC Köln, having once filmed there with ex-player Tony Woodcock, and having seen something like

15,000 of their fans infiltrate the home stands at a Europa League game at the Emirates a couple of years ago. Two of them were sitting right next to me, trying not to be too conspicuous, but the other 14,998 gave themselves away when they took the lead in their first European fixture for 24 years. Just as well it was at Arsenal, not the aforementioned Millwall.

For the first time in a while, I'm in the mood for football, as the Nolans should have sung. As I did on several occasions after my book launch last year and intermittently since, I took part in a podcast last night. My rule now is that I'll say yes to anything that involves talking football and TV, even though it can only be virtual at the moment. Even the most raucous of inner London secondary school classes has informed (and often funny) opinions about running orders and how football is covered, and if just one or two kids try a bit harder in English because I've emphasised its importance, then that's a bonus. Last night, a frighteningly young and clued-up pair – Spurs and West Ham respectively – grilled me about all matters *MOTD* and TV sport. I haven't talked about football for any length of time in a while, so it was an enjoyable experience. I'm still planning to conclude this journal on an appropriate football note, preferably the resumption of the Premier League to bring it full circle, but who knows anymore?

WEEK TEN

Saturday, 16 May 2020

I've had 24 hours away from the news – the latest guesswork surrounding the all-important reproduction (R) rate suggests that it may be close to 1 – any higher than that and cases would be multiplying. If so, England's partial lifting of lockdown this week looks even more unwise. Deputy Chief Medical Officer Jenny Harries, though, contradicted Boris Johnson's last press conference outing, when she said that the R rate isn't the be all and end all. Mind you, she was relaxed about the Cheltenham Festival going ahead, said on 28 March that track and testing was 'not an appropriate mechanism', and boasted of the UK's 'exemplar preparedness' a couple of weeks ago, so who knows? I'm giving up trying to make any sense of these people's pronouncements – we'll know more in two or three weeks' time when the statistics begin to reflect this week's shenanigans.

I've read a whole chunk more of Hilary Mantel's mammoth tome: the barbarous north has swallowed the fake news that King Henry is dead and the hated Cromwell is now in charge, poised to melt down crucifixes and impose bread taxes as he collaborates with foreign governments to ruin Albion. Hmm, it's difficult not to draw parallels with 'Taking Back Control'.

One of two tremendous pieces of TV I've watched in the last 24 hours was more overtly political, but also provided us with several much-needed belly laughs. Charlie Brooker's *Wipe* strand – this incarnation was entitled *Antiviral Wipe* – is one of the few TV formats which can remain unaltered in lockdown. For my money, Brooker is Marina Hyde's chief rival as the sardonic British satirist of our times. His set-up montage featured some appalling COVID complacency and flippancy from early 2020 – mostly Johnson, but also moments to forget when the inquiry gets under way from others, like Professor Vallance. Thereafter, joined (remotely at least) by stalwart talking heads Philomena Cunk and Barry Shitpeas, he just let rip with lines like 'Matt Hancock is your sister's first boyfriend with a car' and 'Professor Whitty looks like a prematurely aged Tintin who's just watched his dog drown'. Brooker's slating of the god-awful celebrity version of 'Imagine' was the pièce de resistance, though: 'If John Lennon were alive, he'd be phoning Mark Chapman to give him his GPS co-ordinates.' Just the cynical bad taste that we, and many of our friends, need right now.

I met Charlie Brooker once: *MOTD*'s autocue specialist, Sophia, also worked on C4's *Ten O'Clock Live* in which he featured. Only Charlie and Roddy Frame – who I met backstage once in the company of his friend, the ex-athlete Roger Black – have ever immediately apologised, on being introduced to me, for knowing nothing about sport. As if they needed to do that: I'd take that straightforward approach any day over the TV executives who insist that they're 'passionate' about sport, then say, 'Who's this chap?' when Clarence Seedorf appears on the monitor in the green room 30 seconds after you've introduced them to his agent. Yes, that actually happened. Charlie wouldn't have had any interest in the other masterly piece of TV I've just watched, but Sophia, one of the world's most vociferous Gooners, certainly would.

In an attempt to provide something new for those who haven't bothered to cancel their subscriptions, Sky Sports are casting far and wide. One such offering was the feature film-length documentary, *'89*. Along with a quite wonderful film BT Sport made to mark Jimmy Greaves's 80th birthday, I've recently seen two British-made sports documentaries of the highest calibre. *'89* was co-produced by my old colleague, Lee Dixon, and told the story of the extraordinary 1988/89 league season in which he featured. Arsenal overhauled Liverpool in injury time at Anfield in the last game of the season, which had been delayed to 26 May by the aftermath of the Hillsborough tragedy. That 'Aguerrroooo' moment in 2012 is the only finish to a top-flight season which has ever come close to matching Michael Thomas's title-snatching goal that evening. I know where I watched it – a hotel room in Nottingham where I'd been running slow-motion replays at an Ashes Test – and I'll always remember Brian Moore's great commentary line, 'It's up for grabs now,' as Thomas bore down on Bruce Grobbelaar, but there were many aspects which I had forgotten. Elton (christened Roger) Welsby presented the live coverage on ITV, with Bobby Robson standing in as studio guest after a late withdrawal. Programme editor Jeff Foulser recalled how he spotted Bobby by the directors' entrance, and persuaded him to bale him out. I remember that feeling, Jeff.

Football-wise, I'd completely forgotten that David O'Leary played in a one-off George Graham defensive reshuffle. The established back four – Dixon, Winterburn, Adams and Bould – who were reunited for the film, were supplemented that evening by O'Leary at sweeper, allowing the full-backs to push up on Ray Houghton and John Barnes. George Graham's coaching was still held in awe by that back four, whose collective spirit, even 30 years later, was something to behold.

I found the same lasting togetherness in evidence when I looked after nine of Celtic's 1967 European Cup-winning team for a *Hearts of Gold* show in the late '80s, or when Hansen and Lawrenson got together with Souness, Dalglish and others from that great Liverpool side. Steve Archibald of Spurs and Barcelona once said, 'Team spirit is an illusion only glimpsed when you win,' which I'm not sure is true. Any gathering of BBC Sport veterans could discuss the comradeship which came from reversals such as losing the *MOTD* contract in 2000, but I guess success does help bonds to tighten.

The way director David Stewart and editor Sam Billinge cut together the famous Michael Thomas goal, especially given the limited isolated angles available back then, thanks to some fantastic anecdotes which those concerned have had 30 years to perfect, made for one of the best archive-based sequences I've ever seen. And to top it all, Ian Wright made me cry (as he did when he was on *Desert Island Discs* telling the story of his teacher Mr Pigden) with his emotional recollection of watching the game on the south London estate where both he and David Rocastle had grown up. The late Rocky was not only a fabulous player, but a role-model and mentor to Wrighty and other youngsters. Rocastle scored a goal against Boro at Highbury in that 1988/89 season, twisting and turning past three or four defenders then lashing home so gloriously that I, and many others in the away end, felt obliged to applaud.

All in all, *'89* was a superb watch, which led me to text Lee to offer my compliments. He replied immediately saying how much fun it had been to work on, and then adding an amusing aside about the fact that Martin Keown would be commentating on Eintracht Frankfurt v Borussia Mönchengladbach later this afternoon. During the endless hours Lee and I sat together watching matches on weekend afternoons, he had a fund of great stories about the rather intense colleague who eventually replaced Steve Bould, as Arsène Wenger built a dynasty around the back four he'd inherited.

I might have to tell one or two of those Keown stories here at some point, but for the time being, I'll give you one Dicko told us about Tony Adams. A month or so after Adams had moved into management at Wycombe Wanderers, Lee phoned him to see how it was going. Naturally, Tony used their mutual experiences at Arsenal as a barometer: 'I started off trying to be Arsene Wènger, radiating calm and putting an arm round their shoulders. That wasn't really working, so I went into George Graham mode: hours of hard training drills and some sergeant-major shouting. Still no joy, so I eventually went the full Bruce Rioch and just started twatting people.'

One thing Adams said in *'89* struck me as apposite, and way beyond its football context, too: 'A good unit is bigger and better than the sum of the individuals.' Political theory talks of 'a collective action problem'. That is, a situation in which all individuals would be better off co-operating but fail to do so because of conflicting perceptions of self-interest. For example, if we want decent public services, it's probably better if everyone who can afford to do so, pays a reasonable amount of tax. However, certain affluent and influential individuals would rather not do so, so we end up with poor infrastructure and the less well-off encouraged to turn on each other.

Which brings us back to 2020 and Trump, Bolsonaro and Johnson, the three rugged individual populists occupying the podium of shame in the daily COVID-19 death toll Olympics. Bolsonaro has now gone through three health secretaries in a month as Brazil spirals out of control. I had a distanced chat this morning with our Brazilian neighbour Aline as she wheeled her bike into the communal garden. She was as sunny as ever, but must be cursing her luck to be stuck in this benighted country while her family are locked down in another. She says she can't even discuss Bolsonaro with her father because, like many older Brazilians, he refuses to see how toxic the man is.

I'm actively avoiding the detail of Trump's latest outbursts, but the asinine branding of something called 'Operation Warp Speed' and a headline I saw about a 'super duper' missile merely confirm that a presidential toddler has forfeited the right to lead the free world. And the little I've seen of UK, specifically English, politics in the last day or so has been more than enough, too. All the parents and teachers of my acquaintance are extremely uneasy about the announced phased return of primary schools from 1 June, and bewildered by the year groups chosen to go first. That is, the reception classes who won't understand social distancing or hygiene, and those in Year 6 who are leaving for secondary school this summer. In the case of my nieces, the elder who's passed her 11-plus would have to go back, while the younger, with her 11-plus to sit in the autumn, stays at home. Utterly bonkers, as well as making childcare arrangements doubly difficult. The grim Gavin Williamson and patsy journalists at the *Daily Mail* and *Telegraph* are frantically trying to turn the public against the teachers. I hope this tactic won't work, but we know from the way Brexit suddenly became an overarching necessity that many people are effectively Homer Simpson: not inherently evil, but all too receptive to any old crap planted in their brains. 'False consciousness', to use another term from political theory.

A Brexit talks headline I stumbled across claimed that the UK has issued the EU with an ultimatum: apparently, it has two weeks to drop its 'ideological stance'. Or what? Are we going to hold our breath until we turn purple? And some absolute imbeciles, doubtless inspired by their gun-toting counterparts in the US, have been protesting against the lockdown in Hyde Park and, in some cases, waving banners linking the virus to 5G masts. Others say it's a 'fake epidemic'. Jeremy Corbyn's brother Piers was one of those arrested. Give me strength. I need a bike ride, then I'm going to watch some football.

A late-afternoon update, with two pieces of news from Germany. The first is sad: Astrid Kirchherr, photographer of the Beatles, creator of their moptop haircuts and former girlfriend to Stuart Sutcliffe, has died in Hamburg at the age of 81. On a happier note, I've just watched Borussia Dortmund thrash Schalke 4-0 to go within a point of Bayern at the top of the Bundesliga. It was initially strange to see the empty stands – a magnificent stadium, minus its Wall of Yellow – but the sheer exuberance of Borussia's football and four brilliant finishes reminded me of what I've been missing. Along with music – I've just assembled a replacement exercise bike, and am about to pick an inaugural playlist – sport really is the 'most important of all of the unimportant things in life'.

Sunday, 17 May 2020

I emerged from the bedroom at 8.30am, and for the first time in living memory, a Sunday morning was entirely silent in this household. Birdsong filled the void, and I found Amanda luxuriating in the bath. She's not watching the Ridge and Marr shows, not least because Michael Gove was scheduled to appear on both this morning, so she knew that scarcely an informative word would be spoken. She's also abandoning the daily press conferences – the informative elements like the international comparisons are disappearing since they reflect badly on the government. Dr Jenny Harries appears to be planning to stand as a Tory candidate at the next by-election, her medical pronouncements having now veered into the overtly political. Rising R numbers worry the teaching unions and most of the rest of us, so despite having spent two months banging on about them, let's just say that they don't matter all that much after all, shall we, Doctor Jenny? Boris Johnson, in particular, has kept referring to those figures, despite never convincing this viewer that he knows his Rs from his elbow.

It was the turn of Frank Spencer lookalike, former fireplace salesman and National Security Council leaker, Gavin Williamson, to stand between the government scientists in the press conference yesterday. I was watching the closing stages of Borussia Dortmund v Schalke when a cryptic message appeared on my phone from Harry, my Teesside poet friend (that's not an oxymoron, by the way). It read, 'I feel like I'm watching an audition for the Scarborough Amateur Dramatics Society.' It was only when Amanda emerged from the bedroom an hour or so later, that I realised that this had been a reference to Spencer-Williamson.

The disgraced and sacked Defence Secretary (May 2019), now Minister for Education (May 2020), had channelled his weird, elocution-lesson drop-out vowels into an appeal to our 'hero' teachers to do as they're told and get back in the classroom. The ones we know are already back, on a rotated basis, teaching the children of essential workers. They don't want to be called 'heroes', nor do they want to catch or spread the virus. Unsurprisingly, though, they trust their unions more than they trust a government which assured everyone that mass gatherings were safe until it turned out that they weren't. Amanda said she actually fell asleep once Williamson started fielding questions and parroted the same 'we're working very hard on that' and 'there'll be an announcement in the coming days' lines which everyone from Hancock to Generick churns out every day. We're done with the press conferences in this household, I suspect.

The fact that it's taken so long for Amanda's patience to snap illustrates a fundamental difference between us. We both try to see the best in people initially, so can share a table with strangers on holiday or meet an old friend's new partner and conduct ourselves accordingly. We agree on the fundamentals of behaviour and unacceptable viewpoints, but whereas I explode on a daily basis and write certain people off fairly quickly, Amanda has a very long fuse. I can bounce back within half an hour (I have to be able to do that, or I'd rant myself to cinders) but when Amanda's had enough of something or somebody, that's it for the rest of time. I suspect she's now finished with anything this government has to say.

This may surprise anyone who knows us (you, sir, at the back – can you at least pretend to be surprised?) but Amanda is usually the steady one in our relationship. The Spot the Cat (Michael tells me that was the name) to my Hong Kong Phooey, if you like, although we can reverse roles once in a while when there's a crisis or I realise I've gone too far. My job as programme editor brought the best out of me on one level: I was always suited to an exam situation, cramming information and thinking clearly as deadlines approached. I could usually keep my worrying internalised, at least when we were on the air and the show needed decisive navigation. However, the stress undoubtedly took its toll somewhere deep inside.

Yesterday, we should have been watching Juliet Stevenson in the play *The Doctor* in the West End, in the company of Amanda's cousin Susie. Amanda mentioned this and reminded me that we owed Susie her money back. I was in the middle of writing my handover note to myself for today, then trying to find any evidence of ticket payment and refund, while also replying to a completely separate message I'd just had from a friend. None of those three things needed to happen that very minute, but my brain imposed arbitrary deadlines; I ballsed up all three elements and got quite angry with myself.

It's absolutely ridiculous, but whether I'm awake or asleep, my brain often goes into a default essay crisis/live programme setting which is completely inappropriate to my post-BBC life, especially in current circumstances. That's where mindfulness should, and on a good day does, step in. Amanda also thinks much of my exasperation and anxiety about the wider world – especially at the moment – is fuelled by a feeling that I should be helping to solve problems, accompanied by the helplessness of knowing I can't. Amanda is a very wise woman. When she reads this – she'll probably scan today's entry for grammar and punctuation errors this evening – I'd like her to know that I'm sorry I exploded yesterday.

Regular reader Daz has been in touch again – he tells me the fine bass part on Fairport Convention's 'Who Knows Where the Time Goes' was played by Ashley Hutchings. I said last week I wasn't going to bother to research it because he'd correct me if it wasn't Dave Pegg, and he has. Like Captain Mainwaring, I'll now claim that it was a deliberate error: 'I was wondering who'd be the first to spot that.' I caused a bit of a stink in a family quiz this week when an incorrect answer was given for the year of Abba's Eurovision win (1973, my arse) so I've been hoisted by my own pedantry. One thing Daz and I do agree on, though, is the quality of those cover versions released by Susanna Hoffs and Matthew Sweet. Daz has been trawling Spotify on my recommendation and thinks their version of 'Train in Vain' stands comparison with the original, his favourite Clash track. I can see this controversial opinion – with which I agree, by the way – causing virtual fisticuffs with other readers, notably Jan and Andrew, the Clement fils.

Incidentally, Andrew was lucky enough to look after Susanna and the other Bangles during a 1980s appearance on *Wogan*. Her looks may have been the first thing we 20-somethings noticed back then – she's still gorgeous, but what a voice. Her version of 'Different Drum', a song I've always loved in its various incarnations, is untouchable. The guy who wrote it, ex-Monkee turned fine singer-songwriter, Mike Nesmith, was bowled over by the Hoffs/Sweet rendition, too. I'm going to trot out some pointless trivia now: Nesmith's mother invented Tippex, Susanna Hoffs' husband Jay Roach directed the *Austin Powers* movies (Susanna made a cameo appearance as 60s singer Gillian Shagwell), *Meet the Parents* and, more recently, *Bombshell.*

Another regular correspondent has been in touch. Niall says he and his wife Penny have also used the government's drive-through testing facilities at the IKEA in Wembley. The results were negative, fortunately, but he says there wasn't another car on the site when they visited a couple of days after we did. Meanwhile, TV reports from care homes show untested, elderly hospital patients who have been dumped on, and looked after by, inadequately protected carers who are still themselves untested.

Then you read that the 130,000 daily tests the government claimed yesterday only equate to 70,000 people, because the figure includes multiple tests on the same person, as well as those which have been posted out but not returned. Recording 70,000 tests a day would still be more than enough in South Korea or Germany (19 and 174 new cases respectively yesterday) where tracking and testing is on top of any small new outbreak, but is clearly nowhere near enough here in the UK. If Martha Kellner's Sky News report from a socially distanced Bundesliga-watching sports bar in Dortmund had been seen more widely, I suspect even the non-political among us would be asking questions.

I've read just one newspaper article today. Andy Burnham, the Mayor of Manchester, has pointed to the elephant in the room in today's *Observer*: 'Far from a planned, safety-led approach, this looks like another exercise in Cummings's chaos theory.' Burnham is no firebrand – the deluded Labour membership chose Corbyn ahead of him in 2015 for precisely that reason – but he's gone further there than even I have done to date. While I've thought throughout this pandemic that Cummings's divisive, sloganeering, vendetta-waging approach was an inappropriate response, I preferred to ascribe the government's shambolic handling to incompetence, and the need to placate the right of their party, rather than to an over-arching Cummings strategy.

Surely this is too chaotic to be anyone's plan? But then you remember that Cummings claims to be guided by the Chinese military strategist Sun Tzu and you wonder. 'Confound your enemies', 'make your opponent look like an unreasonable aggressor', and 'isolate them, break their alliances and morale' may have steered him and Johnson through a referendum and general election, but it isn't working during a pandemic. They need to have the vast majority of the public on their side this time, not the usual 52 per cent or 40 per cent with the remainder seething but impotent.

Burnham is, to an extent, playing to his electorate. The number of confirmed daily COVID-19 cases here in Camden and neighbouring Brent yesterday were the highest for three weeks, so it's not simply a case of London moving at a different speed and dictating to the north. The schools shouldn't be going back here either, and both Transport for London and Manchester's trams were given no advance warning of last Sunday's Johnson porridge. A week on, during the course of the politics shows we couldn't face watching, Michael Gove has apparently said that 'teachers will be safe in schools' and that local authorities should 'look to their responsibilities' after several English councils, including Liverpool, Hartlepool and Gateshead have said that their schools won't be reopening on 1 June. Then again, Gove also blamed NHS clinicians for those COVID patients returning to care homes, claimed that successive Conservative administrations have 'closed the gap' between rich and poor, and the NHS still hasn't seen any of the £350m a week he promised if we voted Leave in 2016.

I don't share Boris Johnson's professed faith in the 'British common sense' of our electorate, but I do think only a minority of the public would trust Gove or Williamson ahead of the BMA, the teaching unions (hardly a gang of Arthur Scargills) and their own intuition. Having tried to home school their own offspring of late, I suspect many parents have developed a new-found respect for the entire teaching profession. After that desperate attempt by Nadine Dorries and friends to smear Keir Starmer as the paedo's friend, the *Mail on Sunday* has tried to mount another diversion. Harry Cole has a front-page story headlined: 'Man of the People? New Labour leader Sir Keir owns land worth up to £10m.' In his distinguished legal career, it turns out that the knight of the realm once earned a few quid. He duly bought a field, and 'is thought to have a stake in a strip of scrubland', adjacent to his parents' house in Surrey, where his parents worked as a toolmaker and a nurse while he attended the local state school. I've added those biographical details since Harry Cole somehow omitted them. If any reader makes it as far as paragraph 14, they'll find a begrudging attempt to mitigate against any libel charge: 'The field was used to house donkeys that Keir's parents rescued and cared for. After his mother lost the ability to walk, the field allowed her to watch the donkeys from her home. The field is not for sale.'

Elsewhere in today's *Mail on Sunday*, an exclusive article by Johnson – or, more likely Cummings – blathers on once more about the 'good sense of the British people'. I've only seen the headline, but I'm not wasting any more precious time – or risking a fuse blowing in my head – by reading the full two-page spread. There are signs of some of that 'good sense' finally prevailing, though. Some *Sun*, *Mail* and *Telegraph* readers may just swallow the notion that worried parents and teachers are traitors, and may even be persuaded to fulminate against the Labour leader for daring to buy a field (imagine the fawning newspaper write-up if Johnson made sure his disabled mum could watch rescued donkeys?) but for the first time, a poll shows that more people disapprove of the government's handling of this crisis than approve.

While it's still staggering that 47 per cent of those who weren't 'don't knows' think they're doing a good job – there really should be a decimal point in there – they're clearly losing goodwill by the day. A comfortable majority think they relaxed lockdown prematurely and 73 per cent feel the government hasn't issued enough guidance. Even 22 per cent of those who voted Conservative in December think their government is handling the crisis badly. Unfortunately, they, and we, are stuck with them for four and a half more years.

The UK's death toll of 468 was the third highest in the world yet again yesterday, behind the US and Brazil. Germany registered just 26 and Denmark, cited by Gove as a country where the schools are open again, had six new deaths. We're in no shape whatsoever to do what two or three newspaper proprietors, Toby Young, 20 mad bastards in Hyde Park and Sir Geoffrey 'I'm all right, Jack' Cilfton-Brown, MP for the Cotswolds, have been demanding. We may have to find that out the hard way in two or three weeks' time, unfortunately. I say unfortunately but really, I mean tragically.

Monday, 18 May 2020

A beautiful warm morning found us driving to Ingram Avenue for another walk on the Hampstead Heath extension. This time we had a walk around Hampstead Garden Suburb, past the rather grand-looking academic hothouse that is the Henrietta Barnett School, named after the suburb's founder. The school overlooks the two elegant Lutyens-designed churches and main square. Lutyens went on to design New Delhi to replace Calcutta as the centre of British rule in India and it remained the capital after independence. We visited in 1999, and it's difficult to believe that its vast avenues and grand buildings lie in the same city as the teeming mass of humanity and assault on the senses which characterise Old Delhi. Back in eerily quiet Hampstead Garden Suburb, the scene looked more like *The Truman Show*. Not a bad thing in this time of social distancing.

I didn't take my phone, so the audio accompaniment to our short drive to and from our walk was BBC Radio 5 Live and another Barnett, the excellent presenter Emma. On the way there, we heard a heart-rending testimony from a care home manager in West Yorkshire who, despite pleading for tests to be carried out, had untested NHS patients discharged into his homes in March, which in turn led to a COVID-19 outbreak among his staff and residents. Seventeen of the latter died and their bodies had to be wrapped in clingfilm as a makeshift hygiene measure. He took great exception, therefore, to Matt Hancock's assertion that a 'protective ring' had been thrown around care homes.

Driving home, we were alerted to the fact that Priti Patel's immigration bill was appearing before the Commons today. Recent events have changed nothing: care workers, along with anyone else who doesn't earn more than £25,600 are not welcome in the brave new post-Brexit world from next January. Naturally, Emma Barnett questioned this approach, though her language, unlike mine, was fit for broadcast.

I've finished the second section of Hilary Mantel's *The Mirror and the Light* and am now even more conscious of the similarities between the revolts of 1536 and 2016. In both cases, Lincolnshire is the epicentre. The Pilgrimage of Grace against the Reformation begins in Louth and spreads to Lincoln and beyond. Nearly 500 years later, every constituency in the county voted with Farage, Gove and co., and Boston recorded the highest Leave vote in the country at more than 75 per cent. In both cases, fury seems to have been founded on fake news: Mantel writes, 'In Essex he [Cromwell] is a swindler, a blasphemer and renegade Jew … while in Carlisle, he is a ghoul who steals children and eats their hearts.'

In our era, we had the 'bendy bananas' and 'one size fits all condoms' invented by Boris Johnson as the *Telegraph*'s Brussels correspondent, then 'Taking Back Control' and the '£350m for the NHS' bus, and still it carries on to this day. *The Sun* ran a story today claiming that Britain 'faces a £380bn bill if Brexit is delayed beyond December'. That figure is considerably higher than the UK's accumulative contribution to EEC/EU finances across our entire 47-year membership. Professor Anand Menon's uncharacteristically blunt assessment is that this is 'maths homework done while drunk or high, or both'.

Meanwhile, David Davis continues to validate an unusually perceptive assessment from Dominic Cummings: namely, that he's 'as thick as mince and lazy as a toad'. Fresh from what I hope is a unique assertion that tax cuts, rather than rises, are needed to help balance what will soon be unprecedented levels of government debt, Davis says that the EU will 'change stance if we stick to a firm line'. This is the man who turned up to his first meeting with Michel Barnier as Brexit Secretary with no notes, paperwork or even writing implement. Like his fellow David – Brent – he merely tapped his head and said, 'It's all up here, mate.'

In recent days, the UK government has given the EU a two-week ultimatum to drop its 'dogmatic stance' and is currently unilaterally drawing up a draft treaty based on its fantasy outcome. I'm thinking of applying the same strategy to my long-standing, but as yet unsatisfied, demand that the Seychelles government gives me a private island.

It's all heading towards a No Deal car crash this winter which will mean tariffs and disrupted food and medicine supplies, to coincide with a predicted second or third COVID-19 spike. The government's only hope is that no one will be able to work out what's caused what. As Marina Hyde put it this weekend, 'Far from taking pause, the Conservatives are embracing the timing with the sweaty gratitude of a guy who knows that the unfortunate fire at a storage unit factory will take care of the corpse he's been storing there.'

My love affair with the Bundesliga turned out to be short-lived. A routine 2-0 win for Bayern Munich at Union Berlin restored their four-point lead at the top of the table, and I fell asleep on the sofa after half-time. It only occurred to me later that I've seen Bayern play this season – in that extraordinary Champions League game which saw Spurs concede seven goals at home for the first time in their 137-year history. Tall Paul, who was sitting next to me, said his goodbyes at 5-2, and went off into the north London night ranting about Mourinho and right-back Serge Aurier, but I stuck it out to witness history being made.

Meanwhile, Celtic have been declared Scottish champions yet again. Bayern, Celtic, PSG and Juventus have rendered four of Europe's historically more interesting leagues rather tedious in recent times. Spain is usually a two-horse race and although the Premier League was over as a contest when curtailed, at least the club out in front on their own haven't been champions since 1990.

In honour of what should have been the last day of the PL season, I watched the recording of an entertaining Lineker/Shearer/Wright debate about the best goals from the Premier League era. The wonderful Dennis Bergkamp ballet routine for Arsenal at Newcastle topped their charts, which seemed fair enough. This was followed by *Match of Their Day* which showed the intercut edits which featured in the two most exciting final days the Premier League has seen: Manchester City snatching the title from neighbours United with two goals in injury time in 2012; and the incredible four-way relegation battle which saw West Brom leap three places off the bottom and relegate Southampton, Crystal Palace and Norwich in 2005.

I was programme editor for both of those shows, frantically making notes throughout the afternoon, keeping commentators informed and then liaising with the producers putting together the packages. I hadn't watched either edit back since, but I thought they still stood up well, and both the guys who cut the packages are now established programme editors. Andy Fraser, who told the City/United story so brilliantly, now runs football shows at the BBC; Mark Demuth, who charted those inordinately complicated relegation twists and turns, is ITV Sport's lead editorial figure these days. Mark had to be particularly professional in 2005 – his edit featured his own team,

Crystal Palace, being relegated by a Charlton equaliser minutes from the end of the season.

Although I knew he was sent off for QPR against his old club, City, before Agüero scored that famous winner, I'd forgotten just how deranged Joey Barton's behaviour was on that final day in 2012. He committed at least four red card offences in one sequence: an off-the-ball elbow to the throat, a vicious stamp on Agüero after he'd been sent off, and then he had to be restrained by team-mates and the opposition's Micah Richards as he tried to pick several more fights while leaving the pitch.

Football Focus presenter Dan Walker is a really nice man: his Christian faith, while it prevents him from working on a Sunday, also makes him try to see the good in everyone. However, when we worked together at BBC Sport, I occasionally chuckled at his special relationship with Joey Barton. Bad boy Joey was generally able to persuade Dan that he'd turned over a new leaf. A sympathetic, and often entertaining, interview would duly be transmitted in *Focus,* only for Barton to transgress again and earn himself another lengthy ban, another rehabilitation would lead to another interview, and so on.

Dan continues to be a fine, natural presenter and an affable presence on *BBC Breakfast* in normal times. The last time I saw the show was in the run-up to last year's general election. Boris Johnson famously hid in a fridge rather than face a Piers Morgan inquisition, but was prepared to endure the comfy chair of Schofield and Willoughby and the plumped cushion of Walker. I have to admit I didn't see all of Johnson's *BBC Breakfast* interview, having switched off in somewhat agitated fashion when he and Dan ended up discussing cheese.

I haven't seen either channel's breakfast coverage of the COVID-19 crisis, either, but government ministers are currently boycotting ITV's *Good Morning Britain* as they have previously *Channel 4 News* and R4's *Today.* I'd argue that's not a great reflection on the government who should be communicating with the public on all possible fronts, especially during a pandemic.

That said, as far as I know, our PM hasn't been seen or heard anywhere at all since last Thursday when he provided his usual sea lion impression during the 'clap for carers'.

Tuesday, 19 May 2020

I foolishly decided that it was my public duty to catch up with the news via my iPad when I woke up this morning. Oh boy; 'US and UK lead push against global patent pool for COVID-19 drugs' was the *Guardian* headline which grabbed my attention. I knew Trump was trying to buy first dibs on any vaccine in his ongoing battle with both China and any vestige of humanity left in his soul, but why would we join him? Well, there's Special Relationship sycophancy and the fact that the EU are lobbying for a global patent waiver, so they must be contradicted at all costs. Then there's the almost certainly deluded belief, perpetrated yesterday in another wave of 'all Brits vaccinated by September' tabloid headlines, that of the 80 different vaccine research programmes under way across the world, our single programme is bound to be the first to bear fruit.

It's far from guaranteed that there'll ever be a COVID-19 vaccine, but I'd be delighted beyond measure if the Oxford University team is ahead of the pack. Even then, it would be horrible to see our government brandish the patent as a political weapon. If any of the other 79 potential vaccines from around the world is manufactured first, we'd deserve to be at the back of the queue if that really is our attitude. If America gets it first, God alone knows what concessions we'd have to make in our much-vaunted trade deal in order to be sold any of it. Goodbye, British farming industry, for starters. And well done to our farmers for voting overwhelmingly for Brexit, by the way.

Elsewhere, I read that Priti Patel, fresh from 'clap for carers on Thursday, call them unskilled and send them home on Monday' (I preferred Craig David's version), has tweeted, 'We're ending free movement to open Britain up to the world.' That distant rotating sound you can hear is George Orwell impersonating a spin dryer in an Oxfordshire graveyard.

I moved on to WhatsApp for some respite. Big mistake, huge. Tall Paul had posted the latest on Trump. He's bragged that he's taking hydroxychloroquine as a COVID-19 preventative, despite overwhelming evidence that it has no effect on the virus, and moreover, can lead to heart failure. We can but hope. Paul also linked to an extraordinary long-form article from the *Financial Times* which assessed the Trump presidency during the pandemic. Most of it is a timeline of well-catalogued disarray and incompetence to rival our own, but some of the details are shocking. Trump's instincts were anti-science from the start and his son-in-law Jared Kushner easily won him over with this argument: 'Testing too many people, or ordering too many ventilators would spook the market, and we just shouldn't do it.'

I've also read a *New York Times* state of the nation article from the weekend – yes, I have had some breakfast, thanks for asking – where one line from a prison secretary and carer for two disabled parents in Marianna, Florida jumped out at me. Of Trump, she said, 'He's not hurting the people he needs to be hurting.' That statement cuts straight to the heart of many social media, and real-life, battles of the last four years. Much of the drive behind Brexit and Trump was a desire to hurt others, whether it was foreigners, London, Washington or liberals. I grew up believing that being liberal was a good thing, but of late, every vaguely empathetic tweet from any well-known Twitter account receives a barrage of abuse about 'virtue signalling', or a meme of a gleeful halfwit drinking from a mug labelled 'salty liberal tears'. Clearly this is a vocal, gloating minority augmented by Russian bots, but it's horrible to see them seemingly deriving comfort from, 'You lost – get over it/suck it up, snowflake.' Those to whom they lent their vote have as yet done nothing about the underlying problems which led those people to that misguided place.

My friend Stu, normally one of the funniest people I know, wrote a truly bleak and world-weary post yesterday: 'Politicians lying: you point it out, then folk (who presumably voted for them) respond with "Who cares?" And you want to say, "Look, they're lying to you as well. Just because you like them doesn't mean you're in on it. If anything, they're laughing at you even more than they are at me."' This isn't how any major democracy should be making people feel in the 21st century.

On a more practical level, I'm becoming aware of a schism developing among certain friends. The Fat Larry's Band quiz convened on Sunday, and during a technical delay with the Kahoot app, the discussion turned to the lockdown. I know that Justin, who I've mentioned on here, is pretty much as one with me and Amanda in having no intention of lifting our own lockdown yet. Other members of the group, while broadly agreeing that our government's response has been poor and that, ideally, they 'wouldn't start from here', just want to get back on with daily life and take the inherent risks, while continuing to shield the vulnerable. Curry Club Tall Paul – who, if anything, dislikes Johnson and Cummings even more than I do – also seems to feel the same way. All of these people are far more immersed in the economy than I am, and are not in any way callous, so it's a pragmatic viewpoint I take seriously.

We'll have to see where the statistics go this week – they've been lower over the last couple of days but the death tally immediately after a weekend is always down. The ONS review of death certificates said today that there were 39,071 deaths where COVID-19 was mentioned in England and Wales alone, up until 8 May. Across the UK, there were 53,000 deaths more than average across the pandemic period to date. The government are still sticking to an overall tally, even 11 days later, of 34,796 for the whole UK. And despite these glaring discrepancies, Grant Shapps and many of the 'suck it up loser' brigade continue to pour scorn on cheating foreigners for allegedly massaging their figures.

I wouldn't be entirely surprised if Belarus or China haven't reported accurately, but frankly, I'd trust pretty much any government in the EU (possibly not Orbán's Hungary) before I'd trust ours. I never thought I'd be saying that when I was growing up in our green and pleasant land, but there you go. Meanwhile, *Daily Mail* readers must be royally confused this morning: having been shrieked at for decades about the wickedness of all things Continental, they're now accosted by a front-page splash which reads, 'Yesterday, 22 EU countries said opening their schools has NOT been harmful.' Quite apart from the spectacular volte-face involved – any ammunition is seemingly legitimate when deployed against 'Britain's militant teaching unions' – all of those countries had substantially lower infection rates than ours when they tentatively reopened their schools. It also hasn't been an unqualified success: France has already closed more than 70 schools and colleges in under a week because of fresh outbreaks. Not that the *Mail* is reporting that angle.

Right, it's 11.30am, so I have half an hour to write about something else. You can't move for anniversaries on social media. Boro's Twitter feed told me yesterday that it was 23 years to the day since our only FA Cup Final appearance. Why exactly would I want to remember that? Roberto Di Matteo killed that game by scoring for Chelsea after 43 seconds, and I later got into a handbags fight with a shaved gibbon in a blue shirt in front of me. My brother and I left before we had to watch Dennis Wise waving the trophy around. It was also 32 years since Boro beat Bradford in the play-off semi-final to set up a rare win against Chelsea, and scary second leg at Stamford Bridge, in the final. And it's 26 years ago today since Bryan Robson was unveiled as Boro's manager for that last season at Ayresome Park. I was slightly more in the loop back then, so I'd known about that appointment for a few weeks, courtesy of John Motson's impeccable contacts.

Meanwhile, a stunning photo on our friend Liz's Facebook page reminds me that it's a year ago today since our farewell dinner on the beach in Bali with the school friends who'd won a week in a villa in a silent auction. When they flew home, Amanda and I headed inland to Ubud for an extra couple of days. Thanks to that stroke of auction luck, and the even luckier timing of the villa booking, Amanda and I extended our trip to the South Pacific and New Zealand to include a fortnight in Java and Borneo prior to meeting the others in Bali. I've had two poignant e-mails in recent days from a couple of fantastic hotels we stayed in while touring Java, telling me they've been shortlisted for the Conde Nast Travel awards. I hope those beautiful establishments survive this awful time. Given the success of Asia in dealing with the virus, they should be able to welcome internal tourism and visitors from neighbouring countries in due course. It might be a long time before we Brits can try anything like that again, but we're so grateful we chose to make that trip in 2019, not 2020.

We now have two exercise bikes parked next to each other on the patio: the original is stuck in a low gear, but Amanda still uses the attached arm exercisers. Then there's the newly assembled one which we've left in a middle gear to try to avoid any more components snapping. I'm back into my 20km in just under half an hour groove. This was aided two nights ago by a Green Day playlist: a great cycling soundtrack in the grand tradition of three-piece bands making an agreeable racket – Cream, Jimi Hendrix Experience, the Jam, Rush, Nirvana – with distinct punk overtones. Their *American Idiot* is my favourite 21st-century album so far, not that I'm familiar with very many others.

Last night, I opted for an esoteric Dylan covers playlist. I've upset many a Dylan aficionado – Bob Willis and my mate Justin, to name but two – by saying that cover versions of his songs are often an improvement on the original. I'd concede that no one quite does bile or world weariness like he can, so his 'Like a Rolling Stone', 'Positively 4th Street' and 'Not Dark Yet' are peerless, but Hendrix and the Byrds, in particular, elevated 'All Along the Watchtower' and 'My Back Pages', among others, to a different plane. Spotify managed to find me a whole series of gems I'd never heard before: a stunning 'She Belongs to Me' by

Beatles associate Billy Preston; Beck's version of 'Leopard Skin Pillbox Hat'; and PJ Harvey's 'Highway 61 Revisited'.

The one which really tickled me though was the Nice's live version of 'Country Pie' which they mashed up with Bach's *Brandenburg Concerto No. 6*. Keith Emerson, later of the somewhat excessive (imho) ELP, gave this full welly on the organ. Hearing it made me feel a lot better about my latest 'spot the song' round when hosting the Poncey Horse Club quiz. I played a mixture of restrained ukulele ('Losing My Religion' by REM) and piano intros (Abba's 'The Winner Takes It All') before turning on the church organ setting for the two-point question finale, and segueing from Procul Harum's Bach adaptation 'A Whiter Shade of Pale' into 'Don't Look Back in Anger' by Oasis. I've only ever messed around with that medley for my own amusement, or maybe Amanda's if she's feeling tolerant, but we're in lockdown and it was my turn to host, so frankly, my gaff, my rules. I can also add in 'No Woman No Cry', 'Go West', 'Altogether Now' by the Farm, Pachelbel's Canon, and many others with a very similar chord sequence and keep it going for some time, but I spared Poncey Horse any further self-indulgence.

It's 11.58am now, the sun is blazing down and I'm off to the bench for another instalment of the unruly north versus Thomas Cromwell and 'that there London'. Only 510 pages to go now, so I'm almost on the home straight.

Wednesday, 20 May 2020

The only movie of my teenage years which rivals *The Life of Brian* for lines many of us quote to this day is *Airplane*. I used the 'that's just what they'll be expecting us to do' runway lights gag to describe the Cummings/UK government chaos theory a while back. Yesterday I was reminded of Lloyd Bridges's under-pressure air traffic controller, and the running gag, 'Looks like I picked the wrong week to quit drinking/smoking/amphetamines/

sniffing glue.' Amanda should add government press conferences to that list. After weeks of torture she finally gives up on them, just before there's a zinger.

Yesterday's looked as unprepossessing as it could be: George 'Useless' Eustice, former UKIP candidate, now Environment Minister, and just the one scientist: Dame Angela McLean, Chief Scientific Adviser to the Ministry of Defence. I decided to swerve it live and watch the *MOTD*-style edited highlights online instead, then got wind that I'd missed a turning of the worm. Or rather, the scientists, sensing the politicians are starting to blame them, are starting to break rank. No doubt still smarting from faceless minister Therese Coffey's media rounds that morning (bar Piers Morgan) where she squarely put the blame for the care home testing fiasco on 'wrong' scientific advice, Dame Angela was clearly having none of it. When BBC health correspondent Sophie Hutchinson asked her what led to the abandonment of testing and tracing on 12 March, Dame Angela's clipped reply was that prioritising hospitals over care homes was unavoidable at that time, given the inadequacy of the testing then available. She pointedly stared at Eustice.

Boris Johnson trumpeting the UK's 'world-class testing' on 3 March, the day he boasted of 'shaking hands with everybody' in a hospital, and four days before he did the same at the Twickenham rugby, now looks foolish and hollow. The UK's tracking and testing certainly won't be proven by 1 June: it might not even work fully by the time the next academic year starts in September. Incidentally, that's the earliest possible month in which our leading public schools are prepared to consider reopening. The *Mail*'s latest meltdown – 'Callous Teacher Union's Plotting Exposed' is today's front-page splash – only rounds on the state sector. Curious that Old Etonian *Mail* editor Geordie Greig should fail to mention that his alma mater – also that of the Prime Minister, of course – is currently two months into a six-month summer holiday. Sorry, it's the 'long vac' there, just like the debating society is 'Pop' and 'Boys' maids' are the cleaners.

Two SAGE scientists have publicly stated that schools shouldn't go back until tracking and testing is up and running. That puts them on the same side as 11 English councils, including one Tory council (Solihull), and my brother who's already written to my nieces' school, saying he's not chancing it given that they share a house with my vulnerable parents. Moreover, Josie already has a place at grammar school for the autumn, so is the wrong niece of the two to be summoned back. They're both doing hours and hours of study online every day as it is, so it would present a risk with very little upside.

In the early days of this journal, I flagged up the likely shortage of NHS ICU beds and ventilators as the crisis grew, so I have a smidgen of sympathy for ministers trying to avoid the kind of health service collapse which had been seen in northern Italy. That BBC Two *Hospital* documentary showed the Royal Free on the brink of being overwhelmed in late March. Once the Nightingale hospitals were up and running and still had almost all their beds available, though, surely suspected and untested elderly COVID-19 patients could have been moved there to protect other care home residents and staff? Lewis Goodall of *Newsnight* has calculated that a staggering eight per cent of all care home residents in England and Wales have died in the last six weeks. Maybe Priti Patel factored in the resultant lower demand for care staff when she refused to exempt them from the unskilled/unwanted category in her Immigration Bill.

Most of the other front pages have bought into the latest cynical distraction, and media manipulation, based around a genuinely good man. Just as the government is coming under the cosh, Captain Tom is getting a knighthood. Presumably they've kept a peerage in reserve for the next time they're in a corner and need another 'look over there' moment for all the Homer Simpsons out there. So, a couple of days' time, probably.

The track and test technology may have to reboot from scratch at some point, judging by some of the early whispers about Dom's cronies' NHS app trial in the Isle of Wight. The app still fails almost all practical, clinical and privacy standards, it seems, and there's a reasonable chance that even if Dom gets its approval past SAGE, some individual members with one eye on a future inquiry may now disown it in public. Meanwhile, private-sector firm Serco have accidentally released the e-mail addresses of some 300 staff recruited to carry out contact tracing, and it's emerged that little or no training has been given to any of those recruited. Serco are the firm who were given the contract for an NHS breast cancer hotline in 2018. The non-medically trained staff were given an hour's briefing and a sheet of FAQs before being expected to field calls from desperately worried women.

Like G4S, whose security duties were handed to the Army in the week leading up to London 2012 when it became clear they were unequipped to fulfil them, Serco win contract after contract from our government. This despite a somewhat chequered track record which includes a £23m fine in 2019 as part of a settlement with the Serious Fraud Office over electronic tagging contracts. Even during a pandemic, the Conservative Party seems unable to tear itself away from its private enterprise = good, public services = bad, dogma. The devolved governments have mostly asked local authorities and public health teams to take charge of tracking and testing, so it's shaping up to be another comparison of England vs the rest.

One delightful by-product of going back on to Twitter has been a reconnection with Peter Reid. He phoned me yesterday afternoon after I'd retweeted an excellent Dominic Cummings compilation video put together by Joe.co.uk. My covering line had been a world weary 'I know far more about this bloke than can possibly be good for me' and Reidy sensed I needed a pep talk. We held forth jointly for 20 minutes about everything from Arron Banks and Carole Cadwalladr, to what he should have done to Boris Johnson in that dressing room, to Peter Shilton having blocked me for challenging his praise for Jacob Rees-Mogg. The upshot was that Reidy was delighted to have me back alongside him in the online trenches. Years of abuse from opposition fans have hardened him to any hostility, so if he can take the flak as a public figure, I figured I should be less sensitive about any nonsense that comes my way. I'm still not sure anything we say or post changes any minds, but 'evil triumphs when good men do nothing' and all that.

Reidy posted something this morning which made me re-assess yesterday's criticism of *BBC Breakfast*. With a simple comment attached – 'They're lying about lying now' – he posted a clip of Louise Minchin interviewing Justice Minister Robert Buckland. She quoted the (aforementioned) comments by Therese Coffey to Dan Walker the previous morning about care homes and tests, all of which had been shown to be inaccurate. Perhaps you really do attract more flies with honey than vinegar: Louise's technique was not unlike that of Keir Starmer's at PMQs; pointing out errors in a tone more suggestive of disappointment than anger, and suggesting that public discourse and trust might benefit from greater honesty and transparency from those who are supposed to be in charge. Buckland responded with utter piffle, naturally, but had the decency to look slightly crushed. Minchin didn't say as much, but sending out Johnson or at least one of the inner sanctum who are privy to the current thinking (such as it is) might help. So Raab, Sunak, Gove or Hancock to face the media every day, instead of the Frank Spencer the fireplace salesman, Useless and Generic would do everyone a favour.

I suspect a more strident version of the same argument may have been used behind the scenes by some of the government's scientists in the last 24 hours: Number 10 (presumably Dom) has been forced to disown Therese Coffey's blame-shifting comments. 'Ministers decide' is the ultimate verdict which may or may not have prevented some members of SAGE from walking. I'm not holding my breath, but perhaps Dom has been forced to wake up and smell the Coffey.

There was another darkly comical aspect to the press conference yesterday. Farmers, the vast majority of whom voted for Brexit, have belatedly worked out that almost all of their fruit and vegetable pickers of late have come for the summer from the EU, to live in tents and earn a pittance for long hours of manual labour, under freedom of movement. On the same day that Priti Patel triumphantly announced that all that nonsense was finally over, Useless Eustice was pleading with the British populace to sign up to a website called Pick for Britain on which Prince Charles, who owns much of the farming land in Useless's home county of Cornwall, also appealed to a Union Jack sense of patriotic duty. The problem is that most people who do believe in 'my country: right or wrong' are too old/pampered to countenance such back-breaking work. The young, who might be up to it, didn't vote for Useless's government, in many cases would like to have enjoyed freedom of movement, and are in no mood to bail out rural communities which predominantly voted to shaft them. And in any case, the Pick for Britain website crashed as Useless was speaking.

Not much else to report, except that it's now properly hot outside. I had to put my panama hat on for the first time this summer yesterday. Reidy is a huge cricket fan, so like me, was lamenting the fact that an almost perfect April and May would have given us uninterrupted leather on willow action and the occasional snooze in the sunshine. I foolishly did yesterday's bike ride in the late afternoon: the sun had gone from that corner of the patio by then, but I downed a precious Lucozade Sport in one gulp when I'd finished and went straight into the shower. Tall Paul has inserted a 1980s and '90s music round into tonight's quiz, having suffered Jan's prog rock questions, then Lee and I mining the '70s, on previous occasions. With the exception of Aztec Camera and the Scottish guitar bands, I more or less stopped listening to new music in about 1983 and only returned in the mid-'90s when playing an instrument seemingly became important again.

I appreciate that not all music in that intervening era was forged by the two e's – electronics and ecstasy – but most of it seemed to be. Of the stuff which wasn't, I liked Johnny Marr's guitar work, but could never stand Morrissey even before he went weird and very right wing. And I just couldn't take Bono at any price after his 'look at me' exhibition during an interminable version of 'One' at Live Aid. As for the Edge, Bill Bailey's magnificent sketch where his guitar pedal breaks and he's left playing 'Jingle Bells' nails it for me.

As a result of my cynicism, though, I missed some absolute gems first time round – I'd woken up by the time Oasis (good if derivative tunes, unspeakably bad lyrics) and the rest appeared but I had to catch up with the Stone Roses and The Cure, for example. I went with The Cure radio for the bike ride yesterday, partly in an attempt to cram ahead of Tall Paul's quiz. It wasn't entirely successful – Duran Duran were always average, and time elapsed does not mean that the Thompson Twins have ceased to be bloody awful one-finger synthesiser dross – but all The Cure tracks were great.

I ended my sweaty 20km to the strains of a song with happy associations, 'Friday I'm in Love'. Sharon Lence, who produced the first BBC Sport show I regularly edited in the early to mid-90s, *Sport on Friday*, doubled up the fine jangly guitar intro to that song and used it for our scene set music. It was a low maintenance, only moderately pressurised, live afternoon show, ideal for would-be editors and directors to get some programmes under our belts. A mixture of outside broadcasts on the day – often horse racing – previews of the weekend ahead and other odds and ends, presented by the late and much-missed Helen Rollason. Occasionally, the vigilant but somewhat intimidating head of sport, Jonathan Martin, would phone the live gallery to keep the young whippersnappers on their toes (you could go a whole World Cup without hearing from senior management under certain subsequent regimes) but I have almost entirely happy memories of that time. And for anyone who worked in BBC Sport for 20 years or more around that period, hearing The Cure always evokes fond thoughts of our colleague Andy Gilbert.

Andy contracted polio as a kid, later won Paralympic swimming medals and became one of our best studio directors. He used crutches to get about but after a few drinks, and especially if anything by The Cure came on, he'd hit the dance floor.

I spoke to Andy just the other week: he, his wife Tanya and daughter Olivia live a mile or so south of here in Camden Town, and we'd normally see them every once in a while. Olivia is an extremely talented footballer, and she and I had a memorable kickabout in Kensington Gardens, which turned into a keepy-uppy competition and a full-scale one-on-one match. I was already in my 50s by then – I used to be able to do 1,000 keep-ups in my heyday – but I could hardly walk after this lengthy session. I was thrilled to be sent a recent video of the whole family's lockdown exploits for charity. Olivia, now 14 years old and training with Arsenal, got the ball off the ground with a funky manoeuvre, unknown in my day, which is apparently called a 'round the world', then nonchalantly did 100 keep-ups in a confined space. Even though this upped the donation I'd pledged, I was delighted to see how she's progressed.

When Andy left BBC Sport a few years ago to set up his own company, our colleague Ian Finch made a fantastic farewell video to which we all contributed, including Lineker, Hansen and co. The soundtrack, inevitably, was provided by The Cure. Its title has taken on extra meaning in these strange times: 'In Between Days'.

Thursday, 21 May 2020

This horrible disease has finally impacted close to home. My cousin Peter sent a message yesterday evening to say that his dad has contracted COVID-19. Uncle Andrew is pushing 80 and, since suffering a serious stroke and then losing his wife, my Aunt Dorothy, has lived for more than a decade in a lovely care home in Bishop Auckland. I'm in no position to assess how the virus arrived at Sandringham House, but it won't have been through indifference from the staff. Suffice to say, Andrew is a gentleman, and indeed a gentle man, and despite his advanced years, is physically and mentally strong, and so far only displaying what's been described as a 'slight cough'.

Even in adversity, Andrew would try to find humour in the macho posturing of the three leaders whose countries still top those daily death toll charts we no longer see at UK press conferences. Trump says the US's number-one status is 'a badge of honour', Bolsonaro has instructed his third health minister in a month to advocate Trump's hydroxychlorine 'cure', and also on the podium and still undisputed European champion, Boris Johnson is trumpeting a 'world-beating track and trace system' which is on its way, honestly. That's the man who only last week claimed that international comparisons were inappropriate who's now using the phrase 'world-beating'.

All three of the aforementioned testosterone-fuelled populists seem to believe that if they say something bombastically enough, it becomes true by definition. To quote a passage I've just read in which Hilary Mantel describes an increasingly erratic Henry VIII, 'The King believes his caprice can alter reality.' The UK could only beat the world at tracking and testing if we can climb in Marty McFly's DeLorean and go back four months, put different people in charge, and somehow upstage South Korea and Germany. A functioning tracking and testing system at some point would suffice – my friend Georgia, who writes about Africa for a living, points out that far from wealthy Tunisia had its citizens install a COVID-19 app in March. There was one death there yesterday, taking their overall tally to 47. Here in the UK, to quote the poem Teesside's Harry Gallagher has posted this morning, 'Just another 363 dead today … hang out the flags … just an airliner jam-packed with everyone you know.'

Meanwhile, Jacob Rees-Mogg has announced that the civility of a remote Parliament is to end at the beginning of June. Not because it's safe to have 650 people descend on London from all over the country to cram into the benches, but rather because Johnson is floundering at PMQs without the usual braying and catcalling behind him. Oh, and the Liaison Committee – the only Commons committee allowed to summon the PM, and which he's swerved the last three times it has called on him to appear – has a new chair. Bernard Jenkin, a very right-wing ERG type, was handpicked by Johnson and duly installed. No scrutiny please, we're British. And the police have just decided that that Jennifer Arcuri business – public money handed over to the woman who gave Johnson 'technology lessons' in her flat – doesn't merit any more of their precious time. So, as so often with him, nothing to see here, everyone.

I've watched no TV whatsoever in the last day or so, but Amanda's friend Juliet pointed us towards yesterday's *More or Less* on Radio 4. The statisticians they interviewed calculated that a UK lockdown taking place even one week earlier (when Germany did it) would have prevented 75 per cent of our death toll. I suspect that analysis won't circulate far beyond our evidence-seeking echo chamber. Having logged on to BBC Sounds, I'm now working my way through some other R4 gems. Amanda and I loved *Down the Line*, the phone-in spoof Paul Whitehouse and co. made a while back, so we'll listen to their lockdown special together at some point. We listened to Graeme Garden's lovely tribute programme to Tim Brooke-Taylor, with contributions from everyone from Eric Idle to Sandi Toksvig, and I followed that up with *Great Lives* presented by Matthew Parris.

Despite working where I did, it's still strange when people I know well are invited on to august Radio 4 shows. Christina Lamb's *Desert Island Discs* was one such programme, and now there's Professor Anand Menon on *Great Lives*. And talking about Leeds United, too. As a Boro fan of a certain age and veteran of some, shall we say, lively visits to the away end at Elland Road, I have a default setting whenever they're mentioned. That Cure radio exercise bike session threw up Joy Division yesterday, so I found myself singing, 'Leeds, Leeds are falling apart again.' And yet even I softened slightly towards them, and Anand's choice, Billy Bremner, while listening to that show.

I knew Anand had some hairy experiences as a Yorkshireman of south-Asian descent in the 1970s and '80s, but had no idea how important Bremner had been in the life of Leeds's first black player Albert Johanneson in the 1960s. Not unlike the Beatles refusing to play to segregated audiences in the southern USA, Bremner's core values shone to the fore, as Johanneson's autobiography revealed. Later, as manager, Bremner pointedly bought two black players – Noel Blake and Vince Hilaire – who had previously been abused by the Leeds crowd, and also championed the supporters' anti-racism movement which helped to drive the National Front's influence out of Elland Road. While as captain, he may have epitomised the dogs of war approach which sometimes sullied a brilliant football team, I now have a far more rounded picture of Bremner the man. I still don't really want the modern Leeds to go up or ever win anything again, having said that.

Elsewhere in the online world, lockdown is still throwing up some musical bonuses. Baron Wood of Anfield is still channelling Ian Anderson. I haven't listened every day but I did catch episode 61, featuring one of my favourite Jethro Tull tracks, 'Cross Eyed Mary' and bloody good it was, too. Chrissie Hynde and guitarist James Walbourne have separately been recording their parts to a weekly Bob Dylan cover: true to form, a decent song, 'Standing in the Doorway' from 1997's *Time Out of Mind* has been raised to a whole other level. Meanwhile, the greatest of all Beatles solo albums, *All Things Must Pass*, by Dylan's old mucker George Harrison, has been raided by Sheryl Crow for a sublime housebound 'Beware of Darkness'. Susanna Hoffs and Matthew Sweet previously covered this wonderful song, which prompted me to learn it on the guitar. I was playing it on the patio after breakfast only this morning, and as seems to happen all too regularly at the moment, the lyrics have taken on even greater meaning in lockdown.

Watch out now, take care, beware of thoughts that linger
Winding up inside your head,
The hopelessness around you, in the dead of night,
Beware of sadness.
Watch out now, take care, beware of greedy leaders.
They take you where you should not go
While weeping Atlas Cedars, they just want to grow and grow
Beware of darkness.

Friday, 22 May 2020

'*Diagnostic tests which involve taking saliva and nasal samples from the same patient are being counted as two tests, not one.*'
– The Telegraph

A fortnight ago today, Amanda and I were tested for the virus at IKEA in Wembley. In a miracle to rival the Biblical loaves and fishes, it seems we managed to increase the government's tally by four. They missed a trick by not recalling us, as has happened to many others. Our household of two people could have counted as 8, 12, 16, anything you want, to get Matt Hancock to that 100,000 tests a day figure. I've even heard ministers claiming 100,000 people a day have been tested, but that hasn't happened once. They're now repeating the previous numerical con trick which counted a pair of protective gloves as two pieces of PPE. Of course, if they'd imposed lockdown just a week earlier, let alone a fortnight earlier when Amanda and I imposed it on ourselves … ah, what's the point?

Then again, that's what they're hoping will happen. The well-informed will say, 'Ah, what's the point?'; the rest just assume the funny blond man and his faceless mates are trying their best. That said, as with Trump and his 'inject disinfectant' theory, even the apolitical may spot the flaw in the exchange I've just seen posted from this morning's *BBC Breakfast*.

Naga Munchetty: 'Are you saying this government genuinely believes teachers are going to stop 10 to 15 five- and six-year-olds from touching each other?' Brandon Lewis, Northern Ireland Secretary: 'It's an opportunity for teachers to explain the importance of social distancing.'

Lewis doesn't have the accent of one who left all that child-rearing stuff to Nanny, but he's clearly unaware of how a reunited reception class will behave, both in the classroom and the playground. I've also listened to Lewis's contribution to Radio 4's *Today* in which he boldly told Nobel Prize-winning scientist Sir Paul Nurse that he was wrong on all matters scientific. It reminded me of a cartoon I once saw where an argument is accompanied by the caption, 'Let me interrupt your expertise with my confidence.'

The government has got two things right in the last 48 hours. It may have taken a great deal of political, journalistic and social media pressure to bring it about, but the families of NHS and care workers from overseas clearly should receive the same death in service benefits as everyone else. And yesterday, the healthcare surcharge for overseas workers was dropped for those same NHS and care families. In my opinion, Keir Starmer has adopted the right tone in response – he's welcomed the government's rethink, and chosen not to bray 'U-turn!' at them. This approach makes it a lot easier for the government – and Boris Johnson, in particular – to think again when they're going down the wrong path. We're going to need plenty of it in the coming weeks, notably in regard to the NHS app.

Away from politics, we listened to *Down the Line* – like Charlie Brooker's *Wipe*, the format can remain unchanged during lockdown – and there were several belly laughs. Phone-in host Gary Bellamy (played by Rhys Thomas) has taken time off during lockdown from his day job at Radio Wickford to dial in from his living room. His wife Melanie is 'self-isolating with her best friend Kieran' a couple of streets away, leaving him with their two screaming children. There followed the usual array of deluded and deadbeat callers, voiced by Paul Whitehouse and other *Fast Show* stalwarts, as well as Lucy Montgomery and Amelia Bullimore. Sadly, the great Felix Dexter has died since the last *Down the Line* was broadcast. First up, a posh woman sounding distraught: 'Every morning I open my laptop with dread and I just can't bear to see the hundreds of new ...poems,' while a West Countryman spoke of the new unity in his community where they're busy setting up roadblocks and booby traps. 'Don't bring your filthy London disease down 'ere!'

The Mirror and the Light is now gathering pace. The death of Jane Seymour has left Cromwell scouring Europe for Henry's fourth wife. Even though I know Anne of Cleves is going to be the fatal error which heralds Cromwell's decapitation, it's somehow still gripping. Hilary Mantel continues to slip in lines clearly intended as a dig at modern England. At one point the Duchesse de Longueville is considered a suitable match and one which will help build alliances with France. Negotiations with the French court break down quickly, however, when it's revealed that she's already promised to James V of Scotland.

The French ambassador and his entourage are then taunted in the streets by London vagabonds. The burning at the stake of Joan of Arc by the English the previous century is the natural basis of these gibes. Cromwell, a sophisticated Europhile, observes sadly, 'You would think they would find a fresher taunt.' 'Two World Wars and one World Cup' anyone? I'm rather hoping a thinly disguised Mark Francois will turn up in the remaining 350 pages to lament the King's next marriage to the German Anne of Cleves.

I accepted an invitation yesterday from an impressive young man called Tom at Brentford FC to take a virtual tour of their new ground. I've been going to Griffin Park regularly since I lived in nearby West Ealing in the late 1980s. Tall Paul and Matt from the Curry Club, who live in south-west London, joined me at the Bees' game with Dirty Leeds in February, and having looked at the pricing scheme, we all mused on buying season tickets for the new stadium. As at Spurs and Arsenal, there'll be a ticket exchange to sell your seat for any games you can't attend, but in Brentford's case that's around £20 a match, instead of £80-plus at the north London superstadia. Plus, the new ground is close to Gunnersbury station which is on the same line as Finchley Road and Frognal station, ten minutes' walk from here. I could leave the house at 2.15pm and still make kick-off.

The new ground looks fabulous, and they've kept the capacity down to 17,000 so it shouldn't become a Wigan or Sunderland (okay, Boro, too) and be half-empty and forlorn if they remain outside the Premier League. The entire project was supposedly financed by the building of 9,000 flats, but who knows where London property prices are headed now? On the football side, they'll accept a 25 per cent downpayment now for the season, but given that no one can say when crowds will be allowed back, they could find themselves refunding even that fraction of their projected revenue by this time next year.

Brentford have still sold most of the new stadium's capacity on that provisional basis, but you can't help but feel sorry for them. I'm pretty sure a number of Football League clubs must be on the brink of folding: unlike the Premier League with its colossal TV deal, staging matches behind closed doors will make them little money, and almost none outside the frequently televised Championship.

League Two has already terminated its season on that basis, though promotion and relegation may end up being settled in the courts. I now think the Premier League probably will return in June, a runaway train set in motion by training having resumed this week. Even so, some players haven't returned, notably Troy Deeney at Watford who has a young child with respiratory problems. Fortunately, Deeney is too popular in those parts for the supporters to turn on him and has a manager in Nigel Pearson, who despite his tough exterior, is enough of a thinker to respect that decision. Pearson has publicly despaired of both Johnson and Brexit, so that seals that assessment for me.

For the Premier League, and those cabinet ministers who have an inkling of what football represents to much of our electorate, the pressure is now on with the Bundesliga having restarted and Serie A seemingly soon to follow. The terrifying implications of having to refund global TV money will also concentrate minds. I still don't trust this country not to balls it up somehow, especially with an infection and death rate currently so much higher than every other European nation. The return of *Match of the Day* proper will take this journal full circle, so from a selfish point of view it would provide a neat, though possibly temporary, end point. I suspect I'll find myself beginning volume two to chronicle a second viral wave and reimposed lockdown later this year.

WEEK ELEVEN

Saturday, 23 May 2020

In those elusive, precedented times, this would have been FA Cup Final day. Instead, the only contest in town is, once more, Dominic Cummings versus all established norms. And he'll probably end up doing a lap of honour with the trophy by 5pm, as Sweet FA happens to him once again.

I'm not going to go into all the details even here, dear reader, but several weeks ago, I was made aware of chatter in the north-east that Cummings had been seen (by a friend of a friend of mine, among others) at his parents' place in Durham during his period of supposed self-isolation. One or two newspapers were looking into it, but needed more verification before they'd publish. I had a trawl around Twitter, picked out a few mentions which sounded like more than just hearsay, including a chap who claimed to have contacted the police, sent them on and thought little more about it. Anyway, the friend in question has connections at the *Daily Mirror* and *Guardian* and, after several weeks of investigation, they have managed to make it stick. I've no idea whether I contributed slightly, or not at all, but I've had a 'thank you' message and they all have my full support either way.

As I write, Cummings's side of the story has only been told in two tweets from the BBC's Laura Kuenssberg. The first of those was a direct rebuttal to a fellow journalist, Pippa Crerar of the *Daily Mirror*, who had posted a link to her paper's story. Laura's 'source' – Dom himself, one assumes – wants us to know that 'the trip was within guidelines. Went to stay with his parents so they could help with childcare while he and his wife were ill – they insist no breach of lockdown.' On the contrary, it clearly was a breach in anyone's language. The government had passed emergency legislation telling those infected to stay at home, with a fine as the penalty for not doing so. Instead, Dom put his four-year-old in a car with two potentially infected adults, and drove 264 miles (petrol? loo break?) to dump the child on his elderly parents.

This morning, he'd remembered some different details, so his conduit Laura passed those on, too: 'Sources close to Cummings say … seems it was his sister who had offered to help with childcare … family stayed in separate house.' By way of balance, Laura has tweeted some dissenting quotes from Labour, and unsourced harrumphing from Tory backbenchers.

I watched the BBC's *News at Ten* last night, breaking my usual rules. What was the main story for Sky and ITV and indeed *Newsnight*, wasn't mentioned in the headlines and was squeezed in for 50 seconds at ten past ten. Laura wasn't on duty, other than as Dom's Twitter messenger, so a reporter I hadn't seen before, Leila Nathoo, gave a decent short summary of the allegations, balanced with Laura's tweet which she read off a sheet of paper. Leila raised the precedent of the Chief Medical Adviser for Scotland who resigned for visiting her second home, while not infected and not in contact with anyone.

Even more tellingly, she referred to Professor Neil Ferguson from Imperial College, who after spending 14 days in isolation having contracted the virus, allowed a visitor into his home. Laura Kuenssberg had been all over that one – 'that's a hell of a story' was her one-line response on Twitter to that scoop. A feeding frenzy encircled the professor – Matt Hancock declared himself speechless, and suggested the police get involved – and Ferguson duly resigned from SAGE. It will be interesting to see whether Hancock is as outraged now it's one of the two most important men in his government who has driven a coach and horses through the guidelines and regulations most of the rest of us have tried to follow.

Those with good memories may recall my exchange with Sarah Sands, editor of *Today*, after Mary Wakefield – Cummings's wife and deputy editor of *The Spectator* – was given a chunk of Radio 4 airtime to read out her treacly account of 'extremely kind man' Dom, and his brush with death during his 'London lockdown'. 'Was he fighting off the bug or heading for the ventilator?' she asked, Mills and Boon-style. Neither, as it turns out – he was dancing to Abba in his parents' garden in Durham. With the son who, in Wakefield's parallel universe, had put on his doctor's uniform to bring hot Ribena to the London bedside of his stricken father.

Having been unable to visit my mother on her 80th birthday last week, I've taken this 'one rule for us' hypocritical disgrace rather badly, as you can probably tell. I'm not alone it seems. My entirely level-headed and reasonable friend Mel has posted the following this morning: 'I've followed every lockdown rule to the letter, I've been living on my own for nine weeks. Today I honestly think, fuck it. Try fining me £1k. I'll offer Cummings as my defence. Whatever I do will be entirely essential for me.'

Or you can listen to Michael Gove on Twitter: 'Caring for your wife and child is not a crime.' This will be the same Michael Gove whose government issued the following guidelines, which became emergency law on 26 March: 'If you or someone you live with has symptoms of coronavirus: do not leave your home for any reason. Order food or medicine online or by phone. Do not have visitors in your home.'

Friday, 27 March was the day brave Sir Dom was filmed bravely running away along Downing Street. He was first sighted in Durham on 31 March. Gove, Johnson and Cummings all made up their own laws and rules to push through Brexit and their current majority: it's their default setting, even when thousands of lives are at stake. Cummings's career appears to be more important to them than the viability of their already creaking lockdown strategy, and ultimately the death toll. And, of course, Parliament has entered a two-week recess, so they'll try to ride this out without opposition scrutiny or any murmurings among their own backbenchers.

Even the civil service has now been roped in: the official Downing Street account has, as I write, published a full description of the extraordinary lengths to which this 'extremely kind' man (according to his wife) went to, in order to endanger his extended family as well as the little people at motorway service stations, sorry, act 'in line with coronavirus guidelines'. Unfortunately, the statement's claim that 'at no stage was he or his family spoken to by the police' is directly contradicted by yesterday's Durham Constabulary statement that 'officers made contact with the owners of that address'. Still, it's not difficult to add the police to the judges, civil service, BBC, Tory rebels, EU, metropolitan elite, Electoral Commission and non-patsy journalists to Classic Dom's list of enemies who must be destroyed.

Oh, and here comes Matt Hancock. Not at all speechless this time: it was 'entirely right for Dom Cummings to find childcare for his toddler'. Childcare a 264-mile drive away? As Dr Rachel Clarke replied, 'In the midst of a pandemic – with the death toll exceeding 55k already – the health secretary and Prime Minister have chosen to tear up vital public health messaging in order to save Dominic Cummings.' It's probably why they recently dropped Dom's slogan 'Stay (at) Home', come to think of it. The malign, grotesque career of one man – not even our official, elected leader – is more important to every single one of these weasels than the lives of any number of members of the public. At least we know where we stand now, if we hadn't worked it out before.

Even Rishi Sunak has now parroted the 'taking care of his wife and child is justifiable and reasonable' horseshit on Twitter. I thought he was the one minister emerging from this crisis with any credit, but he's blown it now as far as I'm concerned. Once a Winchester Head Boy with 12 homes, married to one of India's richest heiresses, always … The mandated message from all of them is effectively, 'If you proles cared about your families like we do, you'd have broken all our rules, too.' Clearly, I was a mug for not going down to visit my mother 30 miles away on her 80th birthday five days after I tested negative. I thought that was a tough, responsible decision, but doubtless Cummings and his eugenicist friends would see me as a genetically inferior member of the herd. Like those Grenfell residents who followed instructions, rather than Jacob Rees-Mogg's version of 'common sense', and perished in their homes as a result.

The overwhelming sentiment – among my friends and contacts at least, most people probably won't even have noticed – is bitter, sardonic mockery, with a worrying overtone of openly saying that there's no point following any of the rules any more. So far today, I've seen 'Lockdown's dull, Hope I get COVID so I can go and stay with my parents.' 'Let's go and ransack Tesco's. Gove says it's no crime to look after your wife and kids,' and 'If the Yorkshire Ripper had gone to Eton, he'd have been let off for trying to build Britain's herd immunity to hammers.'

Laura Kuenssberg has forfeited much of her remaining support, including from Philip Pullman who has previously defended her. Some sample Twitter lines: 'The simplest solution would have been to get Laura Kuenssberg to babysit the source's child', and 'Sources close to Laura Kuenssberg are confirming that sources close to Dominic Cummings have confirmed that she is not resigning.' That last one may well be what will happen. By the time Parliament reconvenes in a fortnight, Rees-Mogg will presumably have filled the backbenches with toffs braying for Bozza, the Number 10 source will (unlike Prof. Ferguson) be sitting on SAGE and briefing Laura as usual, and everyone will have forgotten any of this ever happened.

Well, that was a tiring, but partially cathartic, exercise. I don't have much more to say, except on what should have been FA Cup Final day, I've cast my mind back to a documentary I made with Tony Pastor, whose company is now co-producing those lockdown *MOTD*s, and Graham who's on my distribution list. When the BBC temporarily lost the FA Cup contract, we marked our last final – that Boro debacle of 1997 – with a lovingly made 90 minutes called the *Essential FA Cup Final*, which was shown the previous evening. We interviewed dozens of cup winners and losers from George Mutch, scorer of 1938's winning penalty right through to modern greats.

Somewhere in between was Billy Bremner. His one winner's medal (he lifted the trophy in 1972) and three losers' medals had recently been stolen in a burglary, but he spoke movingly about what a lucky man he'd been and the memories which 'no one can take away'. The footage of him going up to the Royal Box in 1973, after that wildly unlikely defeat by Second Division Sunderland, shows him smiling graciously. Billy died at the age of just 54, later in 1997, the year our documentary was shown. His statue is Elland Road's focal point to this day.

Indeed, the more I hear about him, the more I'm glad my friend Anand alerted me to Bremner's non-footballing qualities in that *Great Lives* programme. My old boss Niall replied to last week's instalment of this journal with the following anecdote from his time as an assistant producer on *Football Focus* in the 1980s. Tony Gubba and Niall went to make a feature with Billy when he was the manager of Doncaster Rovers.

'He was utterly charming and helpful. At the end of the interview he asked, "Is there a fee for this?" I thought, "Here we go again, just bloody typical." I replied, "Yes, £50," and he immediately said, "Don't send it to me, could you please send it to the Doncaster branch of Mencap?"

'No footballer (pre- or post-) ever did that and that's why I remember Bremner as a lovely man as well as a world-class footballer.'

With Niall's permission, I thought that was a tale worth retelling. Memo to self: try to be more like Billy Bremner and not at all like Dominic Cummings. That motto would also allow me to try to hack Cummings and his team of scumbags down – verbally, for now – whenever the opportunity arises. But let's face it, Johnson isn't ever going to sack him. That would be like Orville sacking Keith Harris.

Sunday, 24 May 2020

I'd like to level with you this morning. When I billed this as a London lockdown diary, I may have been a tad economical with the vérité. I've actually spent the last ten weeks motoring up and down to the north-east, visiting my extended family and sampling a variety of beauty spots from Barnard Castle to my in-laws' castle in Northumberland. I've been stimulating the local economy in the process, and by coughing liberally over the proles I've encountered, helped to push the spread of the virus across the region. When I first arrived in late March, it lagged way behind that there London (where I'm obliged to live in an Islington townhouse with a tapestry room, despite my loathing for the metropolitan elite) but now the north-east's boroughs proudly fill the top four places in the national league table. That never happens in that soccerball thing the locals seem to enjoy so much, so I hope they're grateful for my helping to put them on the map.

Not really. I'm still here in Belsize Park, and haven't left the capital since I went to Reading on 19 March, four days before lockdown was imposed. It now appears, according to the *Mirror*'s eyewitness, retired chemistry teacher Robin Lees, that Cummings went for an outing to Barnard Castle during that first infected trip north where he supposedly never left that separate house on his parents' premises. According to both the *Mirror* and *Observer*, Cummings made a second trip to the north-east in mid-April, after he'd returned to work in London, was allegedly seen admiring the bluebells in Houghall Woods and, according to at least one local, even managed a side trip to the in-laws' castle and then up to Alnwick in Northumberland. This may or may not stand up, and potential witnesses are doubtless fearful of the kind of reprisals which forced Johnson's Camberwell neighbours to go into hiding.

I really hope the damage is now done. For the first time since I last felt the tide might be turning – that is, last autumn, before Jeremy Corbyn and Jo Swinson lost their minds and gave Johnson and Cummings the escape route of a general election – I've watched both Sunday politics shows. I'm still leaning towards thinking Johnson isn't going to unplug his Gollum-shaped life support machine, but he's going to struggle to get much else done while this carries on.

I thought Piers Morgan becoming a voice of reason was the most bizarre transformation this crisis could produce. I was wrong. On Sky News's *Sophy Ridge on Sunday*, a man I'd previously regarded with despair – ERG stalwart and ex-junior Brexit minister, Steve Baker MP – said everything I've ever thought about Dominic Cummings. It was like sitting down for lunch with an insider who confirms everything you've suspected about someone you've watched from a distance. Some sample lines: 'Sneering' Cummings is 'burning the PM's capital;' 'Ministers serve at Dominic's pleasure;' 'The only politician he respects is Michael Gove.' Baker acknowledged that Cummings's 'slogans' worked in the 'guerrilla warfare' of Brexit and gaining a majority, but he admitted to profound discomfort with Cummings's 'winning at any costs' mentality, citing the red NHS bus and the 'Turks are coming' posters.

Baker concluded – rightly, in our eyes and those of everyone we've been in touch with in the last 24 hours – that Cummings's round trip north (plus excursions) has made the 'lockdown laws unenforceable', and that he has to go. He even cited one of my favourite quotations, which I used about my own departure from *Match of the Day*; Napoleon's 'The graveyard is full of indispensable men.'

Another unlikely outcome of recent events is that we've ended up feeling a scintilla of sympathy for Grant Shapps and his various other personas. Grant/Michael Green/Sebastian Fox was supposed to be unveiling road improvements worth £280m, both at yesterday's press conference and on this morning's politics shows. Instead, he's faced question after question about Cummings, and found himself saying that the lockdown laws were only guidelines to interpret as you see fit (in which case they've just ceased to function) then implied that Durham police and the eyewitnesses the *Mirror* and *Observer* have found were all mistaken.

Okay, so those are craven, desperate responses, but they put him off his stride so much that he missed an obvious retort: the widening of the A66 he'd wanted to trumpet would have allowed Cummings to cut a good half an hour off that essential round trip from Durham to Barnard Castle. That has to be a good use of 80 per cent of a day's worth of the money the side of Dom's red bus said we'll be getting back from the EU. Sorry, that's going to the NHS, isn't it? Silly me.

Elsewhere on *Ridge*, two people who, in normal times, represent extreme and entrenched viewpoints with which I'd have little sympathy – the DUP's Arlene Foster and Sinn Fein's Michelle O'Neill – sat down to a socially distanced interview at Stormont, and talked like a pair of adults about how they're working together to save as many lives as possible in Northern Ireland. We've been here before, of course, with Ian Paisley and Martin McGuiness, but it's come to something when you look on admiringly as two people like that put aside their differences in a grave crisis, talking honestly about mistakes made, lessons learnt and common humanity.

Churchill and Attlee managed to do likewise the last time England was in this much of a mess, and you could imagine Sunak and Starmer, for example, working together in a crisis. It was impossible, though, during Corbyn's reign, as I suspect it will be for as long as Johnson, and particularly Cummings, are still on the scene. As Steve Baker seems to have confirmed today, Cummings will always pick a fight in an empty room. His nasal sneering at the press pack yesterday – 'I don't care how it looks,' he told the nation – will have done much to harden media and backbench hostility towards him, and made a couple of mild-mannered friends of mine separately say they wanted to climb inside the TV and punch his lights out. In any case, Baker confirmed that Cummings would much rather Gove was his PM, but has presumably been forced to recognise that obvious 'freaks and misfits' don't win elections. The man who somehow did win a referendum and general election (thanks again, Jezza) now needs to recognise that however useless he is on his own, Cummings's toxicity currently leaves him unable to govern.

As I type, dear old Andrew Marr has roped Grant/Michael/Sebastian into as a big tangle as Sophy did earlier. If he doesn't text Johnson immediately after he's off the air to say 'fuck this for a game of soldiers, you're not putting me through that again', he has even less about him than I thought. To quote a memorable Woody Allen line about an ageing roué, 'A haircut masquerading as a man.' Show some backbone, haircut. He's now wittering on about keeping the R below one, to which Marr has not unreasonably asked how that's going to happen if there's now a 'Cummings clause' in the lockdown legislation. This government has to choose between that R (reproduction rate) and Cummings. And the answer needs to be: Rs over Tit.

The last 24 hours have mostly been consumed with playing my own small part in stirring up as much social media heat as possible, passing on ideas for follow-ups, and generally relishing the misfortune of the man I dislike right now more than anyone else on the planet. I'm not proud of feeling that way at my age – and it may not be all that healthy – but I'm afraid it's true.

In the brief time I spent away from following this story, we did manage a couple of virtual link-ups yesterday: one was with Philip who's running BBC Sport from isolation, and he explained the extraordinary work which has gone into making studios, and potentially outside broadcasts, into socially distanced and safe environments. Regardless of some of my misgivings about aspects of BBC News's coverage, BBC Sport has conjured proverbial rabbits out of top hats throughout lockdown.

We also spoke to my first, and to be honest only, previous serious girlfriend (of 30 years ago), Liz, and her partner Dan. They met in Hong Kong, after Liz escaped City law firm Linklaters and now live with their two kids in Switzerland, where Liz works at the UNHCR in Geneva. The four of us had a lovely, and lively, chat as we always do when we get together: Dan worked at UEFA at one point and managed to get Amanda and me into Boro's European final in Eindhoven among other games, and he and I went together to see Stewart Lee insult Brexity Ipswich with some gusto from the stage of the Regent Theatre a couple of years ago. Liz, her ex-flatmate (and my ex-BBC colleague) Margaret had lunch together in December, and we've met up as a foursome and its various permutations throughout the quarter of a century and more that Amanda and I have been together.

Refugee issues never subside, and if anything have become more acute under the pandemic, so Liz has been working flat out, albeit remotely. It sounds like the COVID-19 situation is under control in Switzerland, though: 18 new cases yesterday and just two deaths. Our respective tolls were 2,959 and 282 yesterday. We're just getting used to it, but I've been on Worldometers and added up the totals for all the other western European countries for yesterday and all of them in aggregate don't match our daily figure, for just the one sad country. Liz hasn't lived in the UK since 1992, and although she and Dan are too kind to say so, if it wasn't for their families, I'm not sure they'd visit at all. They still care about the place, though, and are better informed about it than 99 per cent of the people who actually live here.

Finally, some unequivocally good news from the north-east, which – tempting though it is – I'm not going to sully with any further mention of the region's most notorious recent visitor. My cousin Peter's daughter, Becca, reposted a new Facebook entry from the Sandringham Care Home in Bishop Auckland. A smiling Uncle Andrew was holding up a sign saying, 'Missing my family very much. I hope everyone is safe. I'm doing well and causing havoc as usual!' Better sign off, I seem to have something in my eye.

4.40pm update

It looks like Johnson simply cannot survive without Cummings – or possibly, is terrified of any kompromat he might have on him – and is about to announce as much at the 5pm press conference. I'm afraid I've been less than stable this afternoon, and have felt physically ill following this shitshow today. I can no longer face being as well-informed as I've needed to be these last ten weeks.

This country is in absolute ruins, and try as I might, neither I nor anyone else I know can do anything about it.

I need to look after my mental health right now, and give Amanda a break. I may be back at some point if and when I feel able. Until then, thanks for your support and especially friendship, which will endure long after these awful people and times are a distant memory, and for bearing with me. Stay safe. X

Postscript

Sunday, 21 June 2020

I intended to finish this journal with the return of *Match of the Day* proper. I didn't anticipate taking a four-week break first, but there we are. The longest day of the year in what feels like the longest year of our lives has arrived, but at least football is back. The return of Saturday night *MOTD* Premier League highlights was preceded last night by the BBC's first live top-flight game since 1988. With 92 games to be broadcast before the season ends, the BBC has been given some to cover, along with the contracted live broadcasters at Sky, BT and Amazon.

I joined BBC Sport in 1989, so never worked on a live top-flight game, but the son of the man who kindly wrote my foreword made a small piece of history last night to help round the book off. Andrew Clement directed Bournemouth versus Crystal Palace on BBC One, and all went smoothly. Gary Lineker's opening caught the tone perfectly in the spirit of the old line that 'football is the most important of all the unimportant things', and he, Shearer and Wright in the studio, along with Alex Scott in the ground and some excellent videotape sequences, shared poignant pre-match reflections on the events of the 105 days since the show was last on the air. Of which, more later.

The Championship also resumed this weekend. I have a pass to watch relegation-threatened Boro's remaining nine games online, but by the time I'd made the app work on my iPad, late in the first half, they were already 3-0 down at home to Swansea. The only upside of being in the third tier for just the third season in our history would be away days at places like Shrewsbury and Accrington, but going to games probably won't be happening any time soon. Tees-Wear derbies in League One behind closed doors, just as the region's jobs and cynically exploited hopes start to disappear, would be a new low. About the only positive Middlesbrough-related news I can offer is that my emergency attempts to cut Amanda's hair have left it shaped rather like that of our Danish striker of the late 1990s, Mikkel Beck. He always was the prettiest Boro player of the Riverside era, just edging out Phil Stamp and David Wheater.

In retrospect, I think I chose the right time to bow out of my daily Pepys Show. Thanks to the government removing international comparisons from the daily media conference, it's largely gone unnoticed, but the downward slope of the UK's statistics has remained glacially slow, and completely out of kilter with those for the similar-sized European nations. We registered 129 COVID-19 deaths and 1,300 new cases in the 24-hour period announced yesterday afternoon, figures which scarcely merit a mention any more. No other western European nation has registered a three-figure daily death toll or a four-figure new cases tally in the whole of June, but other than those of us who log on to Worldometers every day, pretty much no one knows that or, it seems, realises just how lamentably we're still performing as a country.

The day after I withdrew my co-operation from my journal, and went for a lie down in a darkened room, Dominic Cummings held a surreal media conference in which he claimed his family's day trip to Barnard Castle was merely his way of testing his eyesight before driving back to London. He also managed not to shout or swear for 90 minutes and just about concealed his contempt for the assembled media and wider masses. A by-product, not lost on me after my correspondence with the editor of Radio 4's *Today*, was that Mary Wakefield's lachrymose account of 'extremely kind' Dom's brush with death in London was now not only nauseating, but shown to be an absolute crock from start to finish. No wonder she needed us all to know how hard she'd been praying. It takes some effort to write the most unbelievable article *The Spectator* has run this year, or possibly ever, but the deputy editor has managed it.

Rather like Trump and the disinfectant lunacy, actual common sense – not the mythical British version Johnson had been citing – led many erstwhile supporters of the regime to find the eyesight story ludicrous and therefore to question much of what they'd been told to date. And, like Trump, our government has registered a negative approval rating for its handling of the crisis ever since. Unlike Trump, they don't have to face the electorate for a long time, but even so, I'll be amazed if it's Johnson who does so. His failure to discipline Cummings for riding a wagon train through the government's COVID-19 regulations has proved once and for all that he's Orville to Cummings's Keith Harris. Or Lord Charles to Ray Alan, for older readers. Their entire virus strategy effectively collapsed at that point: the abandonment of social distancing was tangible around here, not least on an unnerving visit I made soon afterwards to our greengrocer. Elsewhere, the beaches were rammed and unofficial raves mobbed as people decided for themselves that they'd been played for mugs for three months by those in charge.

Then the ripple effect of a horrendous event across the Atlantic exacerbated an already fraught situation. George Floyd, a 46-year-old African-American man, was killed (I was going to say 'murdered' but that presupposes the verdict of a jury in a country where some very strange things have happened over the years) by a Minneapolis police officer, Derek Chauvin. Floyd's death, recorded on video, resulted from Chauvin kneeling on his neck for almost nine minutes despite the victim's repeated cries of 'I can't breathe'. The collective memory of centuries of similar racial injustices led to protests, some civil unrest and the possibly the crassest act in the history of the US presidency. Trump had riot police clear a path, with tear gas and flailing batons, through a peaceful protest outside a church close to the White House, to create a photo opportunity of him holding a Bible aloft outside the church. If that didn't alienate at least some of his religious supporters and, along with his abysmal handling of the pandemic, cost him the November election, then I really do give up.

The reaction in the UK was swift, too. Though this particular outrage took place thousands of miles away, it resonated in our own, often unequal, society. As Gary Lineker said, we're unsure, as appalled white middle-aged onlookers, as to exactly what we should do or say, but we all need to be educated about our past and, sadly, present. I saw some crass posts, even from well-meaning people on social media, and some distinctly dodgy ones from the less well-meaning. I posted something to the effect of saying 'All Lives Matter' is like interrupting Martin Luther King to tell him about your dream from last night, and argued with one or two extraordinarily ignorant posters on our local Next Door neighbourhood website, to the point where I eventually deactivated my account. I quite like knowing which shops are open at what times, and whether anyone can recommend a plumber, but not at that price.

The Black Lives Matter rallies were powerful, if tinged for some broadly supportive observers with a little anxiety about the inherent limits to social distancing when large crowds assemble during a pandemic. Premier League football returned with a united statement from the players who all wore Black Lives Matter instead of the names on their shirts, and 'took the knee' at kick-off, in each of the first round of games. No one can freeze out every player in the Premier League for making a statement, in the way that Colin Kaepernick was in the NFL just three years earlier. Sky, BT, and the BBC team, in an outstanding opening segment of the first live *MOTD,* were all unequivocal in their support for the campaign, and their desire to discuss, spotlight and understand the underlying issues. We always tried to handle societal issues sensitively when I worked there, but this went much further and deeper and sent out a forceful message.

I suspect most people outside Bristol learnt something when the statue of slave trader Edward Colston was toppled a fortnight ago. I'd heard of the Colston Hall, but had no idea about the man or the long-standing hurt caused by the immortalisation of him close to Bristol harbour. You can argue that such statues should be removed in a less drastic way – possibly into a museum with a contextual explanation attached. Then you read about the insensitive blocking tactics by some – chief among them, Richard Eddy, a stripey-tied, worryingly young-looking, Conservative Bristol councillor who once posed for publicity shots with a golliwog – and you begin to understand why Colston's statue ended up in the harbour.

Sadly, that incident, and an idiot attaching themselves to a huge Black Lives Matter march in London, then spraying 'racist' on Winston Churchill's statue in Parliament Square, led to the government's most reckless attempt at a dead cat distraction yet. Rachel Sylvester of *The Times* reported last autumn that Dominic Cummings was running focus groups to examine the potential exploitation of 'culture war' issues. With tabloid sales on the wane, and young people generally more relaxed about sexual orientation, gender and racial equality than previous generations, most isms of the past will no longer automatically enjoy majority support when whipped up. According to Sylvester, Classic Dom had identified transgender rights as an area where public attitudes, especially in former 'Red Wall' areas in the north, were out of step with the metropolitan elite he watches with such loathing from the tapestry room window in his Islington townhouse. And hey presto, the *Sunday Times*'s main headline a week ago today read 'PM scraps plan to make gender change easier'.

In another attempt to move away from shaky ground – the pandemic, racism ('picaninnies with watermelon smiles' is not a line you should repeat right now, Bozza) – Johnson had spent the previous week banging on about Churchill. Someone had written something nasty on the plinth of the statue of his hero and Dom's focus groups presumably suggested that pretending there was a sinister plot to have the statue removed would play well with the great unwashed. Several newspapers led with little else all week and Saturday's *Mail* front page screamed 'Set Our Greatest Hero Free' alongside a picture of a protective box which had been put up around Winston in anticipation of trouble on Saturday. Gandhi and Nelson Mandela had been given similar treatment, but somehow that wasn't mentioned anywhere. The reason for the latter precautionary steps is that Tommy Robinson, Britain First and the Democratic Football Lads' Alliance had all answered the prime ministerial whistle and were planning to come to heel to 'protect our statues'.

In the end, 'Robinson' (real name: Stephen Yaxley-Lennon) didn't show, presumably having remembered whatever suspended sentences and probation he's still serving in a long list of criminal convictions, but the self-styled DFLA did. In true *Life of Brian* style, they are a breakaway splinter group who fell out with the original Football Lads' Alliance. I did start to read an account of the parting of the ways, but life's too short. I'm going to hazard a guess that they're about as democratic as the Korean People's Democratic Republic and whichever Kim currently has Trump reaching for his Kim wipes. Britain First and others also rallied to the cause to form a ragbag of what looked for all the world like the middle-aged remnants of the bad old days on the terraces. Cummings, Johnson and his fellow Etonian Geordie Greig of the *Mail* weren't at state school in the 1970s and '80s, nor did they attend gigs, football matches and ropey pubs back then, so they probably haven't met these particular men in the street.

What ensued was entirely predictable to me, the Poncey Horse Club and many other friends. I don't think we foresaw our finest patriots spitting on female picnickers in Hyde Park, or urinating next to a memorial to a police victim of terrorism, but it was never going to be pretty. With no one to fight, and no plastic furniture to hurl around a Continental town square this summer, the tattooed, pot-bellied worst of England attacked the police instead. Of course they did. So, if you put up a handful of lawbreakers from a large legitimate protest versus pretty much everyone taking part in a bovver boys' nostalgic pond-life parade, this incarnation of the culture wars ended in a nil-nil draw. Let's hope it doesn't go to a replay.

As ever, the statues fiasco prompted some dark humour. It was obvious from the photos and clips online that one of the guys standing next to a 'Britian First' (sic) banner in a bra, and with a very obvious piss stain on his bright green shorts, was the same topless man in green shorts who later kicked a policeman in the back close to Westminster Tube station. So, the identification and arrest of Daniel John Allan from Sunderland was not a case for Poirot. A round trip of Cummings proportions, enough beer to make him incontinent and an assault on a policeman in front of the cameras. It just needed another defeat at Wembley (they lost there twice in 2019) for the perfect Mackem day out. What is less funny is his criminal record of 110 convictions, including one for threatening to take two children hostage during a burglary. Still, as Trump (or was it Priti Patel?) said, 'There were a lot of good people on both sides.'

The sight of a handful of the dimmest of Geordies trying to punch police horses at a gathering to 'protect' Grey's monument in Newcastle also allowed one or two of us Teessiders to snigger on social media. Firstly, the statue stands 135 feet above the city streets, so no one was going to push it over, and secondly Grey was Prime Minister when the British Empire abolished slavery, so is not an obvious BLM target to rival Colston. Those who can read had presumably seen a rumour in the *Daily Express* that bonkers Brussels was about to ban Earl Grey tea. Then there was the frankly hilarious sight of a ragbag of tubby bulldog patriots clutching beer cans as they 'protected' George Eliot's statue in Nuneaton. 'Nuneaton' clearly wasn't a reference to how many pies they'd consumed en route, but imagine the outrage when they discovered that George was in drag. David Llewellyn offered the following caption on Twitter: '"Middlemarch" is the greatest novel of the 19th century, charting the monumental shift from agrarian to industrial England and the intellectual sea changes of the Romantic era, and if any Bronte Boys come around here saying different, they'll be shitting teeth for a month.'

A few days later there was another attempt at dog-whistling or the 'War on Woke' to use the ghastly expression apparently doing the rounds among Dom's posse in Whitehall. However, the announced merger of the Department for International Development with the Foreign Office, and implied threat to the UK's overseas aid budget, was completely overshadowed by a 22-year-old Premier League footballer. Matt Hancock had, somewhat desperately, rounded on professional footballers a few weeks earlier for supposedly not pulling their weight. As the most prominent of the leading players who have been doing all manner of good deeds away from the spotlight, Marcus Rashford of Manchester United and England provided the perfect response.

Having partnered with a food distribution charity during lockdown to ensure that three million disadvantaged children in the north-west were fed while their free school meals were unavailable, Rashford sent an eloquent and heartfelt letter to all MPs asking the government to provide those meals nationally throughout the summer. While the Scottish, Welsh and Northern Irish governments signed up, the English government initially refused. As has happened repeatedly of late, ministers were sent out to defend the indefensible – poor old Grant Shapps found himself claiming on ITV that we faced a straight choice between funding cancer treatment and feeding vulnerable children – before there was another hasty U-turn from a shambolic regime.

At least that's how I saw it, and so have a number of commentators who are to the right of me politically. Ex-

Conservative MP Matthew Parris wrote the following of Boris Johnson in *The Times* last week: 'This is not a time when his skills as a self-parodying light entertainer are called for. Sadly, though, he doesn't have any other skills. He broke into Downing Street by clambering up a drainpipe called Brexit.' A Brexiteer journalist, Tim Montgomerie, formerly close to Johnson, wrote of his despair this week, saying that all alternative thinking is terminated in Downing Street as soon as someone says, 'There's no way that Dom would wear that.' I know I may seem mildly obsessed with Cummings, but given the history of the row he had with Nick Clegg over free school meals when he was Michael Gove's Education SPAD, and Johnson's claim that he'd been unaware of Marcus Rashford's hugely publicised campaign until the morning before the U-turn, I would strongly suspect that Classic Dom decided unilaterally that he wasn't going to allow a mere footballer to tell him to feed the kids of the poor and struggling.

The Cummings factor – and the pitiful echo chamber cabinet he constructed to rubber stamp whatever form of Brexit he decrees 17.4 million people wanted – has been central to most of the informed discussions I've heard. The *Today* edition on Thursday morning spoke to two political journalists from traditionally right-wing publications: the long-standing Johnson sceptic Rachel Sylvester of *The Times* and James Forsyth, the political editor of *The Spectator*, and a *Sun* columnist. Both agreed that the Prime Minister is being appallingly served both by his advisers and a low-calibre cabinet of 'nodding dogs'. Rachel Sylvester claimed that while many Tory backbenchers 'despaired' of Theresa May, they now 'despise' Johnson. An interesting question was also raised about the so-called 'Red Wall' new intake of Conservative MPs for places like Bishop Auckland, Workington and Redcar. Will they toe the party line or, like members of the US Congress, try to appease constituents who lent them their vote because of Brexit, and may be increasingly prone to buyer's remorse?

Then there's Laura Kuenssberg. As I proofread the main body of this book, I wondered if I'd been slightly harsh on the BBC's chief political correspondent. Then I read her BBC website blog the morning after the Rashford U-turn. 'Most of us change our minds all the time,' she gushed. 'Maybe this morning you had planned to go for a run, then actually when push came to shove another ten minutes in bed seemed a better idea. Maybe when you grew up you wanted to be an astronaut but then discovered you weren't that good at physics.' As Amanda said, portraying the PM as a child who wanted to be an astronaut may not be as innocuous as Laura thinks it is, and she did eventually conclude rather weedily, 'Too many U-turns and governments can end up going round and round in circles.'

There was no mention in the whole blog, though, of the moral dimension of choosing to feed or not to feed under-privileged children (not quite the same toss of a coin as staying in bed or going for a run) and certainly no mention of Cummings, individual ministers or the growing backbench fury other Westminster watchers are describing. I genuinely don't know whether Laura is too reliant on Cummings, too lightweight to see the deeper issues or has been told to go gently on a government at a time of pandemic, but the net result simply isn't good enough. It's impossible to imagine predecessors like John Cole, or Nick Robinson who chaired that *Today* segment, or current counterparts like Beth Rigby of Sky News writing such a powder puff, non-committal piece during as grave a crisis of governance as we've known.

An official COVID-19 death toll of 42,000, economic collapse on the way, all mass foreign travel off the agenda for the foreseeable future but there are mutterings in government circles of a new royal yacht to 'boost public morale'. In the meantime, Sky News are reporting that a military aircraft is being painted with a giant Union Jack for Boris Johnson's official travel, at a cost of £900,000 from the public purse. Prime Minister Austin Powers will be signing glorious trade deal after trade deal for Global Britain every time he steps down from Air Farce One. And we might as well make the most of our flag before we have to remove the cross of St Andrew. It's almost as if this government is trying to troll the public.

Still, all that totemic twaddle has kept everyone's mind off the pandemic for a while, which was a result of sorts for the government. They quietly admitted on Wednesday that the once vital track and trace app, designed by Vote Leave's data wonks and trialled on the Isle of Wight, had disappeared until winter at the earliest. By Thursday, they'd abandoned the app entirely and will now approach the rank amateurs at Google and Apple with a view to acquiring theirs. If someone who knows very little about technology (me) but had read what more qualified friends were saying, wrote on 5 May, 'I honestly think we'll be on our hands and knees pleading with Google and Apple within weeks, but I'd really love to be proved wrong,' how can it have taken six vital weeks for our actual government to work it out?

Meanwhile, the 20th-century version – a call centre phoning some of the people for whom an infected person has contact numbers – is a million miles short of where South Korea and Tunisia were in March. It's all now in the hands of Dido Harding: wife of a Tory MP, steward of the Jockey Club which went ahead with the 2020 Cheltenham Virus Spreading Festival, and the person in charge of TalkTalk when it breached the personal data of 156,000 customers. But she moves in the same circles as the MP for racing's very own HQ, Newmarket, one … checks notes … Matt Hancock who also just happens to be Health Secretary.

We'll have banished the virus and be back to normality like New Zealand by the time this is published, I'm sure. Gavin 'Frank Spencer' Williamson has only managed to get a tiny fraction of schoolchildren to return before the summer as I write, but the real pillars of learning in our society – the bookies and Sports Direct – have reopened, and Wetherspoons will soon be able to operate once more as a holding pen for the Democratic Football Lads' Alliance. And we may not have a second COVID-19 spike after all. Mostly because we won't have properly seen off the first one, so can just enjoy one long spike instead of messing around like other lesser countries will have done. In any case, as Mr Micawber said in *David Copperfield*, 'Something will turn up.' It always has, to date, in Boris Johnson's chaotic but charmed life, so maybe he'll find a vaccine the next time he rummages through the pockets of his Bullingdon Club frock coat.

And then a No Deal – or Awful Deal – Brexit will be just grandy and dandy. Or at least its devastating effects will be lost within the pandemic, especially now we've decided we'll have no incoming border checks in January. We're going to 'phase them in' over six months, apparently. Hmm. It'll be a different story for our exports, of course, but again the powers that be will be able to blame the resultant ruinous shambles on the virus, and the hedge funds' gigantic disaster capitalist punts will come to fruition. Unless, of course, our Violet Elizabeth Bott style of negotiation – 'we'll scream and we'll scream until we're sick' – wears the EU down to the point while they'll sign anything just to get us out of their lives for good. That outcome would still be dire, just not quite as cataclysmically dire as No Deal.

According to a survey last week, 67 per cent of our electorate doesn't think the economy shrinking by more than 20 per cent in March 'will affect me'. Not only does that help to explain various democratic outcomes in recent years, it also suggests the government and their unsavoury backers may be able to get away with pretty much anything. Speaking of which, it turns out Jennifer Arcuri was just a fictional Jackie Collins character all along, and it looks like three hungry bears ate the long overdue Russia Report. Boris has no doubt promised Carrie he won't be seeing the former again, and none of us will be seeing the latter until 'independence' from the EU is complete, if ever. And speaking of independence, in the unlikely event that you're reading this in 2030, I wonder how Scotland is getting on back in the EU, and just how smoothly the reunification of Ireland went. More triumphs in the pipeline for the current (at time of going to press) leader of the Conservative and Unionist Party and Prime Minister of the United Kingdom.

As I write, the UK has suffered a small setback. Brazil has edged us out of the silver medal position on the podium of global COVID-19 deaths. But, like the runaway leaders the United States, they have a far bigger population than ours, so we're still streets ahead pro rata. Trump, Bolsonaro, Johnson: thank goodness we went for a big personality to keep pace with the big boys of nationalist idiocy, not one of those tedious do-gooder women like Angela Merkel or Jacinda Ardern. One of the few women hitherto allowed around the fringes of power in COVID-raddled UK, England's Chief Nursing Officer, Ruth May, reportedly said she would echo Deputy CMO Jonathan Van Tam in not offering public backing for the Cummings Grand Tour of the North. As a consequence, it seems, neither has appeared at any of the daily briefings since. Van Tam's boss, Chris Whitty, and even Patrick Vallance look like they're being held hostage when they make their rare appearances. I keep expecting Whitty, in particular, surreptitiously to hold up a sign which says, 'I am being treated well, but please send help.'

By the time this goes to press it may well be that they're not appearing at all. Johnson has been dithering about reducing the two-metre social distancing rule for weeks. He'll eventually do it, to help Tim Martin, Mike Ashley and co. return to profitability, and at that point the tenuous claim that 'we're following the science' will finally have bitten the dust, although doubtless someone will try to claim the 'science has changed' as it did (or didn't) over herd immunity. The scientists should walk out at that point if they have anything about them, or they can keep their jobs but become an irrelevance. They're rather obviously already being lined up to take much of the blame instead of the politicians at the eventual Nuremburg-style trial. We may have to wait until 2024 and a change of government for those public recriminations, though. If indeed there is a change of government. You never know with the British public.

Who knows how much of the 'hostage to fortune' speculation above will be borne out? A fair amount of it, I suspect, but then

I'm not one of Cummings's much-vaunted 'super-forecasters', and more to the point I won't be able to re-edit this later to pretend I was right. Cummings tried to do just that on the March 2020 evening he returned to London from Durham and Barnard Castle by inserting a coronavirus 'prediction' into a 2019 blog. Embarrassingly for him, he was rumbled. Maybe he was just testing his eyes again by typing some random hindsight into his keyboard? I know people who've lost all academic credibility for less, but not Classic Dom. Not while he can have you evicted from Whitehall for questioning his omniscience, and indeed omnipotence.

Who knows, Mary Wakefield may even be allowed to write articles again for *The Spectator* in due course. Putting your name to an absolute pile of tripe for that publication has served Rod Liddle, Toby Young and Brendan O'Neill perfectly well for years, so it's only fair that the same rules should apply to a woman. Especially one whose father owns a castle, and has a 'half-black, half-white' horse called Barack, as revealed in a 2017 interview with Field Sports TV. An older, but recently resurfaced, YouTube clip shows Daddy regaling visitors to his castle with his views on the superior breeding genes of the ruling class. 'You can't make a Pekinese puppy from a pit bull terrier,' is one such example, which chimes with the eugenicist views of Andrew Sabisky, his son-in-law's first and thankfully short-lived appointee to Downing Street. There's a book to be written about Sir Humphry Wakefield, why Dom, sloganeer to the masses, chose to marry into his lineage and what the two of them find to talk about over port and cigars once the ladies have withdrawn, but this isn't it.

I long for a future when these people are no longer in charge of our destinies. I'm trying to ration how much I read about their inept handling of this crisis each day – not writing in depth about it every morning has helped – but I'm pretty sure we're going to end up as one of the worst affected countries on the planet, both economically and, more crucially, in terms of lives lost. The government locked down too late, have covered their tracks ever since and are reassuring virtually no one with their incompetent attempts to emerge from lockdown, having already lost the goodwill of most of the population of a battered, angry, weary and divided country.

If there is a second COVID-19 wave, especially in the winter, they'll struggle to reimpose another lockdown, having made such a Horlicks of the first. At least the researchers at Oxford University will have helped cancel out the blundering of some of their non-scientific alumni. Clinical trials have shown that taking dexamethasone will save the lives of a third of those people on ventilators who would otherwise have died. It's a cheap, widely available steroid and means that the UK – albeit not the government – has finally done something of significance to help the world in its battle against the coronavirus.

If the Oxford history graduate and pseudoscientist Cummings is still looking to recruit more super-forecasters, he may be interested in in a post of mine which popped up as a Facebook memory from a year ago this week. Theresa May had announced she was standing down, and I wrote that Johnson 'will be our PM, and will destroy what's left of our reputation, common purpose and economy. There are many people to blame for where we find ourselves – Cameron, Farage, Blair, Corbyn, Murdoch, the uninformed portion of the electorate etc., etc. – but if you think our next PM is going to be anything other than a disaster: a) read the words of his former employer (a Tory) and b) defriend me now, so we don't have to fall out at some later point.'

I very much wish that had turned out to be an unduly gloomy call. I'd only previously been as certain that disaster was about to befall our country when Tony Blair started trying to tell us (and himself) that Saddam Hussein had weapons of mass destruction and, for different reasons, when Leave won the referendum. Far greater super-forecasting than mine was to be found in the lines I attached to that June 2019 post from an article by Max Hastings, Johnson's former boss at *The Telegraph*: 'Boris is a gold medal egomaniac ... His chaotic public persona is not an act – he is indeed manically disorganised about everything except his own image management. He is also a far more ruthless, and frankly nastier, figure than the public appreciates … I would not take Boris's word about whether it's Monday or Tuesday … He is not a man to believe in, to trust or respect … He is bereft of judgement, loyalty and discretion. Only in the star-crazed, frivolous Britain of the 21st century could such a man have risen so high.'

An emphatic and prophetic denouncement from a man who knew Johnson better than most. And written before he became PM, let alone faced a global pandemic.

I am trying to distract myself from it all, honestly. It doesn't help that the calendar has turned into Jim Bowen, regularly telling me to 'look at what you could have won'. T20 evenings at Lord's and The Oval have come and gone in mockingly glorious weather, and we'd now be over a week into Euro 2020. In that elusive parallel universe, I'd have been to both of England's opening fixtures by now, with a trip to Dublin with Amanda to watch a game in between. Two more Wembley fixtures, then a quarter-final in Baku with a side trip to Georgia and Armenia would have awaited us in the coming weeks. Will it all happen in 2021 instead as planned? Will it happen but without dear old infected Blighty? Will travel ever be the same, or even feasible again?

We really haven't changed much about our regime. We're lucky in having that small area of outside space and a large degree of control over how we spend our time, but even as there have been nominal relaxations in what passes for government guidelines, we've stuck to the borough of Camden: some food deliveries, some socially distanced shopping for essentials and a short drive then a long walk three times a week around the further reaches of Hampstead Heath, the now-reopened Kenwood grounds and the woods towards Highgate. We went into lockdown a fortnight before Johnson finally acquiesced and we'll continue to be more cautious than he and his party want us to be. We don't trust them on any level and, to be honest, we're getting by as we are. The phone and Zoom and other means of virtual communication mean we've been in touch with friends and family more than we usually would, and we've politely declined various recent invitations to socialise within current guidelines.

Until or unless we feel it's safe to resume proper treats like foreign travel or going to sport or gigs or the theatre and cinema, the notion of bringing our own refreshments, sitting across a garden from people we've been in touch with anyway, and not being able to go to the toilet until we get home, doesn't really appeal. I have booked our first visit to a drive-in movie – *The Shawshank Redemption* somewhere in Docklands – for early July though, so we'll be leaving the borough for that.

And, of course, we have some football – albeit this weird incarnation – to watch again now, as well as books to read (I finally finished *The Mirror and the Light*, and am now immersed in John Kennedy Toole's *A Confederacy of Dunces*) and we still have TV, that strange world Dick Clement has described where you cringe as people make physical contact with each other and gather in crowds. There's also a faraway place in the here and now where that's happening, too. It's called New Zealand and while it's lucky that it's so remote, it also has something called a leader. The only two new COVID-19 cases they've had in weeks flew in from the UK to attend a funeral.

And then of course, there's music. At my age, I can only keep adding to my repertoire of songs I play by displacing others. In the last couple of weeks, I've been playing Crowded House songs on the guitar after Amanda and I videoed and recorded a personalised rewrite of 'Weather with You' for our Kiwi friend Lijana's birthday. I've also pretty much nailed the solo to 'Live Forever' by Oasis (it's great, but not exactly Jimi Hendrix) and have grown strangely addicted to playing 'Losing My Religion' by REM, plucking the ukulele in place of the original mandolin. Amanda was spared that until I'd got it right.

And there's the daily exercise bike session: 20km now in a regular 27 minutes and 30 seconds, since I discovered a way to set the pace metronomically. Roger Bannister had Chris Brasher, then Chris Chataway, to help him. I have what used to be, until it started popping up everywhere, Amanda's favourite song of all time, 'Heroes' by David Bowie, to start off my daily playlist. Pedalling in time to that glorious swirl of Brian Eno's keyboards, Robert Fripp's guitar and a superb vocal and lyric takes you to a steady 45 kph and it's then just a question of staying at that pace. I only cottoned on to this about a week ago, but I haven't yet tired of hearing that masterpiece once every day. The fact that it only got to number 24 in the UK singles charts is yet another savage indictment of the British public. Amanda's cycling Bowie song of choice these days is 'Station to Station' – three minutes of creeping, sinister weirdness before he lets rip for the remaining seven.

Although Bowie's death in January 2016 set the tone for what seemed at the time to be the most awful year imaginable, in retrospect, checking out before Brexit and then the election of Trump may have been a characteristically smart move on his part. Either way, 'Heroes', and its tale of a lovers' meeting by the Berlin Wall is the greatest musical evocation I know of the triumph of the human spirit over adversity. When it was recorded in Berlin in 1977, there was no way of knowing that the Wall was destined to be pulled down 12 years later.

We're now prisoners of a virus rather than a warped ideology, but we're similarly unable to know how or when this entrapment will resolve itself, or whether we'll taste the true freedom we once knew ever again. For now, we have to take comfort where we can and hope for happier times. We know there's trouble ahead but, as Irving Berlin said, 'While there's music and moonlight and love and romance. Let's face the music and dance.' And, for now at least, there's football, too – *MOTD2* is back on tonight.